Publishing Team Director: Jack Calhoun
Acquisitions Editor: Keri Witman
Developmental Editor: Dennis Hanseman
Production Editor: Brenda Owens
Media Technology Editor: Mary Hufford
Media Production Editor: Kurt Gerdenich
Production House: Pre-Press Company, Inc.
Internal Design: Craig Ramsdell and Sandra Kent, Kent and Co., Cincinnati
Cover Design: Paul Neff Design, Cincinnati
Cover Photo: © Hiroyuki Matsumoto/Tony Stone Images
Photo Research: Cary Benbow
Marketing Manager: Lisa Lysne
Manufacturing Coordinator: Georgina Calderon

Library of Congress Cataloging-in-Publication Data
Farmer, Roger E. A.
      Macroeconomics/Roger E. A. Farmer.
         p. cm.
      Includes index.
      ISBN 0-538-84581-3 (alk. paper)
      1. Macroeconomics. I. Title.
   HB172.5.F36 1998   98-6002
   339—dc21   CIP

123456789   765432109

Printed in the United States of America

I(T)P®

International Thomson Publishing
South-Western College Publishing is an ITP Company
The ITP trademark is used under license.

MACROECONOMICS

Roger E. A. Farmer

University of California—Los Angeles

South-Western College Publishing
an International Thomson Publishing company I(T)P®

Cincinnati • Albany • Boston • Detroit • Johannesburg • London • Madrid • Melbourne • Mexico City
New York • Pacific Grove • San Francisco • Scottsdale • Singapore • Tokyo • Toronto

**To My Son
Leland Edward Farmer:**

"If I were to own this countryside
As far as a man in a day could ride,
And the Tyes were mine for giving or letting…

…I would give them all to my son
If he would let me any one
For a song, a blackbird's song, at dawn."*

*Edward Thomas. "If I Were to Own." *Collected Poems*. New York: Thomas Seltzer, 1921.

Roger E. A. Farmer   *Photograph by Esméralda Lina de Bokay*

Roger E. A. Farmer is a Professor of Economics at UCLA, where he has been teaching graduate and undergraduate macroeconomics since 1988. Prior to coming to UCLA, he held appointments at the University of Toronto and the University of Pennsylvania and visiting positions at Cambridge University and the Innocenzo Gaspirini Institute in Milan, Italy. He is a Fellow of the Center for Economic Policy Research, a Fellow Commoner of Churchill College Cambridge and is currently on leave from UCLA at the European University Institute in Florence.

Professor Farmer is internationally known for his work on macroeconomics. His 1993 book, *The Macroeconomics of Self-Fulfilling Prophecies,* is widely used in graduate programs throughout the world. He has written extensively on macroeconomic and monetary theory, is an associate editor of *Macroeconomic Dynamics,* and serves as Director of the Program for Dynamic Economics, a nonprofit research group based at UCLA.

A CONSENSUS VIEW OF MACROECONOMICS

Until recently, there was much disagreement about the way to go about *doing* macroeconomics. Keynesians analyzed the economy using a theory developed by John Maynard Keynes in the 1930s. Others argued for a classical approach based on *general equilibrium* theory. This disagreement made it hard to teach the subject to undergraduates because a macroeconomics course would vary depending on the point of view of the instructor. Recently, this disagreement has begun to fade as economists recognized that many of the ideas central to Keynesian economics can be understood using the language of equilibrium theory. A consensus is emerging in which most economists recognize that the right language is that of general equilibrium, but that this language is capable of being used to express many different ideas. This book is based on this emerging consensus.

The core of most undergraduate macroeconomics courses is the IS-LM model, which has not been taught in graduate schools for twenty years. Graduate students of macroeconomics learn models that are dynamic; undergraduate students are taught models that are static. Graduate students learn general equilibrium theory; undergraduates are taught Keynesian economics. Many undergraduate treatments of macroeconomics (this is also true, to a regrettable extent, of many graduate programs) have lost touch with data from the real world that our subject was developed to explain. *Macroeconomics* attempts to address each of these issues by providing a grounding in macroeconomics that undergraduates can understand while incorporating the major developments introduced in the last two decades. Because most journalists and policy makers still think in terms of the IS-LM model, the topic cannot (and should not) be ignored in a book of this kind; however, our emphasis lies elsewhere. *Macroeconomics* presents the subject from the viewpoint of general equilibrium theory; it introduces the tools of basic dynamics, and in every chapter it relates theories to data.

DISTINCTIVE FEATURES OF THIS BOOK

There are many books on the market aimed at intermediate students; but none quite like this one. Here are some of the exciting features that make *Macroeconomics* stand out from its competitors.

1. **Data** is emphasized in every chapter. Chapter 2 explains income and wealth accounting and how they are related to each other. It teaches students the magnitudes of wealth, income, and the components of income by presenting figures for the wealth and income of an average American and the relative wealth of different countries and different regions of the world. Chapter 3 shows how to remove the trend from a data series and how to construct scatter plots of one detrended series against another. These scatter plots are used extensively in later chapters to check the implications of simple theories against facts from the historical record.

2. Ideas are introduced in **historical context**. The theoretical section of the book begins, in Part 2, with a classical model based on the idea that demand and supply are always equal. Using this model, it explains data from the 1973 and 1979 recessions. Part 3 contrasts the Keynesian and classical models by demonstrating that data from the Great Depression can be more easily explained by one approach than by another. Part 4 introduces the student to dynamics and explains the budget deficit, growth, the debate over the shifting Phillips curve, and rational expectations.

3. Every chapter uses **the tools of demand and supply** with a consistent theme running throughout—namely, that macroeconomics and microeconomics are both based on the idea that households and firms pursue their own self-interests subject to constraints. This theme is employed even in the chapters on Keynesian economics, in which unemployment is shown to result from an information problem that prevents firms and workers from trading at prices that exhaust all of the gains from trade.

4. The book brings **dynamics** to the intermediate market. It explains **difference equations** using a graphical framework and with a simple example that students can understand and relate to—that is, the economics of the government budget. It also uses difference equations to explain growth and the modern approach to monetary policy.

5. Much of modern macroeconomics has been directed at the causes of growth, and a major paradigm—endogenous growth theory—has absorbed the attention of many of the best minds in the profession. *Macroeconomics* has two chapters on growth and an entire chapter explaining **endogenous growth theory,** using the tools of modern dynamics.

6. The book contains a **modern treatment of rational expectations** and the constraints that it imposes on monetary policy, using examples from the speeches of Alan Greenspan to illustrate the relevance of the theory to the real world.

7. **Extensive reference to Internet sites** is made and information from the Internet is used to illustrate examples or to provide sources for additional research material.

8. Each chapter is illustrated with **boxed examples that draw on practical problems** to illustrate important concepts.

HOW TO TEACH FROM *MACROECONOMICS*

Macroeconomics is designed to allow you to teach at a number of different levels. A knowledge of some basic microeconomics is helpful, although it is not essential because the necessary tools are covered in an appendix. Algebra, in the core chapters, is also relegated to appendices, although there is a section on economic dynamics that makes more extensive use of equations.

Navigating Through the Book

Part 1: Introduction and Measurement	Difficulty Level	Status
1. What This Book Is About	1	Required
2. Measuring the Economy	1	Required
3. Macroeconomic Facts	1	Required
Part 2: The Classical Approach to Aggregate Demand and Supply		
4. The Theory of Aggregate Supply	1	Required
5. Aggregate Demand and the Classical Theory of the Price Level	1	Required
6. Saving and Investment	1	Required
Part 3: The Modern Approach to Aggregate Demand and Supply		
7. Unemployment	2	Required
8. The Demand for Money	2	Optional
9. The Money Supply	1	Optional
10. IS-LM and Aggregate Demand	2	Optional
11. The Open Economy	1	Optional
Part 4: Dynamic Macroeconomics		
12. Debt, Deficits, and Economic Dynamics	4	Optional
13. Neoclassical Growth Theory	4	Optional
14. Endogenous Growth Theory	4	Optional
15. Unemployment, Inflation, and Growth	3	Optional
16. Expectations and Macroeconomics	3	Optional
17. What We Know and What We Don't	1	Suggested

Explanations of Levels

Level 1: This material is self-contained. Chapters can be covered in one lecture if students have already studied microeconomics. Analytic material is covered in graphs, with some algebra in appendices.

Level 2: These chapters are similar to Level 1 chapters but they introduce new ideas that will not be familiar from more basic courses, including externalities (used to explain the natural rate of unemployment) and simultaneous determination of equilibrium in more than one market (the basis of the IS-LM model). Often these chapters will require two lectures for a complete understanding.

Level 3: Level 3 chapters are similar in difficulty to those in Level 2 and may also require two lectures per chapter. They differ from Level 2 chapters because they involve some simple dynamic analysis and the idea of a random variable. Conceptually, this material is no more difficult to convey to students than the ideas underlying IS-LM analysis, although the material is not usually covered at the intermediate level.

Level 4: These are the most demanding chapters in the book. They involve a discussion of difference equations (taught with graphs and demonstrated with examples). Of the three chapters in this group, two (Chapters 13 and 14) deal with economic growth and the third (Chapter 12) deals with the economics of the budget deficit. Chapter 12 is included at Level 4 because it uses difference equations, but it is easy to teach and students are usually highly motivated to learn the material.

WHAT'S IN EACH PART OF THE BOOK

Part 1: Introduction and Measurement

Part 1 consists of three chapters. Chapter 1 introduces three major questions that are covered in more detail later:

1. Why has GDP per person grown at an average rate of 1.6% per year since 1890?
2. Why does GDP per person fluctuate around its trend growth rate?
3. What causes inflation?

Chapter 2 explains how to measure GDP and its component parts and it relates the measurement of GDP to the measurement of wealth. Students learn how to attach numbers to the U.S. and the world economies. How big is GDP? How wealthy is the average American? How large is the U.S. economy relative to the rest of the world? Finally, Chapter 3 explains how to measure time series. What are the regularities that characterize business cycles and how can these regularities be quantified?

Part 2: The Classical Approach to Aggregate Demand and Supply

Chapters 4, 5, and 6 move from a *description* of data to an *explanation* of it. They introduce a classical model of the whole economy that was developed over the course of 150 years. The classical model makes some strong simplifications that are too simplistic to enable it to capture all of the features of a modern industrial economy. There are, however, still features of the data that can be understood with the classical model, and it is useful as a framework for understanding how more complex theories work.

Chapter 4 constructs a model containing all of the features that determine output and employment in an economy operating at full employment. Chapter 5 adds money to this model and explains how inflation and prices are determined. Chapter 6 describes how the capital markets channel funds from savers to investors. By the end of Part 2, students will have learned how to construct models using the equilibrium method—the idea that demand equals supply in each of several markets simultaneously. They will also have seen how equilibrium methods are applied in practice to real-world economic problems: the causes of business cycles, the cause of hyperinflation, and the determination of savings and investment with applications to current issues, such as the aging of the population and the funding of Social Security.

Part 3: The Modern Approach to Aggregate Demand and Supply

Part 3 contains five chapters that go beyond the classical model and incorporate insights from Keynesian economics. Chapter 7 explains unemployment as a market friction in which search is costly. It introduces students to the natural rate of unemployment, which is explained as an equilibrium in which no firm can profit from offering a lower wage or by searching more intensively for the right employee. The Keynesian theory of supply is introduced as the idea that unemployment may be either above or below its natural rate.

Chapters 8, 9, and 10 explain the modern theory of aggregate demand that was developed from ideas in Keynes's *General Theory*. It is presented as a generalization of the classical model of aggregate demand, which recognizes that the propensity to hold money is not independent of the interest rate. This leads to a theory that explains why the position of the aggregate demand curve depends on factors other than the quantity of money.

Chapter 8 makes a generalization about the quantity theory of money that allows the propensity to hold money to depend on the interest rate. Chapter 9 explains how the Federal Reserve Board controls the money supply. Chapter 10 develops the IS-LM model and uses it to derive an aggregate demand curve similar to that of the classical model. The payoff to this generalization is presented as a theory of business cycles, in which recessions may be caused by shifts of both the aggregate demand curve and the aggregate supply curve. Because many variables can shift aggregate demand, including changes in investors' beliefs and changes in fiscal policy, the complete Keynesian model is seen to account for both the pre–World War II experience as well as for recessions in the postwar period. It also provides policy makers with an understanding of how government behavior can influence output and employment over the business cycle.

The last chapter in this section, Chapter 11, explains how demand management must be modified in an open economy. The chapter concentrates on the different kinds of exchange rate regimes and explains the constraints on monetary policy in a world of fixed exchange rates.

Chapters 8 through 11 contain ideas that were extremely influential in macroeconomics from 1940 through the 1970s. *Macroeconomics* takes the position that these ideas are important but not *essential* to an understanding of what has been happening *since* 1970. Their main contribution is to explain the interaction between the capital market and the demand and supply of money that, in turn, helps explain what shifts the aggregate demand curve. The more important recent ideas deal with the dynamics of aggregate demand and supply. These ideas can be understood using the classical theory of aggregate demand based on the quantity theory of money. For this reason, Chapters 8 through 11 are optional and instructors may choose to omit them and jump to the modern theory of expectations and dynamics covered in Part 4.

Part 4: Dynamic Macroeconomics

Part 4 contains five chapters that are united by their concern with economic dynamics. Chapter 12 introduces a graphical representation of a difference equation and uses it to explain the economics of the government budget. This chapter is the least demanding of the five and it can be taught in isolation from the others. It explains why policy makers are concerned with balancing the budget, why balancing the budget has emerged as a problem only in recent years, and why balancing the budget may be even more of a problem in years to come.

Chapters 13 and 14 use difference equations to understand economic growth. Although these chapters are relatively advanced, they are also rewarding because they bring students to the frontier of knowledge on a topic that has absorbed some of the finest minds in economics over the past twenty years. Chapters 15 and 16 extend the neoclassical model to a dynamic setting. Chapter 15 introduces dynamics to the neoclassical model by allowing the nominal wage to change from one period to the next and by adding technical progress. Chapter 16 goes one step further by allowing expectations of future inflation and the nominal wage to be determined endogenously. This chapter introduces the theory of rational expectations and uses it to interpret a speech by Alan Greenspan about the role of monetary policy. Chapter 17 wraps up the book with a summary of the current state of research.

SUGGESTED COURSE OUTLINES

The following suggestions represent different ways in which the material could be organized in a course.

I. Short traditional course   Parts 1, 2, and 3. Part 3 ends with the IS-LM model and aggregate demand. It could be followed with Chapter 12 (the budget deficit) or Chapter 15 (the Phillips curve). Chapter 9 on the money supply and Chapter 11 on the international economy could be omitted.

II. Longer traditional course with expectations   Parts 1, 2, 3, and Part 4, Chapters 15 and 16. This is the same as course *I* but adds material on the dynamics of inflation and unemployment and on modern theories of economic policy. Chapter 12 also fits well with this course. Once again Chapters 9 and 11 are optional.

III. Short course stressing equilibrium theory with rational expectations   Parts 1, 2, Chapter 7 from Part 3, Chapters 12, 15, and 16 from Part 4. This course deals with the Keynesian theory of aggregate supply but skips the IS-LM model and goes straight to expectational dynamics. Chapter 12 is included as an introduction to dynamics. Even though it is a Level 4 chapter, Chapter 12 is easy to teach and fits well as an introduction to discussing inflation and unemployment in Chapters 15 and 16.

IV. Long course stressing equilibrium theory with rational expectations   Parts 1 and 2, Chapter 7 from Part 3, Part 4. This is the same as course *III* but adds growth theory. Chapters 13 and 14 require at least four lectures and perhaps more depending on student abilities.

V. Year-long course at leisurely pace   Parts 1 through 4. The entire book could be taught in a two-quarter (or two-semester) course.

SUPPLEMENTARY ITEMS

To support the *Macroeconomics* text, the following supplementary items are available.

- A **Study Guide**, written by Jang-Ting Guo of the University of California, Riverside, and Shankha Chakraborty of UCLA, provides a variety of review materials and problems that will help students master macroeconomics. Solutions are provided. (ISBN 0-538-85483-9)

- An **Instructor's Manual/Test Bank**, written by Shankha Chakraborty, provides instructor support. For each chapter in the text, the Manual includes outlines plus suggested answers to all of the end-of-chapter problems. The Test Bank includes 30 multiple choice and numerical problems per chapter to use in constructing in-class examinations. (ISBN 0-538-84585-6)
- All of the figures from the text are available in the form of **PowerPoint slides**. (ISBN 0-324-00822-8)
- Both instructors and students will want to visit the *Macroeconomics* **Web site**. It can be accessed by using **http://farmer.swcollege.com/**.

ACKNOWLEDGMENTS

Countless colleagues, students, and friends have given me suggestions and advice in the development of this book. Thanks to all of them. Thanks also to the following reviewers who developed this project with me. Many of them taught from early drafts and provided criticism and feedback that enabled me to improve the final version.

Krishna Akkina
Kansas State University

Jose Lasa Alcides
Universidad Autonoma Metropolitana

Richard Baillie
Michigan State University

Brock Blomberg
Wellesley College

Maureen Burton
California Polytechnic State University

Kevin Carey
American University

Menzie Chinn
University of California, Santa Cruz

Lawrence Christiano
Northwestern University

Wouter den Haan
University of California, San Diego

Michael Donihue
Colby College

Michael Dowd
University of Toledo

John Driscoll
Brown University

Pami Dua
University of Connecticut

Steven Durlauf
University of Wisconsin

Hadi Esfahani
University of Illinois

Windsor Fields
James Madison University

Edward Gamber
Lafayette College

Fred Graham
American University

James Hartley
Mt. Holyoke College

Jack Hou
California State University, Long Beach

Frederick Joutz
George Washington University

Shawn E. Kantor
University of Arizona

Kent P. Kimbrough
Duke University

Jaewoo Lee
University of California, Irvine

Sang-Sub Lee
University of South Florida

Stephen McCafferty
Ohio State University

Norman Miller
Miami University

Peter Montiel
Williams College

Daniel Nuxoll
Virginia Polytechnic Institute

Lee Ohanian
Federal Reserve Bank of Minneapolis

Peter Pedroni
Indiana University

Kevin Reffett
Arizona State University

Matthew Shapiro
University of Michigan

M. Dek Terrell
Louisiana State University

Douglas Waldo
University of Florida

Charles Weise
College of William and Mary

Eric Zivot
University of Washington

During the development of the book the manuscript was transferred from Wadsworth to South-Western College Publishing, and in that process we lost track of some of the reviewers. I apologize to anyone who helped develop the early drafts but whose name does not appear here. Please accept my thanks.

The entire manuscript, while in development, was available on my Web site and I benefited from numerous e-mail exchanges with readers who used the book in its development stages. Thanks to Gbenga Aina, Rick Ashley, Graziella Bertocchi, Marco A. Bittencourt, Kevin Carey, Lawrence Christiano, Peter Dorman, Asif Dowla, Hadi Esfahani, Doug Fisher, Jim Gale, Marc Hayford, Marcos Godinho, Rick Harper, Yannis Ioannides, Yufeng Li, Steve Lee, Jose Alfredo Leite, Thomas A. McGahagan, Phil Meguire (for reminding me that A. W. Phillips was a New Zealander), Giorgio Miele, Giacombo Balbinotto Neto, Minh Tri Ngyuen, Dan Peled, Steve Quinn, Aida A. Rahim, K. Osama Rahman, Nouriel Roubini, Geraldo Edmundo Silva, Abraham Vela (for detailed comments on every chapter), and Thomas L. Wayne for their comments, corrections, and encouragement. My thanks also to Ted Bos and Nathan Newman for letting me link to their Web sites.

Two people deserve special mention—Ken King for persuading me to begin this project in the first place and Dennis Hanseman for guiding it through to completion. Thanks to Elisa Adams for early work on development and the team at South-Western, especially Jack Calhoun, Kurt Gerdenich, Dennis Hanseman, Tom Hilt, Bob Lynch, Lisa Lysne, Tim McEwen, and Brenda Owens. Several generations of graduate students at UCLA helped me as teaching assistants, including Rosalind Bennett, Shankha Chakraborty, Yuan Gao, Jang-Ting Guo, Mariassunta Giannetti, and Michael Ryall. Special thanks to Jang-Ting Guo and Shankha Chakraborty, who have done an outstanding job preparing a Study Guide and an Instructor's Manual to accompany the text. My biggest debt is to my family and friends, especially to my mother Kathleen, my wife Roxanne, my son Leland, Peg and Bernard, Bob and Barbara, and Reg and Carolyn for their love, support, and encouragement as the manuscript evolved from an idea into a reality.

Roger E. A. Farmer
Los Angeles, California
July, 1998

CONTENTS

PART 2   THE CLASSICAL APPROACH TO AGGREGATE DEMAND AND SUPPLY   65

4 The Theory of Aggregate Supply   66

6 Saving and Investment   112

PART 3   THE MODERN APPROACH TO AGGREGATE DEMAND AND SUPPLY   139

7 Unemployment   140

8 The Demand for Money   165

PART 1

Introduction and Measurement

Part 1 consists of three chapters. Chapter 1 introduces the three major questions that we study in the rest of the book: Why has Gross Domestic Product (GDP) per person grown at an average rate of 1.6% per year since 1890? Why does GDP per person fluctuate around its trend growth rate? and What causes inflation? Chapter 2 explains how we measure GDP and its component parts and relates the measurement of GDP to the measurement of wealth. This chapter poses questions such as: How big is GDP? How wealthy is the average American? How large is the U.S. economy relative to the rest of the world? Finally, Chapter 3 explains how economists measure economic time series, focusing on the regularities that characterize business cycles and how these regularities can be quantified.

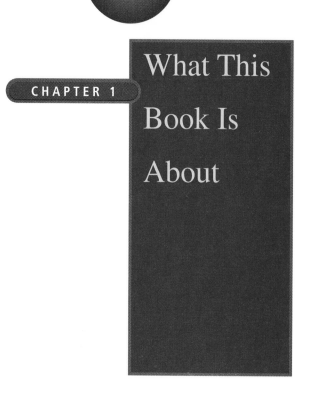

CHAPTER 1

What This Book Is About

❶ INTRODUCTION

A Unified Approach to Macroeconomics

This book is about macroeconomics and the debates between economists who study macroeconomics. The idea of distinguishing between macroeconomics and microeconomics did not take shape until the 1930s, when John Maynard Keynes wrote *The General Theory of Employment Interest and Money.* Keynes tried to explain the working of the economy as a whole. Keynes asked how employment related to prices, how prices and employment were influenced by government policies, and, above all, what the government could do to maintain full employment. Keynes used methods that were very different from those used by the microeconomists of his day, and the novelty of his approach led to the development of two separate subjects, macroeconomics and microeconomics, which remained unconnected for 30 years. More recently economists have recognized that the methods used to study the behavior of individual producers and consumers in markets (**microeconomics**) can also be used to study the working of the economy as a whole (**macroeconomics**). This book explains the modern approach which treats macroeconomics and microeconomics as different parts of one subject using a single method of analysis.

The Three Major Questions

The most important macroeconomic event in this century was the Great Depression. The Depression affected the entire world economy, although its magnitude and timing differed from country to country. In America the Depression began in 1930; in the course of three years unemployment reached 25% of the labor force and the output produced by U.S. workers fell 20% below trend. The economy did not recover from the Depression until 1941, when the United States entered World War II. The Depression was an event of such importance in people's lives that it shaped the way macroeconomists thought about their subject for the next 30 years. The generation of economists who lived through this era became concerned with a single overriding question: What causes economic booms and recessions? The study of this question is called the economics of **business cycles**.

Understanding business cycles is still one of the most important goals of macroeconomics. But although business cycles are important, they are not *the* most important determinant of living standards. The quantity of goods and services produced by the residents of a country is measured by its **real Gross Domestic Product (real GDP)**. Although fluctuations in real GDP are important, a more significant factor affecting economic welfare is the fact that capitalist economies have been experiencing sustained **growth** in real GDP for the past two hundred years. Recently economists have begun to see the Great Depression as a large fluctuation in the growth rate and to search for a common explanation for both fluctuations and growth. The theory of growth focuses on why economies produce more each year on average, whereas the theory of business cycles is about why they do not always produce more.

Figure 1.1 graphs real GDP per person in the United States from 1890 through 1996.[1] There are two features of this graph that you should notice. First, real GDP per person has followed an upward trend since 1890, the first date for which we have reliable estimates. Second, real GDP per person is subject to very big fluctuations around its long-run trend. These two features define the first two questions that we are concerned with in this book.

Although the Great Depression was the most significant economic event to affect Americans in this century, another event of similar importance affected Austrians, Germans, Poles, and Hungarians at the end of World War I—inflation of such enormous magnitude that it is difficult for anyone who has not experienced such an event to comprehend its impact. Prices in Germany in 1923 increased at a rate of 230% per month, which means that every day commodities cost 6% more than they had the day before; workers were forced to spend their pay the day they received it, before the money became worthless. Inflation of this magnitude is called **hyperinflation**, and episodes of hyperinflation are occasional features of economic life today in a number of countries. Examples of countries that have experienced recent hyperinflationary episodes include Israel, where prices increased 400% in 1985; Argentina, where they went up by 700%, and Bolivia, where the annual price increase in 1984 was a staggering 12,500%.

---

1.   The scale of the vertical axis on Figure 1.1 measures GDP using *logarithmic units* and the horizontal axis measures time. We call a graph of this form a *logarithmic graph*. Logarithmic graphs are a useful visual aid for understanding the behavior of rapidly growing variables because they can be used to plot the variable of interest as a straight line. The growth rate of a variable is the slope of this line.

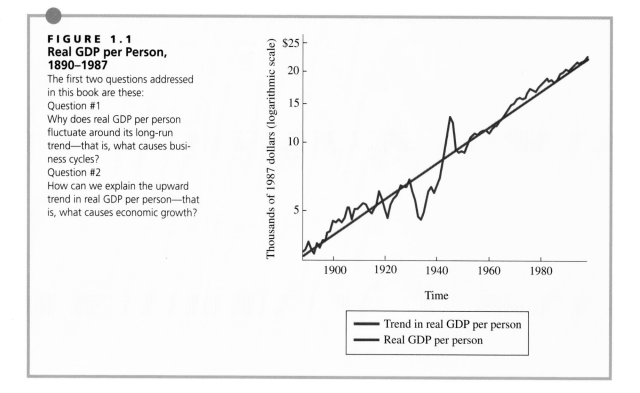

FIGURE 1.1
Real GDP per Person,
1890–1987
The first two questions addressed
in this book are these:
Question #1
Why does real GDP per person
fluctuate around its long-run
trend—that is, what causes business cycles?
Question #2
How can we explain the upward
trend in real GDP per person—that
is, what causes economic growth?

Although we have not experienced hyperinflation in the United States, we have experienced sustained inflation of a more moderate magnitude: prices have increased at an
average rate of 4.5% per year since 1946. Figure 1.2 shows the average price of goods
and services in the United States for each year since 1890 as a percentage of the average
price level in 1987. Before World War II, prices rose, on average, at 1.7% per year; but
since the end of World War II they have showed a persistent tendency to rise at an average annual rate of 4.5%. The effect of this continually compounded price increase
means that a cup of coffee in a restaurant that cost 10 cents in 1946 would cost $1.00 to-
day. The pattern of price changes shown in Figure 1.2 is the third area that we study in
this book.

❷ ECONOMIC GROWTH

Growth Is a Recent Phenomenon

When we reflect on our own experiences of change and adaptation, it is difficult to
imagine life without continual improvements. But economic growth is a relatively recent phenomenon in the span of human civilization. The collapse of the Roman Empire
in the third century was followed by a period of stagnation and decline in living standards that did not substantially improve again in the Western world until the beginnings

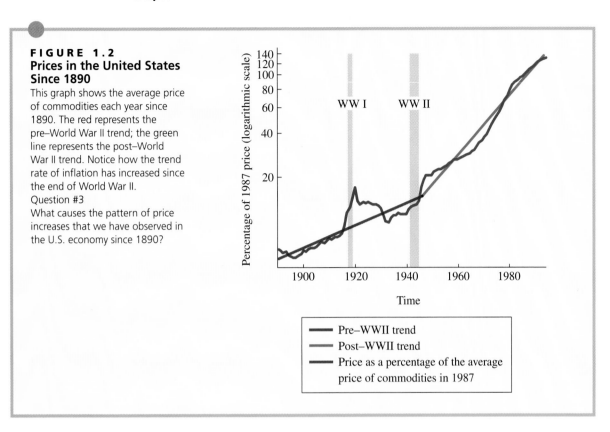

FIGURE 1.2
Prices in the United States Since 1890

This graph shows the average price of commodities each year since 1890. The red represents the pre–World War II trend; the green line represents the post–World War II trend. Notice how the trend rate of inflation has increased since the end of World War II.
Question #3
What causes the pattern of price increases that we have observed in the U.S. economy since 1890?

Pre–WWII trend
Post–WWII trend
Price as a percentage of the average price of commodities in 1987

of modern capitalism in the eighteenth century. Most capitalist countries have experienced an average annual improvement in their standard of living of 1 to 2% for the past two hundred years. The first part of the world to experience economic growth in modern times was the region that today consists of Belgium and the Netherlands, the richest region in the world from 1760 to 1850.[2] In the mid 1800s Great Britain took over as the world's richest economy; and around the beginning of World War I, Britain itself was overtaken by the United States. Today the United States enjoys the world's highest standard of living.

Measuring Economic Growth

The changes in our living patterns that are associated with growth have so many different dimensions that a single index will inevitably miss some of their important features. For example, increased production is often accompanied by increased pollution. Similarly, a single number that represents the quantities of commodities produced in two different countries will miss differences in the quality of life that cannot be measured by market activity. For this reason, you should be wary of comparisons that rank the quality of life on a

2.   Angus Maddison, *Dynamic Forces in Capitalist Development*, Oxford University Press, 1991.

single scale. Economists measure the output available to an entire community with an index of the goods and services produced called **Gross Domestic Product** (GDP). To measure the **standard of living** in a country we divide GDP by the number of people, to arrive at GDP per person.

Real and Nominal Gross Domestic Product

Although GDP is a good way to measure the average dollar value of the goods produced in any year, it is not a good way to measure differences in the average quantities of goods produced over time because GDP can go up from year to year for either of two reasons. First, it may increase because a country produces more goods and services; we call this increase *growth*. Second, it may increase because goods and services cost more money on average; we call this increase *inflation*. To separate the increase in GDP that comes from growth from the increase that comes from inflation, we measure the value of GDP in every year using a common set of prices. These prices are the ones that prevailed in one year, called the **base year.** GDP measured using current prices is called **nominal GDP** and GDP measured using base year prices is called **real GDP**. Increases in living standards are measured by changes in real GDP per person.

Economic Growth and Standards of Living

Just as the real GDP per person can be used to make comparisons across time, it can also be used to compare living standards across countries. The standard of living in most countries grows at a rate of 1 to 2% per year, although the range of growth rates across countries varies from –1% in some of the countries in sub-Saharan Africa to 7 or 8% in Japan, South Korea, and mainland China. Differences in rates of growth across countries may seem like small numbers, but they can have a very big impact on the standard of living because the increase each year is compounded.

You are familiar with compound growth already if you have a bank account that earns compound interest. To get a feel for the importance of compounding, consider the **rule of seventy**, which can be used to gauge how fast a quantity will double in size. To use the rule of seventy, take the growth rate of a variable that is experiencing compound growth and divide it into 70. The result is (approximately) equal to the number of years it will take for that variable to double. For example, suppose that you put $100 into a bank account that pays 10% annual interest. In (70/10) = 7 years, your money will be worth $200.

The effects of compound growth on the living standards of different countries is illustrated in Figure 1.3, which compares the growth performance of the United Kingdom, India, Japan, and South Korea to that of the United States over the period from 1960 to 1992. The vertical axis of this graph measures GDP per person relative to GDP per person in the United States; the horizontal axis measures time. Notice the tremendous differences in living standards across the countries. The average American citizen earns 10 times as much as the average citizen of India and a third as much again as a resident of the United Kingdom. This difference in living standards has persisted over long periods of time for countries such as the United Kingdom and India. Their position relative to the United States has not changed much in 30 years, and the growth rate of per capita GDP has been (roughly) 2% per year in all three countries since 1960.

FIGURE 1.3
GDP per Person as a Percentage of U.S. GDP per Person in Four Selected Countries[3]
Many countries grow at about the same rate as the United States, but the level of GDP per person in these countries is often much lower. The United Kingdom and India are examples of countries in this group. Other countries have experienced rapid growth relative to the United States, and their level of GDP per person has increased substantially in the past 30 years. Japan and South Korea are examples of countries in this group.

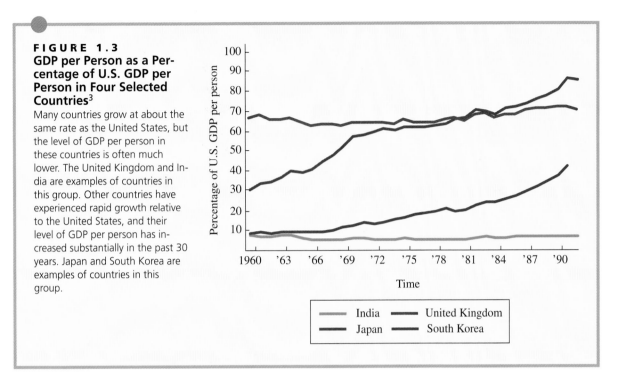

Using the rule of seventy, we can establish that the time needed for the standard of living to double in any of these countries is

$$\frac{70}{2} = 35 \text{ years}$$

Although many countries have grown at about 2% per capita, another group of countries has grown at much faster rates since World War II. A leading example of this second group is Japan, which increased its standard of living at an average rate of 5.5% per year between 1960 and 1992. When we apply the rule of seventy to Japan, it follows that the time it took for the GDP per person to double in Japan was just

$$\frac{70}{5.5} = 13 \text{ years}$$

The difference in the growth rate between the Japanese and the U.S. standard of living may not seem very big, but small differences in growth rates have very big effects when compounded over 30 years. In 1960 the average Japanese citizen earned just 20% of the income of an average American; by 1990 this gap had narrowed to 80%.[3] More

3.   The data in Figure 1.3 is taken from the "Penn World Table" by Alan Heston and Robert Summers. The Heston-Summers data is explicitly designed to make international comparisons of this kind by taking into account the cost of living in different countries using a price index in each country for a comparable "basket" of commodities.

recently, South Korea, Taiwan, Hong Kong, and Singapore have all grown rapidly, and the quality of life of their citizens has increased accordingly. The fastest growing country in the world at present is China, where the GDP grew by 10% in 1992. Although in the 1990s the United States is the richest and most powerful country in the world, this has not always been the case and it was only in the fifteenth century that Europe overtook China as the world's most advanced civilization. The recent growth of China can be attributed to Deng Xiaoping's program of reform, which opened up the Chinese economy to the outside world. Since 1978 China's economic performance has brought about one of the biggest improvements in human welfare anywhere at any time. If China meets its self-imposed targets, by 2002 its GDP will have increased eightfold.

The startling growth of Asian economies has still not challenged the United States's position because rapidly growing economies like China's and Japan's began from a much lower base. But there is no reason to assume that the United States will always be the richest country in the world. If a country can maintain even a small difference in its growth rate over a long period of time, its standard of living will inevitably outstrip those of other nations. Economists are interested in the reasons why economies grow at different rates and have begun to investigate the role of government policies in promoting the economic miracles of Japan, South Korea, Singapore, Hong Kong, and China.

❸ BUSINESS CYCLES

Defining Business Cycles

The data used for macroeconomic analysis consists of macroeconomic variables. A **macroeconomic variable** is an economic concept that can be measured and that takes on different values at different points in time, such as real GDP. Economists measure a number of economic variables over long periods of time, in what are called **time series**. The study of the relationship between different economic time series makes up the data for the scientific study of business cycles.

The most important indicator of economic activity is real GDP. The movements in GDP and the associations of other variables with GDP define the business cycle. When GDP is above trend for a number of time periods in a row, we say the economy is in a **boom**, or an **expansion**; when it is below trend for a number of time periods in a row, we say that the economy is in a **contraction**, or a **recession**.

When economists talk about business cycles, they are not referring to regular periodic motion of the kind that occurs in physical systems. The business cycle is not a *cycle* in the same sense; it has an important random component. But although economic variables move in an irregular way through time, many of them move very closely together. This co-movement is called **coherence**. Coherence is the relationship between variables that accounts for many of the important characteristics of booms and recessions; when, for example, GDP is below trend, coherence implies that unemployment is likely to be high and consumption is likely to be low.

A second distinguishing feature of economic variables is their high degree of inertia through time; a recession in one year is very likely to be followed by a recession in the following year. The tendency of economic variables to display inertia is called **persistence**. Persistence provides a degree of predictability to economic forecasting. Persistence

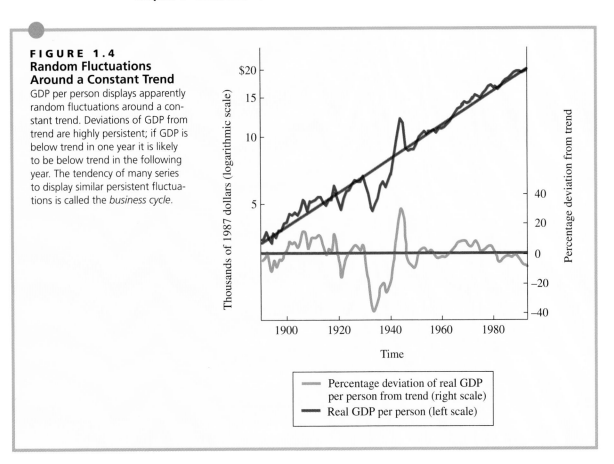

FIGURE 1.4
Random Fluctuations Around a Constant Trend
GDP per person displays apparently random fluctuations around a constant trend. Deviations of GDP from trend are highly persistent; if GDP is below trend in one year it is likely to be below trend in the following year. The tendency of many series to display similar persistent fluctuations is called the *business cycle*.

Percentage deviation of real GDP per person from trend (right scale)

Real GDP per person (left scale)

and coherence together make up the distinguishing characteristics of economic fluctuations that we refer to as business cycles. By identifying the reasons for the coherence of a set of economic time series at a point in time and for the persistence of each of these variables at different points in time, economists hope to be able to explain why recessions occur and how they can be controlled.

Measuring Business Cycles

Many of the time series that economists are interested in display upward trends. GDP, prices, and consumption are examples of variables in this class. Other variables, such as interest rates and unemployment, show no tendency to grow. In order to separate the relationship between the long-run trends in two or more time series from the relationship between their business-cycle fluctuations, we need to define what we mean by *trends* and *cycles*. The process of separating the observations on a single time series into two components, a trend and a cycle, is called **detrending a series**.

Figure 1.4 illustrates the decomposition of GDP into trend and cycles that results from detrending per capita GDP by drawing the best straight line through the points. This technique is called **linear detrending** and is one of three popular methods of breaking a

FIGURE 1.5
Procyclical and Countercyclical Variables

Coherence is the tendency of variables to move together over the business cycle.
The cycle in consumption moves with the cycle in GDP and is therefore *procyclical*.
The cycle in unemployment moves against the cycle in GDP and is therefore *countercyclical*.

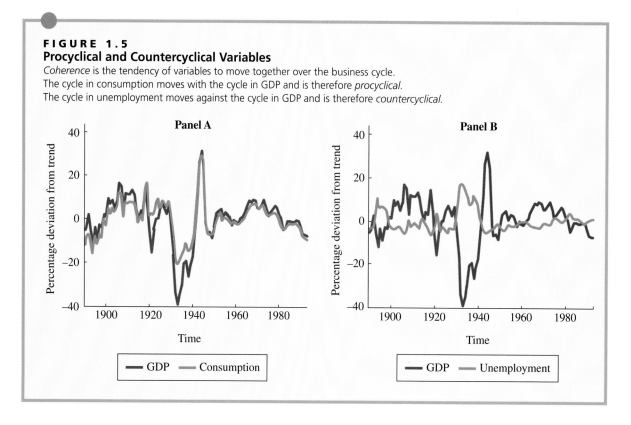

time series into trend and cycles. (We examine two other methods in Chapter 3). Figure 1.5 shows GDP per capita (the blue line) and the deviation of per capita GDP from its linear trend (the red line). Notice that the red line is above zero when per capita GDP rises above its trend and below zero when GDP falls below its trend.

One important feature of the business cycle, as illustrated in Figure 1.4, is that it is irregular. Although many economic variables are irregular, they tend to be irregular in the same way at the same point in time. Graphs of many time series display the same bumps and dips as the detrended per capita GDP series plotted here. Still other time series display exactly the opposite bumps and dips. We capture this idea in economics by developing a measure of the coherence of a time series with GDP. Coherence, remember, is the tendency of two variables to move up and down together.

Coherence can be illustrated by plotting two detrended variables on the same graph. Figure 1.5 illustrates the coherence between consumption and GDP per capita in panel A and between unemployment and GDP per capita in panel B. In each case, the cycle in consumption, unemployment, and GDP has been constructed by removing a linear trend. The cyclical component of consumption is plotted against the cyclical component of GDP per capita in panel A, and the cyclical component of unemployment is plotted against the cyclical component of GDP per capita in panel B. Variables like consumption that move in

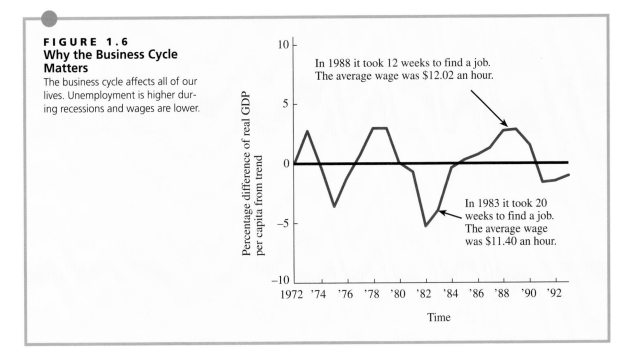

FIGURE 1.6
Why the Business Cycle Matters
The business cycle affects all of our lives. Unemployment is higher during recessions and wages are lower.

In 1988 it took 12 weeks to find a job. The average wage was $12.02 an hour.

In 1983 it took 20 weeks to find a job. The average wage was $11.40 an hour.

the same direction as GDP over the cycle are said to be **procyclical** because they move with (*pro*) the cycle. Unemployment, in panel B, is an example of a variable that tends to be high when GDP is low. Variables like unemployment that move in the opposite direction to GDP over the cycle are said to be **countercyclical** because they move against (*counter* to) the cycle.

Importance of the Business Cycle

Figure 1.6 illustrates some of the differences between the U.S. economy in 1983 in the middle of a recession and the economy in 1988 at a business-cycle peak. In 1988 real per capita GDP was 2% above trend, but in 1984 it was 5% below. In 1988 an unemployed worker could expect to spend about 12 weeks searching for a job and to receive an average wage of $12.02 an hour.[4] But in 1983 a person would need 20 weeks to find a job and would earn only $11.40 an hour (in dollars with comparable purchasing power). If the economy is in recession when you graduate from college you will be paid less and take longer to find a job than if the economy is at the peak of a business-cycle expansion.

4.   From the *Economic Report of the President,* 1993. Real wage data is total economy hourly compensation measured in 1982 dollars, from Table B-42. Unemployment is mean duration, from Table B-39. The trend line used to calculate deviations is the least squares line fitted to the data from 1929 through 1993.

❹ INFLATION

Measuring Inflation

Inflation is the rate of change of the price level from one year to the next and is measured by the percentage increase in an index of prices. Several indices of the price level are in common use; these indices differ according to the bundle of goods included in the index:

1. **The consumer price index (CPI)** measures the average cost of a standard bundle of consumer goods in a given year. The price of each good in the bundle is multiplied by a fraction called its *weight,* and the weighted prices are added up to generate a single number, called the consumer price index. For the CPI the weight of each good in the bundle is its share in the budget of an average consumer.
2. **The producer price index** is also a *weighted average,* but the bundle of goods is selected from an earlier stage in the manufacturing process. For example, the producer price index includes the producer price of wheat and pork, as opposed to the consumer price of bread and bacon.
3. **The GDP deflator** is the most comprehensive price index. It includes all of the goods and services produced in the United States weighted by their relative values as a fraction of GDP.
4. **The GDP price index** is similar to the GDP deflator in that it includes all of the goods and services produced in the United States. It differs from the GDP deflator in the way it weights different commodities.

In this book we typically refer to the rate of change of the GDP deflator when we talk about inflation.[5] The history of the GDP deflator is graphed in Figure 1.7 as the blue line and is measured on the right axis. Figure 1.7 also illustrates the history of inflation. Inflation is related to the GDP deflator in the following way. When the GDP deflator is higher in one year than in the previous year, inflation is positive; when the GDP deflator is lower than in the previous year, inflation is negative. Although inflation has been positive in every year since the end of World War II, there have been significant episodes in U.S. history when the price level fell. The Great Depression is the most striking example although there have been other deflationary episodes, such as at the end of the nineteenth century and in 1920, when prices fell by 20% in a single year.

The Importance of Inflation

In the 1990s in the United States, inflation might seem like a distant problem. The hyperinflations we know about have occurred in countries like Bolivia, Argentina, Austria, and Germany. Although the United States has experienced mild inflation since World War II, the magnitude of this inflation has been dwarfed by those in other countries. Still, U.S. inflation can cause serious problems by disrupting financial contracts. When inflation is unanticipated, as it was in the 1970s, the amount that one person owes to another dwindles in value. Debtors benefit from this kind of inflation but creditors suffer.

---

5.   Recently the Commerce Department has moved to the GDP price index as its price index of choice. We retain the GDP deflator in our discussions because there are longer data series available.

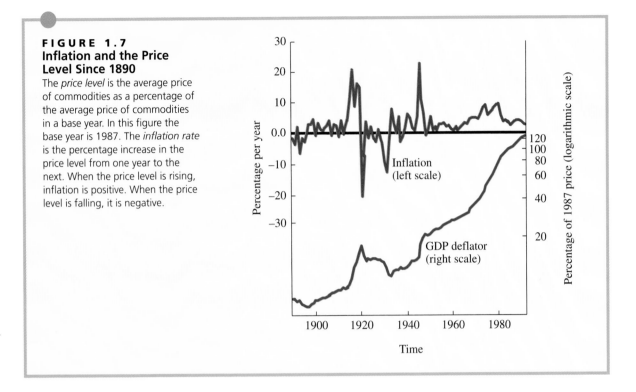

FIGURE 1.7
Inflation and the Price Level Since 1890
The *price level* is the average price of commodities as a percentage of the average price of commodities in a base year. In this figure the base year is 1987. The *inflation rate* is the percentage increase in the price level from one year to the next. When the price level is rising, inflation is positive. When the price level is falling, it is negative.

Inflation increased rapidly from an average of 2% per year in the early 1960s to nearly 10% in 1975. One consequence of this rapid increase in inflation was to deplete the real resources of those on fixed incomes, such as the elderly, and to redistribute these resources to those with large nominal debts, such as young families with fixed-rate mortgages. President Carter failed to win reelection in part as a result of the effects of an unanticipated inflation.

Figure 1.8 illustrates the problems that faced policy makers in the Carter administration. Not only was inflation running at 10% (the highest figure since 1946), but unemployment at the end of the Carter years reached 7.5% and showed no sign of coming down soon. Even when inflation is not in the range of 100 or 200%, it can present a significant brake on economic activity because policy actions taken to lower inflation are also likely to increase unemployment. The link between unemployment and inflation is explored in Chapter 15.

❺ ECONOMIC MODELS

An **economic model** is an artificial economy represented by a set of equations. These equations define the relationships between model variables, each of which is an analog of a real-world variable. A good model of the economy can be used to predict the behavior of economic time series by extrapolating past behavior. Because some of the variables in an

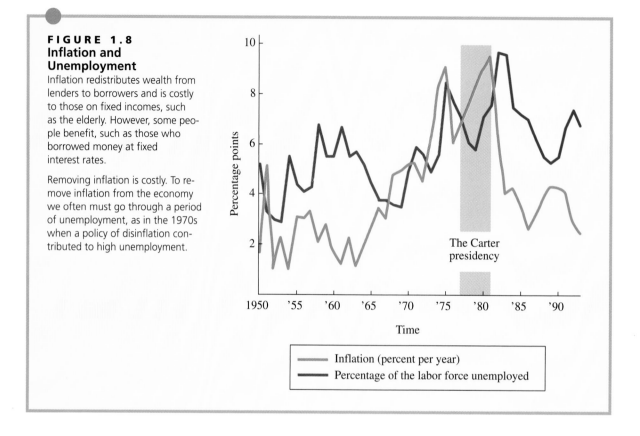

FIGURE 1.8
Inflation and Unemployment
Inflation redistributes wealth from lenders to borrowers and is costly to those on fixed incomes, such as the elderly. However, some people benefit, such as those who borrowed money at fixed interest rates.

Removing inflation is costly. To remove inflation from the economy we often must go through a period of unemployment, as in the 1970s when a policy of disinflation contributed to high unemployment.

economic model have analogs that can be controlled by the government, we may, by manipulating the model variables, learn how to manipulate their real-world analogs to control inflation, reduce unemployment, and increase economic welfare.

The Difference Equation

The main tool that economists use to describe an economic model is an equation that describes how the model variables evolve from one period to the next. An equation of this kind is called a **difference equation**. Difference equations are used in economics to help us to understand the economics of growth and business cycles. Difference equations can also be used to understand the economics of inflation, but, because this topic is more easily explained once we understand the relationships between different economic time series, we confine the discussion in this chapter to how a single variable, GDP per capita, evolves over time.

Figure 1.9 illustrates the way that economists use difference equations to construct economic models. The solid blue curve describes the actual growth of per capita GDP in

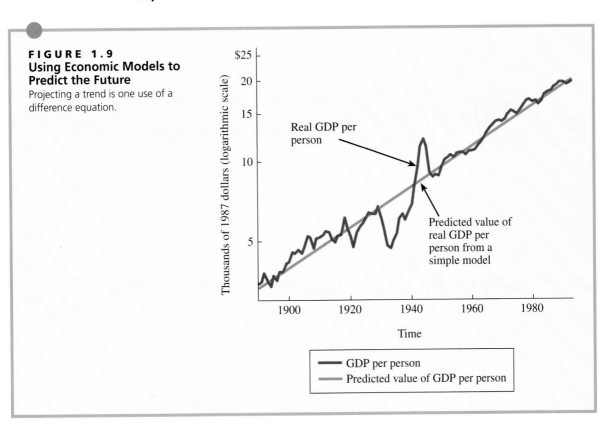

FIGURE 1.9
Using Economic Models to Predict the Future
Projecting a trend is one use of a difference equation.

the United States from 1930 to 1992. The red line is the prediction of a simple model of per capita GDP, where the model predicts that

1.1
$$y_{t+1} = 1.02 \times y_t$$

The variable y_t is per capita GDP at date t, where "t" stands for the year in which GDP is measured. Similarly, y_{t+1} is the GDP one year later. Because the proportional difference between any two years is equal to

$$\frac{y_{t+1} - y_t}{y_t} = \frac{(1.02 \times y_t) - y_t}{y_t} = 0.02 = 2\%$$

the model predicts that GDP will always grow at 2% per year. This equation can be expressed as the statement

The per capita GDP of the United States will be 2% bigger in any given year than it was in the previous year.

Although Equation 1.1 is the simplest possible example of a difference equation, it elegantly represents the idea that the state of the world evolves from one year to the next.

In Part 4 we show how simple difference equations can be used to explain competing theories of growth, business cycles, and inflation. Looking at Figure 1.9 you can see that in some years per capita GDP will be higher than predicted and in other years it will be lower. Although the model will not be right in every year, it may still be right on average. The model can give us a rough guide to future per capita GDP. If we want to improve the ability of this simple model to predict GDP, we must turn to theories of why the economy fluctuates around its trend growth path; that is, we must study the theory of business cycles.

The Rocking Horse Model

Although we refer to the fluctuations in GDP as *cycles,* it is clear from the graph of actual GDP per capita in Figure 1.9 that these cycles are not regular waves of the kind observed in simple physical systems. They have an important random component. For many years economists argued about the best way to model systems like this. In 1933 the Norwegian economist Ragnar Frisch suggested we think of the economy as a **rocking horse** that is being constantly hit by a child with a stick. If the child were to hit the horse just once, it would return slowly to its rest position, rocking back and forth along the way. But if the child were to constantly pound it, in a random manner, the rocking horse would continue to move in a way that depended partly on the motion of the stick and partly on the internal dynamics of the rocker. Frisch suggested that an economy is like the rocking horse: It is constantly hit by an impulse (the child with the stick) but it also has a mechanism for propagating these impulses (the dynamics of the rocker). In 1969 Ragnar Frisch and Dutch economist Jan Tinbergen won the first Nobel prize in economics.

As a description of the behavior of real per capita GDP, Frisch's idea does a pretty good job. Take a look at Figure 1.10 and ask yourself which of the lines is real data and which is artificial data simulated by an economic model. If you think about it, you will realize that the red line is real data because only the line dips in the 1930s (the Great Depression) and rises in 1945 (the end of World War II). But if you didn't know anything about economic history, you would be unable to tell which was real. In this sense the model that simulated the artificial series is a good model of the real world.

Most economists agree that a good place to start modeling the economy is with some version of Frisch's rocking horse analogy, but not about which design of rocking horse is the right one to choose. Frisch's analogy suggests that we can separate economic theories of the business cycle into two parts: one that deals with the propagation mechanism and one that deals with the impulse. Economists disagree about how to model each part.

Unified Theory

Macroeconomics and microeconomics differ more in their topics than in their methods. Macroeconomics concentrates on the working of the economy as a whole and on how it evolves through time. Microeconomics deals with parts of the economy in isolation and with the behaviors that form the foundation for macroeconomic theory. The defining feature of our approach to macroeconomics is that the microeconomics of demand and supply can be used to understand every aspect of the macroeconomy.

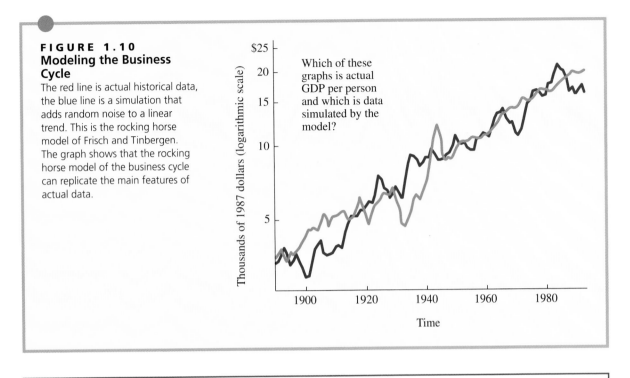

FIGURE 1.10
Modeling the Business Cycle
The red line is actual historical data, the blue line is a simulation that adds random noise to a linear trend. This is the rocking horse model of Frisch and Tinbergen. The graph shows that the rocking horse model of the business cycle can replicate the main features of actual data.

Which of these graphs is actual GDP per person and which is data simulated by the model?

CONCLUSION

Three main issues are addressed in this book: What determines economic growth? What are the causes of business cycles? and What determines inflation?

Economic growth is the persistent tendency of GDP per capita to increase on average in every country in the world. The theory of growth is concerned with why it occurs and why countries grow at different rates. Small differences in growth rates can cause big differences in the standard of living across countries and through time.

The fluctuations in many economic time series tend to move slowly through time; this inertia in a single time series is called *persistence*. The fluctuations in groups of time series move closely together; this co-movement is called *coherence*. The *business cycle* is the tendency of a group of economic series to display persistence and coherence. Business cycles are important because even though living standards on average are increasing over time, GDP per capita may take prolonged dips below trend that last for many years.

The theory of inflation is concerned with why prices have increased at 4.5% on average since World War II. Periods of high inflation, called *hyperinflation,* are very disruptive to economic life. Periods of moderate inflation are also disruptive, particularly when they are unanticipated by those on fixed incomes. Inflation that becomes built into the economy is difficult to control because the same policies that stem inflation also temporarily increase unemployment.

Although the economics of growth, business cycles, and inflation are separate topics, the factors that cause one are related to the factors that cause the others. To understand these topics economists construct economic models, which are systems of equations.

Base year	Inflation
Boom (expansion)	Linear detrending
Business cycles	Macroeconomics
Coherence	Macroeconomic variables
Consumer price index (CPI)	Microeconomics
Contraction (recession)	Nominal GDP
Countercyclical variables	Persistence
Detrending a series	Procyclical variables
Difference equation	Producer price index
Economic model	Real GDP
Gross Domestic Product (GDP)	Rocking horse model
GDP deflator	Rule of seventy
GDP price index	Standard of living
Growth	Time series
Hyperinflation	Weighted average

PROBLEMS FOR REVIEW

1. Using the data on the GDP deflator from the back of the book, calculate the rate of inflation for every year from 1890 through 1996. Which years had the highest inflation rates? Which years experienced the lowest inflation rates?

2. Using the data on real GDP from the back of the book, draw a graph of the logarithm of real GDP against time for the period from 1890 to 1996. Using a ruler, draw the best line through the points. Which years would you classify as recessions? If you had used only the data from 1950 through 1996 to plot the best line, what would your answer be?

3. Assume that the Chinese real GDP per capita is approximately 12.5% of real GDP per capita in the United States. If Chinese per capita GDP grows at 7% and U.S. per capita GDP grows at 2%, how many years will it take for China to catch up with the United States?

4. GDP in 1993 is approximately $6 trillion. If GDP grows by 3% every year for five years, what will GDP be in 1998? (*Hint*: Use your calculator and solve the equation

$$y_{t+1} = 1.03 \times y_t$$

five times, beginning with $y_1 = 6$).

5. Write a brief note (one page) to a friend who is not studying economics, explaining concisely what is meant by

a. growth   b. business cycles   c. inflation

CHAPTER 2

Measuring the Economy

❶ INTRODUCTION

The goal of macroeconomics is to understand how real-world economies operate. We seek to understand the links between variables like growth and inflation, unemployment and interest rates, and government spending and taxes. Our hope is that by understanding these links, we may design policies that improve people's lives. But before we can begin to understand how the world operates, we must measure the data that we want to explain. This chapter covers the measurement of two kinds of data: flow variables, such as GDP and income, and stock variables, such as capital and wealth. We learn how stocks and flows are measured and how flows measure the way that stocks change through time.

The chapter begins with how to decide whether a particular economy is open or closed and how to subdivide it into sectors. We then turn to the measurement of flows, the most important example of which is GDP. A large part of this chapter is concerned with the measurement of GDP and its components. Next we focus on measuring the most important example of a stock, national wealth. Finally, we link wealth accounting and national income.

❷ DIVIDING UP THE WORLD ECONOMY

Open and Closed Economies

The world economy is a fabric woven of many national economies, and although we are sometimes interested in looking at the pattern of the whole, for the most part we study one country at a time. We call the economy of the country that we are interested in the **domestic economy**, and we refer to the collection of all other economies as the **rest of the world.** When a domestic economy is studied in isolation from the rest of the world, it is called a **closed economy**. When we explicitly consider interactions with other countries, we call it an **open economy**. Because all countries in the modern world engage in international trade, there are no real closed economies, but sometimes it is useful to ignore the effects of foreign trade in order to understand how a single economy works.

The United States and Canada together make up only 5% of the world population, but they produce 23% of the world output. Box 2.1 illustrates the tremendous differences between population and GDP by region. Understanding these differences is one of the central tasks of the theory of economic growth (covered in Chapter 13).

Sectors of the Domestic Economy

We often treat the entire U.S. domestic economy as though aggregate variables were chosen by a single decision maker. Treating the entire domestic economy as a single unit is useful when we want to know, for example, how the United States allocates its resources between consumption and investment. For other purposes we break down the economy further into its component parts. One such division is between the **public sector** (government sector) and the **private sector**. This distinction is useful when we want to know how government affects the division of resources between consumption and investment.

WEBWATCH 2.1   **Check out the Commerce Department on the Web**

Established on February 14, 1903, to promote American businesses and trade, the U.S. Department of Commerce is the most versatile agency in government. Its broad range of responsibilities include expanding U.S. exports, developing innovative technologies, gathering and disseminating statistical data, measuring economic growth, granting patents, promoting minority entrepreneurship, predicting the weather, and monitoring stewardship. As diverse as Commerce's services are, there is an overarching mandate that unifies them: to work with the business community to foster economic growth and the creation of new American jobs.

(Quoted from the Commerce Department Web site)

The Commerce Department Web site contains links to a fountain of useful information compiled by the Bureau of Economic Analysis http://www.bea.doc.gov and the Bureau of the Census http://www.census.gov, both of which are divisions of the Commerce Department. The Commerce Department homepage is at http://www.doc.gov.

BOX 2.1
FOCUS ON THE FACTS:
North America and the World Economy

How big is the North American continent (United States and Canada) relative to the rest of the world? That depends on what you mean by size. If big means number of people, North America is relatively small. Its population in 1988 was 270 million, or 5% of all of the people in the world. But although the United States and Canada are relatively small in terms of population, they make up by far the world's largest economic region when measured by goods produced. Combined U.S. and Canadian GDP in 1988 was $4.89 trillion, close to a quarter of the world GDP.

The fact that the United States produces a large fraction of the world GDP means that North American living standards, as measured by per capita GDP, are the highest in the world. Per capita GDP in North America was $17,600 in 1988 as opposed to $1,300 in Africa. North Americans produced nearly 14 times as many goods and services on average as did Africans, and North Americans are correspondingly much richer. The most important reason for higher productivity in North America is that North America has more capital. This is true of both physical capital (highways, railways, roads, airports, factories, and machines) and human capital. High human capital means that the average North American is better educated and in a better position to produce commodities that require a high degree of skill than people of many other regions. Human capital commands high income in the modern world marketplace.

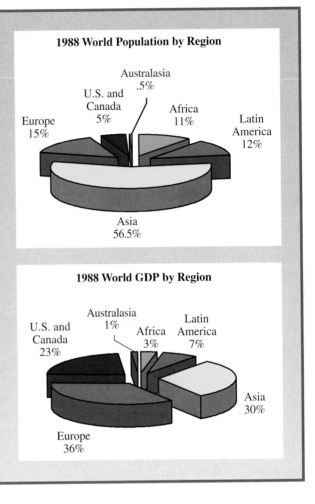

Another useful division breaks the private sector into **households** and **firms**. Firms produce commodities and services, and they own land, factories, and machines. Ultimately, firms are owned by individuals who belong to households. Households buy and sell commodities, supply services to firms, and borrow and lend to the government, to firms, and to other households. The distinction between households and firms is important in models of income determination.

❸ MEASURING GROSS DOMESTIC PRODUCT

Income, Expenditure, and Product

GDP is the most important indicator of the productive capacity of an economy. A comprehensive set of data on GDP and its components is recorded in the system of

National Income and Product Accounts (NIPA), published by a branch of the U.S. Commerce Department called the Bureau of Economic Analysis. The Commerce Department arrives at the GDP using three methods: the income method, the expenditure method, and the product (or value-added) method. To understand how these approaches work in practice, we first need to understand three concepts: final goods, intermediate goods, and value-added.

Gross Domestic Product (GDP) is the value of all final goods and services produced within the United States in a year. **Final goods** are those that are sold directly to final users, as opposed to **intermediate goods** (or inputs), which are produced by one firm and used as an input by another. Some firms produce final goods directly from capital and labor, but most firms also use intermediate goods. A firm that uses intermediate goods adds value because the goods it produces are sold for more than the value of the intermediate goods it buys. The **value added** is the difference between the value of the output that a firm sells and the value of the intermediate goods it used in manufacturing them.

The Circular Flow of Income

Income and output flow around the economy like water through a pipe; this idea, illustrated in Figure 2.1, is called the **circular flow of income**. The purple arrow on the left tracks the flow of **domestic expenditure** by households; the green arrow on the left tracks the flow of commodities and services that households purchase. The purple arrow on the right represents the flow of **domestic income** from firms to households; the green arrow on the right represents the flow of **factor services** that households supply to firms in exchange for this income.

Factor services include labor, the services of land and factories, and the entrepreneurial skills supplied by managers of corporations and owners of small businesses. In reality firms use many kinds of services in the production process, but for the purpose of building models we divide these services into just two types: labor and capital. We call the income that is earned by the supply of labor services **labor income** and the income that is earned from supplying the services of capital **profit**. By adding up all of the income earned by the factors of production we arrive at the **income method of computing GDP**.

Domestic expenditure on final goods and services refers to the purchase of final goods by households and firms. By adding up all of the expenditures on final goods and services we arrive at the **expenditure method of computing GDP**. Pursuing the analogy of water flowing around a pipe, the income and expenditure methods of computing GDP correspond to measuring this flow at different points in the pipe.

Box 2.2 illustrates the third method for computing GDP, the **product** or **value added method**. For each firm in the economy, the product method computes the difference between the value of the firm's output and the cost of its expenditures on intermediate inputs; this difference is called the firm's value added. GDP is the sum of the values added over all firms in the economy.

Consumption, Investment, and Saving

For many purposes we may want to measure the composition of goods that make up GDP. The components of GDP in a closed economy are consumption, investment,

FIGURE 2.1
The Circular Flow of Income
Households spend money on goods and services produced by firms. Firms pay money to households in return for the services of the factors of production (labor and capital).

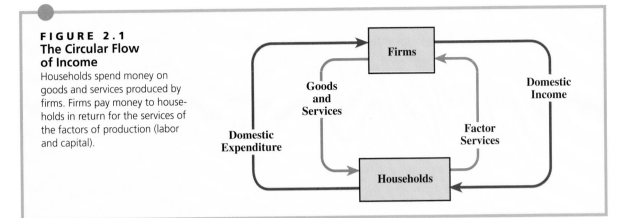

BOX 2.2
Measuring GDP

The household buys bread from the baker and flour from the miller; these are expenditures on *final goods*. The baker buys flour from the miller; these are expenditures on *intermediate goods*. Only final goods production counts as part of the GDP. The miller pays $40 to households for the services of labor and $10 for the services of capital, and uses these services to

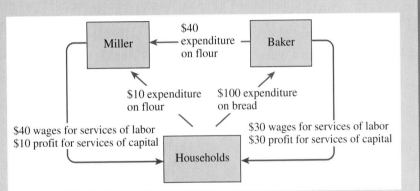

produce flour worth $50. Because the miller does not use intermediate inputs its value added is equal to $50—the same as the value of its product. Because the miller sells its product both to final users (the household) and to intermediate users (the baker), flour is both an intermediate good and a final good. The value of the flour sold to the baker is $40; this part of the production of the miller is an intermediate good because it is used by the baker to produce bread. The value of the flour sold directly to households is $10; this part of the production of the miller is a final good.

The baker combines the $40 of flour that it buys from the miller with $30 of labor services and $30 of capital services that it purchases from households. Using the flour and the services of labor and capital, the baker produces final goods worth $100. Because the intermediate goods purchased by the baker cost only $40, the value added by the baker is $60.

Recall that there are three methods for calculating the value of GDP. The expenditure method adds up the value of all expenditures on final goods and services. Because the household spent $10 on flour and $100 on bread, the expenditure method yields a figure of $110:

$$\text{Expenditure} = \$10 + \$100 = \$110$$

Using the income method, we compute GDP by adding up the income earned by all of the factors of production. The household received $70 in wages and $40 in rents, also yielding a figure of $110:

$$\text{Income} = \$70 + \$40 = \$110$$

To compute GDP using the product method, we sum the value added by every firm in the economy. The miller adds $50 in value and the baker adds $60. Once again this approach yields a value for GDP of $110:

$$\text{Product} = \$50 + \$60 = \$110$$

Productive activity in the domestic economy is a flow that can be measured in three different ways.

and government expenditure. In an open economy GDP includes exports but excludes imports.

We begin by differentiating between consumption and investment goods. **Consumption goods** are commodities like haircuts, movies, beer, and pizza that meet our immediate needs. **Investment goods** are commodities like tractors, power plants, roads, and bridges that help us to produce more goods in the future. In any given year the members of a society will enjoy a higher standard of living if they increase their consumption. But a policy of consuming more in the present is short-sighted because current consumption is at the expense of investment, which can increase the quantity of commodities available for consumption in future years.

Although society as a whole requires capital goods to produce output, households do not directly invest in capital. Instead, they save money by abstaining from consumption and lending resources to banks and other financial institutions. Firms invest when they purchase new factories and machines. To raise money for investment, firms either borrow directly from banks or issue new shares that are sold to households or to other financial institutions in the capital market. Alternatively, firms may finance investment from retained earnings. **Retained earnings** are profits that are used to purchase new capital instead of being returned to shareholders as dividends. Whether a firm finances its investment through retained earnings or through new borrowing, the net effect is the same. Some of the income that could otherwise have been used to purchase consumption goods has instead been channeled into investment. Financial institutions that channel savings from households to firms are collectively referred to as the **capital market**. They include banks, the stock market, pension funds, and savings and loan institutions.

In Figure 2.2 the circular flow model is amended to show this process. Households divide their income between consumption and saving. When they fail to spend all of their income on consumption commodities, they channel the funds through the capital market to borrowers who use the money to buy factories and machines. The amount of income that is invested as opposed to consumed is an important determinant of economic growth because the more resources that a society invests now, the more commodities it will be able to produce later.

Wages and Profits

Because every commodity earns income for the factors that produced it, the GDP of a closed economy is equal to the income earned by its residents. In the NIPA the income earned by the factors of production is broken down into several components. The largest component represents payments to the services of labor; this is called **compensation to employees** and consists of wages and other elements of employee benefits such as the value of health care packages and pension rights. Other categories include net interest, rent, corporate profit, and proprietor's income. In this book we build very simple models in which land and capital are interchangeable and labor is not separated into skilled and unskilled. In these simple models we will distinguish only two types of income, labor income, which we call wages, and capital income, which we call profit. In the United States the share of income earned by labor is approximately two-thirds and the share earned by capital is one-third.

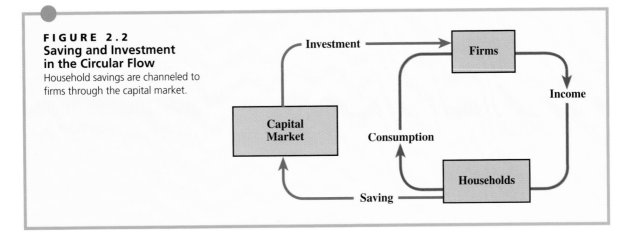

FIGURE 2.2
Saving and Investment in the Circular Flow
Household savings are channeled to firms through the capital market.

❹ THE COMPONENTS OF GROSS DOMESTIC PRODUCT

Although individuals may save more or less than they invest, in a closed economy saving and investment are always equal.[1] In open economies this idea extends to relationships among the government budget deficit, the trade deficit, and private saving.

Saving and Investment in a Closed Economy

Expenditure can be divided into three categories: private consumption expenditure, private investment expenditure, and government expenditure on goods and services. Equation 2.1 defines the relationships among these categories, using the symbol Y to represent GDP, C for private consumption, I for private investment, and G for government purchases of goods and services. This equation is called the **GDP accounting identity**.

2.1
$$Y = C + I + G$$

We can further divide government purchases into government spending on investment goods, I^{GOV}, and government spending on consumption goods, C^{GOV}. Using these terms we can rewrite the GDP accounting identity as follows:

2.2
$$Y = C^{TOT} + I^{TOT}$$

where $C^{TOT} = C + C^{GOV}$ is total consumption by government and the private sector, and $I^{TOT} = I + I^{GOV}$ is total investment.

---

1.   Remember that investment means the accumulation of physical capital, not the purchase of financial assets.

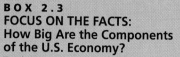

BOX 2.3
FOCUS ON THE FACTS:
How Big Are the Components of the U.S. Economy?
Total consumption (government plus private consumption) has remained roughly constant at 80% of GDP since 1930. Total investment has remained constant at 20% of GDP. In other words, society as a whole uses one-fifth of its resources (the services of labor and capital) to build new factories and machines and to replace old ones.

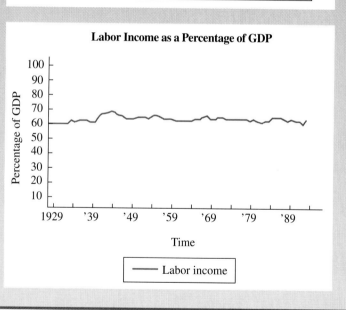

GDP produces income for the factors of production. Ever since we have kept good records, the share of GDP earned by labor has been equal to two-thirds. The remaining third generates income that compensates the owners of land and capital.

In common usage the words *saving* and *investment* are used to mean the same thing. In economics, we use *saving* to mean the part of income that is not consumed and *investment* to mean additions to the stock of capital goods. Using this definition, total saving of the economy is defined as

2.3

$$S^{\text{TOT}} = Y - C^{\text{TOT}}$$

Government expenditure makes up roughly 30% of GDP and has grown substantially since 1929 when government spending accounted for only 10% of GDP. Most of the growth in recent years has been as a result of entitlement programs such as Social Security, Medicaid, and Medicare. Three-quarters of government expenditure is federal; the remainder is at the state and local level.

In 1929 foreign trade accounted for only 4% of GDP; in 1993 the figure was closer to 13%. In 1929 it was possible to argue that, for most purposes, the United States was a closed economy. The growing importance of foreign trade made this assumption steadily less tenable.

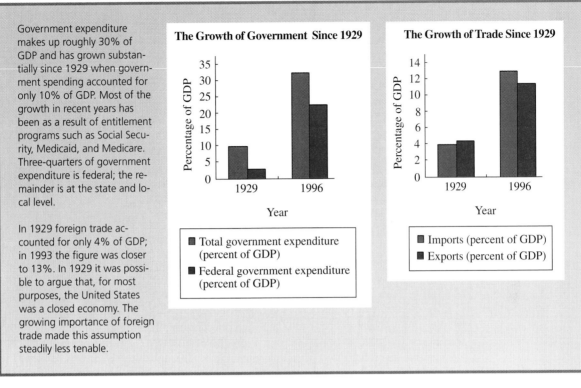

The Growth of Government Since 1929

■ Total government expenditure (percent of GDP)
■ Federal government expenditure (percent of GDP)

The Growth of Trade Since 1929

■ Imports (percent of GDP)
■ Exports (percent of GDP)

If we combine the definitions of the components of GDP from Equation 2.2 with the definition of saving from Equation 2.3, it follows that in a closed economy saving and investment must be equal:

2.4
$$S^{\text{TOT}} = I^{\text{TOT}}$$

Saving and Investment in an Open Economy

Although saving and investment are always equal in a closed economy, this is not true in the real world because countries may invest more than they save by borrowing from abroad. This possibility leads to an interesting connection between two concepts that are frequently discussed in the news: **budget deficit** and **trade surplus**. The amount that the government borrows from the public can have a significant impact on the goods that we import from abroad.

We begin by defining *deficit* and *surplus*. A deficit is an excess of expenditure over income. When a government spends more than it earns, the excess expenditure is the government's budget deficit. When the nation as a whole spends more on foreign goods and services than it earns by selling exports, the excess of expenditures over income is the nation's trade deficit. Because the nation earns income by selling exports and spends accumulated assets by purchasing imports, the trade deficit is equal to imports minus exports.

In recent years the government has typically spent more than it earns; the difference has been made up by accumulating debt. This is not always the case; in some years government revenues exceeded expenditure. When this happens, we say that the government budget is in surplus. Because a budget surplus results in an accumulation of government assets, we also refer to a budget surplus as government saving.

When exports exceed imports we say that the nation enjoys a trade surplus. Because the trade surplus is equal to the difference of exports over imports, we also call this **net exports;** the value of net exports is also commonly referred to as the **balance of trade.** Table 2.1 lists these definitions and their mathematical relationships to each other. Notice in particular that a deficit is just a negative surplus; we often use the terms deficit and surplus interchangeably.

To study the relationship between saving and investment in an open economy, we begin by amending the national income accounting identity to allow for the fact that some of the expenditure of U.S. residents is on imported goods and that some of the goods produced in the United States are sold to foreign countries. This leads us to add an additional term to Equation 2.2 to account for the difference between the value of the goods sold abroad and the value of the goods imported:

2.5
$$Y = C^{\text{TOT}} + I^{\text{TOT}} + NX$$

where NX represents net exports and is defined as exports (EX), minus imports (IM). Putting this equation together with the definition of total savings (Equation 2.3) produces an equation that relates savings to investment in an open economy:

2.6
$$S^{\text{TOT}} - I^{\text{TOT}} = NX$$

Equation 2.6 says that when a country saves more than it invests at home, saving results in a flow of commodities out of the country; that is, exports exceed imports. These resources may either be invested abroad in new factories and machines in foreign countries, or they may be consumed by foreigners, who incur a debt that must be repaid in future years.

Government and the Private Sector

Total saving can be divided into government and private saving. To define private saving we first need to introduce a term for the income that is available to the private sector after the government takes out taxes and puts back transfer payments to individuals and firms. This concept, called **disposable income**, is defined as

2.7
$$YD = Y + TR - T$$

where YD is disposable income, TR is **transfer payments,** and T is **taxes.** We can now define private saving as

2.8
$$S = YD - C$$

TABLE 2.1
Concepts Used in Budget Accounting

Concept	Symbol	Definition	Category
Imports	IM		
Exports	EX		
Trade Surplus (Net Exports) (Balance of Trade)	NX	$NX = EX - IM$	Foreign Trade
Trade Deficit (Net Imports)	$-NX$	$-NX = IM - EX$	
Government Purchases	G		
Transfer Payments	TR		
Government Revenues (Taxes)	T		Government Budget
Government Budget Deficit	D	$D = G + TR - T$	
Government Budget Surplus (Government Saving)	$-D$	$-D = T - G - TR$	

If we put the definitions of private saving and disposable income back into Equation 2.6 and use the earlier definitions of total saving and total investment, we arrive at the following breakdown of saving and investment between public and private sectors[2]

2.9
$$(S - I) + (T - TR - G) = NX$$

This equation tells us about the interaction of the government, the private sector, and the rest of the world. The term $(S - I)$ represents private saving; $(T - TR - G)$ is government saving. In recent years the U.S. government budget has been in deficit (government saving has been negative) because the government has spent more than it takes in taxes. Equation 2.9 demonstrates that there are two ways the government can do this: It can

---

2.   From Equations 2.7 and 2.5 we have $YD = C + I + G + NX + TR - T$. But from the definition of private savings, Equation 2.8, $YD = S + C$. Putting together these two expressions and rearranging terms gives us Equation 2.9.

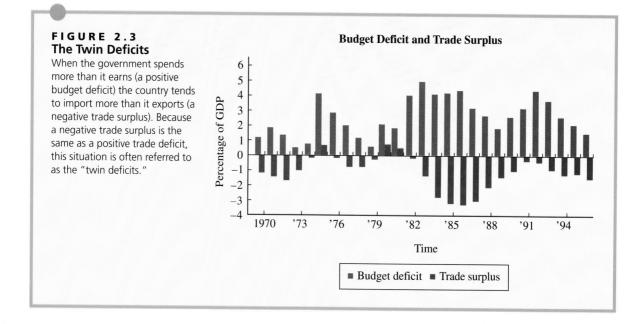

FIGURE 2.3
The Twin Deficits
When the government spends more than it earns (a positive budget deficit) the country tends to import more than it exports (a negative trade surplus). Because a negative trade surplus is the same as a positive trade deficit, this situation is often referred to as the "twin deficits."

borrow from U.S. residents—this happens when private saving (S) is greater than private investment (I)—or it can borrow from the rest of the world—this happens when imports (IM) are greater than exports (EX) and hence net exports (NX) are less than zero. If the government borrows mainly from domestic residents, we expect private saving to be greater than private investment, because domestic residents save to buy newly issued government bonds. If, on the other hand, domestic residents are unwilling to supply all of the resources required to fund government expenditure, we would expect to see a negative trade surplus, $NX < 0$, because the economy as a whole imports goods to fuel its excess demand for commodities.

Figure 2.3 shows the history of the budget deficit and the trade surplus in the United States since 1970. In the 1980s the Reagan administration cut taxes and increased defense expenditures, thereby raising the budget deficit. This increase in the budget deficit was paid for by borrowing in the capital market: The government sold bonds to the public. If U.S. citizens had responded to this increase in government debt by saving more, there would have been no adverse consequence for the trade surplus. However, much of the increased government debt was purchased by foreigners. This shows on Figure 2.3 as a larger negative trade surplus at about the same time as the increase in the budget deficit. Partly because Americans cannot borrow from abroad forever without eventually repaying the debt, large government budget deficits are perceived to be a problem. This is one major reason why we have begun to balance the budget again in the 1990s by reducing public expenditures. The effect of the budget balancing measures of the Clinton administration, in partnership with the Republican Congress, can be seen in Figure 2.3 as budget deficits that have clearly declined as a percentage of the GDP since 1992.

❺ MEASURING WEALTH

The concepts used to measure GDP and its component parts are examples of flows. In this section we look at the measurement of wealth. Wealth is a stock and is measured by a system of balance sheet accounting.

Stocks and Flows

There are two kinds of economic variables: stocks and flows. A **stock** is a variable measured at a point in time; a **flow** is a variable measured per unit of time. A flow is often the rate of change of a stock. An important economic example is the relationship of government debt, a stock, to the government budget deficit, a flow. If the government deficit is equal to $100 billion per year, the government debt will grow bigger by $100 billion *each and every year.* Table 2.2 illustrates the relationship between a stock and a flow using the example of Jane Chavez, an economics student who spends more each month than she earns by borrowing against her credit card.

At the beginning of the year Jane has a zero balance on her credit card. Every month she runs up bills that exceed her repayments to the credit card company by $100. Jane's deficit is $100 per month. This is a flow. Each month that her deficit equals $100 Jane's debt to the credit card company increases by the amount of the deficit. Jane's debt is a stock. Jane runs a constant deficit, so the stock of her debt grows each month, and by the beginning of May she has accumulated a debt of $500.

Real and Financial Assets

The capital owned by an individual or firm is called a **real asset**. The wealth of an individual may consist not only of capital but also of less tangible items, such as promises by someone else to repay resources in the future. Promises to deliver resources in the future are called **financial assets**.

TABLE 2.2
The Credit Card Statement of Jane Chavez

	Excess of Charges Over Payments (Flow)	Credit Card Balance (Stock)
Beginning Balance		$0
January	$100	$100
February	$100	$200
March	$100	$300
April	$100	$400
May	$100	$500

An individual who promises to deliver goods in the future incurs a **financial liability**. The individual who buys the promise gains a financial asset. An example of a financial asset is a mortgage on a house. A private individual borrows money from a bank by signing a mortgage. The mortgage represents a financial liability to the household, but to the bank that holds the mortgage it is a financial asset. An important feature of financial assets is that, in a closed economy, every financial asset is someone else's financial liability. One implication of this is that although a financial asset represents wealth to an individual agent, it does not represent wealth to the whole economy. In a closed economy the sum total of all financial assets and liabilities is zero.

In an open economy financial debts and liabilities do not equal zero because some individuals and firms borrow or lend abroad. In 1993, for example, U.S. financial assets in foreign countries were equal to $11,000 per person, whereas the value of U.S. assets owned by foreigners amounted to $12,600 per person. As a nation, we were in debt to the rest of the world to the tune of $1,600 per person.

Balance Sheet Accounting

The total wealth, or **net worth**, of an agent is the sum total of her assets (both real and financial) minus the sum of her financial liabilities. The method used to keep track of the assets and liabilities of the households and firms in an economy is called **balance sheet accounting**. Table 2.3 shows how balance sheet accounting is used to record the assets and liabilities of John Chen, a professor of economics. John has two real assets, a house worth $100,000 and a car worth $20,000. He also owns a bank account. The bank account is an example of a financial asset because it represents a loan to the bank. On the liability side of his balance sheet, John has a mortgage and an auto loan.

It is conventional to separate a person's real and financial assets by drawing a horizontal line across the balance sheet. Above the line we record the real assets and below the line we record the financial assets. John's real assets (his house and his car) are worth $120,000 and his financial asset (a bank account) is worth $5,000. Offsetting these assets he has financial liabilities in the form of a mortgage on his house for $80,000 and a loan on his car worth $5,000. Subtracting his liabilities from his assets we arrive at John's *net worth,* which is equal to $40,000. By convention, net worth is recorded on the liabilities side of the balance sheet—it is a liability that you owe to yourself—guaranteeing that the total value of assets and liabilities add up to the same amount. John's assets and liabilities each add up to $125,000.

American National Wealth

We have seen how to apply balance sheet accounting to an individual; in this section we apply it to the United States. National wealth consists of the value of its land and natural resources, its accumulated physical structures in the form of houses, factories, machines, roads, bridges, and other public infrastructure, and the skills and knowledge of its people. Collectively we refer to all of the tangible physical resources as physical capital and to the skills and knowledge of the people as human capital. Because the value of human capital is difficult to measure, it is often ignored in measuring wealth. In the rest of this book, unless stated otherwise, the term *capital* is used exclusively to mean physical capital.

TABLE 2.3
An Example of Balance Sheet Accounting

The dashed line separates real assets from financial assets.

John Chen				
Assets		**Liabilities**		
House	$100,000			
Car	$ 20,000			
Bank		Mortgage	$ 80,000	
account	$ 5,000	Auto Loan	$ 5,000	
		Net Worth	$ 40,000	
	$125,000		$125,000	

How great is our national wealth? In 1993 the value of the nation's capital stock plus the value of all of the land in the United States was equal to $24.75 trillion.[3] Because there are approximately 250 million Americans, the share of the nation's wealth owned by the average American was $99,000. Of course there is no such person as the "Average American" and no individual owns exactly $99,000 at every stage of life, but this figure makes the wealth of the U.S. economy much easier to comprehend. The balance sheet of the average American, obtained by adding up the real assets and liabilities of the entire population and dividing by the number of people, is reported in Box 2.4.

⑥ THE LINK BETWEEN GROSS DOMESTIC PRODUCT AND WEALTH

Wealth accounting measures stocks, and income accounting measures flows; the NIPA can be used to show how the stocks of real and financial assets of the different sectors of the economy change from one year to the next. The key to this relationship is the fact that a flow can be used to measure the change in a stock.

Gross Versus Net Domestic Product

We can invest in new capital by producing new capital goods, such as factories, houses, and machines, but not all investment creates new capital; some investment is necessary each year to offset the deterioration through normal wear and tear of the existing stock of capital. The portion of gross investment that contributes to increases in the stock of capital is called **net investment**. The portion that is devoted to replacing worn out capital is called **depreciation**.

---

3. The *Economic Report of the President,* 1994, Table B–112, using data compiled by the Board of Governors of the Federal Reserve, reports a figure of $18.5 trillion for aggregate private wealth. We have added an estimate of $6.25 trillion to account for public capital. This estimate is based on the assumption that government assets are roughly twice the size of government debt (R. Eisner and P. J. Pieper, "A New View of the Federal Debt and Budget Deficits," *The American Economic Review,* March 1984, pp. 11–29. See Table A1, p. 25.)

BOX 2.4
FOCUS ON THE FACTS:
The Wealth of the Average American

Table A shows the balance sheet of the average American in 1993. The average American had a net worth of $97,400, with $99,000 worth of physical assets, such as land, houses, buildings, and machines. Offsetting these physical assets were $1,600 of debts to the rest of the world.

Tables B and C break down the balance sheet of the average American into assets and liabilities accumulated by the private and public sectors. Table B shows that the private sector owned $74,000 in physical assets in the United States: land, houses, factories, and machines. In addition to owning U.S. assets, Americans invest around $10,000 per person overseas, shown in Table B as ownership of foreign financial assets. In addition, foreigners invest in the U.S. economy. Foreign ownership of private U.S. assets is now larger than U.S. ownership of foreign assets. Americans also lend to their government to the tune of $10,800 per person.

Table C shows that about one-quarter of U.S. physical assets are publicly owned. These assets consist of roads, schools, government enterprises, public parks, and other government capital. The extent of these assets has been estimated to be roughly twice the size of government debt, which is itself considerable. In 1993 the government owed roughly $12,800 per person, of which $10,800 was owed to U.S. citizens and the remaining $2,000 to foreigners.

TABLE A:
The Balance Sheet of the Average American

	Assets	Liabilities	
Physical assets	$99,000		
		$ 1,600	Net debt to foreigners
		$97,400	Net worth
	$99,000	$99,000	

TABLE B:
U.S. Private Sector

	Assets	Liabilities
Physical assets	$74,000	
U.S. ownership of foreign assets	$10,000	
Foreign ownership of U.S. assets	....	$10,600
Loans to U.S. government	$10,800	
Net worth	....	$84,200
	$94,800	$94,800

TABLE C:
U.S. Government

	Assets	Liabilities
Physical assets	$25,000	
Govt. ownership of foreign assets	$ 1,000	
Debt to U.S. citizens	....	$10,800
Debt to foreigners	....	$ 2,000
Net worth	....	$13,200
	$26,000	$26,000

TABLE 2.4
Gross Versus Net Domestic Product

Per Capita Expenditure in 1993 dollars		Per Capita Flow ($ per Year)	Percent of GDP
Consumption (Government Plus Private)		$21,300	84%
Gross Investment (Government Plus Private)		4,400	17
Net Exports		(− 300)	(−1)
Gross Domestic Product per Person	**$25,400**	**25,400**	**100**
Gross Investment		4,400	20
Depreciation	−3,000	−3,000	12
Net Investment		1,400	5
Net Domestic Product per Person	**$22,400**		88

Linked with the idea of net investment is that of **Net Domestic Product (NDP)**, which is a measure of the maximum output of the economy that is available for consumption without running down the stock of capital. Table 2.4 shows the connection between GDP and NDP. From this table we can see that, in 1993, the average American produced goods and earned wages and profits equal to $25,400, spent $21,300 on consumption goods, and spent $4,400 on investment goods. These investment expenditures are divided into two parts: replacement of worn out capital (depreciation), listed as $3,000, and creation of new capital goods (net investment), listed as $1,400. Because the average American must invest at least $3,000 to maintain the existing capital, the maximum income that he or she can produce on a continuing basis is $22,400, the measure we call Net Domestic Product.

Stock and Flow Accounting

In this section we demonstrate how the flows recorded in the NIPA accounts show up as changes in the balance sheets of the U.S. economy from one year to the next. As an example we use a summary statement of the U.S. private sector and public sector balance sheets from January 1993 and January 1994, together with the NIPA flow accounts for the year beginning on January 1, 1993 and ending on January 1, 1994. These three sets of accounts appear in Table 2.5.

The first panel of Table 2.5 represents the balance sheet of the average American in January of 1993. At the beginning of the year, assets total $99,000 in the form of physical capital, but net worth is only $97,400. The discrepancy arises from the fact that in January

TABLE 2.5
How Balance Sheets Are Linked to the National Income and Product Accounts
This balance sheet represents the net asset position of the average American at the beginning of 1993.

Balance Sheet of the Average American on January 1, 1993

Assets		Liabilities	
Real assets	$99,000		
		Net foreign debts	$ 1,600
		Net worth	$97,400
	$99,000		$99,000

This income statement shows how the average American allocated income during the year.

The average American consumed $21,300, saved $4,100, and borrowed $300 from abroad. Gross investment was equal to $4,400, but only $1,400 represented a net addition to the capital stock. The difference was the result of the $3,000 of gross investment used to replace worn out capital.

Income and Expenditure of the Average American, 1993

Total income......................................	$25,400
Consumption.............................	21,300
Saving	4,100
Net foreign borrowing...............	300

Capital Accumulation of the Average American: 1993

Beginning-of-year real assets............	$ 99,000
Depreciation..............................	−3,000
Gross investment........................	4,400
End-of-year real assets...............	100,400

This balance sheet represents the net asset position of the average American at the beginning of 1994. Notice that U.S. capital is greater than in 1993 by the addition of $1,400 net investment. Net worth is less than real assets because part of the capital stock is owned by foreigners.

Balance Sheet of the Average American on January 1, 1994

Assets		Liabilities	
Real assets	$100,400		
		Net foreign debts	$ 1,900
		Net worth	$ 98,500
	$100,400		$100,400

of 1993 the average American had net foreign liabilities of $1,600 as a result of borrowing from abroad to finance past expenditures.

The second panel of Table 2.5 shows that between January 1993 and January 1994 the average American earned $25,400 with $21,300 allocated to consumption goods and $4,400 to investment. Because $3,000 was used to replace depreciated capital, this investment resulted in a net increase in capital stock of $1,400. This net increase in capital is reported on the last panel of Table 2.5 as an increase in real assets from $99,000 in 1993 to $100,400 in January of 1994. The 1994 balance sheet also shows that the average American's net worth increased from $97,400 in 1993 to $98,500 in 1994. The increase in net worth is less than the increase in real assets because part of the increased capital was purchased with borrowed funds.

CONCLUSION

The world economy is a collection of national economies, each of which can be analyzed as open or closed. The domestic economy can be further divided into a public sector; and the private sector can, in turn, be divided into households and firms.

The most important measure of the productive capacity of an economy is GDP, which can be measured in three ways: the income method, the expenditure method, and the product method. The GDP of a closed economy is equal to consumption plus investment. In an open economy it equals consumption plus investment plus net exports. GDP, consumption, investment, and net exports are examples of flows—that is, variables that are measured per unit of time. U.S. GDP in 1993 was roughly $25,000 per person, of which 80% was consumed and 20% invested.

The wealth of an economy is a stock, a variable measured at a point in time. Wealth consists of real assets and financial assets. A real asset is a tangible commodity such as land or a machine; a financial asset is a promise by someone else to deliver commodities to you in the future. U.S. national wealth in 1993 was roughly $99,000 per person.

There are two kinds of investment: gross and net. Gross investment is net investment (additions to capital) plus depreciation (replacement of worn out capital). Wealth and net investment are related to each other since net investment is an addition to wealth.

KEY TERMS

Balance of trade

Balance sheet accounting

Budget deficit

Capital market

Circular flow of income

Closed economy

Compensation to employees

Consumption goods

Depreciation

Disposable income

Domestic economy

Domestic expenditure

Domestic income

Expenditure method of computing GDP

Factor services

Final goods

Financial asset

Financial liability

Firms

Flow

GDP accounting identity

Households

Income method of computing GDP

Intermediate goods

Investment goods

Labor income

National Income and Product Accounts (NIPA)

Net Domestic Product (NDP)

Net exports

Net investment

Net worth

Open economy

Private sector

Product method of computing GDP (value added method)

Profit

Public sector

Real asset

Rest of the world

Retained earnings

Stock

Taxes

Trade surplus

Transfer payments

Value added

PROBLEMS FOR REVIEW

---

1. Which of the following items are stocks and which are flows?

consumption   transfer payments

Gross Domestic Product   capital

government debt   interest payments on the debt

government budget deficit   Net Domestic Product

2. Using the information from Box 2.1, calculate the relative GDP of the average resident of Africa, Latin America, Asia, Europe, and the United States and Canada. Let the United States and Canada equal 1 and find the fraction of U.S. GDP produced by residents of each of these regions.

3. How large is per capita government debt in the United States? How large is consumption as a fraction of GDP? How large is saving as a fraction of GDP?

4. The following balance sheets record the wealth of an average citizen of the Kingdom of Liliput in 1993 and 1994.

Balance Sheet Account of the Average Liliputian

1993		1994	
Assets	Liabilities	Assets	Liabilities
Capital $10,000		Capital $_ _ _ _	
Government debt $7,000	Net worth $_ _ _ _	Government debt $_ _ _ _	Net worth $_ _ _ _
$_ _ _ _	$_ _ _ _	$_ _ _ _	$_ _ _ _

Per Capita National Income and Product in Liliput (1993)

GDP	$5,000
Consumption	$2,600
Government spending	$1,200

All figures are in Liliputian dollars.

a.   What was the per capita gross investment in Liliput during 1993?

b.   Economists in Liliput have estimated that 10% of capital depreciates each year. What was the per capita net investment in Liliput in 1993?

c.   What was the value of per capita Net Domestic Product?

d.   What was the value of the capital stock at the beginning of 1994?

5. The following figures represent gross investment in Liliput during the 1970s. All figures are in 1970 dollars. (Liliput uses 1970 as the base year for its GDP calculations.)

1970 $1,000

1971 $ 800

1972 $1,200

1973 $ 500

1974 $ 900

At the end of 1969 the stock of capital was equal to $5,000. Assuming depreciation of 10% per year, calculate the capital stock in 1977.

6. John Brown owns a car worth $20,000 and a bank account worth $2,000. John lent his wife, Joan, $17,000. Joan owns a car worth $11,000 and jewelry worth $2,000. Between them, John and Joan own a house worth $100,000 and have a mortgage equal to $90,000. Joan has a bank account worth $1,000 and credit debts of $700. Using this information, prepare a balance sheet for John, for Joan, and for the Brown family. (You may assume that the house and the mortgage are apportioned equally between John and Joan.)

7. An economy has two firms. Households own all of the labor services and all of the capital, which they rent out to the firms. Firm A produces sugar using labor services worth $10 and capital services worth $20. It sells $5 worth of sugar to households and $25 worth of sugar to firm B, a bakery. The bakery produces cakes worth $80, which it sells directly to households. Households earn $30 in wages from firms A and B combined.

  a.   What is the value of GDP in this economy?

  b.   What is the value added by firm A?

  c.   What is the value added by firm B?

  d.   How much does the household earn in profit from firms A and B combined?

  e.   What is the total value of intermediate goods produced in this economy?

8. Write a short essay explaining the difference between stocks and flows. Give at least three examples of stocks and flows to illustrate how they are related to each other. Your examples may be drawn from physical or social systems, but at least one example should be economic.

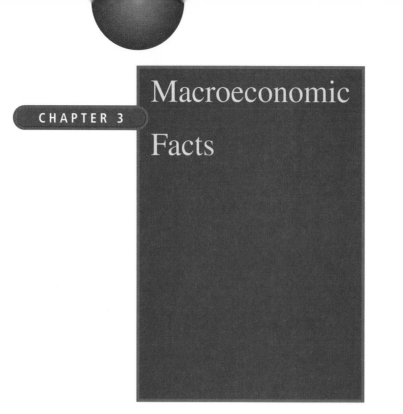

CHAPTER 3

Macroeconomic Facts

❶ INTRODUCTION

Unlike many of the natural sciences, in macroeconomics we cannot conduct experiments. Instead, we must collect data by recording observations of variables as they occur. If we collect enough data, we may uncover regular patterns of behavior by averaging observations over many instances of similar events. For example, we could average the unemployment rate and the inflation rate during every recession. Although each recession is different, on average the relationship between unemployment and inflation during all recorded recessions may display a pattern.

The regularities in economic data are of two kinds: relationships between the growth components in different variables and relationships between the cycles. We differentiate growth from cycles by removing the trend from a variable. Then we use three methods to uncover hidden patterns in the data: linear detrending, flexible detrending, and differencing. The relationship between variables can be described by persistence, which records how closely a variable is related to its own past history, and coherence, which measures how closely two variables are related to each other. The ability to measure persistence and coherence enables us to document the regularities in economic data that economists refer to as the business cycle.

Once we have learned about the methods used to quantify the relationships between variables, we can more carefully define the way that we measure unemployment and inflation. Keeping unemployment and inflation down is a primary goal of economic policy; understanding what we are measuring is important if we are to grasp the benefits and costs of alternative strategies for controlling them.

❷ TRANSFORMING ECONOMIC DATA

Measuring Variables

The principal units of data for macroeconomics are the values of a variable at different dates, in a time series.[1] Time series can measure GDP, unemployment, the interest rate, and the supply of money, for example. Time series go up or down as the economy prospers or falls into recession. Some fluctuate more than others. Some move up when others move down. By learning how time series related to each other in the past, we may be able to predict how the economy will behave in the future. Some variables, such as the money supply or government spending, are directly controlled by government and it may be possible to control them in ways that influence other important variables. An example is macroeconomic stabilization policy, which attempts to reduce the fluctuations in unemployment by controlling government spending and interest rates.

Time series are collected by a number of government agencies. Much of the data we study in this book are collected by the Commerce Department, which is responsible, among other things, for measuring GDP and its components. The Federal Reserve System

---

WEBWATCH 3.1   **Where to Find the Economic Report of the President**

The University of California maintains an electronic gateway, the *GPO gate*, from which you can access a wealth of federal documents electronically. The GPO gate (short for Government Printing Office) provides access to the full-text databases made available by the GPO Access service of the Government Printing Office in Washington, D.C. The following quote is from their Web page, at http://www.gpo.ucop.edu/index.html.

Welcome to GPO Gate, the University of California's gateway to federal information. GPO Gate is a World Wide Web interface to the Government Printing Office's suite of databases known as GPO Access. GPO Access databases contain the full text of selected information published by the United States Government. GPO Gate is designed to help citizens easily access the laws, regulations, reports, data and other information provided through the GPO Access system. Among the growing list of titles available are the Federal Register, the Congressional Record, Congressional Bills, United States Code, Economic Indicators, and GAO Reports.

The *Economic Report of the President* is part of the GPO data base; the 1997 edition can be found at http://www.gpo.ucop.edu/catalog/erp97.html.

---

1.   We also record observations on many categories of a variable at a point in time; data like this is called a *cross section.* An example might be the GDP of every country in the world in 1993.

publishes time series of industrial production, monetary aggregates, and interest rates, and the Bureau of Labor Statistics publishes data on employment, wages, and other labor market statistics. A good summary of all this information is the *Economic Report of the President,* published by the Council of Economic Advisers every February.

Separating Growth from Cycles

Data are measured at different intervals. Some data are annual (recorded once a year), some are quarterly (available every three months), and some are monthly (recorded once a month). There are even some financial data series that are available by the minute, such as the prices of stocks on the New York Stock Exchange. Before economists analyze annual, quarterly, or monthly time series we typically transform the data in some way to make it more amenable to analysis. Examples involve removing the seasonal[2] part of a time series or removing a trend.

The **trend** in a time series is the **low-frequency** component of the series. The deviation of the series from its trend (the part of the series that moves up and down over the business cycle) is called the **high-frequency** component. **Detrending** decomposes a time series into the sum of its high and low frequency components. The theory of economic growth focuses on what determines the low-frequency movements in economic time series, and the theory of business cycles studies the causes of their high-frequency movements.

Removing a Trend

The most common detrending method works by fitting a trend line to a set of points and defining the cycle to be the differences between the original series and the trend. Before we fit a trend to economic data we typically take the logarithm of the original series. The following example explains why.

Suppose that a variable, Y, is growing at a constant, compound rate. **Compound growth** (also called **exponential growth**) means that annual increments to the series themselves contribute to growth in subsequent years. Examples involve population growth (our children grow up and have children of their own) and compound interest earned on a bank account (the interest on the account itself earns interest). To make the example concrete, think of Y as the value of a bank account that was equal to $1 in 1890 and that earned compound interest of 5% per annum. Variables that grow at a constant rate explode over time because the increases each period are themselves multiplied by the growth rate. The result is a variable that has exponential growth.[3] Figure 3.1 (panel A) illustrates an exponentially growing series and its logarithm. Note that the graph of the logarithm of Y is a straight line. A short primer on logarithms and how to manipulate them is included in Appendix B at the back of the book.

2.   The seasonal component of a time series is the part that goes up and down with the seasons. For example, the money supply goes up at Christmas when people demand more cash for Christmas shopping; GDP goes down in August when many people are on vacation. In this book we deal mainly with data reported at the annual frequency, so the issue of removing seasonal fluctuations does not arise. Each number in an annual time series represents a variable for a whole year.
3.   **Mathematical Note:** If a bank account that earns compound interest i was worth Y_t in year t, it would be worth Y_{t+1} in year $t+1$, where $Y_{t+1} = Y_t(1+i)$. Variables like this are said to be growing exponentially because, as the length of a period becomes small, the formula that describes the value of the account is given by $Y_t = \exp(it)Y_0$, where Y_0 is the initial amount invested and Y_t is the value of the account at date t.

FIGURE 3.1
How to Construct a Linear Trend

The logarithm of a growing variable is a straight line when plotted against time. The red curve, measured on the left axis, shows the value of a bank account each year from 1890 to 1996 if $1 were invested at 5% compound interest. The blue line shows the *logarithm* of the value of this account.

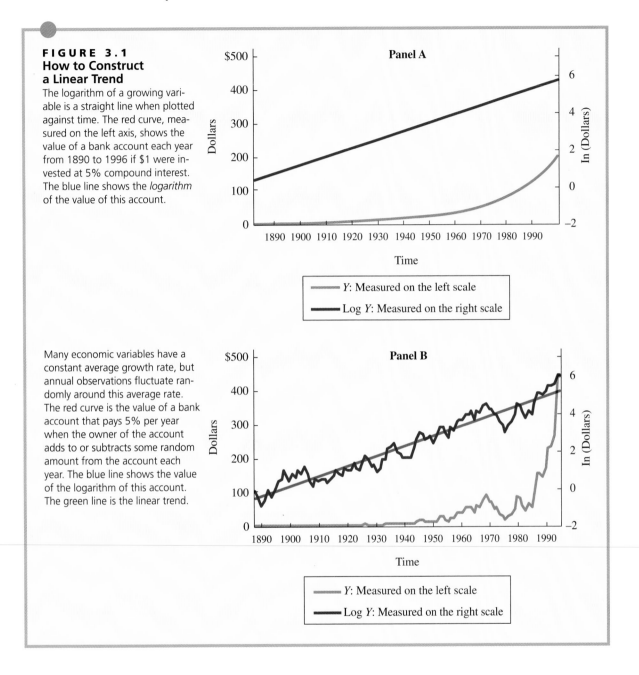

Many economic variables have a constant average growth rate, but annual observations fluctuate randomly around this average rate. The red curve is the value of a bank account that pays 5% per year when the owner of the account adds to or subtracts some random amount from the account each year. The blue line shows the value of the logarithm of this account. The green line is the linear trend.

Many variables in economics have an underlying growth rate that is constant, but they fluctuate randomly around this underlying rate from one year to the next. Suppose, for example, that in some years the owner of the bank account adds money to the account and in other years withdraws it. If additions and withdrawals are random and equal to zero on average, then the value of the bank account will fluctuate around a trend. Panel B of Figure 3.1 illustrates this idea.

The red line in the bottom panel is the value of the account in dollars and the blue line is its logarithm. Notice that although Y itself moves up and down around a curve, the logarithm of Y fluctuates around a straight line. Many time series fluctuate in this way. The goal of detrending is to separate the movements in these variables that occur because of an underlying trend growth rate from the movements that occur because of random fluctuations around this trend. Linear detrending accomplishes this task by fitting the best straight line through the graph of the logarithm. The fitted line is called the **linear trend** and the deviations of the log series from the fitted line is called the **linear cycle.** The linear trend is the low-frequency component of the series and the linear cycle is the high-frequency component.

Detrending Methods

Although the linear trend is relatively simple to construct, it has the disadvantage that the trend itself is assumed constant. Many economists believe that the trend reflects an underlying growth rate that changes slowly from one decade to the next. These economists prefer to fit a **flexible trend.** Instead of fitting a straight line through the logarithm of a variable, flexible detrending fits a curve.[4] If a series is detrended using the linear method, the series itself may depart from its underlying growth rate for long periods of time. Linear detrending does not allow these protracted departures from trend to alter our view of the underlying growth rate. In contrast, flexible detrending interprets protracted departures from the linear trend as swings in the underlying growth rate.

A third method of revealing the high-frequency relationship between time series is to look at growth rates of data rather than at the raw data itself. This method, called **differencing,** defines the cycle in a variable to be the percentage change in the original series. For example, the differenced value for GDP in 1987 is given by the formula

$$\text{DGDP}_{1987} = \frac{\text{GDP}_{1987} - \text{GDP}_{1986}}{\text{GDP}_{1986}}$$

where DGDP is the differenced data and the subscript 1987 refers to the year.

The Importance of Detrending

Detrending reveals relationships between time series that exist at one frequency but not at another. Figure 3.2 illustrates this idea by comparing the raw data on unemployment and real GDP with the detrended series. Panel A of this figure plots the raw data series on unemployment and GDP; panel B plots the high-frequency component of GDP against unemployment using linear detrending to detrend the series. The raw series do not appear connected, because at low frequencies unemployment fluctuates around a constant level whereas GDP has an upward trend. A graph of unemployment against GDP would reveal no particularly striking relationship between them.

Although unemployment and GDP are unrelated at low frequencies, they are quite strongly related at high frequencies. The high-frequency relationship is revealed in

---

4.   One popular flexible detrending method, called the Hodrick–Prescott filter, is commonly used by a group of economists from the real business cycle school.

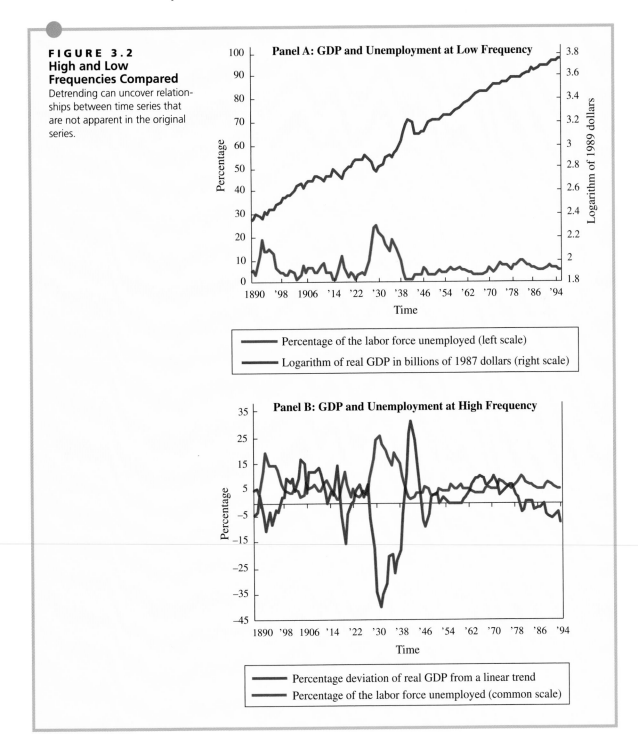

FIGURE 3.2
High and Low Frequencies Compared
Detrending can uncover relationships between time series that are not apparent in the original series.

panel B of Figure 3.2, which reveals that unemployment and the cycle in real GDP move quite closely together in opposite directions. Only by detrending real GDP could we have uncovered this important economic fact. For this reason, detrending is an important component of the macroeconomist's toolkit.

❸ QUANTIFYING BUSINESS CYCLES

One tool used to describe business cycles is the **correlation coefficient,** which measures the strength of a statistical relationship. The correlation coefficient is used in two ways: to measure the strength of a relationship between two variables and to measure the strength of the relationship between a single variable and its own history. We call the strength of a relationship between two variables their degree of **coherence.** We call the strength of the relationship between a single variable and its history its degree of **persistence.** The tendency of many economic time series to display coherent, persistent swings from one period to the next is the business cycle.

Peaks and Troughs

The common features of business cycles are peaks, troughs, expansions, and recessions. GDP displays a tendency to cycle around a growing trend. A business cycle **peak** is the point at which the growth rate of GDP begins to decline, and a business cycle **trough** is when it starts to increase again. The period between a trough and the subsequent peak is called a business cycle **expansion,** and the period from the peak to the subsequent trough is called a **recession.** Figure 3.3 illustrates each of these concepts on a stylized picture of a business cycle.

Real data do not display the kinds of regularities suggested by Figure 3.3. The regularities in economic data are statistical rather than deterministic. No two business cycles are exactly alike, so their regularities must be uncovered by looking at the average behavior of data over many different expansions and contractions. By applying one of the three methods of removing a trend, we can study the average relationships between the high-frequency components of economic time series. The regularities in these average relationships are the business cycle facts that must be explained by economic theory.

The Correlation Coefficient

The fact that economic data is not perfectly regular can be modeled by equations that contain random elements. These random elements may be caused by our inability to properly measure the variables we study or they may reflect our inability to capture the true complexity of the world. In either case, an equation that links two variables will contain a random term that in some years will be positive and in other years negative. When we plot one variable against another on a graph, the random elements that we are unable to account for will show up as discrepancies between the observations that we plot and the true relationship that we are trying to measure. When these random elements are strong, two time series that are theoretically linked may in practice seem to be unrelated to each other. When these random elements are weak, the relationship between the two time series will show up clearly in a graph. One way of measuring the strength of the linear relationship

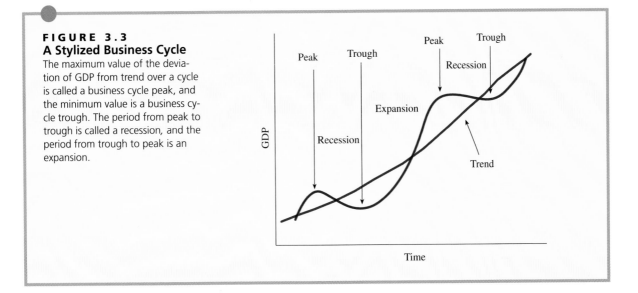

FIGURE 3.3
A Stylized Business Cycle
The maximum value of the deviation of GDP from trend over a cycle is called a business cycle peak, and the minimum value is a business cycle trough. The period from peak to trough is called a recession, and the period from trough to peak is an expansion.

between two variables is to plot a graph on which each point represents a particular year and to see how closely the points on the graph lie to a straight line.[5] A graph in which each point represents an observation from two different variables at a given time is called a **scatter plot**.

Statisticians have developed a way of quantifying the relationship between two variables in a scatter plot with a single number, called the correlation coefficient.[6] It measures how closely a scatter plot lies to a straight line. The symbol used to represent the correlation coefficient is ρ_{xy}. Figure 3.4 illustrates the use of the correlation coefficient to measure the strength of the relationship between two sets of variables, consumption and GDP, and unemployment and GDP. Consumption and GDP are positively correlated, whereas unemployment and GDP are negatively correlated. Notice that the cycles in consumption and GDP lie around a positively sloped straight line. Not every point is exactly on the line, but the line itself represents a good approximation of the relationship between the two variables. Unemployment and GDP, on the other hand, lie along a negatively sloped straight line.

5.   A linear relationship between two variables x and y can be expressed by an equation of the form $y = a + bx$, where b represents the slope of a graph of y against x and a is the intercept with the y axis. Although there is no reason to believe that all economic relationships are linear, in practice, most applied work uses a linear equation as a first approximation.
6.   The correlation coefficient is defined by the formula

$$\rho_{xy} = \frac{\sum_{i=1}^{n}(x_i - \bar{x})(y_i - \bar{y})}{\sqrt{\sum_{i=1}^{n}(x_i - \bar{x})^2}\sqrt{\sum_{i=1}^{n}(y_i - \bar{y})^2}}$$

where a bar over a variable denotes its arithmetic mean. In practice, the correlation coefficient is calculated using high-speed computers.

FIGURE 3.4
Positively and Negatively Correlated Variables
Panel A plots the cycle in real GDP against the cycle in total consumption. These points tend to lie around a positively sloped line. The correlation coefficient between consumption and GDP is 0.94.

Panel B plots the cycle in real GDP against the cycle in unemployment. These points tend to lie around a negatively sloped line. The correlation coefficient is −0.71.

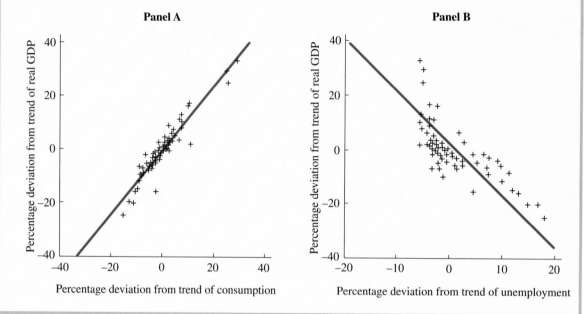

Persistence

You frequently read in the newspapers that GDP is forecast to increase by 1.3% next month, or that unemployment is going to go down by 3 points. You may have wondered where these numbers come from and whether you should have any faith in them.

Persistence means that if we plot the value of the deviation of GDP from trend in one year against its own value in the previous year, these deviations from trend lie along a straight line. Figure 3.5 constructs this plot for real GDP. The fact that the data tends to lie close to a straight line means that if we know the value of GDP at date t (where t is some number that indexes the year), then we will be able to predict relatively accurately what it will be equal to at date $t + 1$ (a number that indexes the subsequent year). The best forecast of GDP predicts that the deviation next year of GDP from trend will be equal to the point that lies exactly on the best straight line through the scatter of past points. This forecast will not be 100% accurate because the points do not lie *exactly* along a straight line, but it will be more accurate the closer the points are to a straight line.

There is a simple quantitative way of measuring how accurate our forecasts are likely to be. By looking at the correlation coefficient between a variable and its past values, we

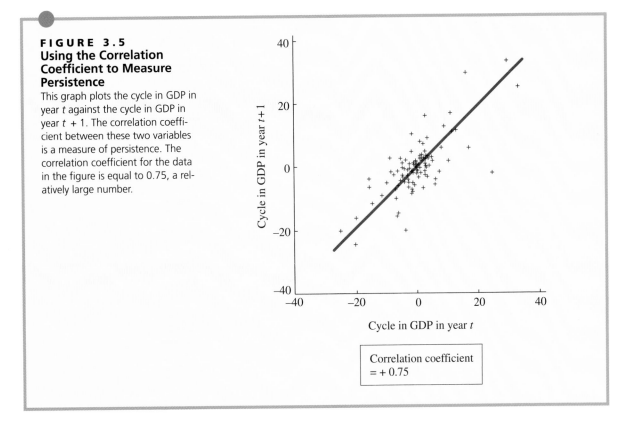

FIGURE 3.5
Using the Correlation Coefficient to Measure Persistence
This graph plots the cycle in GDP in year *t* against the cycle in GDP in year *t* + 1. The correlation coefficient between these two variables is a measure of persistence. The correlation coefficient for the data in the figure is equal to 0.75, a relatively large number.

Correlation coefficient
= + 0.75

can quantify what we mean by persistence. If the correlation coefficient is close to +1, then a big deviation from trend will persist for a long time; if it is close to zero, the series will quickly return to trend. The correlation coefficient for the data in Figure 3.5 is equal to 0.75, which is a relatively large number. Data that shows no persistence would have a correlation coefficient with its own past of zero.[7] Modern economic forecasting models exploit the tendency of economic data to display persistence, so the fact that many economic time series display a high degree of persistence accounts for the success of economic forecasters over relatively short forecast horizons.

Coherence

A second important feature of economic time series is that they tend to move together; this tendency is called *coherence.* Economists classify time series according to whether they move in the same direction or the opposite direction to GDP. If a time series goes up when GDP goes up (and down when it goes down), we say the series is **procyclical.** A series that moves in the opposite direction to GDP is **countercyclical.**

7. The technical term for persistence is *autocorrelation.* If a time series is (strongly) correlated with its own past values, we say that it is (strongly) autocorrelated.

BOX 3.1
The Sign of ρ

When a scatter of points tends to lie around a positively sloped line, the correlation coefficient is a positive number; when they tend to lie around a negatively sloped line, it is a negative number.

The points in Panel A tend to lie around a line with a positive slope. In this example the correlation coefficient is a positive number between 0 and +1.

The points in Panel B tend to lie around a line with a negative slope. In this example the correlation coefficient is a negative number between 0 and −1.

The points in Panel C do not seem to have any strong relationship with each other. In this example the correlation coefficient is equal to 0.

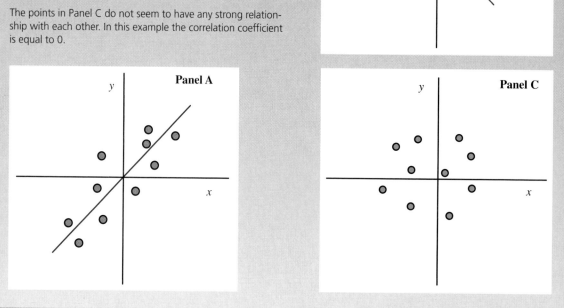

Consumption and investment are examples of procyclical time series variables; other time series variables are countercyclical, such as unemployment. Just as we used the correlation coefficient between GDP and its own past values to measure persistence, so we can use the correlation coefficient between two time series to measure coherence. If two time series move very closely together in the same direction, they have a correlation coefficient that is close to +1. In this case we say that they display high positive coherence. If two time series move very closely together in opposite directions, they have a correlation coefficient that is close to −1 and we say that they display high negative coherence.

Although coherence can be used to define the degree to which any two series are related, to define the ups and downs of the business cycle we use GDP as a reference series. Although many of the time series that we study are either highly procyclical or

BOX 3.1 *(continued)*
The Magnitude of ρ
The magnitude of the correlation coefficient measures the strength of the linear relationship among the points in a scatter diagram. The closer the points lie to a line, the closer ρ is to 1.

The points in Panel A lie exactly on a positively sloped straight line. In this example the correlation coefficient is equal to +1.

The points in Panel B tend to lie close to a positively sloped straight line, but the relationship is not exact. In this case the correlation coefficient equals +0.9.

The points in Panel C also lie around a positively sloped straight line, but the relationship is not as strong as in panels A and B. In this case the correlation coefficient equals +0.5.

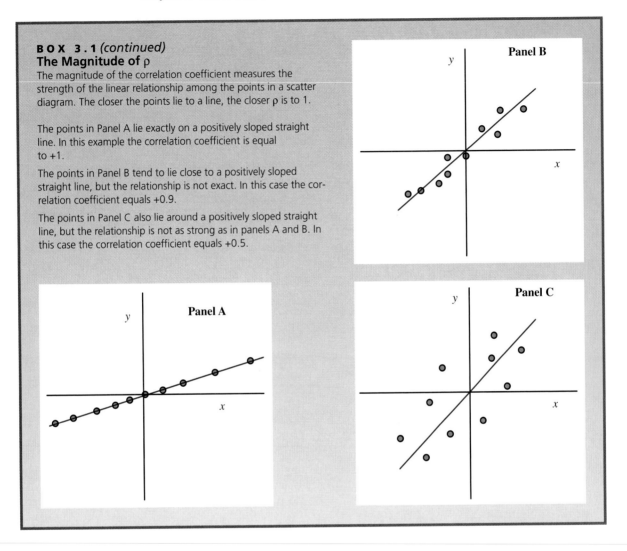

highly countercyclical, other series do not display strong comovements in either direction. Table 3.1 summarizes the ways that the correlation coefficient is used to catalog the behavior of time series over business cycles.

To summarize, we say that two time series (any two time series) are coherent if their scatter plot lies close to a straight line. The degree of coherence is measured by the absolute value[8] of a single number, called the correlation coefficient. If the points in the diagram cluster very close to a straight line with a positive slope, the correlation coefficient is very close to +1; if they lie very close to a line with a negative slope, the correlation

8.   **Mathematical Note:** The absolute value of a number is its magnitude, regardless of its sign. For example, +7 has the same absolute value as −7.

TABLE 3.1
Coherence and Business Cycles

The absolute value of the correlation coefficient between two arbitrary time series measures their degree of *coherence*.

	Correlation Coefficient	Degree of Coherence	Scatter Plot
X and Y are two arbitrary time series.	$\rho_{XY} > 0$	$+\rho_{XY}$ X and Y are positively correlated.	Slope is positive.
	$\rho_{XY} < 0$	$-\rho_{XY}$ X and Y are negatively correlated.	Slope is negative.

When a time series has a positive correlation coefficient with GDP it is *procyclical*. When it has a negative correlation coefficient with GDP it is *countercyclical*.

	Correlation Coefficient	Meaning	Scatter Plot
X is GDP and Y is some other time series.	$\rho_{XY} > 0$	Y is procyclical.	Slope is positive.
	$\rho_{XY} < 0$	Y is countercyclical.	Slope is negative.

coefficient is very close to -1. When a series has a high correlation coefficient with its history, we say that it is persistent. A time series with a positive correlation coefficient with GDP is procyclical; one with a negative correlation coefficient with GDP is countercyclical.

④ MEASURING UNEMPLOYMENT

The unemployment rate is an indicator of economic activity that is highly correlated with the high-frequency movements in GDP. To understand how unemployment is measured, we will introduce two new concepts: the labor force and the labor force participation rate.

Participation and the Labor Force

The Bureau of Labor Statistics, the agency responsible for collecting employment data, recognizes three activities: A person may be *employed, unemployed* or *out of the labor force*. People who are working or looking for work are part of the **labor force**. People who are not employed or who are not looking for a job are out of the labor force. They may be retired, they may be performing unpaid work in the home such as housekeeping or child rearing, or they may be wealthy enough that they do not need to work to support themselves.

The labor force, expressed as a percentage of all of the civilian adult population over the age of 16, is called the **labor force participation rate**. In 1992 the labor force consisted of approximately 126 million people, out of a civilian adult population of roughly 191 million people. The participation rate for 1992 was equal to 126/191, or 66.1%. The participation rate is an important economic variable, because one of the major ways in which families vary the number of hours they supply to the market is by deciding how many members of the household will participate.

Employment and Unemployment

There are two important measures of labor market activity: the **employment rate** and the **unemployment rate**. The employment rate is the fraction of the population employed. The unemployment rate is the fraction of the labor force looking for a job. Box 3.2 shows that the employment rate has increased since 1960, and at the same time the unemployment rate has drifted higher. The two facts are consistent with each other because more people are in the labor force now than in the 1950s, mainly as a result of increasing numbers of women finding paid employment, outside the home.

Of the 126 million people in the labor force in 1992, 7.1% were unemployed (see Table 3.2). Unemployed people are by definition searching for a job. Some may be temporarily between jobs, but some have been unemployed for very long periods of time. This is particularly true in Europe, where unemployment insurance programs are more generous than in the United States. In 1989 only 13% of unemployed Americans had been searching for a job for 12 months or longer. In Germany the comparable figure was 40%, in the United Kingdom 47%, and in Italy 58%.[9] In other words, over half of the unemployed in Italy had been looking for a job for more than a year!

Some economists focus on the unemployment rate in their models of economic activity; others focus on the employment rate. The main difference between these two measures of labor market activity is that employment varies when the participation rate changes—the unemployment rate does not.

❺ MEASURING INFLATION

Inflation is the average rate of change of the price level. The correlation coefficient can be used to document the history of inflation and its coherence with GDP. The distinction between real and nominal GDP can be used to provide a comprehensive measure of the price level called the GDP deflator. We measure inflation as the percentage change in the GDP deflator from one year to the next.

Price Indices

In Chapter 1 we mentioned four measures of the price level: the consumer price index, the producer price index, the GDP deflator, and the GDP price index. The reason there are four measures of the price level is that the economy produces more than one good and the

9.   Data is from *O.E.C.D. Employment Outlook*, Organization for Economic Cooperation and Development, 1991.

B O X   3 . 2
FOCUS ON THE FACTS:
Labor Force Participation Since 1950

Panel A shows that the unemployment rate has been rising since 1950.

Panel B shows that the employment rate has also been rising.

Panel C explains that employment and unemployment both increased because the participation rate increased.

There is an active debate in macroeconomics about whether the unemployment rate, as opposed to the employment rate, is the more interesting variable to try to understand. The difference between the employment rate and the unemployment rate would not matter very much if the two measures of activity in the labor market always moved in opposite directions. But as A through C show, unemployment and employment since 1960 have *both* been increasing. The reason for this apparently anomalous fact is that the unemployment rate is defined as the percentage of the labor force who are looking for work but are not currently employed, whereas the employment rate is the percentage of the population who are employed. Since 1965 the labor force has increased substantially, mainly as a result of the increase in participation by women.

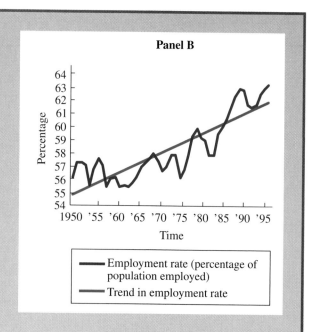

Panel B

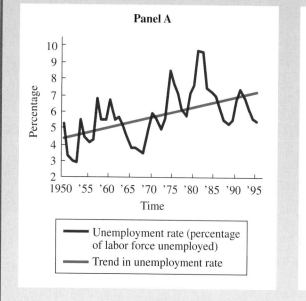

Panel A

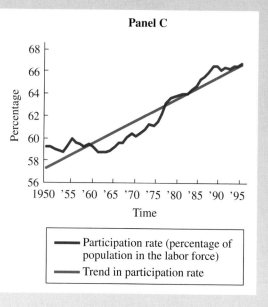

Panel C

TABLE 3.2
Employment Statistics

	Definition	Number of People (in thousands)	% of Population	% of Labor Force
Civilian Adult Population	Everyone in the United States over 16 and not in the armed forces	190,759	100%	151%
Employed	Everyone who worked full-time during the past week or was on sick leave or vacation	117,036	61.4% (employment rate)	92.9%
Unemployed	Everyone who did not work in the previous week but looked for work during the past four weeks	8,992	4.7%	7.1% (unemploy-ment rate)
Civilian Labor Force	Employed plus unemployed	126,028	66.1% (participation rate)	100%
Out of the Labor Force	Everyone who did not work during the previous week and did not look for work during the previous four weeks	64,731	33.9%	51%

From *Economic Report of the President*, Government Printing Office, 1993. All figures are for January 1992.

relative prices of different goods change from one year to the next. A price index is an attempt to capture the average value of a large number of commodities measured in units of money. By attaching more or less importance to one commodity or another in the averaging process, we arrive at different measures of the average price.

The importance of a commodity in the construction of a price index is measured by its weight. A price index is a weighted average of the prices of many different commodities, where weights are constants that are multiplied by each price and which sum to one. For example, if an economy produces apples, oranges, and bananas, a price index could be constructed by taking one-third the price of apples plus one-third the price of oranges plus one-third the price of bananas. In this case the weight attached to each commodity would be one-third. Alternatively, we might notice that consumers eat more apples than oranges and give more weight to apples in our construction of an index; in this case we might set the weight on apples equal to one-half and the weight on bananas and oranges equal to one-quarter. Different price indices are constructed by averaging the values of different bundles of commodities and by using different weights.

In this book we always measure the price level using the GDP deflator, an index that is constructed by taking the ratio of nominal GDP to real GDP in any given year. This index weights the price of each commodity by the commodity's relative value as a proportion of

BOX 3.3
The Consumer Price Index and the Deficit

This figure shows how a 1% correction in the CPI would alter the path of the federal budget deficit.

When inflation began to occur on a regular basis in the 1970s people started to index their financial contracts to the Consumer Price Index. Many wage agreements, for example, include automatic pay increases if the CPI goes up, and almost a third of federal spending, mainly in the form of retirement programs, is directly indexed to the CPI. Changes in the CPI also affect federal revenues because income tax brackets are indexed. The indexation of inflation makes it critical to get the numbers right because a 1% point increase in the CPI can change the budget deficit by as much as $6.5 billion.

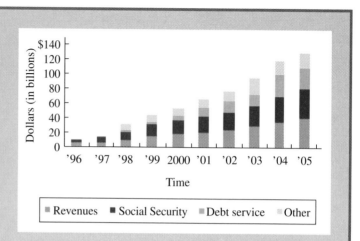

Recently, many economists have argued that the CPI overstates inflation by as much as 1% per year, although estimates range from as little as 0.2% to 1.5%. Overstatement of inflation occurs because consumers adjust their spending habits more rapidly than the CPI updates the basket of goods that it uses to measure inflation. Consumer habits change from month to month but the CPI updates its basket of commodities every ten years. In the past decade the mix of goods purchased by the average household has changed quite dramatically as new technology has made old products obsolete. Microwave ovens and personal computers were unheard of a couple of decades ago, but now they are common items in the budget of many Americans.

To assess the importance of the problem, the Senate Finance Committee commissioned five economists, led by Michael Boskin of Stanford University, to study the issue. They concluded in a report published in September of 1997 ("Toward a More Accurate Measure of the Cost of Living") that in recent years the CPI has overstated the true increase in the cost of living by 1.5%. They also projected the bias forward and concluded that the CPI could overstate inflation by as much as 2% in coming years. Even using the more conservative estimate of a 1% bias, correcting this bias would reduce projected inflation from 3% per year to 2% per year. Because the CPI is used to decide how much to pay in pensions and how much to alter tax brackets from one year to the next, the effect of this correction would be to lower the projected budget deficit by $140 billion by 2005. This amounts to one-third of the projected budget deficit, according to the figures released by the Congressional Budget Office.

Source: "Advisory Commission to Study the Consumer Price Index. Towards a More Accurate Measure of the Cost of Living." Washington, D.C. GPO, 1997.

GDP. The U.S. Commerce Department has recently replaced the GDP deflator with the GDP price index, which uses a more sophisticated weighting method. We will retain the GDP deflator as our measure of the average price level because it is available for a much longer period of time.

Measuring the GDP Deflator

To show how GDP is constructed, let's study a simple example based on a hypothetical economy called Econoland. Econoland produces just two commodities, beer and pizza.

TABLE 3.3
Measuring Real and Nominal GDP (An Example)

	1993 Base Year		1994		1995	
	Quantity	Price	Quantity	Price	Quantity	Price
Beer (cans)	25	$2	25	$4	50	$4
Pizza (slices)	30	$2	30	$4	60	$4
Nominal GDP	$(2 \times 25) + (2 \times 30) = \$110$		$(4 \times 25) + (4 \times 30) = \$220$		$(4 \times 50) + (4 \times 60) = \$440$	
Real GDP	$(2 \times 25) + (2 \times 30) = \$110$		$(2 \times 25) + (2 \times 30) = \$110$		$(2 \times 50) + (2 \times 60) = \$220$	
GDP Deflator	100		200		200	

Table 3.3 illustrates the quantities and prices of each of these commodities for three years, 1993, 1994, and 1995. In 1993 Econoland produced 25 cans of beer that sold for $2 each and 30 slices of pizza that sold for $2 a slice to generate a nominal GDP of $110. Because 1993 is the base year used by the Econoland Department of Commerce to measure real GDP, the real GDP in 1993 was also $110 dollars.

In 1994 Econoland suffered inflation and prices doubled, although the economy experienced no real growth. Because prices doubled, nominal GDP went up from $110 to $220, but because the economy did not produce any more real commodities, the index of real GDP stayed the same at $110. Real GDP is constructed by weighting the quantities produced in 1994 using the prices that prevailed in the base year, 1993.

The situation in 1995 was somewhat different because the central bank of Econoland managed to get inflation under control. The central bank policy was so successful that prices in 1995 remained the same as in 1994. 1995 was also a very good year for growth, and the people of Econoland managed to double their production of beer from 25 to 50 cans, and their pizza production went up from 30 to 60 slices. This doubling of output had the same effect on nominal GDP as the doubling of prices between 1993 and 1994. The nominal GDP in 1995 was twice as large as in 1994. But because the doubling of GDP in 1995 was real, rather than nominal, real GDP doubled as well.

The final line of Table 3.3 illustrates how the GDP deflator is constructed from the figures for real and nominal GDP; it is simply the ratio of one to the other. In 1994 nominal GDP went up because prices doubled, even though all quantities remained the same. This increase in prices is reflected in an increase in the GDP deflator, which increases from 100 in the base year, 1993, to 200 in 1994. In 1995, GDP again doubled, but this time the increase arose because the economy produced more of everything. As one would hope, in this case the GDP deflator remained equal to its 1994 level at 200, reflecting the fact that the average level of prices was the same in 1995 as in 1994.

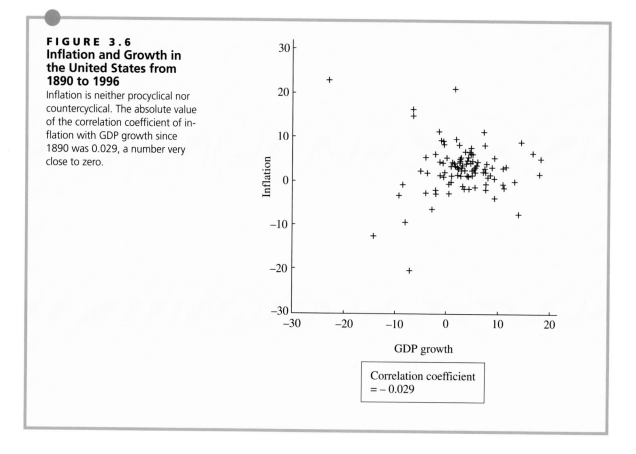

FIGURE 3.6
Inflation and Growth in the United States from 1890 to 1996
Inflation is neither procyclical nor countercyclical. The absolute value of the correlation coefficient of inflation with GDP growth since 1890 was 0.029, a number very close to zero.

Correlation coefficient
$= -0.029$

Inflation and the GDP Deflator

To measure the **inflation rate** we divide the increase in the price level from the previous year to the current year by the price level in the previous year and multiply by 100. For example, to compute the inflation rate in 1994

3.1
$$\text{Inflation in 1994} = \left(\frac{P_{1994} - P_{1993}}{P_{1993}}\right) \times 100$$

where P_{1994} is the GDP deflator in 1994 and P_{1993} is the GDP deflator in 1993. If we plug in the numbers from Econoland Table 3.3 we find that Econoland inflation in 1994 was equal to 100%.

Inflation and the Business Cycle

Recall that a variable is procyclical if it is positively correlated with GDP and counter-cyclical if it is negatively correlated. Many time series are strongly procyclical (consumption, for example) or strongly countercyclical (unemployment, for example). Inflation is an exception to this rule. Figure 3.6 presents the data on inflation and GDP growth for the

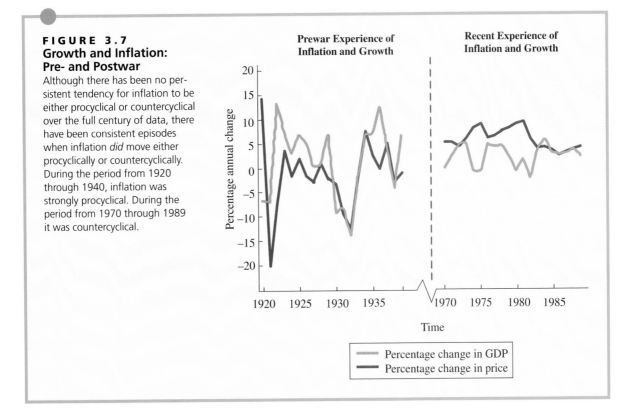

FIGURE 3.7
Growth and Inflation: Pre- and Postwar
Although there has been no persistent tendency for inflation to be either procyclical or countercyclical over the full century of data, there have been consistent episodes when inflation *did* move either procyclically or countercyclically. During the period from 1920 through 1940, inflation was strongly procyclical. During the period from 1970 through 1989 it was countercyclical.

years 1890 through 1996. Notice that inflation over the century is neither procyclical nor countercyclical; its coherence with GDP is only 0.029, a number that is not significantly different from zero.[10]

Although inflation has been weakly correlated with GDP over the century, there have been periods of history when the price level has been either strongly procyclical or strongly countercyclical. Figure 3.7 illustrates this point by isolating two historical episodes. The left-hand side of the figure shows how inflation was associated with growth during the period from 1920 through 1940. This period includes the Great Depression, and it was the behavior of prices during the Depression that led John Maynard Keynes to predict that inflation would be procyclical.

However, procyclical movements in prices have not been characteristic of more recent experience. Real business cycle theory sees the Depression as an unusual event, remarkable for its differences rather than its similarities with other, more typical, episodes of business cycles. Real business cycle theorists assert that most business fluctuations occur as a result of changes in productivity, and their theories predict that inflation should be countercyclical, as it has been in post-war data. They point to the two largest

10. Significance is a well-defined statistical concept. To say that the correlation coefficient is not significantly different from zero means that there is so much variation in the recorded observations that we can have no confidence in the statement either that ρ_{XY} is positive or that it is negative.

post-war recessions, which were triggered by increases in the world price of oil in 1973 and again in 1979.[11]

If inflation sometimes moves procyclically and sometimes countercyclically, perhaps some recessions are caused by the factors isolated by Keynes and some are caused by supply shocks.

CONCLUSION

Economic data are recorded by time series. To analyze time series we split them into a low-frequency component (the trend) and a high-frequency component (the cycle). The three principal ways of decomposing a time series are linear detrending, flexible detrending, and differencing.

Detrending allows us to uncover relationships between time series that hold at one frequency but not at another. We measure the strength of the statistical relationship between two series with the correlation coefficient. A time series that has a high correlation coefficient with its history is persistent; two series that have a high correlation coefficient with each other are coherent. Coherence can be positive (both series go up and down together) or negative (one series moves up as the other moves down). If a series is positively correlated with GDP, it is procyclical; if it is negatively correlated with GDP, it is countercyclical. The business cycle is the tendency for many economic time series to be persistent and coherent with GDP.

Unemployment and employment are two different measures of economic activity. The employment rate is the percentage of the population that are employed; the unemployment rate is the percentage of the labor force that are unemployed. Because the labor force increased in the United States after World War II, the employment rate and the unemployment rate both increased at the same time. The unemployment rate is countercyclical and highly coherent with GDP.

Inflation is the rate of change of a price index. There are four principal price indices; we use one of them, the GDP deflator, because it is comprehensive and available for long periods of time. The GDP deflator is the ratio of the value of GDP valued at current prices to the value of GDP valued at base year prices. Inflation was procyclical before World War II but has been countercyclical since then.

KEY TERMS

Coherence	Detrending
Compound growth (exponential growth)	Differencing
Correlation coefficient	Employment rate
Countercyclical	Expansion

11. Thomas F. Cooley and Lee Ohanian, "The Cyclical Behavior of Prices." *Journal of Monetary Economics*, 3 No. 105:439–472.

Flexible trend   Peak
High frequency   Persistence
Inflation rate   Procyclical
Labor force   Recession
Labor force participation rate   Scatter plot
Linear cycle   Trend
Linear trend   Trough
Low frequency   Unemployment rate

PROBLEMS FOR REVIEW

1. List three methods for detrending a time series and explain briefly how they differ. What is detrending used for in macroeconomics?

2. Explain what is meant by each of these terms:

a. A recession

b. An expansion

c. A business cycle peak

d. A business cycle trough

3. The Kingdom of Fruitland in Southern Europe produces two commodities: apples and oranges. The following data represents total production in Fruitland for the five-year period from 1985 through 1989.

Date	Price of oranges	Price of apples	Quantity of apples	Quantity of oranges
1985	$3	$2	2,000	1,000
1986	$4	$4	2,350	1,150
1987	$5	$7	2,400	1,200
1988	$7	$8	2,500	1,200
1989	$12	$10	2,700	1,250

For each year from 1985 to 1989

a. Calculate nominal GDP in Fruitland

b. Calculate real GDP, using 1985 as the base year

c. Calculate the GDP deflator

For each year from 1986 through 1990

d. Calculate the inflation rate

e. Calculate the growth rate

Draw a graph with GDP on the vertical axis and time on the horizontal axis. Using your judgment, draw a line through the points to represent the trend in GDP and read off the cycle from your graph. According to your analysis, which years in Fruitland were years of recession and which were years of expansion?

4. This statistical experiment is designed to demonstrate the difference between purely random data and persistent data. Take a die and roll it thirty times. For each roll, record the number that you throw on a time series. Now plot the value of the number (from one to six) on throw $t + 1$ against the number that you score on throw t.

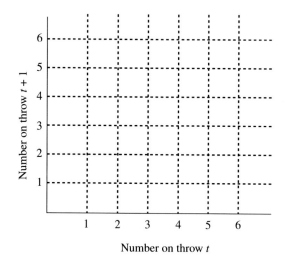

Explain any difference that you see between your graph and Figure 3.5.

5. Consider the following data set from the economy of Legonia:

Year	GDP	Consumption	Unemployment
1900	15	5	4
1901	25	22	3
1902	35	13	2
1903	40	27	1
1904	35	33	2

a.   Plot a graph of consumption against GDP and one of unemployment against GDP. Are consumption and unemployment procyclical or countercyclical?

b.   The average (arithmetic mean) value of a variable, $\bar{x}$, is defined by the formula

$$\bar{x} = \frac{\sum_{i=1}^{n} x_i}{n}$$

where n is the number of observations and i indexes each individual observation. Using this formula, calculate the average GDP, the average consumption, and the average employment in Legonia.

c.   The correlation coefficient is defined by the formula

$$\rho_{xy} = \frac{\sum_{i=1}^{n}(x_i - \bar{x})(y_i - \bar{y})}{\sqrt{\sum_{i=1}^{n}(x_i - \bar{x})^2}\sqrt{\sum_{i=1}^{n}(y_i - \bar{y})^2}}$$

Using this formula, calculate the correlation coefficient of consumption with GDP and employment with GDP in Legonia. Which series is more strongly correlated with GDP?

d.   Construct a measure of the degree of persistence of GDP in Legonia. How persistent is GDP?

6.   In 1982 the economy of Legonia had 25,000 people, of whom 20,000 were in the labor force. The unemployment rate was 10%. In 1992 the economy had 30,000 people, of whom 25,000 were in the labor force. The unemployment rate was 12%. For each year

a.   How many people were unemployed?

b.   What was the participation rate?

c.   What was employment per person?

Show that the unemployment rate and employment per person both increased between 1982 and 1992. Explain how this happened.

7.   Consider the following time series:

a.   Unemployment

b.   Total consumption

c.   Exports

d.   Imports

e.   Total investment

Which of these series are procyclical? Which are countercyclical?

8.   Write a short essay explaining the main defining characteristics of business cycles. Your essay should explain how business cycle data can be random and yet still display regularities.

PART 2

The Classical Approach to Aggregate Demand and Supply

In Chapters 4, 5, and 6 we move from a description of data to an explanation of it. We study the *classical model* of the economy, which was developed over the course of a hundred and fifty years, beginning in the late eighteenth century and ending in the early part of the twentieth century.

Chapter 4 deals with the labor market and the theory of aggregate supply. Chapter 5 deals with the classical theory of inflation, and in Chapter 6 we study the classical model of the capital markets.

Overall, Part 2 looks at aspects of the equilibrium method—the idea that demand equals supply in each of several markets in the economy simultaneously. This method can be applied to real-world economic problems.

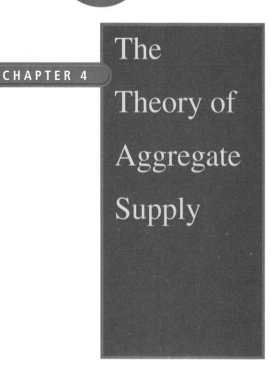

The Theory of Aggregate Supply

① INTRODUCTION

In this chapter, and in the two chapters that follow, we build a model of the entire economy based on the ideas of the classical economists. Classical economists developed their theories over the span of about eighty years, beginning with Adam Smith in 1776 and ending with John Stuart Mill in 1848. Following Mill, a group of neoclassical economists including Stanley Jevons in England and Leon Walras in France, developed the marginal utility theory. The combined ideas of the classical and the neoclassical economists constitute the classical theory of aggregate demand and supply.

② PRODUCTION AND THE DEMAND FOR LABOR

Let us imagine for a moment a society in which all output is produced from labor and capital, and in which everyone has the same preferences. Macroeconomists use such imaginary societies in order to avoid specific issues that concern the distribution of resources in society and instead focus on overall economic activity. These economies are called **representative agent economies**, and economists often refer to the representative agent as Robinson Crusoe, after the hero in Daniel Defoe's novel.

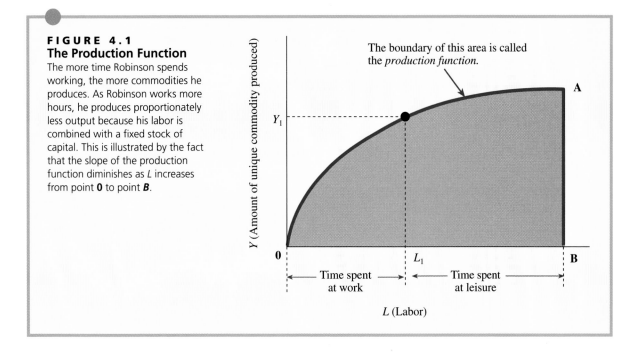

FIGURE 4.1
The Production Function
The more time Robinson spends working, the more commodities he produces. As Robinson works more hours, he produces proportionately less output because his labor is combined with a fixed stock of capital. This is illustrated by the fact that the slope of the production function diminishes as L increases from point **0** to point **B**.

The boundary of this area is called the production function.

Y (Amount of unique commodity produced)

Y_1

L_1

Time spent at work

Time spent at leisure

L (Labor)

The Production Function

Production is the activity of transforming resources such as labor and raw materials into finished goods. A method for transforming resources into finished goods is called a **technology**. Figure 4.1 illustrates a technology in which a single commodity, Y, is produced using the services of labor, L. Reading from left to right, the horizontal axis measures the amount of time that Robinson Crusoe spends working; reading from right to left, beginning at point **B**, it measures the amount of time he spends at leisure. The distance **0B** is the total time available (24 hours a day). The longer Robinson Crusoe spends working, the more commodities he is able to produce. For example, he may decide to spend **0–L_1** hours at work and L_1–**B** hours at leisure. The distance **0–Y_1** measures his output.

Robinson Crusoe's feasible choices, given the state of his technology, are called his **production possibilities set**, and the boundary of this set is the **production function**. In Figure 4.1 the production possibilities set is the blue shaded area **0–A–B**. The points on the production function (boundary of this set) are clearly better than the points inside the set because these points deliver the maximum number of produced commodities for any given input of labor time. The production function is upward sloping, reflecting the fact that Robinson Crusoe can produce more goods by working harder. The slope gets flatter as he puts in more effort, reflecting the fact of diminishing returns.

Diminishing returns occur because labor time is combined with other fixed resources. If we think of Robinson Crusoe literally as the hero in Daniel Defoe's novel, the resources at his disposal might be fixed by the quantity of animals on Crusoe's desert island. The more time Robinson Crusoe spends working, the smaller the marginal return on this work will be, because he will eventually deplete the island's stock of animals and will have to work longer and harder to catch the remaining ones. In a modern industrial economy there is an analogous reason why the production function gets flatter as we work harder. As the labor time of more and more workers is combined with a fixed stock of capital and land, the additional labor becomes relatively less productive.

Markets and Firms

Robinson Crusoe's island may seem a long way from a modern market economy, but we can add a simple element of trade to illustrate the classical theory of markets. First, imagine a number of identical agents or families. Each family operates a **firm**, an entity that buys labor services and combines them with capital to produce output. Labor services and output are traded with other families and firms in a **market**, a network of traders who buy and sell from each other. To distinguish this economy from the Robinson Crusoe economy, no family can use its own labor in the family firm nor can it consume the goods that it produces. In the real world these are realistic assumptions simply because we do not typically produce the same commodities that we consume.

Competition and the Determination of Wages and Prices

In a market economy firms buy labor, households sell labor, and each household and firm has the opportunity to trade with thousands of other agents. Classical theory assumes that no individual can influence prices. In our example there are only two commodities, labor and the produced good, so this assumption means that no household or firm is able to influence the wage or the price level.

In the real world wages are set by firms, but the extent to which firms are able to vary their wage rates is strictly limited by competition. For example, if a large corporation offers a wage of $3 an hour when every other firm is paying $5 an hour for identical work, the corporation is unlikely to find many people willing to work. The more alternative options there are available to workers, the less influence any one firm will have in setting wages. When the market consists of many buyers and sellers, each of whom is trading a small fraction of total market sales, the power of any single buyer or seller to influence price will become arbitrarily small. In this case economists say that the market is perfectly competitive, or simply a **competitive market**.

The Nominal Wage and the Real Wage

In this chapter we do not try to explain why money is used or how money prices are set; this is the subject of Chapter 5. Instead we assume that all trade takes place through barter of labor for commodities, and we measure wages in units of commodities. The amount of the final commodity that a firm must give up in order to purchase an hour of labor time is called the **real wage**, and it is denoted by the symbol ω.

In the real world we do not typically exchange labor directly for final commodities; instead we sell our labor for money and use the money to buy goods. But the *real wage* is still a useful concept. Let w stand for the wage rate in dollars per hour (called the **nominal**

wage) and let P stand for the price of a commodity in dollars. We can define the real wage, ω, as w divided by P.

$$\omega = \frac{w}{P}$$

Maximizing Profits

The classical theory of production assumes that markets are competitive. Firms choose how much labor to hire, taking wages and prices as given, in order to try to make as much profit as possible. The firm's profits, π, are equal to the value of the commodities supplied by the firm, Y^S, minus the cost of hiring labor to produce these commodities. Profits are defined in Equation 4.1. The left-hand side of the equation is the profit that the firm will realize if it sells Y^S units of commodities and pays ω commodities per hour to each of its workers.

4.1	π	=	Y^S	$-$	ωL^D
	Profits of the family firm		**Commodities supplied**		**Cost of labor demanded**

The competitive assumption implies that the firm has no choice about how much to pay its workers. If it tries to pay less than ω, no one will want to work for the firm. There is no point in paying more than ω because the firm can hire as many hours of labor as it requires, providing it is willing to pay these workers the market wage.

Figure 4.2 graphs the equation that defines profits, and can be used to maximize profit. The blue lines in the figure are **isoprofit lines**. Each line has a slope equal to the real wage, ω, and every point on the same line gives the firm equal profit. This profit, measured in units of the commodity, is represented by the point where the isoprofit line meets the vertical axis. The job of the manager of the firm is to decide how much labor to hire and how much output to sell. Obviously the manager would like to sell as much output as possible, since every unit sold will contribute to profits. But the amount the firm can sell is constrained by the amount that it can produce, given the labor that it hires. A combination of output sold and labor demanded, which is physically possible given the constraints of the technology, is called a **feasible combination**.

On Figure 4.2 the feasible points are those combinations of Y^S and L^D that lie within the boundary of the production possibilities set: the blue shaded area. The combination of output sold and labor demanded that gives the firm the maximum possible profit is represented by the point where one of the isoprofit lines is exactly tangent to the production function, yielding a profit equal to π_2. Of the three isoprofit lines in the figure, the line that cuts the axis at π_2 represents the highest feasible profit. The line that cuts the vertical axis at π_3 has higher profits than π_2 but does not intersect the feasible set. The line that cuts the axis at π_1 has many feasible points, but none of them yields as much profit as π_2.

The Labor Demand Curve

The assumption that firms maximize profit lets us derive a relationship between the wage and the quantity of labor demanded. If the real wage is plotted on the vertical axis of a

FIGURE 4.2
Maximizing Profits
Firms choose the combination of output and labor that maximizes profits. This combination is found by picking the highest isoprofit line that also contains a point in the production possibilities set.

These lines are called *isoprofit lines*. Each isoprofit line represents combinations of labor demanded and output supplied that give the firm the same level of profit: Higher lines give the firm higher profits. The formula that describe each line is given by the equation $Y^S = \pi + \omega L^D$.

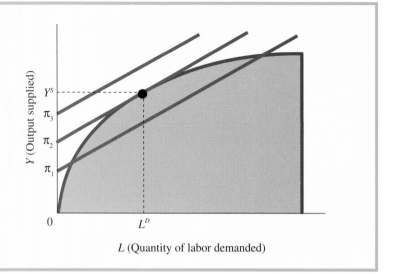

graph and the quantity of labor demanded is plotted on the horizontal axis, this relationship, called the **labor demand curve**, is downward sloping.

Figure 4.3 plots the labor demand curve. Panel A depicts a relatively high value of the wage measured in terms of commodities, ω. Given this relatively high value of the real wage, the firm will demand a relatively low amount of labor, L_A^D, and to produce a correspondingly low level of output, Y_A^S. Given the high real wage, the firm will also make a small profit, represented by π_A. Panel B shows that when the real wage is low, the firm will demand a relatively high quantity of labor and supply a large quantity of output. Panel C puts these two situations together by plotting the real wage against the quantity of labor demanded.

❸ THE DEMAND FOR COMMODITIES
AND THE SUPPLY OF LABOR

To derive the demand for commodities and the supply of labor, we rely on the idea that households derive utility from consuming commodities and from enjoying leisure (spending time relaxing). **Utility** is an index number that records whether a household prefers one combination of goods to another. More of each good gives us more utility; the utility function tells us how much more. We measure utility on a graph by drawing curves, called **indifference curves**, that indicate combinations of different bundles of goods that make us equally happy. A short refresher course on indifference curves is contained in the Appendix on page 87.

Since time spent working takes away from time spent enjoying leisure, we can think of work as bad; more work gives us less utility. We will use this idea to show how the household chooses its supply of labor and its consumption from a limited set of options.

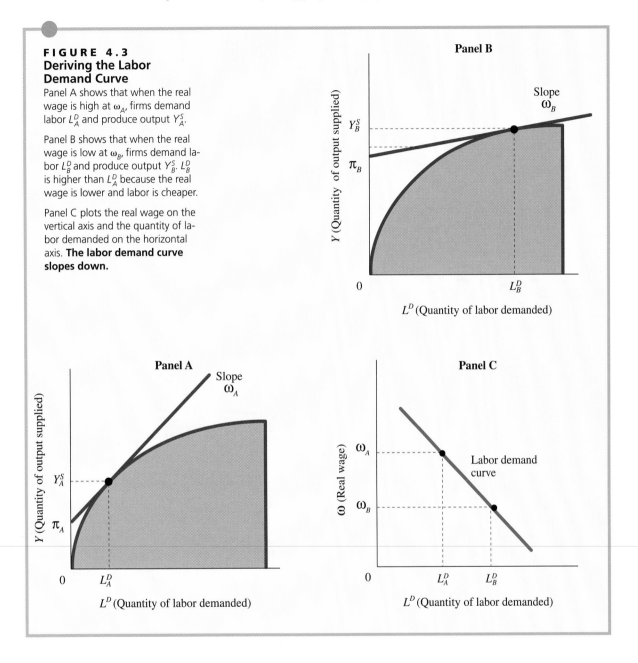

FIGURE 4.3
Deriving the Labor Demand Curve

Panel A shows that when the real wage is high at ω_A, firms demand labor L_A^D and produce output Y_A^S.

Panel B shows that when the real wage is low at ω_B, firms demand labor L_B^D and produce output Y_B^S. L_B^D is higher than L_A^D because the real wage is lower and labor is cheaper.

Panel C plots the real wage on the vertical axis and the quantity of labor demanded on the horizontal axis. **The labor demand curve slopes down.**

Maximizing Utility

Think of a family that both owns a firm and sends family members out to work for other firms in the economy. Perhaps the parents own and operate a small business, but their daughter works in a factory down the street. The family as a whole must decide how many commodities to demand and how much labor to supply to the market. We'll use Y^D to

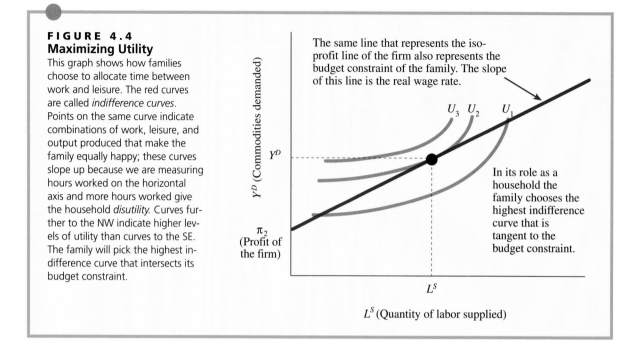

FIGURE 4.4
Maximizing Utility
This graph shows how families choose to allocate time between work and leisure. The red curves are called *indifference curves.* Points on the same curve indicate combinations of work, leisure, and output produced that make the family equally happy; these curves slope up because we are measuring hours worked on the horizontal axis and more hours worked give the household *disutility.* Curves further to the NW indicate higher levels of utility than curves to the SE. The family will pick the highest indifference curve that intersects its budget constraint.

The same line that represents the iso-profit line of the firm also represents the budget constraint of the family. The slope of this line is the real wage rate.

In its role as a household the family chooses the highest indifference curve that is tangent to the budget constraint.

represent the household's demand for commodities and L^S to represent the quantity of labor supplied. In Chapter 6 we inquire more deeply into whether the commodities demanded by households are consumed or invested, but for now we will suppose that consumption and investment affect preferences in the same way, and we will refer to them collectively as commodities demanded.

Families may purchase commodities with income from two sources. First, households own firms and the ownership of firms yields profits. Second, households supply labor and earn income by sending one or more of their members out to work in the market. To express the tradeoff between more commodities demanded and more labor supplied to the market, the household must examine its **budget constraint**, represented by Inequality 4.2.

4.2
$$Y^D \leq \omega L^S + \pi_2$$

Demand for commodities   **Income from selling labor**   **Profit from the family firm**

Figure 4.4 illustrates the household's decision problem. The family must pick how much labor to supply and how many commodities to demand. Once it receives its share in profits from the ownership of the firm, the household will know how much nonlabor income is available to be spent on consumption goods; in Figure 4.4 these profits determine the point where the household budget constraint cuts the vertical axis. This point represents the commodities that the household could purchase even if it chose not to supply any labor.

An indifference curve is a locus of pairs of commodities demanded and labor supplied that yield equal utility. Household labor supply and household demand for commodities can be found by picking the point on the highest possible indifference curve that is also within the household's budget set. In Figure 4.4 the chosen point is represented as $\{Y^D, L^S\}$ where the indifference curve labeled U_2 is tangent to the budget constraint. The household would prefer to choose a point on the indifference curve U_3, because U_3 represents combinations of commodities consumed and labor supplied that yield higher utility. But to get from U_2 to U_3 the household must either work less or it must consume more. Neither of these options is feasible because additional consumption goods can only be purchased at the expense of extra work. The indifference curve U_1 has many feasible points because it intersects the budget set in a number of places, but points on the indifference curve U_1 yield strictly lower utility than points on the indifference curve U_2.

The Labor Supply Curve

The assumption that households maximize utility leads us to a relationship between the wage and the quantity of labor that households choose to supply. If the real wage is plotted on the vertical axis of a graph and the quantity of labor demanded on the horizontal axis, this relationship, called the **labor supply curve**, is upward sloping.

Figure 4.5 plots the labor supply curve. Panel A depicts a relatively high value of the real wage ω_A. Given this relatively high value, the household will supply a relatively high amount of labor, L_A^S, and demand a correspondingly high level of commodities, Y_A^D. Panel B shows that when the real wage is low, the household will supply a relatively small quantity of labor and demand a small quantity of commodities. Panel C puts these two situations together by plotting the real wage against the quantity of labor supplied.

Factors That Shift Labor Supply

Utility theory not only predicts that the labor supply curve will slope up, it also predicts factors that shift the labor supply curve: income taxes and wealth.

Taxes reduce the supply of labor by lowering the wage received by households. For example, when a household is in the 30% tax bracket, it receives only $7 of every $10 earned. The remaining $3 is paid to the government in taxes. Although many of us feel overtaxed, Americans actually pay a much lower fraction of their wages in income taxes than residents of many other countries. The top tax bracket in the United States was cut to 28% in 1988. New legislation in 1993 increased the top tax rate to 39.6%, but this top rate only applies to incomes above $250,000 per year, a tiny fraction of U.S. taxpayers. Even this top rate is low compared with European rates, which can be as high as 70 or 80%.[1]

A second important variable that influences labor supply is wealth. Families that are independently wealthy are less likely to work long hours. Similarly, as society gets richer, we all tend to consume more of all commodities, including leisure. Increased wealth thus shifts the labor supply curve to the left. As households get richer, if all other things remain equal, they work lower hours. Wealthy people do not need to work to maintain their

---

1.   To learn more about economic policies in other countries, you might investigate the Organization for Economic Co-operation and Development. Webwatch 4.1 shows you how to reach the OECD on the Internet.

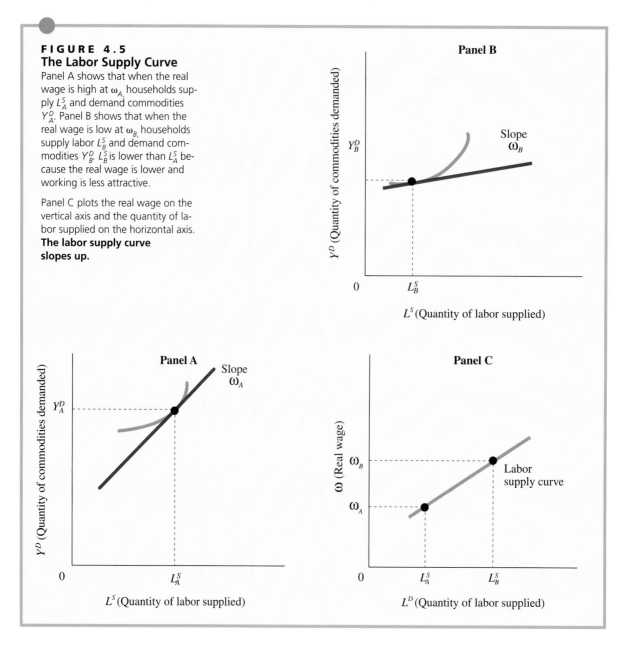

FIGURE 4.5
The Labor Supply Curve
Panel A shows that when the real wage is high at ω_A, households supply L_A^S and demand commodities Y_A^D. Panel B shows that when the real wage is low at ω_B, households supply labor L_B^S and demand commodities Y_B^D. L_B^S is lower than L_A^S because the real wage is lower and working is less attractive.

Panel C plots the real wage on the vertical axis and the quantity of labor supplied on the horizontal axis. **The labor supply curve slopes up.**

lifestyles, and many rich families do not engage in regular employment. Of course this does not mean that all wealthy people do not work; many of the richest families in America acquired their wealth precisely because of the long hours they put into building up their businesses. For the most part, however, we would expect to see that those with large inherited fortunes are less likely to be working long hours in paid employment. Box 4.1 compares work habits in the United States with those in Great Britain and Germany.

BOX 4.1
FOCUS ON THE FACTS:
Why Do Americans
Work So Much?

Many Americans think they work too hard. Certainly Americans work longer and harder now than they did in 1975. What's more, the United States is one of the few countries where hours worked per person have increased in recent years. The trend in Britain and Germany, for example, is to take longer vacations and to work fewer hours. In the United States the opposite is the case.

One possible explanation is that Americans have different preferences. Faced with a choice of working harder or forgoing luxuries, Americans prefer to work. Europeans are more likely to forgo luxury items and to opt instead for longer vacations and more time at home with their families.

An alternative explanation to that of different preferences is the fact that, on average, Americans face a much lower marginal tax rate than Europeans (the marginal rate is the rate that you pay for an extra hour worked). The top tax bracket in the United States is 39.6%, whereas in Britain it is 40% and in Germany it is 53%. Taxes reduce the incentive to work because the family receives a smaller wage for any given input of effort.

Employment and Wages

Wages have grown by a factor of 5 in the past hundred years but the employment rate has remained roughly constant. The reason is that we are wealthier today than we were in 1890 and households choose to consume more leisure as a result. The effect of raising wealth tends to reduce labor supply but the effect of rising wages tends to increase it. The two effects offset each other in the data.

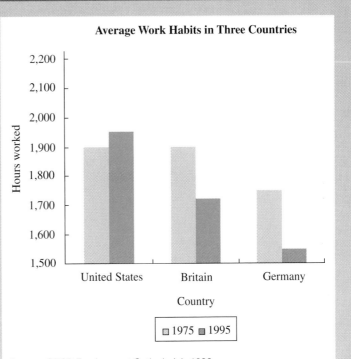

Average Work Habits in Three Countries

□ 1975   ■ 1995

Source: *OECD Employment Outlook*, July 1996

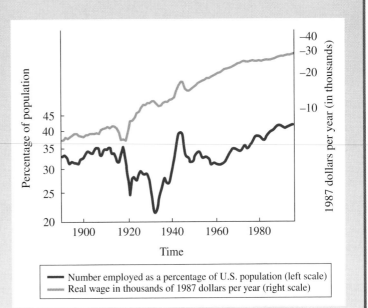

— Number employed as a percentage of U.S. population (left scale)
— Real wage in thousands of 1987 dollars per year (right scale)

WEBWATCH 4.1   Check out the OECD

The Organization for Economic Co-operation and Development, based in Paris, France, is a unique forum permitting governments of the industrialized democracies to study and formulate the best policies possible in all economic and social spheres.

The OECD differs from other intergovernmental organizations in three respects:

- As it has neither supranational legal powers nor financial resources for loans or subsidies, its sole function is direct co-operation among the governments of its member countries.
- At the OECD, international co-operation means co-operation among nations essentially on domestic policies where these interact with those of other countries, in particular through trade and investment. Co-operation usually means that member countries seek to adapt their domestic policies to minimize conflict with other countries. Governments frequently seek to learn from each others' experience with specific domestic policies before they adopt their own courses of action, whether legislative or administrative.
- By focusing the expertise of various OECD directorates and of various member government departments on specific issues, the OECD approach benefits in particular from a multidisciplinary dimension. The organization deals both with general macroeconomic and with more specific or sectoral issues.

Quoted from the OECD Web page at **http://www.oecd.org.** You can obtain a wide range of international statistics from the OECD. For example, the data on international tax rates quoted in Box 4.1 came from the OECD in Figures, available at **http://www.oecd.org/about/oecd_in_figures.htm.**

If greater wealth shifts the labor supply curve to the left, perhaps we should expect to see that hours worked drop over time. In fact, this is not true: The employment rate has been roughly constant in a century of data. In fact, the effect on labor supply of increasing wealth is offset by the fact that the real wage has also risen. The effect of wealth on labor supply is called a **wealth effect**. The effect on labor supply of a higher real wage is called a **substitution effect**. The employment rate has been roughly constant in a century of data because the wealth and substitution effects balance each other out.

❹ THE CLASSICAL THEORY OF AGGREGATE SUPPLY

It is time to put together the theories of the demand and supply of labor to show how the classical economists believed that output, employment, and wages are determined. The **classical theory of aggregate supply** explains these variables.

Putting Together Demand and Supply

The labor demand and supply curves in Figure 4.6 illustrate the choices of the household and the firm. In the classical model the labor market is assumed to be in equilibrium.

FIGURE 4.6
Labor Market Equilibrium
At wage ω_1 households supply L_1^S hours of labor and firms demand L_1^D hours; the quantity supplied exceeds the quantity demanded.

At wage ω_2 households supply L_2^S hours of labor and firms demand L_2^D hours; the quantity demanded exceeds quantity supplied.

Only when $\omega = \omega^E$ does the quantity demanded equal the quantity supplied. Then the labor market is in equilibrium and employment equals L^E.

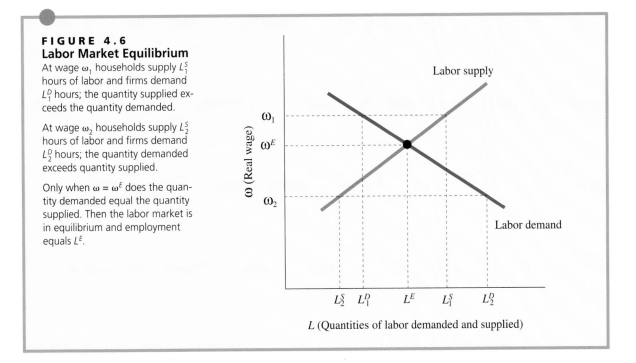

L (Quantities of labor demanded and supplied)

The real wage and the level of employment are determined by the point of intersection of the labor demand and supply curves, denoted by ω^E and L^E, where the superscript E stands for equilibrium. The equilibrium values L^E and ω^E depend in practice on the nature of the technology and of the preferences of the households; these features of the economy determine the positions and the slopes of the labor demand and supply curves.

For any value of the wage, households and firms make plans that express the amount of labor and commodities they would like to buy and sell. For some values of the wage, firms plan to buy more labor than households plan to sell; for other values the opposite occurs. For most values of the wage, the plans of households and firms are mutually inconsistent.

For example, Figure 4.6 depicts a relatively high value of the wage measured in terms of commodities, ω_1. Given this relatively high value of the real wage, the firm will choose to demand a low amount of labor, L_1^D, and households will supply a large amount, L_1^S; in this case supply will exceed demand. Alternatively, if the wage is low at ω_2, the firm's demand for labor will exceed household supply. Only at the **equilibrium real wage**, ω^E, are the quantities demanded and supplied equal to each other. The values of labor and commodities at which the quantities of labor and commodities demanded equal the quantities of those supplied is called a **competitive equilibrium allocation**.

What Is Special About the Equilibrium?

It seems reasonable to ask why classical economists focus on the equilibrium point rather than some other real wage at which demand is not equal to supply. The answer is that the equilibrium wage is the only one at which there are no mutually beneficial gains from trade.

Suppose, for example, that every firm in the economy was offering to pay a wage of ω_1 which is greater than the equilibrium real wage ω^E. In this situation there would be some workers who would be unable to find a job at the market wage because when ω is above its equilibrium level, more hours of labor will be offered for sale than are demanded by firms. The classical theorists assumed that, in this situation, an unemployed worker would offer to work for less than the going wage. Since a firm could profitably hire such a worker, trades would willingly be made by both parties. Similarly, firms that are already employing workers would be in a strong bargaining position. They would be able to force their workers to accept lower wages by firing those who refuse and replacing them with workers who are currently unemployed.

Suppose, on the other hand, that the real wage is at some level ω_2 that is less than the equilibrium real wage ω^E. In this case firms would be trying to hire more hours of labor than was being supplied by households. A firm that was unable to find enough labor would try to lure workers away from other firms by offering to pay a higher wage. Workers that already had jobs at lower wages would be in a strong bargaining position and would be able to threaten to leave and move to some other firm for a higher wage. The only wage at which there is no pressure to either raise or to lower the wage is the real wage, ω^E, at which the quantity of labor demanded is exactly equal to the quantity supplied.

Walras Law

The classical theory of aggregate supply determines the quantity of goods produced as well as the quantity of labor employed; but so far we have focused exclusively on the market for labor. How do we know that when the demand is equal to the supply of labor it will simultaneously be true that the demand is equal to the supply of commodities? The answer is that, in our simple example, there are only two things that are being traded: produced commodities and labor. Every offer to buy labor is simultaneously an offer to sell commodities, because the firm uses commodities to pay wages. A similar argument holds for households. An offer to supply labor to the firm is simultaneously an offer to buy commodities. If every household is happy with the amount of labor that it is supplying, it must simultaneously be happy with the amount of goods that it is purchasing. Similarly, if every firm is happy with the amount of labor it is demanding, it must simultaneously be satisfied with the amount of goods that it is selling.

This idea can be extended to more complicated examples of economic models in which there are many goods being bought and sold. This extension is called **Walras Law**, after the French economist Leon Walras (1834–1910).[2] In an economy in which firms produce many different types of commodities, we can define an equilibrium in much the same way as we do in the one-commodity world. Firms choose how much labor to demand and how much of each commodity to produce to maximize profits. Households choose how much labor to supply and how much of each commodity to demand to maximize utility. The competitive assumption is that households and firms take all prices as given. For arbitrary prices, supply will not equal demand for any commodity or for labor. In this multi-

---

2.   You can find out more about Walras Law on the Internet at
http://www.ecom.unimelb.edu.au/ecowww/rdixon/wlaw.html.

commodity world, Walras Law says that if demand equals supply for all but one of the commodities and for labor, then supply must also equal demand for the last commodity.

Who Holds the Money?

It probably has not escaped your notice that the economy we have described is quite different from the world in which we live. Some of the simplifications that we made are probably not very important, but others are critical.

The firms and households in our model do not use money: instead they directly barter labor for commodities. In more complicated examples of the classical theory there may be many different commodities and many different types of people, but the theory still does not integrate money into the theory in a satisfactory way. It is possible to define the price of output in terms of money and call it P; similarly it is possible to define the price of labor in the model and call it w. This doesn't change the fact that nobody in the classical model cares about w or P directly, they care only about the rate at which they can trade labor for commodities. The answer to the question who holds money in the classical theory of aggregate supply is nobody does.

If no one holds money, you might wonder how the classical theory of competition could be extended to discuss prices in terms of money. We address this in Chapter 5.

❺ USING CLASSICAL THEORY

Economists explain data with models, sets of mathematical equations that explain how variables are related to each other. Some variables, called **endogenous variables**, are explained within the model; others, called **exogenous variables**, are explained outside the model. The **solution to a model** is a set of equations, one for each endogenous variable, that expresses the endogenous variables as functions of the exogenous variables.

By matching up the predictions of our models with observations from the world, we evaluate our theories. When models make false predictions we change or refine them in ways that improve our understanding of the world. In this section we evaluate the classical theory by examining its answers to one of the fundamental questions of macroeconomics: What drives business cycles?

Business Fluctuations

According to the classical theory of employment and GDP, the explanation of business fluctuations lies with the factors that determine equilibrium in the labor market. There are three of these factors: technology, endowments, and preferences.

Preferences, Endowments, and Technology

The level of employment is determined by equality of demand and supply in the labor market. It follows that the factors that cause fluctuations in the level of output are those that cause shifts in the demand curve or the supply curve of labor. Two factors that shift labor demand are improvements in the productivity of technology and increases in the endowment of resources. A factor that shifts labor supply is changes in preferences.

Consider the effect of a productivity improvement that arises from the discovery of a new technology. Improvements of this kind are occurring continuously and may have differing effects on the labor market depending on their relative impact on the marginal products of capital and labor. Suppose, as an illustration, that a new technique is discovered that makes labor more productive, such as mass production in the automobile industry at the turn of the century. After the advent of mass production, firms were willing to pay a higher real wage for any given quantity of labor because, by using the new techniques, they were able to produce more commodities from each hour of labor employed.

The effect of a productivity improvement is depicted in Figure 4.7. Before the improvement, the economy produces output from labor with production function 1. After the improvement it produces output more efficiently with production function 2. The introduction of the new technology causes the labor demand curve to shift from labor demand 1 to labor demand 2 as firms compete more vigorously to hire the existing supply of labor. As the labor demand curve shifts to the right, the intersection of labor demand and supply curves moves up and to the right along the labor supply curve. As firms try to attract additional workers into the labor force, they must pay a higher wage to persuade households to supply additional hours of labor. The amount that the real wage rises depends on the slope of the labor supply curve. In sum, the productivity improvement increases employment to L_2^E and the real wage to ω^{E2}.

The top panel of Figure 4.7 illustrates the impact of a new technology on the supply of commodities. Aggregate supply goes up for two reasons. First, more workers are drawn into the labor force, causing GDP to increase as labor hours increase. Second, the production function shifts up, causing the quantity of output produced to increase even if labor remains unchanged. These two effects combined raise aggregate supply from Y^{E1} to Y^{E2}.

A second cause of an increase in equilibrium GDP would be the discovery of new deposits of natural resources. A natural gas discovery, for example, would increase the productivity of labor and create new jobs as firms seek to mine the deposit. The economy's stocks of natural resources, including the time of its people, are called its **endowment**. The fact that these resources are in fixed supply is responsible for the production function displaying diminishing returns to scale. The discovery of a new natural resource shifts the production function the same way a new invention does, and it has similar effects on the real wage, employment, and aggregate supply.

The final factor that shifts aggregate supply is a change in household preferences. Figure 4.8 shows what would happen if households decided spontaneously to supply more labor for any given value of the real wage. This increase in labor supply, represented as a shift to the right of the labor supply curve, lowers the equilibrium value of the real wage and increases equilibrium employment and GDP. An example of an increase in the supply of labor, due to mainly noneconomic factors, is the increase in participation rates for women since the end of World War II. In 1948 the female participation rate was 32.7%; by 1993 this figure had increased to 57.9%.

The Real Business Cycle School

Recently, the classical model has been revived by a group of economists led by Edward C. Prescott at the University of Minnesota. The classical revival is called the **real business cycle** (RBC) school because these economists believe that 70% of post–World War II

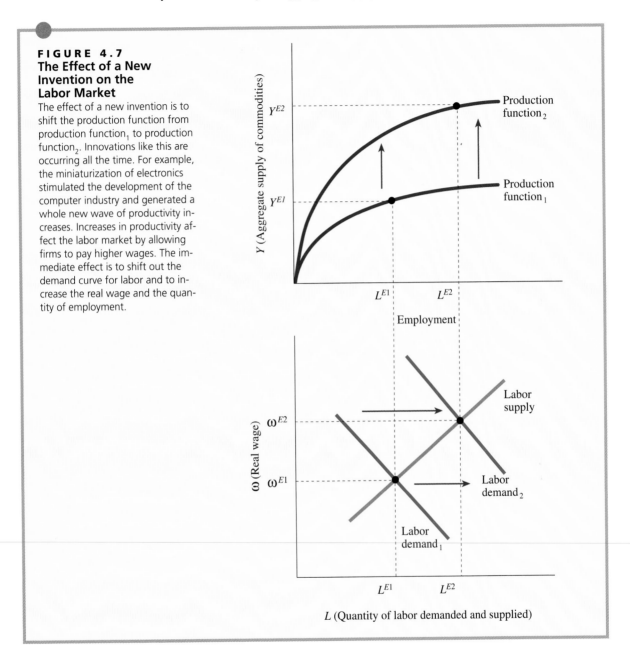

FIGURE 4.7
The Effect of a New Invention on the Labor Market
The effect of a new invention is to shift the production function from production function₁ to production function₂. Innovations like this are occurring all the time. For example, the miniaturization of electronics stimulated the development of the computer industry and generated a whole new wave of productivity increases. Increases in productivity affect the labor market by allowing firms to pay higher wages. The immediate effect is to shift out the demand curve for labor and to increase the real wage and the quantity of employment.

business cycles can be explained by random shocks to technology (see Figure 4.9). If this claim is accepted, it has important implications for the design of economic policy. The predominant belief in the immediate post-war period was that business cycles were inefficient and that it was the role of government to try to prevent these fluctuations. The view implied by the RBC models is different because, in the RBC economy, economic fluctuations are the unavoidable responses of optimizing agents to changing productive

FIGURE 4.8
The Effect of a Change in Tastes on Employment and Output
In the 1960s and 1970s women began to enter the labor force in much greater numbers than they had in previous decades. The effect was to increase employment and allow the U.S. economy to produce greater output.

The graph shows the theoretical impact of an increase in labor supply. A shift in household preferences causes the supply curve to shift from labor supply 1 to labor supply 2. The immediate impact is to increase employment and lower the real wage below what it otherwise would have been.

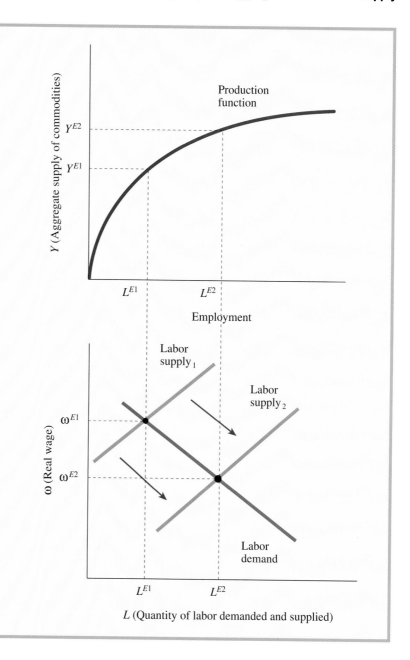

opportunities. In the RBC economy there is no role for policy because the agents themselves cope with economic fluctuations in the most efficient way possible.

The initial reaction to the RBC model was mixed. Many macroeconomists were overtly hostile to the revival of the classical model. In the past 15 years, however, the methodology advocated by RBC economists has become much more widely accepted.

FIGURE 4.9
Real Business Cycles

The real business cycle economists, led by Edward C. Prescott
at the University of Minnesota,
believe that random fluctuations
to technology account for 70%
of post-World War II business
cycle fluctuations. They back up
their claims by simulating business cycles in model economies
and showing that the fluctuations in the simulated models
mimic the features of the actual
data.

In these graphs the left panels
are actual data and the right
panels are simulated time series
from a business cycle model in
which all fluctuations arise as a
result of shocks to technology.
In each case the blue line is GDP
and the red line is consumption
(in the top graphs), investment
(in the middle graphs) and employment (in the bottom graphs).

The RBC model does a fairly
good job of mimicking the statistical properties of the actual
data.

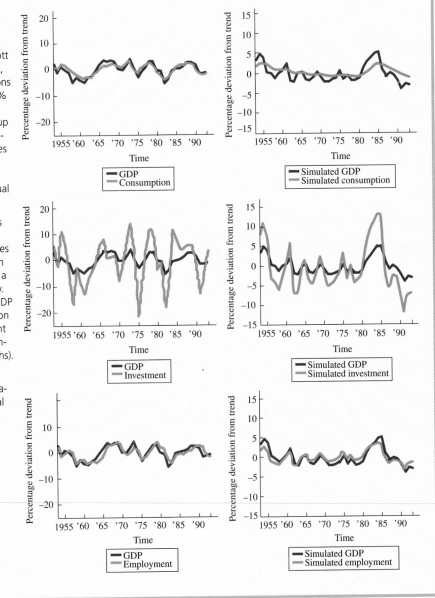

This does not mean that every macroeconomist today believes that all business cycles are
efficient responses to fluctuations in productivity. But the idea that demand equals supply
is now widely used by modern researchers in macroeconomics.

Although the impact of the RBC school has been important, their ideas have not overtaken the mainstream of the economics profession, partly because, although the RBC

WEBWATCH 4.2   **Edward C. Prescott and James Tobin: What Two Leading Economists Think About Real Business Cycles**

The Region

The Region is a magazine published quarterly by the Federal Reserve Bank of Minneapolis. The Minneapolis Fed is closely linked with the economics department at the University of Minnesota, and the research department at the Fed has a group of macroeconomists who are strongly supportive of real business cycle ideas.
http://woodrow.mpls.frb.fed.us/pubs/ordform.html.

   The Region is an excellent source of articles on modern research topics in macroeconomics, many of which you will be able to understand without a Ph.D. It also publishes interviews with leading macroeconomists. You can find an interview with Edward Prescott, in which he explains his views on real business cycles, at
http://woodrow.mpls.frb.fed.us/pubs/region/int969.html.

   Not all economists agree with Prescott. James Tobin, for example, a leading Keynesian economist and winner of the Nobel Prize in Economics in 1981, thinks that unemployment is a significant problem in the post-war period and that the economy typically produces less than its potential because many people are unable to find a job at the prevailing wage. You can read an interview with Tobin and find out how he responds to Prescott at
http://woodrow.mpls.frb.fed.us/pubs/region/96-12/tobin.html.

---

model provides a partial explanation of economic fluctuations, it is not the whole story. The principal causes of business fluctuations in classical models are changes in technology, endowments, and preferences. Although it is likely that some of the fluctuations we observe from one year to the next are due to these factors, it is unlikely that all of them can be explained in this way. The main indication that supply factors are not the whole story is the history of prices and output during the Great Depression. The classical model predicts that the price level should be countercyclical. During the single largest output fluctuation this century, it was strongly procyclical.

A second reason that many economists are skeptical of the RBC model is that it pays little or no attention to unemployment. In RBC models, as in the classical model, all fluctuations in employment arise as the result of voluntary household decisions to vary the quantity of hours they supply to the market. There is no room in these models for workers who are unable to find a job. Although unemployment has not been as important in post-war America as it was during the Great Depression, one would hope that a theory of macroeconomics could explain both pre-war and post-war data with a single model.

CONCLUSION

The idea of equilibrium explains how employment, output, and the real wage are determined. The real wage is the wage measured in units of commodities. Firms maximize profits and demand more labor when the real wage falls. The relationship between the real wage and the quantity of labor demanded is called the labor demand curve. Households maximize utility and supply more labor when the real wage rises; the relationship between the real wage and the quantity of labor supplied is called the labor supply curve. Classical economists believed that employment is determined by the point at which the demand curve and supply curves of labor intersect.

Recently, an influential group of economists, the real business cycle school, has argued that we should not dismiss the classical model too quickly; these economists believe that the Great Depression was an unusual event and that most of the time the classical model does a good job of explaining economics.

KEY TERMS

Budget constraint
Classical theory of aggregate supply
Competitive equilibrium allocation
Competitive market
Constrained maximization problem
Diminishing returns
Endogenous variable
Endowment
Exogenous variable
Equilibrium real wage
Feasible combination
Firm
Indifference curve
Isoprofit lines
Labor demand curve

Labor supply curve
Market
Nominal wage
Production
Production function
Production possibilities set
Real business cycle (RBC)
Real wage
Representative agent economies
Solution to a Model
Substitution effect
Technology
Utility
Walras Law
Wealth effect

PROBLEMS FOR REVIEW

1. Explain in a paragraph or two what economists mean by the difference between the real and the nominal wage.

2. A representative agent has preferences

$$U = Y - L$$

and produces using a technology

$$Y = 8L^{\frac{1}{2}}$$

where L is labor supply and Y is the production of the commodity. Suppose that the agent is endowed with 4 units of time (units of labor).

   a. Draw a graph of the agent's production function.

   b. What would be the real wage in a competitive equilibrium?

c. What would be the amount of the good produced in equilibrium?

d. What would be the real wage in equilibrium? Does this depend on the technology? If not, why not?

e. Suppose that the agent is endowed with only one unit of time. Repeat your answers to parts (a) through (d).

3. Perfect competition is just one way of allocating resources. Some economists have argued that a centrally planned economy should be able to do at least as well as the market mechanism because the allocation of commodities can be rationally planned. Can you think of anything that might be wrong with this argument?

4. Suppose you are the manager of a firm that produces output, Y, from labor, L, using the production function

$$Y = L$$

a. Suppose that you can hire as much labor as you like for a real wage of ½ a commodity per hour. If you want to maximize profits, how much labor would you try to hire?

b. Now suppose that the real wage is equal to 2 commodities per hour. How much labor would you try to hire? What if the wage were equal to one commodity per hour?

c. Using your answers to parts (a) and (b), draw a diagram with the real wage on the vertical axis and the firm's demand for labor on the horizontal axis.

5. (This question requires calculus.) In a representative agent economy the production function is given by

$$Y = 2L^{\frac{1}{2}}$$

and Robinson Crusoe's preferences are given by the utility function

$$U = Y - L$$

a. Draw a graph of the production function plotting Y on the vertical axis and L on the horizontal axis. Draw at least two typical indifference curves and show the feasible point that yields the highest utility.

b. Assume that Robinson runs a family firm in a market economy using the same production function that you used in part (a). Find the marginal product of labor for this economy. (*Hint*: Use calculus to find an expression for the slope of the production function.)

c. By equating the slope of the production function to the real wage, find an expression for the demand curve for labor as a function of the real wage.

d. Draw a diagram with the labor on the horizontal axis and output demanded on the vertical axis. Plot an indifference curve for the household on this diagram and label its slope. Suppose that the household is endowed with **B** units of time. How many units will it supply to firms in a competitive economy if the real wage is less than the slope of the indifference curve? If the real wage is greater than the slope of the indifference curve? If the real wage equals the slope of the indifference curve?

e. Using your answer to part (d), draw a diagram with the real wage on the vertical axis and the household's supply of labor on the horizontal axis. Use it to plot the household's labor supply curve for this economy. Using your answer to part (c), plot the firm's demand for labor on the same diagram.

6. Read the interviews with James Tobin and Edward C. Prescott in *The Region* magazine. Briefly summarize the views of each of these economists on the causes of business cycles. Do they agree with each other? If not, explain their main points of disagreement.

APPENDIX: A QUANTITATIVE EXAMPLE OF EQUILIBRIUM

This appendix provides an optional quantitative example of the classical model for readers with a mathematical background. The example uses some simple calculus.

Suppose that Robinson Crusoe has a utility function given by

4.3
$$U = Y - \frac{L^2}{2}$$

Y is the output that Robinson consumes and L is his work effort. Let the production function be

4.4
$$Y = 3L^{\frac{1}{3}}$$

Now consider how a firm would operate in a market if its technology were given by Figure 4.1. The firm's problem is

4.5
$$\max \pi = Y - \omega L, \quad \text{such that} \quad Y = 3L^{\frac{1}{3}}$$

This is an example of a **constrained maximization problem**. There are several ways of solving problems like this; one of the simplest is to substitute the constraint (in this case the production function) directly into the profit function. This leads to the expression

4.6
$$\max \pi = 3L^{\frac{1}{3}} - \omega L$$

Using calculus to set the derivative equal to zero, we find the optimal choice of L, called L^D, is given by

4.7
$$(L^D)^{-\frac{2}{3}} - \omega = 0$$

Equation 4.7 can be rearranged to give the labor demand function

4.8
$$L^D = \frac{1}{\omega^{\frac{3}{2}}}$$

It also follows that the maximum value of profits that can be earned by the firm (π^*) are given by

4.9
$$\pi^* = 3(L^D)^{\frac{1}{3}} - \omega L^D = \frac{3}{\omega^{\frac{1}{2}}} - \frac{1}{\omega^{\frac{1}{2}}}$$

Now we need to solve the problem of the household to find the labor supply curve. This problem is represented by Equation 4.10.

4.10
$$\max Y - \frac{L^2}{2} \quad \text{such that} \quad Y = \omega L + \pi^*$$

Substituting from the budget constraint into the utility function gives

4.11
$$\max \omega L + \pi^* - \frac{L^2}{2}$$

and setting the derivative of utility equal to zero, we find that

4.12
$$L^S = \omega$$

which is the labor supply curve for this economy. The equilibrium wage is found by equating demand and supply:

4.13
$$L^S = L^D \quad \text{implies} \quad \omega^E = \frac{1}{\omega^{\frac{3}{2}}}, \quad \text{or} \quad \omega^E = 1$$

When we substitute ω^E into 4.12 and 4.8, it follows that

4.14
$$L^D = L^S = 1$$

CHAPTER 5

Aggregate Demand and the Classical Theory of the Price Level

❶ INTRODUCTION

The classical theory of the price level is sometimes called the quantity theory of money or the classical theory of aggregate demand. It was developed in the last part of the nineteenth century and the early part of the twentieth century, although early versions of the theory can be found in the work of David Hume, an eighteenth-century Scottish economist.

Why should you be interested in a theory that is now almost two hundred years old? First of all, there are some questions for which the classical theory still provides very good answers. The most important of these is the classical explanation for the cause of inflation, particularly where the rate of inflation is, or has been, very high, such as Brazil, Bolivia, Argentina, and Israel. Classical theory works well in high-inflation countries for the same reason that Newton's theory of gravity works well at velocities that are well below the velocity of light. Both theories are wrong in some dimensions, but sometimes the dimensions in which they are wrong are not important.

The second important reason for studying the classical theory is that it can help you understand how modern intertemporal equilibrium theories work. These theories build on the classical theory by being more explicit about the factors that lead households and firms to vary their demands and supplies for labor through time. The classical theory makes some invalid simplifications, but it is a good idea to start with simple concepts and learn about the complicated ones later.

Last but not least, it is worth learning the classical theory of aggregate demand and supply because the classical theory has been incorporated into the **neoclassical synthesis**, the theory used by almost all economic journalists and policy makers to understand the economy today.

❷ THE THEORY OF THE DEMAND FOR MONEY

The **classical theory of the price level**, or **classical theory of aggregate demand**, is a hybrid that adds a theory of money to the classical theory of aggregate supply, which we studied in Chapter 4. To integrate money into this theory we begin with the budget constraint of a family in a static, one-period economy, and we show how this constraint is altered when a family engages in repeated trade through time, using money as a medium of exchange.

The Historical Development of the Theory

The classical theory of aggregate demand is a modern name for the **quantity theory of money**. The quantity theory of money was an attempt to explain how the general level of prices is determined. It has a long history, dating back at least as far as David Hume (1711–1776), whose delightful essay *Of Money* is still relevant to modern economics. Later economists who worked on the quantity theory include the American Irving Fisher (1867–1947) and the English economist Alfred Marshall (1842–1924). The approach we take in this chapter is based on Marshall's work, because it was Marshall who first argued for an explicit treatment of money using the framework of demand and supply.

The Theory of the Demand for Money

To understand why people use money, the classical theorists extended their static theory of the demand and supply of commodities by constructing a **theory of the demand for money**. Just as a household demands goods up to the point where the marginal benefit of an additional purchase of a commodity equals its marginal cost, so, the classical theory of the demand for money argues, people "demand money" up to the point where its marginal benefit equals its marginal cost. Money is a durable good and it is not consumed the way butter or cheese is consumed. It is more like a television set or a refrigerator that yields a flow of services over time. Just as a television set yields a flow of entertainment services, so money yields a flow of **exchange services** that increase the convenience of buying and selling goods. The cost of holding money is the opportunity cost of foregoing consumption of some other commodity; the marginal benefit is the additional usefulness gained by having cash on hand to facilitate the process of exchange.

Let us examine both the costs and benefits of holding money, beginning with the costs. Our first task is to show how holding money can reduce the household's ability to buy other commodities by examining the budget constraint of the household in a monetary economy. If households continue to use money when holding money is costly, they must be gaining some benefit. This benefit was assumed by the classical theorists to be proportional to the volume of trade.

WEBWATCH 5.1   **An Interview with Milton Friedman**

The most influential modern figure in monetary economics is Milton Friedman of the University of Chicago. In the period immediately after World War II, the dominant paradigm was Keynesian economics. Many of Keynes's followers argued that money was relatively unimportant as a determinant of inflation and that instead inflation was caused by strong trade unions. Friedman was largely responsible for reviving the classical idea that inflation is caused by changes in the quantity of money. His ideas on money and inflation appear in "The quantity theory of money—a restatement," in *Studies in the Quantity Theory of Money* (University of Chicago Press, 1956).

You can find an interview with Milton Friedman, in which he discusses contemporary economic issues ranging from the role of government in society to monetary union in Europe, in *The Region*, the magazine of the Federal Reserve Bank of Minneapolis. The interview is available online at http://woodrow.mpls.frb.fed.us/pubs/region/int926.html.

Budget Constraints and Opportunity Cost

Money imposes an **opportunity cost** because the decision to use money reduces the resources available to be spent on other goods. In Chapter 8 we discuss the opportunities for borrowing and lending, modifying the analysis of the opportunity cost of holding money. But for the moment we assume that money is the only asset available to households as a store of wealth. In our simple model, the opportunity cost of holding money arises from the fact that if the household were to choose not to hold money, it would instead be able to purchase additional commodities. In the next two sections we illustrate this idea by contrasting the budget constraint in a static model (in which all exchange takes place at a point in time) with the budget constraint in a dynamic model (in which exchange takes place at different points in time). The purpose of these two sections is to show how the use of money imposes a cost on consumers by reducing the resources available to purchase other commodities.

BUDGET CONSTRAINTS IN A STATIC BARTER ECONOMY

The type of economy we studied in Chapter 4 is called a *static barter economy*. The word *barter* means that commodities are directly exchanged for one another without the use of money. The word *static* means that the economy lasts for only one period of time: agents exchange labor for commodities, they produce and consume, then the world ends.

We can rewrite the budget constraint faced by families in the static barter economy by introducing a notation to refer to the prices of commodities and labor in terms of money. This notation uses the symbol P to refer to the money price of commodities and the symbol w to refer to the money wage.

5.1
$$PY^D = P\pi + wL^S$$

Demand for   **Profit**   **Labor**
commodities   **income**

Equation 5.1 is the household budget constraint in a static barter economy. In this economy, no money changes hands and no family uses money for trade, but money can be used as an accounting unit. To illustrate how this accounting device would work, suppose that you were to offer your labor services to a farmer who owns an orchard. The farmer offers to pay $5 an hour, and he sells his apples for 20 cents each. Rather than accept $5 an hour, you could equally well agree to accept 25 apples an hour. The real wage, ω, in this economy is 25 apples an hour, the money wage, w, is $5 an hour, and the price of commodities, P, is 20 cents an apple. The budget constraint in the barter economy, given in Equation 5.1, expresses relative prices by quoting labor and commodities in terms of money, even though money is never used in exchange.

BUDGET CONSTRAINTS IN A DYNAMIC MONETARY ECONOMY

How would this budget constraint be altered in a world in which money *must* be used in exchange? The classical theorists argued that since the typical family does not buy commodities at the same time that it sells its labor, during an average week the family has a reserve of cash on hand to facilitate the uneven timing of purchases and sales. This argument involves an important change to the family's budget constraint because, by thinking of purchases and sales as separated in time, the classical theory is explicitly modeling production and exchange as an ongoing dynamic process rather than as a static one.

$$5.2 \qquad M^D \quad + \quad PY^D \quad = \quad P\pi \quad + \quad wL^S \quad + \quad M^S$$

| Demand for money | Demand for commodities | Profit | Labor income | Supply of money |

Equation 5.2 takes into account the use of cash by adding two additional terms to the budget constraint. M^S represents the money that the family owns at the beginning of the week; we call this the household's *supply of money* because it will be supplied by the family during the week to other families in the economy in exchange for commodities. M^D is the money that the family owns at the end of the week; we call this the family's *demand for money* because it represents cash that the family chooses to keep on hand at the end of the week so that it will be able to buy and sell commodities in the future. The supply of money owned by the household at the beginning of the week is like additional income that is available to be spent on commodities. The demand for money at the end of the week is like a demand for any other commodity, because the decision to keep cash on hand from one week to the next reduces the funds that the household has available to spend on produced goods. Because the household's supply of money could be used to purchase additional commodities, the decision to hold money imposes an opportunity cost on the household. The lost opportunity that arises from holding money is the additional utility that could have been gained by purchasing additional commodities.

The Benefit of Holding Money

If households continue to hold money, and if that money imposes a cost, then money must also yield a benefit. To classical theorists this benefit was the advantage that comes from being more easily able to exchange commodities with other families in the economy; in other words, money is a generally acceptable medium of exchange.

Consider the process of exchange in a barter economy. Suppose that an individual is a seller of good X and a buyer of good Y; we will call him Mr. Jones. For example, good X might be "an economics lecture" and good Y "a haircut." In the barter economy Mr. Jones must find a second individual, Mr. Smith, who wants both to sell good Y and to buy good X. This problem is called the **double coincidence of wants**; it implies that in a barter economy it would be necessary for Mr. Jones, if he wanted a haircut, to find a barber who wanted to hear an economics lecture. Exchange is greatly simplified if everyone agrees on a commodity that they will accept in exchange, not for its own sake, but because by convention others also will accept this commodity. This is the purpose of money.

Classical theorists argued that the stock of money that the average household needs at any point in time is proportional to the dollar value of its demand for commodities. Households that purchase a higher value of commodities each week will, on average, need to keep more cash on hand. The constant of proportionality between the average stock of cash held by the household during the week and the value of its flow demand for commodities is called the **propensity to hold money** and it is represented in the demand for money equation by the symbol k.

5.3
$$M^D = k \times PY^D$$

| **Demand for money** | **Propensity to hold money** | **Nominal value of the quantity of commodities demanded** |

The classical demand for money, Equation 5.3, expresses this idea symbolically. The symbol M^D represents the stock of cash that the household plans to hold at the end of the week, k is the propensity to hold money, and P times Y^D is the nominal value of the commodities that will be purchased during the week.

Notice that the demand for money in the classical theory is the relationship between a stock (money on hand) and a flow (weekly purchases of commodities). The theory predicts that a person who earns $200 a week will, on average, carry half as much cash and keep half the checking account balances as a person who earns $400 dollars a week. Because the theory describes the relationship between a stock and a flow, the constant k has units of time: the number of weeks of income that the average family carries in the form of money. Using a measure of money called $M1$ (mainly cash and checking accounts), the propensity to hold money in the postwar United States has been equal to ten weeks on average, although k has been falling since the end of World War II.

Aggregate Demand and the Demand and Supply of Money

The classical theory of the demand for money was used by classical theorists to explain more than the use of cash in exchange. By putting a theory of the demand for money together with the assumption that the quantity of money demanded is equal to the quantity of money supplied, classical theory explains the quantity of commodities demanded by households at a given price level. This relationship between the aggregate demand for commodities and the price level is called the classical theory of aggregate demand.

A critical step in the development of the classical theory of aggregate demand is the assumption that the quantity of money demanded is always equal to the quantity of money supplied. To understand the logic behind this assumption, suppose instead that, on average, families hold more cash each week than they needed to buy and sell commodities. When a household finds that it has more money on hand than it needs, it can plan to buy

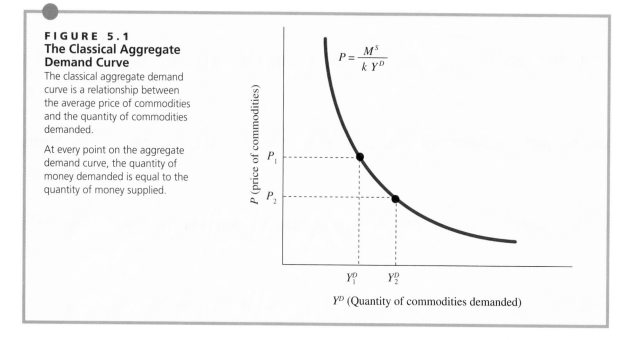

FIGURE 5.1
The Classical Aggregate Demand Curve

The classical aggregate demand curve is a relationship between the average price of commodities and the quantity of commodities demanded.

At every point on the aggregate demand curve, the quantity of money demanded is equal to the quantity of money supplied.

more commodities than it would purchase during a normal week. But although a single household can reduce its money holdings by planning to buy more commodities, the community as a whole *cannot* reduce its money holdings in this way because every attempt to buy a commodity by one family must necessarily lead to an accumulation in the cash held by another. For the community as a whole the demand for money must always be equal to its supply. The fact that the demand for money must equal its supply can be used to develop a theory of how the aggregate demand for commodities varies with the nominal price. This relationship between price and the flow of GDP demanded is called the **classical aggregate demand curve**.

5.4
$$P = \frac{M^S}{k \times Y^D}$$

Price level $= \dfrac{\textbf{Supply of money}}{\textbf{Propensity to} \times \textbf{Aggregate demand}}$
$\phantom{\textbf{Price level} = \dfrac{}{}}\textbf{hold money} \quad \textbf{for commodities}$

Equation 5.4 is the equation of the classical aggregate demand curve, and Figure 5.1 graphs this equation, plotting the price of commodities on the vertical axis and the quantity of commodities demanded on the horizontal axis. Although the graph in Figure 5.1 is called an aggregate demand curve, it is not a demand curve in the sense the term is used in microeconomic theory. It is an equation that shows how the price level would have to be related to the level of GDP if the quantity of money demanded and the quantity of money supplied were equal. As we move along the aggregate demand curve from left to

BOX 5.1
FOCUS ON THE FACTS:
What Is Money?

Barter is uncommon today, but has it ever been the dominant mode of exchange? How did the use of money come about? What kinds of monies have existed historically and what kinds are likely to exist in the future[1]?

In much of the world the use of money in exchange is so commonplace that we cannot conceive of exchanging commodities in any other way. But it has not always been this way, and even today in certain countries in Africa 60% to 70% of transactions are carried out without the use of money. Barter remained the rule over very large areas between the fifteenth and eighteenth centuries, and at the time of the American revolution barter was common. The following quote comes from Clavier and Brissot, two well-known figures in the French revolution:[2]

Instead of money incessantly going backwards and forwards into the same hands, it is the practice here [in America] for country people to satisfy their needs by direct reciprocal exchanges. The tailor and the bootmaker go and do the work of their calling at the home of the farmer who requires it and who, most frequently, provides the raw material for it and pays for the work in goods.

Monetary exchange developed throughout the world as, gradually, three metals, gold, silver and copper began to be used regularly in the process of exchange. The use of copper was generally restricted to low-value transactions within a country, and gold and silver were used primarily in international trade.

The origin of monetary exchange has recently been studied using the tools of modern game theory. In a series of papers, Nobu Kiyotaki of the London School of Economics and Randall Wright of the University of Pennsylvania have explored the idea that the use of a single commodity might arise spontaneously, using the assumption that individuals maximize utility. Kiyotaki and Wright's models are good examples of the modern approach to economics, which derives implications about macroeconomics using microeconomic tools. Interestingly, in Kiyotaki and Wright's models barter can coexist with monetary exchange just as it did historically.[3]

Why might we be interested in the origins of money and what use would this information be to modern policy makers? These questions are important because money is not static – it is constantly evolving. For example, credit cards are widely used today but they were unheard of twenty years ago. The classical theory of aggregate demand still forms the basis for our modern understanding of the causes of inflation. The theory implies that to prevent inflation we must control the supply of money, but to do this effectively we must know what money is. By studying the origins of money, modern researchers hope to learn how currency might evolve in the computer age.

1.   An excellent discussion of the historical development of money can be found in *The Structures of Everyday Life* by Fernand Braudel, Siân Reynolds, Trans. Harper and Row, 1981. The book was first published in France under the title *Les Structures du quotidien: le possible et l'impossible*, Paris: Librairie Armand Colin, 1979.
2.   Braudel, op cit., p. 447.
3.   Nobuhiro Kiyotaki and Randall Wright, "On money as a medium of exchange." *Journal of Political Economy 97* (August , 1989): 757–775.

right, the nominal value of GDP is constant. Since the quantity of money demanded is proportional to nominal GDP, each point along the aggregate demand curve is associated with the same demand for money. The position of the curve is determined by the requirement that the quantity of money demanded at each point on the curve is exactly equal to the nominal money supply; that is, at every point on the classical aggregate demand curve, the quantity of money demanded and the quantity of money supplied are equal.

To understand why the aggregate demand curve slopes downward, suppose that the price is at P_1 and the quantity of commodities demanded is at Y^D_1. If the price were to fall to P_2, the average family in the economy would have more cash on hand than it needed to buy and sell commodities during the week, because a given number of dollars would now be able to finance a greater flow of transactions. Each family would try to eliminate its excess cash by planning to purchase additional commodities. As households try to eliminate this excess supply of money by purchasing additional commodities, the economy experiences an increase in the aggregate quantity of commodities demanded, and thus the aggregate demand curve slopes downward.

❸ THE CLASSICAL THEORY OF THE PRICE LEVEL

The Role of Price Level in the Theory of Aggregate Supply

The classical theory of aggregate demand and supply is a complete explanation of the factors that determine the level of employment, the level of GDP, the relative price of labor and commodities (the real wage), and the prices of labor and commodities in terms of money (the nominal wage, w, and the price level, P). In this section we fill in the remaining part by explaining how the classical theory of aggregate supply can be amended to accommodate the fact that trades take place using money as a medium of exchange. We explain the role of the price level in the theory of aggregate supply using three diagrams: the labor demand and supply diagram, the production function diagram, and the aggregate supply diagram.

The Price Level and the Labor Demand and Supply Diagram

Assume that the labor demand and supply decisions of households in a dynamic monetary economy are the same as the decisions that would be made in a static barter economy. This assumption, used by classical economists to simplify the theory of aggregate supply, is valid under certain strong simplifications about the way that people make choices. These simplifications are replaced in the modern theory of dynamic equilibrium, discussed in Chapter 17.

In Figure 5.2 the labor demand and supply curves plot the choices of the household and the firm. In the classical model the labor market is assumed to be in equilibrium. The real wage and the level of employment are determined by the point of intersection of the labor demand and supply curves, denoted by $(w/P)^E$ and L^E, where E stands for equilibrium. The important feature of the classical analysis is that households and firms care only about the real wage, because the ratio of w to P indicates how many commodities the household will receive for a given labor effort. The equilibrium values of L^E and $(w/P)^E$ depend in practice on the nature of the technology and the preferences of the households, since these features of the economy determine the positions and the slopes of the labor demand and supply curves.

The Production Function Diagram

The second step in the classical theory of aggregate supply is to determine the supply of output. For a given level of employment, this is determined by the production function.

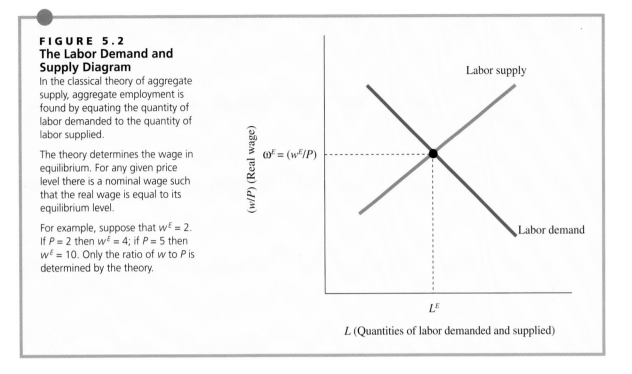

FIGURE 5.2
The Labor Demand and Supply Diagram
In the classical theory of aggregate supply, aggregate employment is found by equating the quantity of labor demanded to the quantity of labor supplied.

The theory determines the wage in equilibrium. For any given price level there is a nominal wage such that the real wage is equal to its equilibrium level.

For example, suppose that $w^E = 2$. If $P = 2$ then $w^E = 4$; if $P = 5$ then $w^E = 10$. Only the ratio of w to P is determined by the theory.

The higher the level of employment, the greater the supply of output. Figure 5.3 reproduces the production function. The equilibrium supply of output, Y^E, is the amount of output that would be produced when the demand is equal to the supply of labor; that is, when the labor input is equal to L^E. This particular value of output is determined by the characteristics of the production function and the preferences of the households.

The Aggregate Supply Diagram

The final step is to determine how the supply of output is related to the money price of commodities. Since the quantities of labor demanded and supplied are both determined by the real wage, there is no relationship between the price of commodities and the supply of output. In other words, a classical economy will supply exactly Y^E units of commodities per week whatever the dollar price of commodities. When the price increases, the nominal wage increases proportionately, leaving the real wage, the quantity of employment, and the supply of commodities unchanged.

The diagram in Figure 5.4 illustrates the classical theory of aggregate supply by plotting the price of commodities on the vertical axis and the aggregate supply of commodities on the horizontal axis. Because there is no relationship between the price of output and the aggregate supply of commodities, this graph is a vertical line at the level of output Y^E. At every point on this vertical line, the quantity of labor demanded is equal to the quantity of labor supplied.

FIGURE 5.3
The Production Function
Once the real wage and the level of employment have been determined by the labor market diagram, the supply of output is determined from the production function.

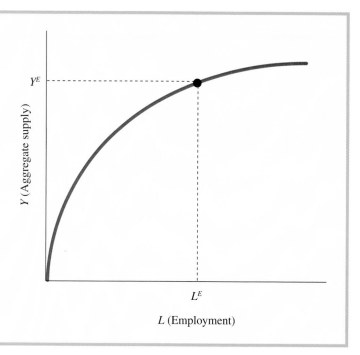

FIGURE 5.4
The Classical Aggregate Supply Curve
In the classical theory, the equality of demand and supply in the labor market determines the real wage. For any price level, there is a nominal wage at which the labor market is in equilibrium. The quantity of output supplied is determined only by preferences, endowments, and technology. Thus, aggregate supply does not depend on the price level.

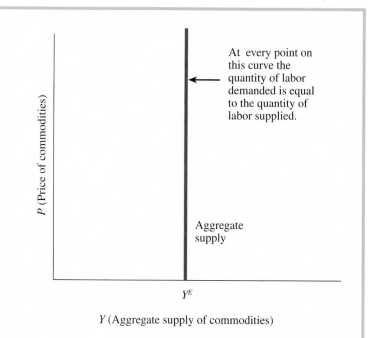

The Complete Classical Theory of Aggregate Demand and Supply

We have used three diagrams to show how the classical theory of aggregate supply determines the real wage, the level of employment, and the aggregate supply of output. Figure 5.5 puts these three diagrams together to illustrate how the price level, output, and employment are determined in the complete classical system. Panel A plots the aggregate demand and supply curves on a single diagram; panel D is the labor demand and supply diagram; panel C is the production function; and panel B has a line at 45° to the axis that is used to take vertical distances from panel C and plot them as horizontal distances on panel A. We use this panel to translate the supply of output, determined by panels C and D, to the aggregate demand and supply diagram in panel A.

The following analysis explains why the aggregate supply curve is a vertical line. Beginning with panel A, pick an arbitrary value of the price of commodities. Call this arbitrary value P_1. To find a point on the aggregate supply curve we must find the quantity of output produced when the price level equals P_1. To establish a value for the quantity of output supplied, we turn to panel D, the labor demand and supply diagram. From panel D we find that, whatever the price of commodities, the equality of the quantity of labor demanded with the quantity of labor supplied will result in L^E hours of labor being traded at a real wage of $(w/P)^E$. To find the equilibrium supply of output, we may read off the quantity of GDP produced, when L^E hours of labor are employed, from the production function on panel C. The final step is to use the line with slope 45° in panel B to translate the distance Y^E from the vertical axis of panel C to the horizontal axis of panel A. This step establishes that the point $\{P_1, Y^E\}$ is on the aggregate supply curve.

To find a second point on the aggregate supply curve, we could begin with a value of the price that is either lower or higher than P_1. Once again we find that the equality of the quantity of labor demanded with the quantity of labor supplied will require the household to supply exactly L^E hours of labor. The critical step in this argument is the fact that the quantities of labor demanded and supplied depend on the real wage and not on the nominal wage or the price level. If the price level doubles, a labor market equilibrium will exist in which the nominal wage is twice as high. This equilibrium will have the same employment level and the same quantity of output supplied as the labor market equilibrium at the price level P_1. Because the equilibrium quantity of employment depends only on the real wage and not on the price level, the assumption of labor market equilibrium generates the same supply of output for every possible value of the price level.

Classical Theory and the Neutrality of Money

An important proposition follows logically from the classical assumptions that all markets are in equilibrium. In the classical model, the aggregate supply curve is vertical. A vertical aggregate supply curve implies that a fall in aggregate demand will cause a fall in the price level and will leave all real variables unaffected. Since the demand for money is proportional to the demand for commodities, a 10% fall in the supply of money is predicted to lead to a 10% fall in the price level and a 10% fall in the nominal wage. The proposition that nominal variables will move in proportion to changes in the quantity of money and that real variables will be invariant to these changes is referred to as the **neutrality of money**.

FIGURE 5.5
Equilibrium in the Complete Classical System

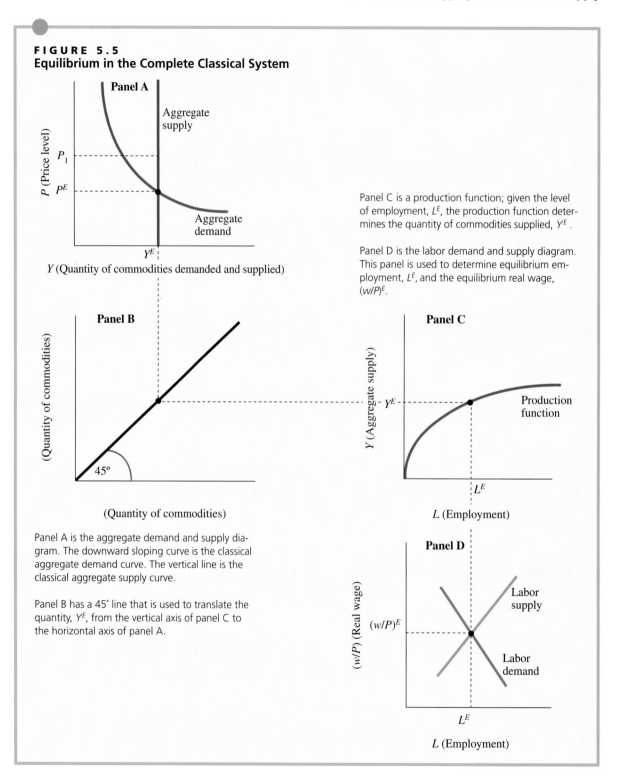

Panel C is a production function; given the level of employment, L^E, the production function determines the quantity of commodities supplied, Y^E.

Panel D is the labor demand and supply diagram. This panel is used to determine equilibrium employment, L^E, and the equilibrium real wage, $(w/P)^E$.

Panel A is the aggregate demand and supply diagram. The downward sloping curve is the classical aggregate demand curve. The vertical line is the classical aggregate supply curve.

Panel B has a 45° line that is used to translate the quantity, Y^E, from the vertical axis of panel C to the horizontal axis of panel A.

Figure 5.6 illustrates the response of output, employment, the real wage, and the price level to a reduction in the quantity of money, predicted by the classical model. Suppose that the average family begins each week with $500 cash. During the week it receives labor income and profits, and it purchases commodities from other families equal to the value of its income. In a typical week the stock of cash held by the family at the end of the week will equal its stock of cash on hand at the beginning. Consider how this economy would respond to an exogenous event that reduced the stock of cash in circulation. In practice there are several ways this might happen; in our discussion we suppose that the government removes $100 from the average family.[1] The week the money supply contracts, the outlays of the average family will be higher than usual because it must both finance its purchases and pay $100 to the government. If it were to maintain its normal spending pattern, the family would end the week holding only $400 in cash. This would not be consistent with equality of the demand and supply of money, because the family requires $500 in cash at the end of the week to meet its future need for money as a medium of exchange. In the classical economy, the family tries to return its cash holdings to normal by spending less on goods and services, but although a single family can choose to hold $500 in cash, the economy as a whole cannot.

Figure 5.6 shows the household's reduction in spending as a leftward shift in the aggregate demand curve in panel A. Before the reduction in the stock of money, the aggregate demand curve is AD_1 and the equilibrium price of commodities is P_1^E. After the fall in the stock of money, the aggregate demand curve is AD_2 and the equilibrium price is P_2^E. To restore equality between the quantity of commodities demanded and the quantity of commodities supplied, the price level must fall by the same proportion as the stock of money, since the demand for money is proportional to GDP. Once the price level has fallen, the household is content to hold the lower quantity of nominal balances. The real wage, the quantity of employment, and the quantity of commodities supplied are not affected by a drop in the nominal supply of money because they are each determined by technology, endowments, and preferences. The proposition that real variables are unaltered by a drop in the money supply but nominal variables fall in proportion is called the neutrality of money.

❹ USING THE CLASSICAL THEORY TO UNDERSTAND THE DATA

In Chapter 4 we evaluated the predictions of the classical model for the theory of business cycles. In this section we turn our attention to the predictions of the classical theory of the price level. How well does the theory enable us to understand the problem of inflation?

The Classical Explanation of Inflation

Classical theory determines the price level as the point of intersection of the aggregate demand curve with a vertical aggregate supply curve. Because inflation is the percentage rate of change of the price level from one year to the next, this theory also explains inflation.

---

1.   In practice most changes in the stock of money are accomplished by actions of the central bank, called *open market operations*. An open market operation involves the sale of interest-bearing bonds to the public. In return for bonds, the public surrenders some of its money back to the central bank. The public ends up holding more bonds and less money.

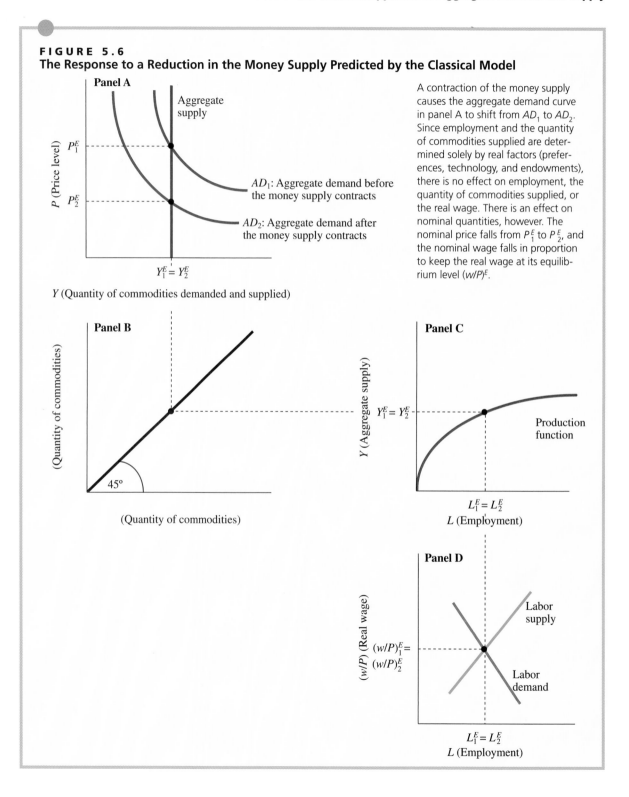

FIGURE 5.6
The Response to a Reduction in the Money Supply Predicted by the Classical Model

A contraction of the money supply causes the aggregate demand curve in panel A to shift from AD_1 to AD_2. Since employment and the quantity of commodities supplied are determined solely by real factors (preferences, technology, and endowments), there is no effect on employment, the quantity of commodities supplied, or the real wage. There is an effect on nominal quantities, however. The nominal price falls from P_1^E to P_2^E, and the nominal wage falls in proportion to keep the real wage at its equilibrium level $(w/P)^E$.

TABLE 5.1
The Factors That Determine the Price Level

The Quantity Equation of Money: $P = \dfrac{M^S}{kY^E}$

k	Propensity to hold money	This is assumed to be constant by the classical theory.
Y^E	Aggregate supply	This grows at a rate determined by preferences, technology, and endowments.
M^S	The money supply	This grows at a rate determined by the government in a modern economy.

Table 5.1 describes the dependence of the price level on the propensity to hold money, the aggregate supply of commodities, and the quantity of money supplied. The equation at the head of this table takes the aggregate demand curve, Equation 5.4, and replaces the quantity of commodities demanded by Y^E, the equilibrium quantity of commodities supplied. The equation expressed in this way is called the **quantity equation of money**. Table 5.1 lists the factors that, according to the quantity equation, are possible causes of increases in the price level: the propensity to hold money, the equilibrium quantity of commodities supplied, and the supply of money.

The first factor that could be responsible for changes in the price level is k. Because classical theory assumes k to be constant, this explanation can be ruled out. The second factor that could cause changes in the price level is the level of aggregate supply. But in order for changes in aggregate supply to be responsible for inflation, output would have to fall continuously through time. This would be equivalent to a continuous leftward shift of the aggregate supply curve. In fact, most countries' economies have been growing through time, which would tend to cause the price level to fall. The only remaining possible explanation of inflation is an increase in the stock of money, which would cause the aggregate demand curve to keep shifting right over time.

Equation 5.5 writes out the quantity equation in the form of proportional changes.[2] Assuming that k is constant, the classical theory predicts that the rate of inflation, $\Delta P/P$, should be equal to the rate of money growth, $\Delta M^S/M^S$, minus the rate of growth of output, $\Delta Y^S/Y^S$.

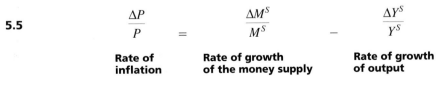

5.5 $\qquad \dfrac{\Delta P}{P} \quad = \quad \dfrac{\Delta M^S}{M^S} \quad - \quad \dfrac{\Delta Y^S}{Y^S}$

Rate of inflation   **Rate of growth of the money supply**   **Rate of growth of output**

2.   The notation ΔX, where X is any economic variable, means the change in X from one year to the next. The notation $\Delta X/X$ means the change in X divided by the level of X; that is, the proportional change in the variable X.

Before the middle of the twentieth century, money was backed by precious metals, usually gold or silver. During this period, no government could issue money unless it had enough gold or silver in the treasury to meet the demands of the public to convert their paper currencies back into gold. In the seventeenth century, with the discovery of gold in the New World, European economists recognized that there was a connection between increases in the stock of money and increases in prices. These early empirical observations gave an impetus to the development of the quantity theory of money.

Since the 1930s, the world monetary system has been uncoupled from precious metals, and in the postwar period there is nothing backing the currency in any country in the world other than the promises of each nations' central bank. In some countries, such as the United States, the United Kingdom, and Japan, the nation's central bank has maintained a relatively tight control over the supply of money, and these countries have experienced relatively low inflations. In other countries, such as Israel, Argentina, and Brazil, the central bank has printed money to finance government expenditure programs instead of raising government revenues by taxation. These countries have experienced very rapid inflations. The different experiences of three low-inflation countries and three high-inflation countries are illustrated in Figures 5.7 and 5.8.

Figure 5.7 plots money growth and inflation for the period from 1960 through 1988 for Japan, the United Kingdom, and the United States. In none of these countries has inflation over this period exceeded 25%. The figure illustrates that even in low inflation countries there is a connection between money growth and inflation, although this connection is not particularly strong because real GDP growth and changes in the propensity to hold money have been almost as important as the rate of money creation in determining the rate of inflation.

Figure 5.8 plots money growth and inflation in Argentina, Israel, and Brazil over the same period. Here, the scale of the vertical axis runs from zero to 800% per year. These are all examples of countries that have experienced very high inflation. Notice that in the high-inflation countries there is a very close connection between the rate of money creation and the rate of inflation.

The connection between money growth and inflation is strong in countries with very high inflation because the movements in the propensity to hold money and movements in real GDP growth are very small relative to the huge movements in the stock of money. Control of the money supply by the central bank is essential if a country is to avoid the very high inflations such as occurred in Brazil in 1987. These periods of very high inflation are extremely disruptive to the lives of ordinary people.

Assessing the Classical Explanation of Inflation

The main feature of the classical explanation of inflation is the concept of a demand function for money that is stable over time; the stability of the equation is represented by the classical assumption that the propensity to hold money, k, is a constant. There have been two principal challenges to the classical explanation. The first claims that k is not, in fact, a constant and that inflation is just as frequently due to changes in k as to increases in the supply of money. According to this challenge, an increase in the supply of money is just one of the possible causes of inflation, and there is no reason to single out changes in the money supply over and above other causes of inflation.

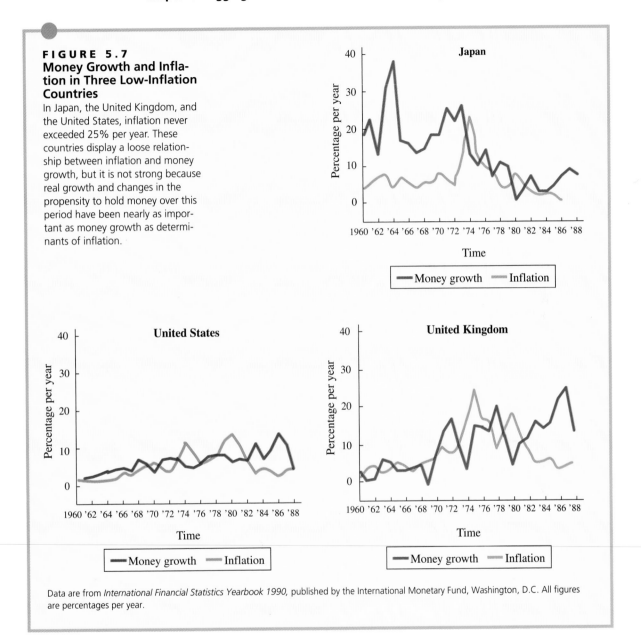

FIGURE 5.7
Money Growth and Inflation in Three Low-Inflation Countries
In Japan, the United Kingdom, and the United States, inflation never exceeded 25% per year. These countries display a loose relationship between inflation and money growth, but it is not strong because real growth and changes in the propensity to hold money over this period have been nearly as important as money growth as determinants of inflation.

Data are from *International Financial Statistics Yearbook 1990*, published by the International Monetary Fund, Washington, D.C. All figures are percentages per year.

The criticism that *k* is not a constant is factually correct. Figure 5.9 tracks the history of the propensity to hold money in the United States. Notice that *k* has been as high as 15 weeks of income and as low as 7 weeks. The fact that *k* has varied through time is a valid criticism of the simple classical theory of inflation, but it is not a fatal criticism. Modern theories of inflation rescue the classical explanation of the demand for money by providing

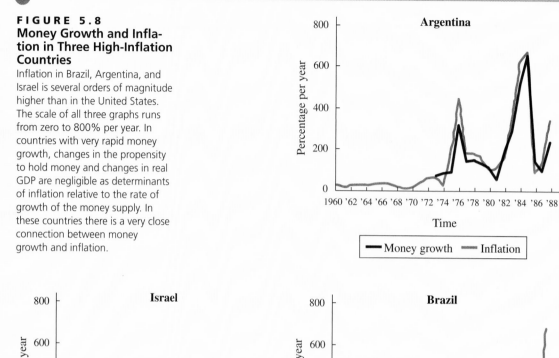

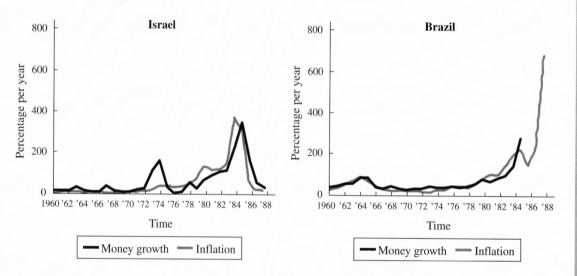

Money Growth and Inflation in Three High-Inflation Countries
Inflation in Brazil, Argentina, and Israel is several orders of magnitude higher than in the United States. The scale of all three graphs runs from zero to 800% per year. In countries with very rapid money growth, changes in the propensity to hold money and changes in real GDP are negligible as determinants of inflation relative to the rate of growth of the money supply. In these countries there is a very close connection between money growth and inflation.

an explanation of exactly how k varies through time. As long as k moves in a predictable way, the theory can be used to explain the cause of inflation. When we return to the modern theory of aggregate demand in Chapter 8, we show that there is a predictable relationship between k and the rate of interest.

A second challenge to the classical explanation of inflation recognizes that there is indeed a connection between inflation and money growth but asserts that classical economists have the direction of causation wrong. In other words, inflation causes money growth and not the other way around. This criticism is most often stated in the form of a political or sociological explanation of inflation that denies the economic assumption that the rate of

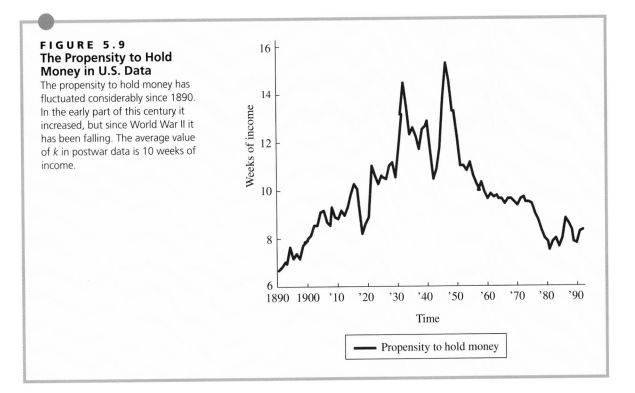

FIGURE 5.9
The Propensity to Hold Money in U.S. Data
The propensity to hold money has fluctuated considerably since 1890. In the early part of this century it increased, but since World War II it has been falling. The average value of k in postwar data is 10 weeks of income.

money growth can legitimately be considered an exogenous variable.[3] Critics of the economic explanation of inflation argue that the growth of trade unions is responsible for the spread of inflation. As unions put upward pressure on wages, wage gains are in turn fed into prices. The increases in the stock of money that are often observed to accompany inflation are explained as the accommodating response of a central bank that raises the rate of money growth in order to avoid a recession. The main problem with this criticism is that there is no strong correlation between the growth of trade union power and inflation.

Perhaps the most troubling aspect of the classical theory of aggregate demand is its failure to explain the Great Depression, when output fell 20% below trend and prices were strongly procyclical. In the classical model (Figure 5.10) the aggregate supply curve is vertical and the aggregate demand curve is shifted only by changes in the stock of money. A leftward shift of the aggregate demand curve would lower prices but would not cause a drop in output because of the vertical aggregate supply curve. A leftward shift of the aggregate supply curve would lower output but would be expected to *raise* prices. The failure of the classical model to easily account for the fact that prices were procyclical during the Great Depression led to the development of Keynesian economics, a topic that we take up in Chapter 7.

3. Political theories of inflation based on union pressure are called *cost push* theories. Cost push theories were influential in the 1960s, although more recently they have become less popular. A good example of the cost push view can be found in P. J. Wiles: "Cost inflation and the state of economic theory." *Economic Journal* 83 (1973) 377–398.

FIGURE 5.10
Classical Theory and the Great Depression
If the aggregate demand curve shifts left, the price level will fall but output will not.

If the aggregate supply curve shifts left, output will fall but the price level will rise.

During the Great Depression, output and the price level both fell together. The classical model cannot easily explain how this happened.

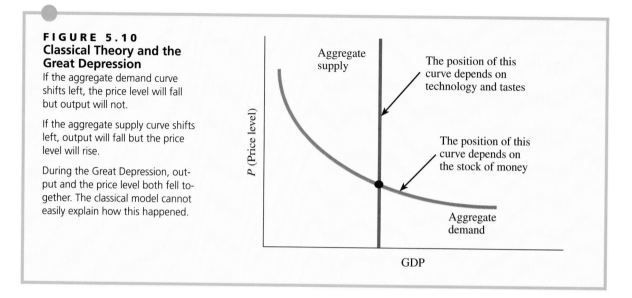

CONCLUSION

The quantity theory of money, the classical theory of the price level, and the classical theory of aggregate demand are different names for the same theory. The theory assumes that the use of money in exchange has costs and benefits. The cost is the resources tied up in cash that could be used to purchase additional commodities. The benefit is the utility yielded by the use of money to bridge the uneven timing of purchases and sales. The theory assumes that the quantity of money demanded is proportional to GDP with a constant k: the propensity to hold money.

To move from a theory of the demand and supply of money to a theory of aggregate demand, we assume that, for the community as a whole, the quantity of money demanded must always equal the quantity supplied. If the price level falls, the real value of the existing stock of money will increase and individual families will experience an excess supply of cash. As they attempt to spend this excess cash, the aggregate quantity of commodities demanded will increase.

The classical theory of aggregate demand can be combined with the classical theory of aggregate supply to explain how output, employment, the real wage, the nominal wage, and the price level are determined. The classical theory implies that if the nominal quantity of money is doubled, all nominal variables will also double but all real variables will remain unchanged. This is called the neutrality of money.

The classical theory of the price level works well for countries that are experiencing very rapid inflations, such as Argentina, Israel, and Brazil. It works less well in low-inflation countries such as the United States, the United Kingdom, and Japan. The reason that it does not work well in these countries is that in reality the propensity to hold money is not a constant. In high-inflation countries, movements in k are swamped by movements in the money supply; in low-inflation countries, this is no longer so. The biggest problem with the classical theory is that it cannot explain why prices were procyclical during the Great Depression.

KEY TERMS

Classical aggregate demand curve
Classical theory of aggregate demand
Classical theory of the price level
Double coincidence of wants
Exchange services
Neoclassical synthesis

Neutrality of money
Opportunity cost
Propensity to hold money
Quantity equation of money
Quantity theory of money
Theory of the demand for money

PROBLEMS FOR REVIEW

1. Explain in a paragraph or two what economists mean by the difference between *real* and *nominal*.

2. The following data are from the U.S. economy for the 1980s. GDP is measured in trillions of dollars per year and $M1$ is a measure of the stock of money measured in trillions of dollars.

	1980	1981	1982	1983	1984	1985
GDP	2.7	3.0	3.1	3.4	3.8	4.0
$M1$	0.41	0.44	0.47	0.52	0.55	0.62

  a. Calculate the value of the propensity to hold money, k, for each year.

  b. What units is k measured in?

  c. Draw a graph of k against time. Was k approximately constant for this period?

3. An economy produces output using the technology

$$Y = L$$

and the representative agent has a utility function given by

$$U = \log(Y) + \log(1-L)$$

  a. How much output would be produced in equilibrium?

  b. How much labor would be employed in equilibrium?

  c. If the price level were equal to $6 per unit of output, what would the nominal wage be in equilibrium?

  d. If the stock of money were equal to $20 and the propensity to hold money equals 1, what would the price level be in equilibrium?

4. Explain briefly why the classical model of aggregate demand and supply has trouble accounting for the Great Depression.

5. This question is based on Milton Friedman's views, as expressed in his interview in *The Region.*

   a.   Does Friedman think that the Federal Reserve System should be made more powerful? If not, why not?

   b.   Why, according to Friedman, is Federal Deposit Insurance no longer useful?

   c.   Why does Friedman think that monetary union in Europe will be unsuccessful?

   d.   Does Friedman agree with the RBC economists?

   e.   Why does Friedman think that more episodes of high inflation and hyperinflation are likely in the world in the next decade?

6. What is meant by the "opportunity cost of holding money"?

7. What is meant by "the neutrality of money"?

8. What is the quantity theory of money and how is it related to the theory of aggregate demand?

9. Why does the aggregate demand curve slope down? What is held constant at every point on the aggregate demand curve?

10. Give examples of changes in preferences, endowments, and technology that would be expected to raise the price level. Have any events of this kind been important in the United States in recent history?

APPENDIX: A QUANTITATIVE EXAMPLE OF AGGREGATE DEMAND AND SUPPLY

In this appendix we use the example from the appendix to Chapter 4 to show how the price level is determined. In that example, the production function of a typical firm was given by

4.4 $$Y = 3L^{\frac{1}{3}}$$

and the labor demand curve was given by the formula

4.8 $$L^D = \frac{1}{(w/P)^{\frac{3}{2}}}$$

where we have substituted (w/P) for the real wage, ω. The labor supply curve was given by

4.12 $$L^S = \frac{w}{P}$$

where once again we have written the real wage as the ratio of the nominal wage to the nominal price of commodities. The equality of demand and supply requires that

5.6
$$(w/P)^E = 1$$

which is the number that represents the equilibrium real wage. Notice that neither P nor w is determined individually; it is only their ratio that is set in the labor market. To find the classical aggregate supply curve we must substitute the equilibrium real wage into the labor demand equation to establish that

5.7
$$L^E = 1$$

Replacing L^E in the production function, we can find the classical aggregate supply curve

5.8
$$Y^E = 3$$

To complete the classical model, suppose that the propensity to hold money, k, is equal to 2, and the stock of money, M^S, equals 600. The classical aggregate demand curve is given by the equation

5.9
$$P = \frac{M^S}{kY^E}$$

Plugging in the numbers for M^S, k, and Y^E, the equilibrium price level in this economy can be found to be

5.10
$$P^E = \frac{600}{2 \times 3} = 100$$

Finally, since

5.11
$$(w/P) = 1$$

the equilibrium money wage in this economy is given by

5.12
$$w^E = 100$$

CHAPTER 6

Saving and Investment

❶ INTRODUCTION

This chapter applies the classical model of demand and supply to the capital market. The theory argues that the rate of interest is a price that equates the demand for investment to the supply of saving, and this theory is widely accepted by economists of all persuasions, even those who do not believe that the classical model should be applied to the labor market.

The starting point for classical economics is the representative family. In the classical model, consumption, investment, GDP, and employment can be viewed as if they were chosen by a family that decides how hard to work and how much to save, based on its rational assessment of the costs and benefits of reallocating resources. The decision to re-allocate time between work and leisure results in employment fluctuations that are highly correlated with GDP. The decision to re-allocate production between consumption goods and investment goods provides a way of redistributing commodities through time. Classical economists believe that business fluctuations are caused by a series of shocks to technology that alter the productivity of labor in a random way from one year to the next. These shocks are transmitted to the capital market through changes in investment, and they cause saving, investment, and the interest rate to go up and down during the business cycle in an apparently random way.

Keynesian economists do not accept that changes in investment are caused by fundamental shocks to the productivity of technology, but they do accept the classical view that explains how these shocks are transmitted to the rate of interest. A Keynesian would take the view that investment moves up and down over the business cycle because of the irrational beliefs of individual investors. But although Keynesians do not agree with classical economists as to the cause of investment shocks, they do accept much of the analysis of how investment shocks feed into saving and the rate of interest.

❷ SAVING, INVESTMENT, AND THE CAPITAL MARKET

Saving occurs when households choose not to spend part of their income. Investment occurs when firms purchase new capital equipment. Because the decision to invest is made by firms and the decision to save is made by households, there must be a mechanism for channeling funds from savers to investors. This mechanism is the capital market.

Saving and Investment

What are the facts about consumption, saving, and investment? Figure 6.1 illustrates the annual detrended observations on U.S. GDP, consumption, and investment per person since the end of the Korean War in 1953. In each panel, the solid blue line is GDP, measured as percentage deviations from a flexible trend. The solid red lines measure consumption and investment per person, also as deviations from trend. Notice that consumption and investment are strongly procyclical, but they differ considerably in how much they move up and down over the business cycle.

Table 6.1 measures the smoothness of each of these time series using a statistical measure called the standard deviation.[1] Roughly speaking, the standard deviation is the average difference from the average. A series that is constant has a standard deviation of zero; a series that moves around a lot has a high standard deviation. Table 6.1 shows that GDP has a standard deviation of 2.58, consumption has a standard deviation of 1.97, and investment has a standard deviation of 8.67. This gives us a convenient way of quantifying what it means for a series to be more volatile than another; a more volatile series has a higher standard deviation. Consumption is three-quarters as volatile as GDP. Investment is over three times as volatile as GDP.

Animal Spirits or Fundamentals?

Why is investment so volatile? There are two possible answers. According to the classical economists, investment fluctuates because firms respond to changes in technology; this is called a **fundamental** explanation because in classical theory, output and employment are determined by the fundamentals: preferences, endowments, and technologies. An example of a fundamental explanation for an investment boom would be an invention that requires an investment in new kinds of machines to exploit the invention. Some economists believe

---

1.   **Mathematical Note:** The standard deviation is given by the formula

$$\sigma_x = \left(\frac{\sum\limits_{i=1}^{n} (x_i - \bar{x})^2}{n-1} \right)^{\frac{1}{2}}, \text{ where } \bar{x} = \frac{\sum\limits_{i=1}^{n} x_i}{n} \text{ is the arithmetic mean.}$$

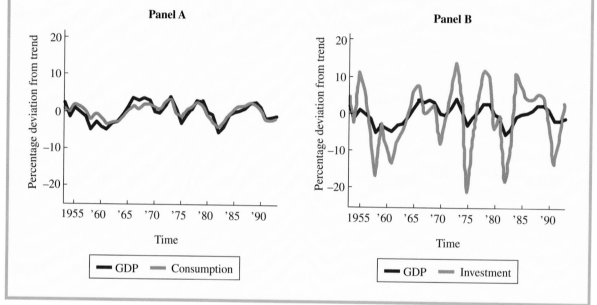

FIGURE 6.1
Consumption, Investment, and GDP in the United States
These graphs illustrate the history of the business cycles in consumption, investment, and GDP in the United States since 1953. In each case, the blue line is the deviation of GDP from a flexible trend.

Panel A plots the deviation of consumption from trend as the red line; notice that consumption does not move up and down as much as GDP.

Panel B plots the deviation of investment from a flexible trend as the red line; notice that investment moves up and down much more than GDP.

that fundamentals, particularly the invention of new technologies, are the most important source of business fluctuations. This is the basis for the real business cycle school, one of the leading modern explanations for the causes of business cycles.

A second possibility, one suggested by John Maynard Keynes, is that highly volatile investment does not reflect changes in preferences, endowments, or technology. Instead, it represents changes in the mass psychology of investors. Keynes called the mass psychology of investors **animal spirits**. Followers of Keynes believe that animal spirits lead to

TABLE 6.1
How Smooth Is Consumption?

	GDP	Consumption	Investment
Standard deviation	2.58	1.97	8.67
Standard deviation relative to GDP	1.00	0.76	3.34

variations in output and employment that could be avoided if investment were more efficiently coordinated. Therefore, they favor the implementation of government policies to
stabilize the business cycle. This Keynesian view in favor of government intervention is in
contrast to the policy prescription of the new classical economists, who believe that business cycles are a necessary and unavoidable feature of the workings of a market economy.

Consumption Smoothing

Why is consumption so smooth? Although Keynesian and classical economists differ as to
the cause of volatile investment spending, they agree on the reason why consumption is
smooth. Consumption is smooth because households borrow and lend in the capital market in an effort to redistribute their income more evenly through time.

We can illustrate consumption smoothing with an example. Suppose that you are faced
with two possible consumption plans over a two-year horizon. In plan A you get to eat five
meals a day in the first year and only one meal a day in the second year. In plan B you get
to eat three meals a day for two years. Consumption smoothing means that most people
would prefer plan B to plan A, even though they get to consume the same quantity of food
in both plans.

To understand how **consumption smoothing** works in a classical model, consider
how Robinson Crusoe would respond to changing productive opportunities. Suppose that
he grows grain each year, but his productivity fluctuates with the weather. In some years
the weather is favorable and he grows a relatively large amount of grain. In other years the
harvest is bad and he grows relatively little. If we associate the harvest in this economy
with GDP, we would observe fluctuations in Crusoe's GDP from year to year, in response
to changes in productivity.

Suppose that in one year Crusoe gets a particularly good harvest. If he prefers a
smooth consumption plan, his best response to a good harvest is to store the excess grain,
over and above a normal year's consumption, in order to distribute it more evenly over future years. Because there are many more years in the future than in the present, this stor-
age plan implies that Crusoe's consumption will rise by less than the increase in GDP. The
grain he stores would be recorded as investment, so an economist observing the Robinson
Crusoe economy would see investment fluctuate much more, in relative terms, than GDP.
This underlies the classical explanation of the relative volatilities of consumption, investment, and GDP over the business cycle.

Borrowing Constraints

Keynesian economists agree on the basic logic that the capital market is used by households to smooth income, but they do not agree that the market works as well as it could.
Some economists point out that although aggregate consumption is smoother than income,
it is not as smooth as it could be, and the real business cycle model predicts that consumption should be much less volatile than it actually is. A possible reason for this is that although it is relatively easy to lend money to firms, it is extremely difficult to borrow
money without security. Many people have low incomes early in life and high incomes
later in life, once they have an education and work experience. Often, we prefer to borrow
more money when we are young than we are able to. The reason that it is often difficult to
borrow is that it is hard for banks to enforce repayment later in life.

❸ THE THEORY OF INVESTMENT

We now explore the theory of investment and saving by developing a demand and supply diagram. The demand curve, called the **demand for investment**, plots the quantity of investment demanded on the horizontal axis and the rate of interest on the vertical axis. The supply curve, called the **supply of savings**, plots the quantity of savings supplied on the horizontal axis and the rate of interest on the vertical axis. We explain the determination of the rate of interest and the quantity of resources saved and invested by arguing that the capital market is typically in equilibrium at the point where these two curves intersect. By developing an explanation of the factors that shift the demand curve for investment and the supply curve of savings, we can explain the co-movements of investment, saving, and the rate of interest that we observe in the data.

The Production Possibilities Set

We begin by asking how Robinson Crusoe would make decisions if he were both a producer and a consumer. We illustrate the options available to Robinson Crusoe with a production possibilities set in which inputs and outputs occur at different points in time.

Once we introduce time explicitly into Robinson Crusoe's decision problem, he must decide not only how much to produce but also how to allocate his produced commodities between consumption goods and investment goods. For example, a few hours spent producing a fishing net will reduce the current production of fish but will greatly augment Robinson Crusoe's ability to catch additional fish in the future. Exactly the same kind of decision must be made in an advanced industrial economy, when resources are switched between the production of factories, roads, and houses to the production of food, entertainment, and other nondurable consumer goods.

We represent the opportunities for investment as Robinson Crusoe's **intertemporal production possibilities set**. This set is the shaded blue region on Figure 6.2. The distance **OA** represents the resources available to Robinson Crusoe to be divided between consumption and investment. The horizontal axis of the diagram measures two things. Reading from left to right, beginning at point **O**, it measures the quantity of commodities that Robinson Crusoe invests. Reading from right to left, beginning at point **A**, it measures the quantity of commodities he consumes. For example, suppose that Crusoe chooses to invest the resources **OB** and to consume the resources **BA**. In this case he leaves himself the resources **OE** to be divided between consumption and investment in the future.

The production possibilities set has an upward-sloping frontier because the more Crusoe invests in the present the greater his income will be in the future. Moving from left to right, beginning at point **O**, the slope of this frontier gets flatter, reflecting the assumption of diminishing returns. Diminishing returns means that, as Crusoe spends more time building tools, each additional tool is marginally less productive than the one before. For example, building one spear may be very useful to him because it will increase his ability to hunt. But building a second spear will be less useful, because it would only be useful once the first one had become blunted. In a modern industrial society, diminishing returns to investment holds because society as a whole has a fixed stock of people. Building extra factories and machines increases the productive capacity

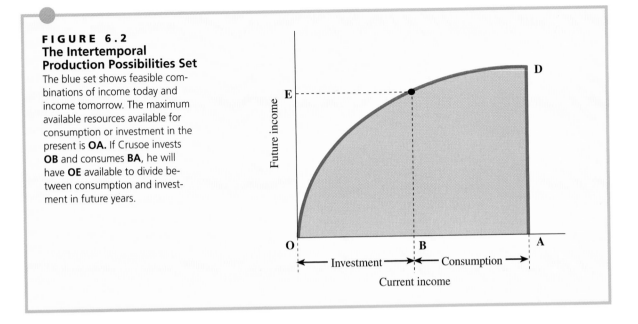

FIGURE 6.2
The Intertemporal Production Possibilities Set
The blue set shows feasible combinations of income today and income tomorrow. The maximum available resources available for consumption or investment in the present is **OA**. If Crusoe invests **OB** and consumes **BA**, he will have **OE** available to divide between consumption and investment in future years.

of the economy, but only to the extent that there are not enough people left to operate them.

The Real and the Nominal Rate of Interest

In modern economies most borrowing and lending contracts are denominated in dollars. But it has not always been this way; in medieval times, for example, it was common to borrow and lend commodities. A farmer might lend ten sacks of flour to his neighbor. If the farmer required his neighbor to repay eleven sacks one year later, we would say that the **real rate of interest** was 10% per year.

If the farmer in this example had been living in an economy in which money was a commonly used medium of exchange, instead of lending ten sacks of flour he might have lent money. Let's suppose that one sack of flour costs $5. Instead of borrowing ten sacks of flour, an equivalent way of financing would be to borrow $50 and to repay $55 in one year. In this case we say that the **nominal rate of interest** was 10%.

As long as the price of flour is the same next year as this year, a loan denominated in units of flour is equivalent to a loan denominated in dollars. But when the price of commodities changes from one year to the next, the real rate of interest is calculated from the nominal rate of interest by subtracting the rate of inflation. The relationship between the real interest rate, the nominal interest rate, and the rate of inflation is given in Equation 6.1, where we use the symbol r to mean the real interest rate, i to mean the nominal rate of interest, and $\Delta P/P$ to mean the rate of inflation.[2]

2.   The symbol Δ means "the change in." $\Delta P/P$ is the proportional change in the price level, which is the definition of inflation.

6.1 $$r = i - \Delta P/P$$

| **Real interest rate** | **Nominal interest rate** | **Rate of inflation** |

For the rest of the chapter we talk exclusively about the real interest rate and assume that loans are denominated in units of commodities.

Maximizing Profits

The classical theory of production assumes that markets are competitive. Firms borrow current resources in the capital markets and invest those resources in factories and machines. Classical theory assumes that firms choose how much labor to demand in order to maximize profits, so the classical economists applied the same logic to the decision about how much to invest. In the future, the factories and machines are used to produce commodities that are sold in the market. The profit of the firm is the difference between the value of the output that they produce and the principal and interest on the borrowing that they engage in to purchase current investment goods. Firms invest up to the point at which the output produced by an extra unit of investment is equal to its cost.

Borrowing and Investment

The classical theory of saving and investment assumes that firms and households can borrow and lend freely at a single rate of interest, called the **market rate**. Borrowing and lending take place in the capital market. Let's suppose that the market rate is r and that a firm can produce output tomorrow of value Y from an investment of I resources today. In this case, the profit of the firm is given by the formula in Equation 6.2.

6.2 $$\pi = Y - (1 + r)I$$

| **Profits of the firm** | **Value of future sales** | **Cost of borrowing** |

Figure 6.3 graphs this equation, illustrating the decision that would be made by a profit-maximizing firm. The blue lines in the figure are isoprofit lines. Each line depicts Equation 6.2 for different values of profit. The slope of each line is equal to one plus the rate of interest $(1 + r)$; this is the cost of borrowing a unit of resources today measured in units of resources in the future. Every point on the same line gives equal profit. This profit, measured in units of commodities tomorrow, is represented by the point where the isoprofit line meets the vertical axis.

Firms would like to make as much profit as possible by selling the maximum possible output for the smallest possible investment, but they are constrained by the fact that they must choose a combination of investment and sales that is feasible, given existing technology. The feasible points are represented by the blue shaded area on Figure 6.3. The feasible combination of output and investment that gives the firm the maximum profit is the point where one of the isoprofit lines is exactly tangent to the production function, yielding profit equal to π_2. Of the three isoprofit lines drawn in the figure, the line that cuts the axis at π_2 is the line with highest profit that contains a feasible point.

FIGURE 6.3
Maximizing Profits

Firms choose the investment that maximizes their profits. The blue set describes the feasible choices of value tomorrow and investment today. Higher investment yields higher value, but the benefit of additional investment is diminishing. Diminishing returns are reflected in the fact that the slope of the production function gets flatter as the firm invests additional units.

The blue lines are isoprofit lines. Each isoprofit line represents combinations of investment today and value of commodities produced tomorrow that give the firm the same profit. Higher lines give the firm higher profits. The formula that describes each line is given by the equation

$$Y = \pi + (1 + r)I$$

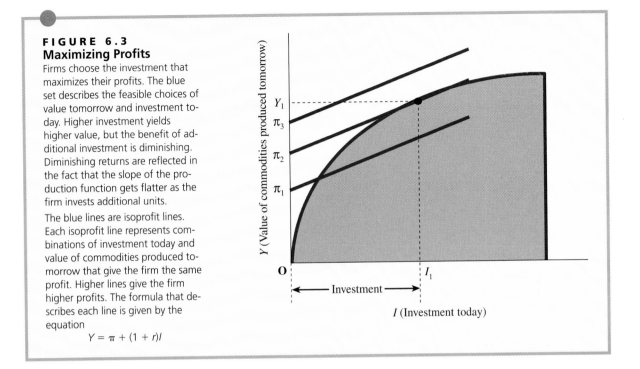

The line that cuts the vertical axis at π_3 has higher profits, but it does not intersect the feasible set. The line that cuts at π_1 has many feasible points, but none of them yields as much profit as π_2.

The Investment Demand Curve

We can use the assumption that firms maximize profit to derive a relationship between the real rate of interest and investment. If the real interest rate is plotted on the vertical axis of a graph and investment on the horizontal axis, this relationship, called the **investment demand curve**, is downward sloping. Since firms must borrow in the capital market to raise the funds necessary to invest, the investment demand curve also determines the demand for borrowing by private firms in the economy as a whole.

Figure 6.4 derives the investment demand curve on a diagram. Panels A and B illustrate the decisions that would be made by a profit-maximizing firm for two different values of the interest rate. On panel A the interest rate, represented on this diagram by the slope of the isoprofit line, is high and equal to r_A. The graph shows just the line that maximizes profit and is tangent to the production function at point **A**. Because r_A is relatively high, the firm chooses to invest a relatively small amount in the present and to produce a correspondingly low level of output in the future.

Panel B shows what happens when the interest rate falls from r_A to r_B. The interest rate r_B is lower than r_A, and this is reflected in the fact that the budget constraint is flatter in

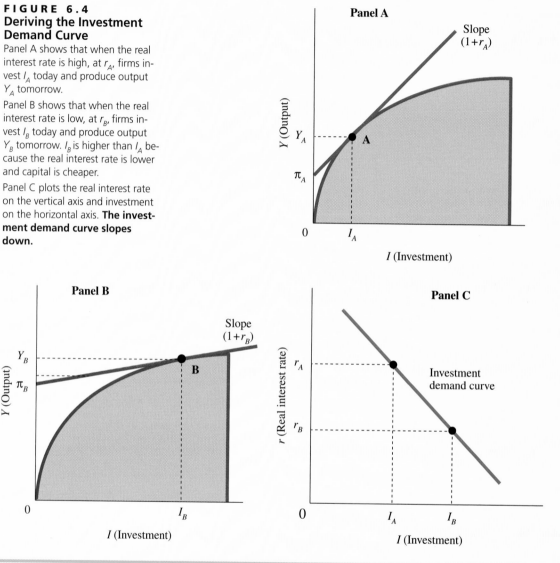

FIGURE 6.4
Deriving the Investment Demand Curve

Panel A shows that when the real interest rate is high, at r_A, firms invest I_A today and produce output Y_A tomorrow.

Panel B shows that when the real interest rate is low, at r_B, firms invest I_B today and produce output Y_B tomorrow. I_B is higher than I_A because the real interest rate is lower and capital is cheaper.

Panel C plots the real interest rate on the vertical axis and investment on the horizontal axis. **The investment demand curve slopes down.**

panel B than in A. The fact that the interest rate is lower means that the cost of investing is less, and firms choose a relatively high amount of investment. Panel C plots the interest rate on the vertical axis and the quantity of investment demanded on the horizontal axis. The downward sloping line on the graph in panel C is the *investment demand curve*. Because the firm demands more investment when the interest rate falls, the investment demand curve slopes down.

④ HOUSEHOLDS AND THE SAVING SUPPLY CURVE

Indifference Curves

The application of indifference curves to the problem of saving is called the **intertemporal utility theory**, and it forms the basis for most modern explanations of how income is divided between consumption and saving. Intertemporal utility theory argues that, given the choice, families would prefer consumption to be evenly distributed across time. Just as preferences between leisure and consumption are represented by indifference curves on a graph of leisure plotted against consumption, so preferences for consumption between periods are represented by indifference curves on a graph of present against future consumption.

The Intertemporal Budget Constraint

Not only can we use a budget constraint to illustrate the opportunities available to a family for trading leisure for consumption, we can also use a budget constraint to represent the trades available to the family at different points in time. Suppose that instead of consuming its income, the family puts it into the capital market by lending to another family or to a firm. In return, the family receives resources in the future, with interest. Because we receive interest on our savings, income that is saved for the future may purchase more future consumption goods than present ones. The amount of additional goods that we can buy in the future grows with the rate of interest. In this sense, the rate of interest is the price at which consumption in the present can be exchanged for consumption in the future.

Present Value

Just as the capital market can be used to transfer resources from the present to the future, so can it be used to transfer resources from the future to the present. When you borrow against future income, the amount you can borrow is its **present value.**

For example, suppose John Smith, an economics student, will inherit $10,000 next year when he turns 21. John would like to spend his inheritance on a used car, but he is impatient and unable to wait until next year. If he buys the car right away, the bank manager will lend him

$$\frac{1}{(1 + r)} Y = \frac{1}{1 + 0.1} \$10,000 = \$9,901$$

which is the sum that can be exactly repaid with $10,000 in one year if the interest rate is 10%. When the rate of interest is positive, future commodities are cheaper than current commodities; this is reflected in the fact that the present value of future income is lower than the income itself.

Borrowing and Lending to Smooth Consumption

A family can use the capital market to redistribute its resources through time. Let's use Y_1 to mean present income and Y_2 for future income. You might like to think of "the present" as the working life of two adults and "the future" as their retirement. If the family does

FIGURE 6.5
Maximizing Utility
Over Time
This graph shows how families choose to allocate resources over time. The red curves are intertemporal indifference curves. Points on the same curve indicate combinations of present and future consumption that make the family equally happy. Curves further to the Northeast indicate higher levels of utility than curves to the Southwest. The family will pick the highest indifference curve that intersects the budget constraint.

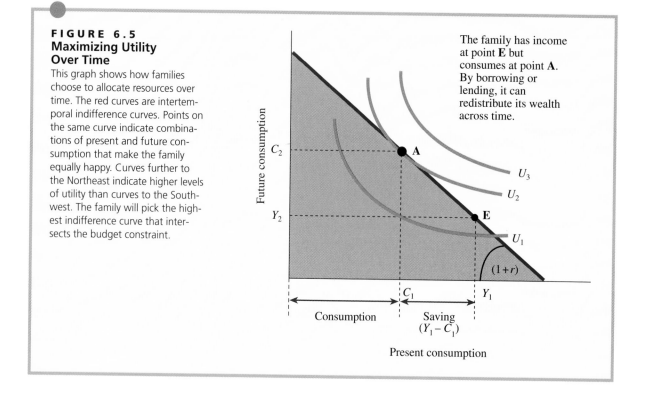

The family has income at point **E** but consumes at point **A**. By borrowing or lending, it can redistribute its wealth across time.

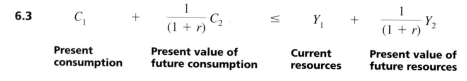

not save, it will be forced to reduce its consumption upon retirement. But by using the capital market, it can buy financial assets that will pay off with interest in old age. The Inequality 6.3 is the constraint on lifetime choices that comes from the use of the capital market to smooth consumption. This inequality, called the **intertemporal budget constraint,** places a bound on the amount of consumption that is available over a family's lifetime.

6.3
$$C_1 \quad + \quad \frac{1}{(1 + r)} C_2 \quad \leq \quad Y_1 \quad + \quad \frac{1}{(1 + r)} Y_2$$

| **Present consumption** | **Present value of future consumption** | **Current resources** | **Present value of future resources** |

The intertemporal budget constraint places an upper bound on the amount that a person can consume over his or her lifetime. The left side of the constraint adds the values of present and future consumption; that is, it represents the value of the goods that a person consumes at every point in life, valued in terms of current consumption goods. The right side adds the values of present and future income; that is, it is the value of the income that a person earns at every point in life, valued in terms of current consumption goods. The price of future consumption is $1/(1 + r)$, where r is the interest rate.

Figure 6.5 puts the indifference curves and the budget constraint together using a diagram first made popular by American Irving Fisher in the 1920s. The horizontal axis measures consumption in the present; the vertical axis is consumption in the future. The shaded purple set illustrates those combinations of consumption in the two periods that are available by borrowing and lending at a fixed interest rate, r; the frontier of this set is the boundary of the family's budget constraint. Consumption and saving are found by picking the point on the highest possible indifference curve that is also within the budget set. On Figure 6.5 the chosen point is represented as $\{C_2, C_1\}$, where the indifference curve labeled U_2 is tangent to the budget constraint. At this point the family saves the amount $(Y_1 - C_1)$ and uses these savings to augment its future income Y_2.

Why does the family choose the point $\{C_1, C_2\}$ rather than some other feasible consumption plan? The household would prefer to choose a point on the indifference curve U_3 because U_3 represents combinations of consumption in the present and consumption in the future that yield higher utility. But there are no feasible points on the indifference curve U_3, and to get from U_2 to U_3 the household would need to be wealthier. The indifference curve U_1 has many feasible points because it intersects the budget set in a number of places. But none of these feasible points will be chosen because points on the indifference curve U_1 yield strictly lower utility than those on U_2.

The Saving Supply Curve

In the intertemporal theory of utility, households choose to allocate resources through time to smooth their consumption. But as with all commodities, individuals can be persuaded to consume more or fewer future (or current) goods by changing their relative price. In the classical theory of saving and investment, the interest rate goes up or down to reflect the relative scarcity or abundance of commodities. If commodities are likely to be plentiful in the future because people expect technology to be productive, this will be reflected in a low price for future consumption. But the price of future consumption is $1/(1 + r)$, and a low price means a high interest rate. It is a high interest rate that persuades people to save more and to choose to defer their consumption until a date at which commodities are plentiful.

To illustrate the relationship between saving and the interest rate we graph the saving supply curve, plotting the interest rate on the vertical axis and the quantity of saving supplied on the horizontal axis. This is panel C in Figure 6.6. To derive the graph in panel C, we draw the two utility diagrams in panels A and B. These diagrams plot current and future consumption on the axes and illustrate, with indifference curves and budget lines, the quantity of saving supplied for two different values of the rate of interest.

The graph in panel A illustrates a low rate of interest, r_A. Panel B illustrates a high interest rate, r_B; in both graphs the interest rate is represented by the slope of the budget line, and the income of the household is the same and equal to $\{Y_1, Y_2\}$. The household can always choose to consume its income in each period, and thus the budget line always goes through the point $\{Y_1, Y_2\}$; this is labeled on both graphs as point **E**. On graph A the relative price of future consumption is high (the interest rate is low), so the household chooses to weight its consumption relatively heavily toward the present. This is reflected in low future consumption, high current consumption, and low saving, represented by the distance S_A. On graph B the relative price of future consumption is low (the interest rate is high), and the household chooses high future consumption and high saving, S_B.

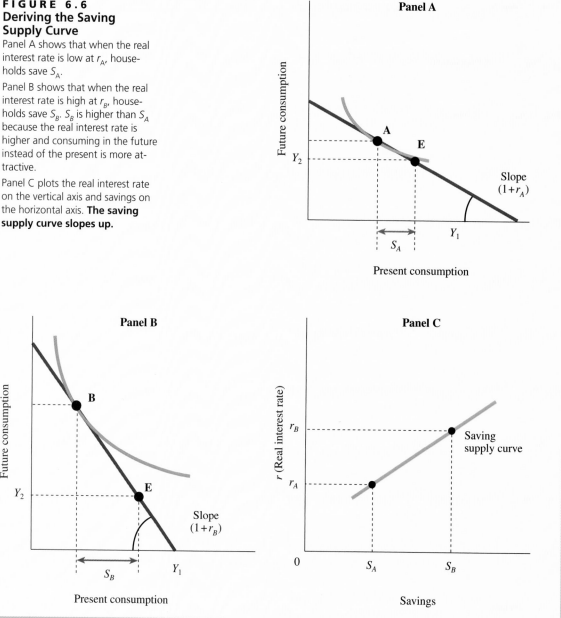

FIGURE 6.6
Deriving the Saving Supply Curve

Panel A shows that when the real interest rate is low at r_A, households save S_A.

Panel B shows that when the real interest rate is high at r_B, households save S_B. S_B is higher than S_A because the real interest rate is higher and consuming in the future instead of the present is more attractive.

Panel C plots the real interest rate on the vertical axis and savings on the horizontal axis. **The saving supply curve slopes up.**

Panel C combines the information from graphs A and B by plotting the interest rate on the vertical axis and the supply of saving on the horizontal axis; the red line is called the **saving supply curve.** When the interest rate goes up, the quantity of savings supplied increases and so the saving supply curve slopes up.

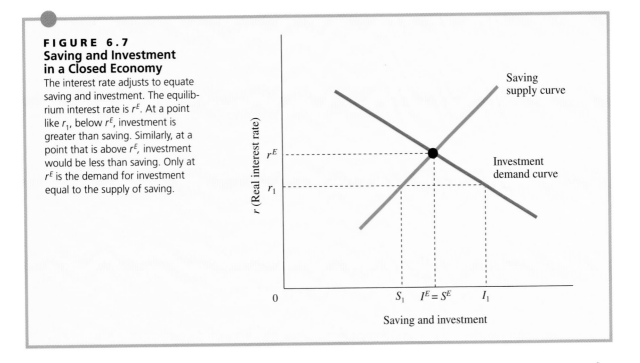

FIGURE 6.7
Saving and Investment in a Closed Economy
The interest rate adjusts to equate saving and investment. The equilibrium interest rate is r^E. At a point like r_1, below r^E, investment is greater than saving. Similarly, at a point that is above r^E, investment would be less than saving. Only at r^E is the demand for investment equal to the supply of saving.

⑤ EQUATING DEMAND AND SUPPLY

By putting the theories of investment and saving together, we can explain how the capital market allocates resources between different points in time. We begin by looking at how the rate of interest adjusts to equate saving and investment in a closed economy. Then we modify this theory to account for trade in the international capital markets in an open economy.

Saving and Investment in a Closed Economy

Figure 6.7 shows how the interest rate, saving, and investment are simultaneously determined. The saving supply curve represents the funds that are flowing into the capital market from households. This flow of saving is channeled through banks, savings and loan institutions, pension funds, and direct ownership of shares by individual investors. When the interest rate goes up, households are more willing to wait to consume. This increased willingness to defer consumption is translated into an increase in funds available for corporations to borrow.

The investment demand curve represents the funds flowing out of the capital market to firms that borrow the money to build new factories and machines. This curve is downward-sloping because, when the interest rate falls, it is cheaper to borrow money and investment becomes more profitable. The model predicts that the interest rate will be equal to r^E, and that saving and investment will be equated at $S^E = I^E$.

BOX 6.1
FOCUS ON THE FACTS

The investment function slopes down; the saving function slopes up. By studying how the interest rate is correlated with investment, we can figure out whether fluctuations in the interest rate are caused by shifts in the demand curve for investment or shifts in the supply curve for savings.

Panels A and B show the relationship between investment growth and the rate of interest in the United States during the 1970s. Panel A is a time series and panel B is a scatter plot. During the period from 1970 to 1980, the investment demand curve was relatively stable, and most movements in investment were caused by movements of the supply curve of savings. This is apparent from the fact that most of the points in panel B lie around a downward-sloping line. The two major recessions during this period were caused by sharp increases in the price of oil in 1973–1974 and again in 1978–1979. These recessions caused the supply curve of saving to shift to the left and triggered movements along the investment demand curve.

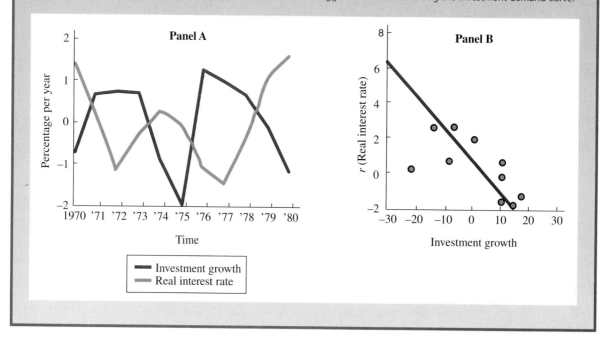

What would happen if the interest rate were different from r^E? Suppose it were equal to r_1, a value that is lower than r^E. At r_1 the quantity of investment demanded is equal to I_1, but the quantity of saving supplied is only equal to S_1; at this interest rate investment exceeds saving and some firms will be unable to borrow all of the funds that they need. Some of these firms will offer to pay a higher rate of interest, and, as the interest rate increases, additional funds will be channeled into the market from savers. If the interest rate were higher than r^E, the reverse situation would occur: Saving would be higher than investment and some savers would be forced to accept a lower rate of interest. Only at r^E is the capital market in equilibrium.

Productivity and the Investment Demand Curve

Two leading contenders for the causes of business cycles are the classical view, made popular in recent years by Edward Prescott, and the animal spirits theory of John Maynard

BOX 6.1
(continued)

Panels C and D show the relationship between investment growth and the rate of interest in the United States during the 1980s. During this period, the investment demand curve was very unstable, and swings in investment caused movements up and down the supply of savings curve. The situation depicted in panel B has been the rule over most of recent U.S. history. Investment has been by far the most volatile component of GDP. Consequently, the rate of interest and investment have been positively correlated. In modern business cycle theories, shifts in the investment demand curve are the most important source of business cycle fluctuations. Keynesian economists believe that these swings arise from animal spirits. Real business cycles economists believe that they arise from productivity shocks.

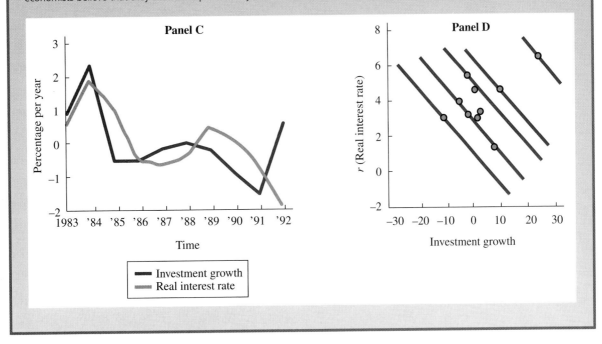

Keynes. Both of these theories have the same implications for the movements of investment and the interest rate.[3]

To illustrate the classical view of business cycles, suppose that a new invention makes investment more productive. A good example would be the invention of the personal computer in the 1970s, which spurred a rash of new developments in the consumer electronics industry. Figure 6.8 shows that a productivity increase causes the firm to demand more investment for any given rate of interest.

Panel A illustrates the production function. Panel B shows the investment demand curve and the saving supply curve. The interest rate begins at r_1; this is an equilibrium interest rate for which savings equals investment. After the increase in productivity, the firm demands more investment for every possible interest rate. On the graph in panel A, the productivity improvement causes the production function to shift up from production

---

3.   Although the animal spirits theory and the real business cycle theory have similar implications for investment and savings, they have very different implications for the role of economic policy. Because of this policy difference, it is important to find ways of separating them. Much current research effort is being directed to this question.

FIGURE 6.8
Productivity and the Investment Demand Curve
An increase in productivity will shift the investment demand curve to the right.

Panel A shows that an increase in productivity shifts up the production function. Before the technology improvement, the interest rate is r_1. The firm uses production function $_1$ and invests $I_1(r_1)$. After the productivity improvement, if the interest rate stayed at r_1 the firm would use production function $_2$ and invest $I_2(r_1)$.

Panel B shows that the interest rate does not stay at r_1 because it is no longer an equilibrium. The effect of the productivity improvement is to shift investment demand from curve 1 to curve 2. In equilibrium, the increase in productivity will raise the interest rate to r_2.

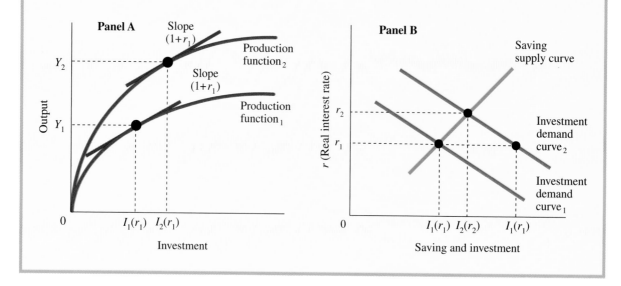

function 1 to production function 2. On the graph in panel B it causes the investment demand curve to shift to the right. If the interest rate were to remain at r_1, panel B shows, investment would go up to I_2 (r_1); but at this interest rate saving is no longer equal to investment. Instead, the shift of the demand curve causes the equilibrium interest rate to increase to r_2, and this increase causes households to save more. The new equilibrium is at $\{r_2, I_2(r_2)\}$, for which investment is higher than before the productivity increase and the interest rate has also gone up.

Animal Spirits and the Investment Demand Curve

Because investment and production do not take place at the same time, investors may make mistakes. Keynes believed that it is not possible to make rational calculations about the probability of the future success of an investment, and he thought that irrational swings of optimism and pessimism might be more important driving forces in the stock market than fundamentals. From the point of view of an investor, a new technology such as the personal computer is unproven, and investments that are made on the basis of mis-

BOX 6.2
Saving and the Baby Boom
How can we use the theory of saving and investment to understand the effect of the Baby Boom on the economy?

Panel A shows that between 1939 and 1970 there was a big shift in the savings supply curve as the Baby Boom generation grew up, got jobs, and started to save. The effect of the increased saving was to lower the interest rate and stimulate investment.

Panel B shows what will happen as the Baby Boom generation retires. The saving supply curve will shift back to the left. The effect of this shift is likely to be felt in lower investment and a higher rate of interest.

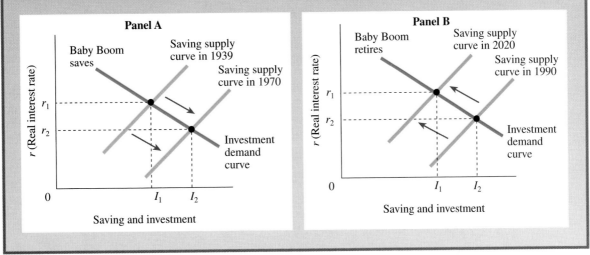

taken beliefs about future productivity have the same effect on the capital market as investments that later turn out to be profitable. History is littered with examples of investments that failed.

The swings in animal spirits that Keynes talked about were not rational in the sense that we use that term in economics today. (We cover rational expectations in Chapter 16.) Recently, researchers have studied the idea that swings in optimism and pessimism may be fully rational. Rational animal spirits occur when the beliefs of investors are self-fulfilling because they cause changes in prices that justify the original belief. Self-fulfilling beliefs are one of the exciting new research topics that economists are researching today.

The Baby Boom, Pensions, and Savings

An important reason to save is to provide income for retirement. In the period immediately following World War II, the United States experienced an increase in the birth rate because many couples had deferred marriage and the birth of children until the end of the war. The postwar spurt of births caused a bulge in the population called the Baby Boom. As the Baby Boom generation ages, it causes changes in the demand and supply of all kinds of commodities, from schools and universities to fast food, music, and clothes. One of the most important effects of Baby Boom demographics, illustrated in diagrams in Box 6.2, is on saving and investment.

TABLE 6.2
Pensions as a Percentage of Wages in Selected Countries

	1939	1980
Canada	17	34
Germany	19	49
Italy	15	69
United Kingdom	13	31
United States	21	44

Source: Max Alier, *Essays on pension reform,* Ph.D. thesis, UCLA, 1997.

Along with the Baby Boom came a windfall for the postwar economy as a flood of productive, tax-paying workers entered the labor market. Governments throughout the world took advantage of the increased tax revenues to institute new entitlement programs. One of the most important of these new spending programs was the universal establishment of government-funded pensions.

Table 6.2 shows the ratio of the average pension to the average wage for 1939 and 1980. We see from this table that in the United States, pensions increased from 21% of the average wage in 1939 to 44% of the average wage in 1980. Pensions in 1980 were more than twice as generous as in 1939. In Italy they were more than four times as generous. Generous pensions would not be a problem if governments had wisely saved the taxes of the young and invested in the stock market. Instead the pension contributions of the young were used to pay the pensions of the current old. This was politically very popular in the

WEBWATCH 6.1   **Read About Pension Reform in *The Economist***

An excellent source of articles on current issues in macroeconomics is *The Economist* magazine. You can subscribe to the economist print edition or you can find an electronic version at http://www.economist.com.

At the time of writing, selected articles from *The Economist* were available at http://www.enews.com/magazines/economist/archive.

I used this resource to read about pension reform in the United Kingdom by downloading "The Great Pension Debate," an article published in *The Economist* July 19th, 1997 by downloading the article from an archive at http://www.enews.com/magazines/economist/archive/07/970719-002.html.

You can guarantee access to *The Economist* by subscribing to their electronic edition or you can find the hard print version in your college library.

TABLE 6.3
Government Debt and Pension Liabilities as Percent of GDP in 1990

	Net Conventional Debt	Net Pension Liabilities
Canada	52	121
Germany	22	157
Italy	100	259
United Kingdom	27	156
United States	35	90

Source: Max Alier, *Essays on pension reform,* Ph.D. thesis, UCLA, 1997.

postwar period because it seemed as if everyone was a winner. Now the Baby Boom generation is aging and there are not enough young people to pay the pensions that they think they are owed.

The aging Baby Boom problem is particularly serious in countries with generous pension systems. Pension commitments to the old represent an implicit source of government debt, and in most countries this debt is greater than conventional government liabilities. Table 6.3 shows conventional government debt together with this implicit pension debt for five Organization for Economic Co-operation and Development (OECD) countries.

In the United States conventional debt was 35% of GDP in 1990, but implicit pension debt was three times that size. Although the U.S. situation is bad, it is by no means the worst case; in Italy, for example, net pension liabilities are 259% of GDP. Many governments are beginning to recognize the big problem and are taking steps to rectify it. In Chile, for example, after a pension reform in 1981 the Chilean government invests the savings of its young workers in the capital market. This way of paying pensions is called **fully-funded**. When today's Chilean workers retire, the government will be able to pay their pensions from the interest income it makes on the money that it has invested for them. The United States and the United Kingdom are looking into the possibility of enacting similar reforms.

❻ SAVING AND INVESTMENT IN AN OPEN ECONOMY

We can now modify the theory of saving and investment to explain borrowing and lending in the world capital market for the case of an open economy. The difference between the open economy and the closed economy models is that in the open economy domestic saving does not equal domestic investment, and the deficit is made up by net borrowing from abroad.

FIGURE 6.9
Saving and Investment in an Open Economy

Panel A shows saving and investment in the domestic economy. At interest rate r_1, total domestic investment (private plus government) is greater than total domestic saving. The difference between domestic investment and domestic saving is paid for by borrowing the amount NB_1 (net borrowing) in the world capital market. If the world interest were to increase to r_2, total domestic saving would be greater than total domestic investment. In this case net borrowing would be negative as funds flowed *from* the United States to the world capital market.

Panel B plots the U.S. demand for capital and the world supply of capital on the horizontal axis and the world interest rate on the vertical axis. In equilibrium, U.S. investment exceeds U.S. saving. The difference is made up by net borrowing from abroad, NB_E.

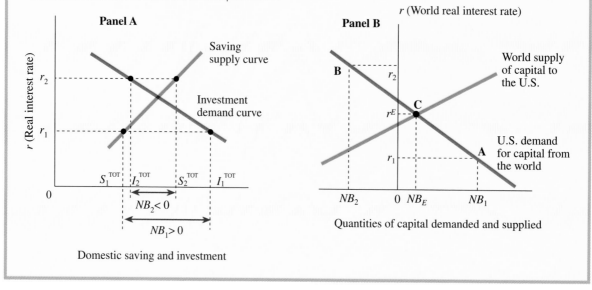

Equilibrium in the World Capital Market

Figure 6.9 illustrates how equilibrium in the world capital market is determined. Panel A reproduces the domestic savings and investment diagram from Figure 6.7. We use this diagram now to show how much money the domestic economy will borrow from abroad for different values of the world rate of interest. For example, suppose that the United States can borrow and lend to the rest of the world at a rate of interest equal to r_1. Panel A shows that when the interest rate is equal to r_1, the United States will demand investment of I_1^{TOT} and U.S. savers will supply savings of S_1^{TOT}. The superscript "TOT" reminds us that we are dealing with *total* investment and *total* savings, that is, with private plus government investment and savings. Because I_1^{TOT} is greater than S_1^{TOT}, at this rate of interest the United States will be a net borrower from the rest of the world. The amount borrowed is denoted NB_1. Suppose instead that the world interest rate is r_2. Panel A shows that for this interest rate U.S. investors will demand I_2^{TOT} and U.S. savers will supply S_2^{TOT} to the world capital market. Because I_2^{TOT} is less than S_2^{TOT}, panel A shows that for this interest rate the United States will be a net lender to the rest of the world. This is represented by the fact that net borrowing, NB_2, is less than zero.

Panel B plots a downward-sloping line for the U.S. demand for capital from the world. This is the difference between domestic investment and domestic saving for different values of the world interest rate. For example, when the interest rate is r_1, domestic investment is greater than domestic saving. This information is plotted on graph B as point **A**. The vertical axis of the graph represents the interest rate in the world capital market. The horizontal axis measures the quantity of capital demanded and supplied on the world market. When the interest rate is equal to r_1, the domestic demand for capital (the difference between domestic investment and domestic saving) is equal to NB_1. When the interest rate is r_2, the domestic demand for capital is equal to r_2, and the United States will be a net saver because domestic investment, I_2^{TOT}, is less than domestic saving, S_2^{TOT}.

What determines the world rate of interest? We can find an investment and a savings curve for every country in the world. If we put together all of the other country's savings and investment curves, we can find out how much the rest of the world is prepared to lend to the United States for different values of the world interest rate. The resulting curve, called the **world supply of capital**, slopes up because when the interest rate is higher, other countries are more willing to lend to us. Equilibrium in the world capital market occurs at the point at which the world supply of capital equals the domestic demand for capital. On panel B this occurs at point **C** when the world interest rate is equal to r^E and U.S. demand for capital is equal to NB^E. We have drawn this graph so that at r^E, the domestic demand for capital, is positive, reflecting the fact that the United States is a net borrower from the rest of the world.

World Saving and the Government Budget Deficit

In Chapter 2 we showed that the U.S. trade deficit increased in the 1980s at the same time that the U.S. government began to run large budget deficits. Figure 6.10 shows how we can use the saving and investment diagram to explain these facts.

Panel A in Figure 6.10 shows that, in the 1980s, the U.S. budget deficit increased from less than 1% of GDP in 1979 to over 4% of GDP in 1986. At the same time the trade surplus became negative and the real interest rate went up. The theory of saving and investment has a simple explanation for these facts. The Reagan administration increased government expenditures on defense and at the same time cut taxes, causing a big increase in the budget deficit. The effect was to increase the U.S. demand for capital in the world capital markets and to drive up the interest rate throughout the world. Because the funds that were borrowed by the government were used to buy goods and services, the increase in net U.S. borrowing from abroad led to a decrease in net exports and a negative trade surplus.

CONCLUSION

We can use the tools of demand and supply to study the allocation of commodities across time. Investment is a way of transferring goods from the present to the future and is determined by firms to maximize profit. Saving is a way of deferring consumption and is determined by households to maximize utility. The interest rate is the relative price of current

FIGURE 6.10
The Budget Deficit, Trade Surplus, and Interest Rate

Panel A shows that the trade deficit and the budget deficit increased simultaneously in the 1980s.

Panel B explains why this happened, using the theory of saving and investment. The increase in the budget deficit shifted the U.S. demand for capital from curve 1 to curve 2. This occurred because the U.S. government increased its demand for capital. The shift in the demand for capital caused the interest rate to increase from r_A to r_B, and it sucked in funds from the world capital market, increasing net borrowing from NB_A to NB_B. The increased borrowing from abroad resulted in a flow of goods into the country and net exports went down, resulting in a trade deficit (a negative trade surplus).

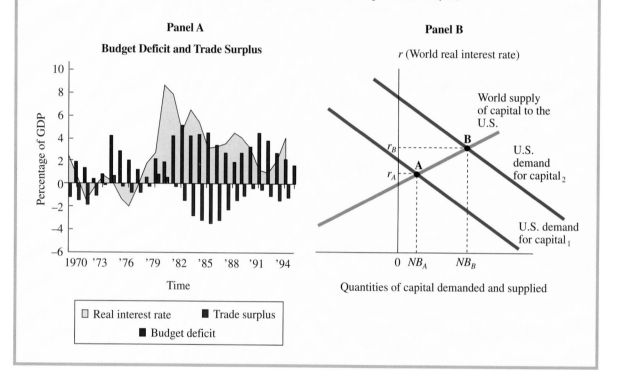

and future commodities and is determined in the capital market at the point at which the quantity of investment demanded equals the quantity of savings supplied.

Over the business cycle, investment is very volatile and consumption is relatively smooth. New classical economists of the real business cycle school believe that investment fluctuates in response to changes in productivity caused by new inventions. Keynesian economists believe that many of the changes in investment are due to changes in the beliefs of investors, called animal spirits. Both groups believe that the model of the demand and supply of capital can be used to explain the determination of the rate of interest.

The apparatus of the demand and supply of capital helps us to understand the effect of the Baby Boom on the interest rate and investment. The aging of Baby Boomers can be expected to raise the interest rate and cause a reduction in investment. We can also use it to study the effect of U.S. government borrowing on the capital market and the interaction between the budget deficit and the trade deficit.

KEY TERMS

Animal spirits
Consumption smoothing
Demand for investment
Fully-funded pensions
Fundamentals
Intertemporal budget constraint
Intertemporal production possibilities set
Intertemporal utility theory

Investment demand curve
Market rate
Nominal rate of interest
Present value
Real rate of interest
Saving supply curve
Supply of savings
World supply of capital

PROBLEMS FOR REVIEW

1. Which series is more volatile, investment, consumption, or GDP? What statistic is used to measure volatility?

2. How do classical and Keynesian economists differ in their explanations of the fluctuations in investment that we see over the business cycle? Do Keynesians and classical economists also disagree about the way that changes in investment are translated into changes in the interest rate?

3. Was investment positively or negatively correlated with investment during the 1970s? How did the correlation change during the 1980s? How can you use this observed correlation to infer the causes of interest rate fluctuations over these two different periods?

4. Explain what classical economists mean by a *productivity shock*. How should a productivity shock affect investment, the rate of interest, and savings? Why should it have each of these effects?

5. How could you tell whether an increase in investment is due to fundamentals or to animal spirits? Can you think of a way of distinguishing between these two explanations?

6. Suppose that the nominal interest rate remains constant, but firms expect that there will be increased inflation in the future. How will this expectation of future inflation affect investment? Explain your reasoning.

7. Suppose that the interest rate is 5% per year. Calculate the "present" value in 1990 of the following:

   a.   A $1,000 inheritance to be received in 1991.

   b.   A $1,000 inheritance to be received in 1992.

   c.   A lottery win that pays $1,000 each year in 1991, 1992, and 1993.

   d.   A lottery win that pays $1,000 every year forever.

8. Suppose that households have the preferences described in the appendix but have 1 unit in the present and 1 unit in the future instead of 2 units in the present. Find an expression for the savings supply curve in this case. Do households save more in this case when the interest goes up? Why is your answer different from the case solved in the appendix?

9. Find an expression for the investment function when technology is given by the function

$$Y = I$$

Can savings have an effect on the interest rate if this is the technology? If not, why not?

10. Read the article "The Great Pension Debate" in *The Economist*, July 19, 1997.

   a. Explain the difference between a fully-funded and a pay-as-you go social security system.

   b. What is the main task of the recent government review of pensions in the United Kingdom?

   c. What were the main criticisms, leveled by Labour, of the pension reforms that had been proposed by the Tories before the recent election in the United Kingdom?

11. Write a brief essay (no more than two pages) outlining the similarities and differences between the classical theory of aggregate supply and the classical theory of saving and investment. Which is more controversial and why?

APPENDIX: THE MATHEMATICS OF SAVINGS AND INVESTMENT

In this appendix we study a simple example that illustrates the mathematics of intertemporal utility maximization. Suppose that a family's utility can be represented by the function

6.4 $$U = C_1 \times C_2$$

Suppose also that the family earns 2 units of commodities in the present and nothing in the future. The family's budget constraint is

6.5 $$C_1 + \frac{C_2}{(1 + r)} = 2$$

The family wants to maximize its utility, subject to the budget constraint, by choosing C_1 and C_2. We can substitute from the budget constraint for C_1 to turn this into a maximization over one variable, C_2

6.6 $$\max_{C_2} \left(2 - \frac{C_2}{(1 + r)} \right) \times C_2$$

To solve this problem, we take the derivative of utility with respect to C_2 and set it equal to zero

6.7
$$\frac{\partial U}{\partial C_2} = \left(2 - \frac{C_2}{(1 + r)}\right) - \frac{C_2}{(1 + r)} = 0$$

which leads to the solution

6.8
$$\frac{C_2^*}{(1 + r)} = 1$$

C_2^* is the future consumption that maximizes utility and is divided by $(1 + r)$ because future consumption must be valued in terms of present consumption. This solution says that the family will choose to consume half of its wealth in the future. Using the budget constraint, we can also show that

6.9
$$C_1^* = 1$$

which says the family will consume the other half of its wealth in the present. We can also find out how much the family saves by subtracting consumption from income, which equals 2:

6.10
$$S^* = 1$$

This is the family's supply curve of saving. For these preferences we say that savings are *inelastic* with respect to the interest rate because a higher rate of interest has no effect on saving.

Now suppose that firms use the technology

6.11
$$Y = 2I^{\frac{1}{2}}$$

Profits are given by

6.12
$$\pi = Y - (1 + r)I$$

Firms choose I to maximize profit. We can find the solution to their problem by substituting from the technology, Equation 6.11, into Equation 6.12 that defines the isoprofit line

6.13
$$\max_{I} \pi = 2I^{\frac{1}{2}} - (1 + r)I$$

To solve this we must differentiate with respect to I and set the derivative equal to zero. This leads to the expression

6.14
$$\frac{1}{I^{*\frac{1}{2}}} = (1 + r)$$

which we can invert to give the investment demand function

6.15
$$I* = \frac{1}{(1 + r)^{\frac{1}{2}}}$$

Putting together Equations 6.15 and 6.10 leads to an expression that can be solved for the equilibrium interest rate in a closed economy:

6.16 $\dfrac{1}{(1 + r^E)^{\frac{1}{2}}} = 1$ *or* $(1 + r^E) = 1$ *or* $r^E = 0$

Plugging this solution back into the investment demand curve, Equation 6.15, tells us that this is indeed an equilibrium, because when $r = 0$, firms demand one unit, which is exactly the same as the supply of savings from Equation 6.10.

PART 3

The Modern Approach to Aggregate Demand and Supply

Part 3 contains five chapters that go beyond the classical model to develop a more modern understanding of the theory of aggregate demand and supply. We begin, in Chapter 7, with two ways of understanding unemployment, and we develop the Keynesian theory of aggregate supply.

In Chapters 8, 9, and 10 we study a modern approach to the theory of aggregate demand. This approach is based on ideas from Keynes's book *The General Theory of Employment Interest and Money*. Chapter 11, the last chapter in Part 3, explains how the idea of demand management must be modified in an open economy.

CHAPTER 7

Unemployment

❶ INTRODUCTION

This chapter is about unemployment and the factors that cause it to vary over the business cycle. Economists first began a systematic study of unemployment during the Great Depression, when Keynes challenged the orthodox view that the economic system tends quickly to return to full employment equilibrium. Before the Great Depression, the most pressing macroeconomic problem was how to maintain a stable currency. Keynes himself wrote extensively on this subject, in part stimulated by the deep social problems that were caused by hyperinflation in Germany, Austria, Poland, and Hungary at the end of World War I. But in the late 1920s, unemployment in England quickly increased to unprecedented levels, and in 1929 the stock market crashed in the United States, heralding the transmission of the Great Depression from Europe to North America. For the next decade the Western world experienced an economic catastrophe that caused economic theorists to completely rethink the classical model.

What is unemployment? In the simple classical model, studied in Chapter 4, there is no room for any such concept. Several modern theories offer explanations for unemployment. We will study one model that incorporates elements from each of these theories into a framework similar to the classical theory of the labor market, studied in Chapter 4.

Why does unemployment vary systematically over the business cycle? The Keynesian view of the Great Depression argues that government bears much of the responsibility for the extent and duration of the Depression. To understand why this is so, we must first study the Keynesian connection between unemployment and fluctuations in the price level. We will also learn some facts about unemployment, drawn from different countries and different historical episodes, that have a direct bearing on the theory we have developed and the policies that have been put forward as ways of dealing with structural problems in the labor market.

❷ UNEMPLOYMENT

There are two dimensions to the problem of explaining unemployment. First, the problem of explaining why anyone is unemployed at all. In simple accounts of the classical model, the quantity of labor demanded is always equal to the quantity of labor supplied. This seems so obviously false that the classical theory may appear to have no merit. But, as we will see shortly, classical economics can easily be adapted to allow for unemployment. The more difficult question is why unemployment moves in a systematic way with other business cycle variables and, in particular, why unemployment and the price level moved sharply in opposite directions over the period from 1929 through 1940. We will return to this issue later and construct a theory that can account for these facts, a theory that forms the basis for much of modern understanding of the problems of business cycle movements as they relate to government policy.

Frictional Unemployment

Explaining why there is *any* unemployment does not require particularly deep insight. Even the economists before Keynes recognized that the idea that demand equals supply in the labor market does not necessarily imply that there is no unemployment, since unemployment might result simply from labor turnover. Unemployment of this kind is called **frictional unemployment**.

Figure 7.1 presents a dynamic view of unemployment as a process whereby there are continual flows in and out of the labor market. Because it takes time to find a job, there is always a pool of unemployed people. To understand how positive unemployment can be consistent with the equality of the quantities of labor demanded and supplied, it is important to recognize that the demand and supply curves of labor are flows, like the water flowing into and out of a tank. But unemployment is a stock, like the water sitting in a bathtub. If we turn up the faucet but leave the plug out of the bath, the level of water in the bath will increase until the extra pressure causes the outflow to once more equal the inflow. The model we develop next says something similar about the labor market.

❸ APPROACHES TO EXPLAINING UNEMPLOYMENT

Efficiency Wages

Ever since Keynes wrote his *General Theory*, economists have been trying to interpret what he said. Keynes was above all a practical man, and the policies he advocated to alleviate the Great Depression worked. But the microeconomics of his theory were never

FIGURE 7.1
**Flows Through
the Labor Market**
The quantity of labor demanded
can equal the quantity of labor
supplied and yet there can still be
unemployment.

The quantities of labor demanded
and supplied are flows, like water
flowing into a tank. Unemployment is a stock, like the water in
a bathtub.

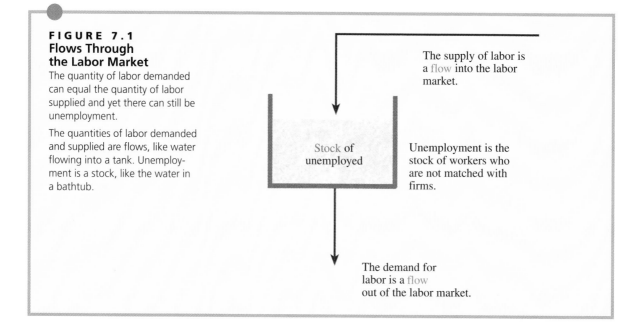

The supply of labor is
a flow into the labor
market.

Stock of
unemployed

Unemployment is the
stock of workers who
are not matched with
firms.

The demand for
labor is a flow
out of the labor market.

spelled out, and the attempt to make sense of Keynesian economics in terms of the theory of rational behavior has occupied a vast amount of the time of his followers. One of the leading modern theories of Keynesian unemployment is the theory of **efficiency wages**, which explains unemployment as a situation in which the real wage is too high and hence the quantity of labor supplied typically exceeds the quantity demanded. Economists who developed this theory believe that the stock of unemployed contains more people than can be explained merely by frictional unemployment arising from the transition between jobs. They argue that firms pay more than they need to to ensure that workers do not shirk.

Efficiency wage theory argues that there are two components to the productivity of a worker. First is the time that he or she spends on the job; this can easily be measured and firms and workers can contract over wages. A second component of the productivity of a worker is how much effort he or she puts into the task. It is a fact of life that some workers are more conscientious than others, and a firm that has a happy, conscientious workforce will likely also make more profits. According to the theory of efficiency wages, it is often to the advantage of the firm to offer to pay more than the real wage at which demand equals supply, because by paying a high wage the firm can afford to choose only the better workers. In turn, the workers work harder because they stand to lose their jobs and enter the pool of involuntary unemployed if the firm finds that they have been shirking.

Nominal Rigidities and Menu Costs

In the efficiency wage theory, the real wage is too high. An important component of the Keynesian theory of unemployment, on the other hand, rests on the assumption that the nominal wage is too high because nominal wages and/or nominal prices are slow to adjust to restore equilibrium. When nominal wages or prices are slow to adjust, we say that the economy experiences a **nominal rigidity**. Recent research in macroeconomics has been directed at explaining why nominal rigidities seem to be prevalent in many market economies. The question is a difficult one, since there would seem to be large gains to be had by individual traders from setting prices correctly.

An imaginative answer to the problem of nominal rigidities has been given by George Akerlof and Janet Yellen of the University of California at Berkeley and by Greg Mankiw of Harvard University. They have argued that the costs of setting the wrong price may be very small to the individual firm, but the effect is cumulative to society as a whole. Mankiw calls this idea **menu costs**, arguing that the small cost of rewriting price lists may outweigh the benefit to the individual firm of revising prices regularly to reflect market conditions. When the actions of many different firms are added up, the wrong employment decision by one firm may cause a second firm to make additional mistakes in its allocation of resources. The fact that a decision by one firm may adversely affect the decisions of another is an example of an **externality**.[1] Such externalities may pile up and, even though the menu cost to an individual is small, have a large impact on society.

Nominal Rigidities and Wage Contracts

One approach that has been suggested to explain nominal rigidities is that labor is typically traded by contract where the nominal wage is set in advance for a period of two to three years. Because new wage contracts are not typically revised at every firm at the same time, in any one year there will be a rigidity built into the average money wage that follows from the fact that existing contracts cannot immediately be revised. John Taylor of Stanford University has demonstrated that a model with overlapping contracts, where some percentage of the wage agreements are renegotiated each period, can explain why changes in the nominal money supply may have persistent effects on output.

Search Theory

The approach we take to unemployment in this book is closest to a theory called **search theory**, which studies the process by which workers and firms are matched with each other, a process that is costly and time-consuming. Although much of the work in search theory is highly abstract, some of it can easily be incorporated into a model similar to the one we have studied so far in this book. The advantage of adding a search model to the classical model of the labor market is that we can see how unemployment may result as a natural consequence of the frictions inherent in the trade process.

❹ REASONS FOR UNEMPLOYMENT

Although our theory of unemployment is mainly drawn from search theory, we also use a number of other approaches that have been developed by Keynesian economists in the

---

1.   An externality occurs when an action by one actor affects the profits or the utility of another.

sixty or so years since the publication of *The General Theory*. At the root of our theory of unemployment is an interpretation of Keynes' writings that was first laid out by an American-born economist, Don Patinkin, who spent much of his working life at Hebrew University in Jerusalem.[2]

To understand search theory, consider the following analogy drawn from my experience as a parent. Every Easter, my wife and I run an Easter egg hunt for the children on our street. Just in case you've never taken part in an Easter egg hunt, it involves hiding a large number of colored eggs (these days the eggs are usually plastic and contain small toys made in China), in various places in a garden where small children can't get into too much trouble. Then you take a group of children and watch while they find as many eggs as they can in as short a time as possible. The Easter egg hunt is a little like the U. S. labor market, with the eggs as workers and the children as firms.

Typically, we hide a number of eggs in very obvious places so that the youngest children will have a chance of finding something. We also hide eggs in very obscure places and try to camouflage them in flowers, bushes, and trees to make them difficult to find. Often, we even forget ourselves where some of them are. Given that the children have a limited time to find the eggs, there are usually a number of eggs that remain unfound. These eggs are our unemployed workers.

A second thing you will quickly realize if you think about organizing an Easter egg hunt is that the more children you invite, the more eggs you should hide. If, by chance, a number of uninvited children turn up at the last moment (small brothers and sisters, friends and other hangers-on, for example) you will notice a number of things about the success of the event. First, more eggs will get found (there will be less unemployment), and second, each child will have to look harder and longer to find any given compliment of eggs. Since small children quickly get frustrated when the eggs are hard to find, this will probably result in each child finding fewer eggs.

A Model of Search

A model of the labor market based on a simple theory of search has a lot in common with an Easter egg hunt. To keep ideas as simple as possible, suppose that firms must find new workers every period; and to keep ideas concrete, suppose that a period is equal to one week. On the demand side of the labor market assume a large number of firms, each of which faces a production function like the one graphed in Figure 7.2. We can derive a relationship between the real wage and the demand for workers by firms that is very similar to the demand curve in a classical model, the difference being that in the search model each firm must set up an employment department with a search cost of C units.

In our model we suppose that the cost of hiring to any individual firm is independent of its scale, so that the activities of an individual firm will not typically have a big impact on the labor market as a whole. Search cost C includes the costs of setting up an employment department, advertising for workers, and sending recruiters round to colleges and universities to ensure that the firm hires the best workers available. These recruiting costs

---

2.   Patinkin's book, *Money Interest and Prices,* was the first to systematically integrate Keynes' *General Theory* with the classical theory of markets.

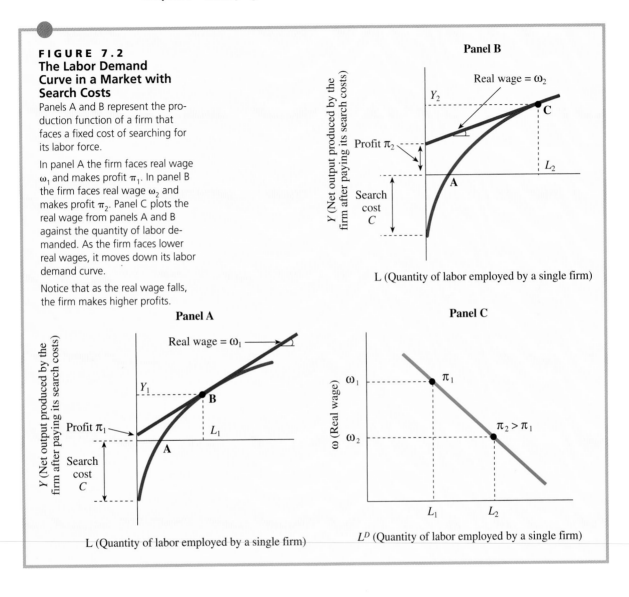

FIGURE 7.2
The Labor Demand Curve in a Market with Search Costs

Panels A and B represent the production function of a firm that faces a fixed cost of searching for its labor force.

In panel A the firm faces real wage ω_1 and makes profit π_1. In panel B the firm faces real wage ω_2 and makes profit π_2. Panel C plots the real wage from panels A and B against the quantity of labor demanded. As the firm faces lower real wages, it moves down its labor demand curve.

Notice that as the real wage falls, the firm makes higher profits.

Panel B

Real wage = ω_2

Y_2

C

Profit π_2

A

L_2

Search cost C

Y (Net output produced by the firm after paying its search costs)

L (Quantity of labor employed by a single firm)

Panel A

Real wage = ω_1

Y_1

B

Profit π_1

L_1

A

Search cost C

Y (Net output produced by the firm after paying its search costs)

L (Quantity of labor employed by a single firm)

Panel C

ω_1

π_1

ω_2

$\pi_2 > \pi_1$

ω (Real wage)

L_1 L_2

L^D (Quantity of labor employed by a single firm)

are bigger in a boom, when it is harder to find workers, than in a recession, when the typical firm can afford to be very choosy about whom to employ.

The employment decisions made by a firm in an economy with search costs will be similar to those of a classical firm. The manager must choose how many workers to hire in order to maximize profit:

7.1

$$\pi \quad = \quad Y \quad - \quad \omega L \quad - \quad C$$

| Profits of the firm | Commodities supplied | Cost of labor demanded | Search cost |

Unlike the classical model, the search model firm must make enough profit to cover its search cost in order to stay in business. Figure 7.2 illustrates this problem in two different situations.

In panel A the firm faces a relatively high real wage, ω_1; in panel B it faces a low real wage, ω_2. In both cases the blue curve represents the production function, after accounting for the fact that the firm must set up a recruiting office (this is the search cost) that costs C units of real resources, before it can produce output. The point **A** in panels A and B represents the minimum amount of labor that must be employed by the firm before it has any output at all. If it hires less labor than **A**, it will not produce enough output to cover the cost of its recruiting efforts.

In Chapter 4 we showed that the firm will maximize profits at the point where an isoprofit line is tangent to the production function. This occurs on panel A at the point **B**, and in panel B at point **C**. Recall that the slope of an isoprofit line is equal to the real wage. This explains why the slope of the isoprofit line is flatter in panel B than in panel A: Panel B depicts an economy with a lower real wage. There is a second important feature that you should take note of in Figure 7.2: the lower the real wage, the higher the profit. In the diagram the profit of the firm is represented by the intercept of the isoprofit line with the vertical axis. Notice that this intercept increases as the real wage falls. In panel A, when the real wage is equal to ω_1, profit is equal to π_1. In panel B, when the real wage is lower at ω_2, profit is higher at π_2.

Panel C plots the real wage against the quantity of labor employed by the firm. When the real wage is high, ω_1, the firm employs a relatively small quantity of labor, L_1; when the real wage is low, ω_2, it employs a relatively high amount of labor, L_2. The downward locus of points that passes through $\{\omega_1, L_1\}$ and $\{\omega_2, L_2\}$ is the labor demand curve and, as shown in Chapter 4 (and again demonstrated here), *the labor demand curve slopes down*. A second important feature of this figure that we once more need to stress is that, assuming that the search cost C is fixed, the profit of the firm increases as one moves down the labor demand curve from ω_1 to ω_2.

The Aggregate Labor Market and the Natural Rate of Unemployment

Up until now we have assumed that the cost of hiring workers is equal to a fixed number, C. In reality, the cost of hiring workers depends on the number of other firms that are also looking for workers. This is just like the Easter egg hunt, where each child has to look a little harder when little Johnny brings along his little brother and three friends, all uninvited. To formalize the idea that costs depend on market conditions, let's use the symbol $\underline{L}$ to mean the number of workers employed (on average) by all of the other firms in the economy, and the symbol L to mean the labor employed by one particular firm. The important element in the search model then is that C depends on $\underline{L}$ and that this cost increases as unemployment decreases. In terms of the Easter egg hunt, the last few eggs are very hard to find. The fact that search costs increase as employment increases means that, in the search model, firms cannot profit in equilibrium by hiring unemployed workers at a lower wage. There is an equilibrium rate of unemployment, called the **natural rate of unemployment,** illustrated on Figure 7.3.

In panel A of Figure 7.3, the downward-sloping curve is the labor demand curve for the economy as a whole. The vertical red line is the supply of labor; to keep things simple we assume that the labor supply does not depend on the real wage, so we may draw the labor supply curve as a vertical line. In the graph two values of the real wage are ω^* and ω^E.

FIGURE 7.3
Profit, the Real Wage, and the Natural Rate of Unemployment
This figure illustrates how the natural rate of unemployment is determined.

Panel A illustrates the demand and supply of labor. In the classical model there are no search costs and employment is at L^E, where the quantity of labor demanded equals the quantity supplied. In the economy with search costs employment is at L^*, where no firm can profit by offering to buy labor at a lower wage. The real wage is at ω^*, above the classical real wage, ω^E, and U^* people are unemployed. This is called the *natural rate of unemployment*.

Panel B illustrates why ω^* does not fall to clear the labor market. If firms hire more workers they increase the costs of other firms. This increase in costs lowers profits. When $\omega = \omega^*$, no firm can make extra profit by offering a lower real wage.

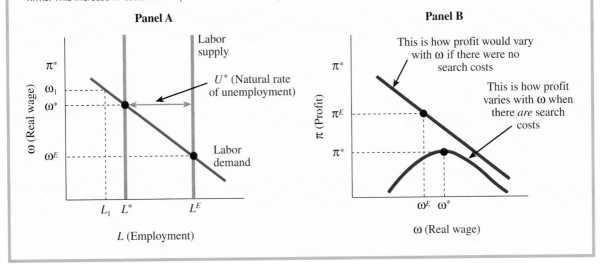

The wage ω^E is the one that would prevail in a classical model, in which there are no search costs. The wage ω^* is the one that prevails in the economy where search is costly.

Notice that, because ω^* is above ω^E, unemployment in the search economy is equal to U^*. The level of unemployment that occurs when $\omega = \omega^*$ is the natural rate of unemployment.

What's "Natural" About the Natural Rate

Suppose for a moment that search costs, C, were fixed and that they did not depend on how many people were searching. In this case if $\omega = \omega^*$ there would be unemployed people prepared to work for less than ω^*. It follows that one of the firms in the economy could employ more people at a lower wage and, because profit increases as we move down the labor demand curve, the firm would benefit from increasing employment. In the classical economy there is a powerful incentive for firms to hire unemployed workers and pay them lower wages. This process of hiring unemployed workers and paying them lower wages would continue, in the classical economy, until all of the unemployed had jobs, that is, until $\omega = \omega^E$ and the quantity of labor demanded equaled the quantity supplied.

Let's see now how this argument falls apart in the economy where search costs change with the number of searchers. Let's start at a real wage, ω_1, that is higher than ω^*. At this real wage unemployment is higher than the natural rate U^* and, just as in the classical economy, there is an incentive for firms to employ more workers and to offer them a lower real wage. The economy is a lot like the classical economy because hiring extra workers doesn't make much difference to the search costs of other firms—there are still plenty of workers to go around. This is a bit like an Easter egg hunt when there are a lot of eggs but not many children.

The economy is not like a classical economy when unemployment falls because it becomes more difficult for firms to hire workers. The cost C that was assumed fixed in the classical model begins to go up as aggregate employment, $\underline{L}$, increases. This additional cost works in the opposite direction of the forces that cause profit to increase as the real wage falls. Eventually, the number of unemployed workers becomes so small that the increased costs of searching for workers outweighs the benefit to the firm of lower wages. When this point is reached, the real wage is equal to ω^*, unemployment equals U^*, and L^* workers are employed. We call these terms the *natural real wage*, the *natural rate of unemployment*, and the *natural level of employment*.

Panel B of Figure 7.3 illustrates how profit depends on the real wage in the case of a classical model and of a search model. The downward sloping purple line shows that profit falls with the real wage when there are no search costs. The purple curve that achieves a maximum at ω^* shows how profits depend on the real wage when the costs of the firm increase with aggregate employment. Why does this curve slope up for low levels of the real wage but slope down for high levels? The answer to this question is the key to understanding why there is a "natural" rate of unemployment.

When the real wage is very high, search costs are not very important; as the wage falls, profits increase because firms benefit from lower labor costs. But as aggregate employment increases, the additional search of each firm makes it harder to find new workers, and the cost C to each individual firm increases. Eventually, as the economy gets close to full employment, the congestion costs of more searchers dominates the private benefits to the firm of paying lower wages. At this point, profit begins to decline as the real wage falls further. The point at which no firm would profit if the wage were to rise or fall is the real wage ω^*, the natural real wage, and when the level of unemployment at ω^* is U^*, the natural rate of unemployment.

⑤ UNEMPLOYMENT AND THE BUSINESS CYCLE

In this section we move beyond the natural rate and study the more important issue of why unemployment varies systematically over the business cycle. In particular, it is important to understand what happened during the Great Depression, when unemployment increased to 25% of the labor force and, at the same time, the nominal price level fell. The Keynesian theory of unemployment[3] addresses this issue by arguing that there are nominal rigidities and that the money wage and/or the money price level are slow to adjust to their equilibrium levels. According to this theory, the natural rate of unemployment can be viewed as a description of the long-run equilibrium of the economy. When there is a

3. Much of the theory of unemployment was constructed by the Keynesian economists who came after Keynes. Whatever Keynes intended to say, the interpretations of Keynes' ideas by his followers have taken on a life of their own, and it is these interpretations that form the basis for modern theories of unemployment. The distinction between Keynes and Keynesians was first made by Axel Leijonhufvud, a Swedish economist who spent much of his career at UCLA and is now at the University of Trento in Italy.

change in an exogenous variable, such as the money supply, the adjustment from one equilibrium to another does not take place instantly, and, in the period of adjustment from one equilibrium to another, unemployment may be either above or below its natural rate.

Unemployment and Changes in the Price Level

The natural rate describes a situation where the nominal wage and the price level are "just right," meaning that no firm could profit from offering a different nominal wage. The main innovation that Keynes introduced to the theory of employment was to argue that this situation, in which the wage and the price level are "just right," is a very unusual one in practice, and that firms and households are typically trading in a situation other than this.

What does it mean for the wage to be "wrong"? Let's study a hypothetical situation to find out how an economy could get into a situation where the wage or the price is wrong. We'll begin by assuming that employment is at the natural rate and that the real wage is equal to ω^*. Suppose that at this initial equilibrium the nominal wage paid by firms is equal to some number, say w_1, and the price level is equal to some other number, say P_1, so that $\omega^* = w_1/P_1$. This situation is illustrated on Figure 7.4, which also shows that when unemployment is at the natural rate, L^* people are employed.

Now suppose that the price level increases from P_1 to some higher level P_2. Later we will ask why the price level might increase, but for now we will take it as given and ask how firms and workers react to the situation. In the classical model we saw that an increase in the price level would immediately be met by an increase in the nominal wage to restore equilibrium between the quantity of labor demanded and the quantity supplied. But Keynesians argue that this process of nominal wage adjustment takes time and that, in the short run, the wage will remain at its nominal level, w_1. Because the price level has risen, the nominal wage of w_1 is now lower in real terms than the natural real wage ω^*, and firms will respond by increasing their recruiting operations, thus creating more new jobs each period. Because the same number of new workers are flowing into the labor market, the fall in the price level will result in a reduction in unemployment from U^* to U_2. The effect of an increase in the price level from P_1 to P_2 is illustrated in panel A of Figure 7.4.

Panel B illustrates what would happen if, beginning from the same situation in which unemployment is equal to its natural rate, U^*, the price level were to fall from P_1 to some lower level, P_3. Once again, we assume that the nominal wage remains at w_1 and so the real wage is higher. Firms now expect to make lower profits and cut back on their recruiting efforts. Employment falls from L^* to L_3 and unemployment increases above the natural rate.

Unemployment and Aggregate Supply in the Short Run and the Long Run

An important idea in the Keynesian theory of unemployment is that the quantity of output produced responds to a change in the price level differently in the short run than in the long run. In the short run the nominal wage is slow to adjust, and changes in the nominal price level are met by changes in the level of unemployment. In the long run, however, the nominal wage adjusts fully and the level of unemployment returns to the natural rate.

Figure 7.5 illustrates this idea by linking changes in the price level with changes in the aggregate quantity of commodities supplied. If the price level increases above P_1, because

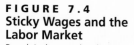

FIGURE 7.4
Sticky Wages and the
Labor Market

Panel A shows what happens in the
search model if the price level increases to P_2. Because the nominal
wage is slow to adjust, the increased price level causes the real
wage to fall. Employment rises to
L_2 and unemployment falls to U_2,
below the natural rate.

Panel B illustrates what happens if
the price level falls to P_3. Because
the nominal wage is slow to adjust,
the lower price level causes the real
wage to rise. Employment falls to
L_3 and unemployment rises to U_3,
above the natural rate.

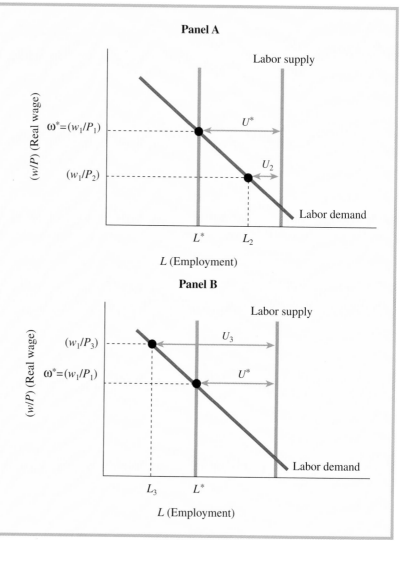

the nominal wage is fixed in the short run, the increase in the price level causes a reduction in the real wage. As the real wage falls, firms hire more workers and the level of unemployment falls below the natural rate. Figure 7.5 shows that when unemployment is
equal to the natural rate, the level of output is Y^*. It also shows how much output would
be produced if the price level were to rise to P_2. Figure 7.4 illustrates that when the price
level rises to P_2, employment rises to L_2. Figure 7.5 shows that when the price level is P_2,
firms supply the quantity of output Y_2. Y_2 is greater than Y^*, because at P_2 the real wage is
lower than at P_1 and firms are willing to employ more workers.

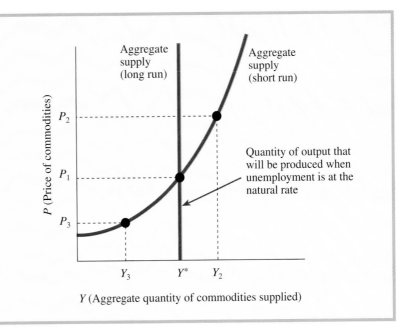

FIGURE 7.5
Aggregate Supply in the Short Run and the Long Run
This graph shows how aggregate supply responds to changes in the price level.

In the short run, the nominal wage is slow to change and a change in the price level causes the real wage to change.

If the nominal price rises, the real wage falls and output rises above Y^*. If the nominal price falls, the real wage increases and output falls below Y^*. In the long run the nominal wage is fully flexible and output equals Y^*.

A similar process applies when the nominal price level falls below P_1. In this case, because the nominal wage is fixed in the short run, the reduction in the price level causes the real wage to increase and firms hire fewer workers. The unemployment rate increases above the natural rate because fewer workers are employed. Figure 7.4 illustrates that when the price level falls to P_3, then employment falls to L_3. Figure 7.5 shows that when the price level is P_3, firms supply the quantity of output Y_3. Y_3 is less than Y^*, because at P_3 the real wage is higher than at P_1 and firms are less willing to employ workers.

Getting from the Short Run to the Long Run

In the long run, we have argued, there is a natural rate of unemployment and the quantity of output supplied is the quantity that will be produced when unemployment is equal to the natural rate. In the short run, the nominal wage is sticky and changes in the price level cause changes in the real wage. As real wages go up or down, firms change the intensity with which they search for new workers, and unemployment rises above or falls below the natural rate. So how does the economy move from the short run to the long run?

Figure 7.6 illustrates the adjustment process on two diagrams. Panel A, a labor market diagram, demonstrates that when the price level is equal to P_2, unemployment is below the natural rate and when the price level is equal to P_3, it is above the natural rate. The red arrows illustrate what happens through time as the nominal wage begins to change. There are two forces at work in the adjustment process. One represents the effect of changes in

FIGURE 7.6
Moving from the Short Run to the Long Run

Panel A: In the labor market, if the price level is too high, at P_2, the real wage is too low and unemployment is below the natural rate. Some firms find it profitable to offer higher nominal wages to attract workers. As the nominal wage rises, employment falls until unemployment is back at the natural rate U^*. If the price is too low, at P_3, the real wage is too high and unemployment is above the natural rate. Some firms find they can increase profit by offering lower nominal wages. As the nominal wage falls, employment rises until unemployment is back at the natural rate U^*.

Panel B: The natural rate is a point where no firm could make higher profits either by offering higher or lower wages to workers.

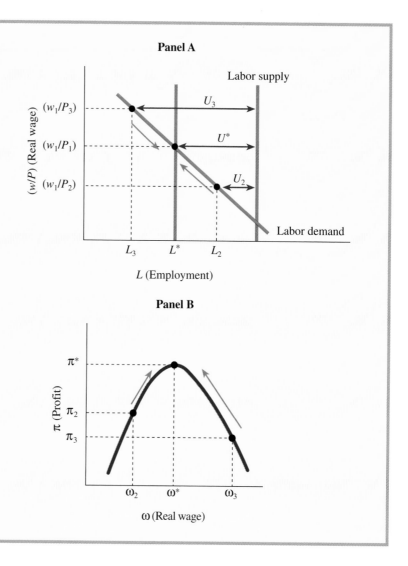

the real wage on a term that we call **private profits.** Private profits are the profits that accrue to the firm independent of search costs. The second is the effect of the real wage on search costs when other firms expand, making it harder for any individual firm to find workers. These two effects can be stated as

7.2 $$\pi \quad = \quad Y(\omega) - \omega L(\omega) \quad - \quad C(\omega)$$

Total profits   **Private profits**   **Search costs**

Each of these terms changes as the real wage falls. Private profits, represented by the intercept in Figure 7.2, get bigger as the real wage falls because the firm can hire addi-

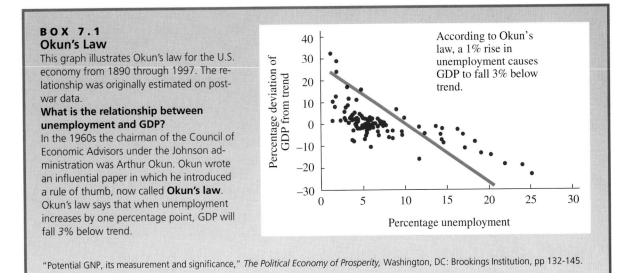

BOX 7.1
Okun's Law
This graph illustrates Okun's law for the U.S. economy from 1890 through 1997. The relationship was originally estimated on postwar data.
What is the relationship between unemployment and GDP?
In the 1960s the chairman of the Council of Economic Advisors under the Johnson administration was Arthur Okun. Okun wrote an influential paper in which he introduced a rule of thumb, now called **Okun's law**. Okun's law says that when unemployment increases by one percentage point, GDP will fall *3%* below trend.

According to Okun's law, a 1% rise in unemployment causes GDP to fall 3% below trend.

(Graph axes: vertical axis "Percentage deviation of GDP from trend" ranging from –30 to 40; horizontal axis "Percentage unemployment" ranging from 0 to 30.)

"Potential GNP, its measurement and significance," *The Political Economy of Prosperity,* Washington, DC: Brookings Institution, pp 132-145.

tional workers for less money and pay its existing workers less. The net effect, as we showed in Figure 7.2, is that lower real wages increase profitability.

In the classical model search costs are absent, and the effect of the real wage on private profits is the only factor driving hiring decisions in the labor market. In the model with search costs, however, as the real wage starts to fall and firms try to hire more workers, the costs imposed on other firms in the economy increase because there is congestion in the hiring process. These costs get larger the closer the economy gets to full employment. They are captured in Equation 7.2 by the term $C(\omega)$.

In panel B of Figure 7.2 we graphed Equation 7.2. This graph illustrates the fact that, at the natural rate of unemployment U^*, no firm can profitably offer to raise or lower the wage, even though there are still some unemployed workers. Adjustment from the short run to the long run occurs as firms change the nominal wage in response to "tight" or "loose" conditions in the labor market, where "tight" means that unemployment is below the natural rate and "loose" means it is above.

Unemployment and the Neutrality of Money

Our model of unemployment incorporates an important insight from Keynesian economics: that the price level and the nominal wage may not always be at the 'right' level, and as a consequence unemployment may fluctuate over the business cycle. This idea has important consequences for one of the central propositions of classical economic theory, the proposition that money is neutral.

Recall that the neutrality of money is a statement about what one expects will happen if the supply of money changes. In the classical model a 10% fall in the supply of money will result immediately in a new equilibrium in which all nominal variables are also lower by 10% and all real variables are unaltered. This is what it means for money to be neutral. Keynes did not disagree with the proposition that the neutrality of money would hold in the long run. Instead, he argued that the establishment of a new equilibrium might take a very long time. To understand why money might not be neutral in the short run we must analyze the effects of a fall in the money supply in a model where search is costly and where it takes time for the nominal wage to restore the natural rate of unemployment.

The insight that the labor market might not always be in equilibrium in the classical sense was one of the most important ideas that Keynes introduced to macroeconomics. But it was not his only contribution. A second very important contribution was Keynes' theory of aggregate demand, which explains how factors other than the money supply can shift the aggregate demand curve. The Keynesian theory of aggregate demand is covered in Chapters 8 through 10. But in order to understand how just one of these factors, the supply of money, can affect unemployment we do not need the full apparatus of Keynesian aggregate demand.

How would the complete economy respond to an announcement by the government that every family must pay $100 to the government? Suppose that the economy begins from an equilibrium in which unemployment is equal to the natural rate and let w_1 be the nominal wage, P_1 be the price level, L^* be equal employment, and Y^* represent GDP. Further suppose that the average family begins the week with $500 and that during a normal week it plans to spend its income on commodities, ending the week with the same stock of cash that it started with. But this week the government takes away $100 from the family. The family must therefore plan to spend less than its usual amount on commodities in order to have enough income to give to the government. We can represent the reduction in the money supply as a leftward shift in the aggregate demand curve, as the family now has less cash to spend on goods and services. This is represented on Figure 7.7 as the shift from demand curve AD_1 to AD_2, on panel A.

As in the classical model, the reduction in the stock of money causes a reduction in aggregate demand as families plan to hold less money at the end of the week. Unlike the classical model, the fall in the supply of money does not cause all nominal variables to fall in proportion, since the nominal wage is slow to adjust. Instead, the reduction in aggregate demand causes a fall in employment and production as the economy moves down the aggregate supply curve. The fall in employment is represented on panel D as the shift from L^* to L_3 as the real wage rises from (w_1/P_1) to (w_1/P_3). Unemployment increases from U^* to U_3.

How is the short-run price level P_3 determined? This is found in panel A as the point at which the new aggregate demand curve AD_2 intersects the short-run aggregate supply curve. If wages were to adjust immediately downward, the fall in demand would cause the nominal wage and the price level to fall in proportion, and unemployment would remain at the natural rate. But in the Keynesian model the nominal wage stays temporarily at w_1 and the real wage is driven up to (w_1/P_3). The level of employment is equal to the quantity of workers hired by firms at the higher real wage.

❻ UNEMPLOYMENT AND ECONOMIC POLICY

How does the Keynesian theory of unemployment fare as an explanation of the data? To address this question we examine some facts about labor markets, beginning with the labor market in the United States during the Great Depression.

FIGURE 7.7
The Response to a Reduction in the Money Supply Predicted by the Search Model
A contraction of the money supply causes the aggregate demand curve in panel A to shift from AD_1 to AD_2. If the money wage cannot fall below w_1, the economy moves down the aggregate supply curve to the point $\{P_3, Y_3\}$. Employment falls to L_3^D (equal to the quantity of labor demanded) and involuntary unemployment equal to U_3 is created.

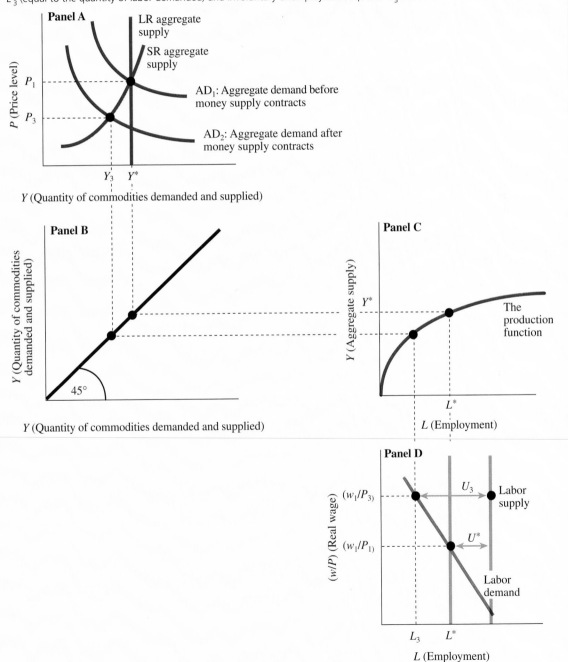

The Labor Market in the Great Depression

During the Great Depression the price level fell by 30% and unemployment increased by 25%. Keynes argued that the combination of these events was inconsistent with the classical notion of equilibrium, and he constructed an alternative explanation showing that the level of unemployment can be very high over long periods of time. Because the Keynesian theory of the Great Depression assumes that the nominal wage does not fall fast enough to restore full equilibrium in the labor market, one test of the theory is to ask how much wages moved during the 1930s. Box 7.2 shows that wages fell almost as much as prices during the Depression. But although the nominal wage fell, it did not fall as fast as the price level. Keynesian economists argue that although the nominal wage fell, it did not fall fast enough to restore unemployment to its natural rate.

Unemployment in North America and Europe

Unemployment in North America has fluctuated in the range of 6 to 7% in recent years. Although this may seem high, in many European countries it is higher still and shows no sign of falling soon. Further, there are aspects of European unemployment that make it a more troubling social problem than it might be in North America. For example, in Europe 40% of the unemployed have been out of work for more than a year, whereas only 11% in the United States have been unemployed for a year or more. One group of workers that fares very badly in Europe are the young. In Spain nearly 50% of youths under 24 years are out of work; in Italy and France the figure for youth unemployment is close to 25%.

A second dimension of the European labor market is that unemployment is particularly high amongst those without skills. This is not true to the same extent in North America, where the unskilled find low-paying jobs. Over the past two decades in North America, the gap between wages earned by high- and low-skilled workers has widened, but aggregate unemployment has remained roughly stationary. Edward Leamer of the University of California, Los Angeles, points out that the gap between garment workers (a low-skill occupation) and those in machinery, metals, or electronics has increased by a factor of 20% since 1960.[4] In Europe, the gap between high- and low-paid workers has not changed as much, but unemployment, particularly amongst the low-skilled, has risen dramatically. What might account for these disparate changes in Europe and North America? One explanation is that there has been a change in the composition of the demand for labor over the past thirty years in the industrialized countries that has favored the skilled over the unskilled. Because of differences in the structure of the European and North American labor markets, this change has caused different effects in the two regions. Some of the key differences are discussed in Box 7.3.

The change in labor markets in industrialized countries has taken the form of an increase in the demand for the services of skilled workers as opposed to unskilled workers. Education is much more valuable in today's labor market than it was twenty years ago. There are two competing explanations for this. The first is that changes in technology favor highly skilled workers over unskilled workers. For example, the level of education required to work in the modern computer industry as a software engineer is greater than the level of education required to operate a sewing machine. The second explanation is that because industrialized

---

4.   See Edward Leamer, "U.S. wages, technological change, and globalization," *Jobs and Capital,* Milken Institute for Jobs and Capital Formation, Summer 1995. This is available at
http://www.mijcf.org/Policy/jobs_capital/jc1995_3/a01.html
on the Milken Institute Web site.

BOX 7.2
FOCUS ON THE FACTS: Wages and Prices in the United States During the Great Depression

Panel A illustrates the behavior of the nominal wage and the price level during the Great Depression. It is clear that a strict application of the Keynesian theory of aggregate supply is not consistent with the evidence since, although the price level fell, the nominal wage fell by almost as much. But this evidence does not lead us to reject the Keynesian theory, because it is possible that the nominal wage did not fall *enough*. The critical Keynesian assumption is that, in response to a drop in aggregate demand, the real wage rises above its equilibrium level. This can occur if the nominal wage is completely inflexible, but it might also occur if the nominal wage falls less than proportionately to the drop in the supply of money.

Panel B shows what happened to employment and the real wage during the 1930s. Notice that although the fraction of the labor force employed fell from 96% in 1929 to 75% in 1932, the real wage actually rose slightly during this period. Keynesians explain this by arguing that the nominal wage did not fall enough to restore full employment.

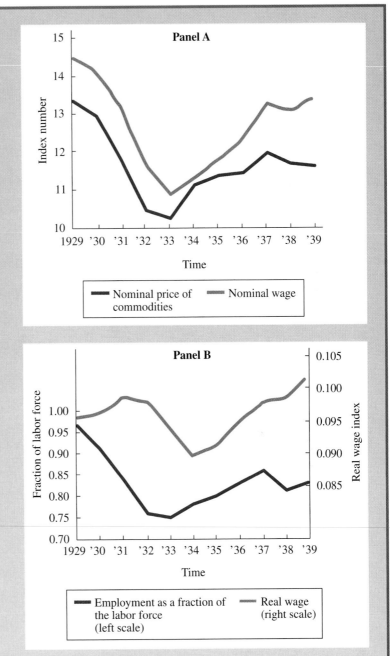

The nominal price level is a price index, the GDP deflator. The nominal wage is constructed by dividing the total wage bill from the GDP accounts by an index of employment (the number of full-time-equivalent employees). The wage index has then been normalized (multiplied by 10) to fit onto the same scale as the price index.

BOX 7.3
Unemployment and Labor Market Rigidities

Table A shows that unemployment in several European countries is much higher than in the United States. Furthermore, higher European unemployment has persisted for a long period of time. According to the theory of the natural rate, these long-term differences across countries must be related to the factors that determine the natural rate, and among the factors that contribute to a high natural rate of unemployment are labor market rigidities that arise as a result of job legislation designed to protect employment.

Table A	Unemployment		
	1983–96	1983–88	1989–94
France	10.4	9.8	10.4
Germany (W)	6.2	6.8	5.4
Italy	7.6	6.9	8.2
Spain	19.7	19.6	18.9
United Kingdom	9.7	10.9	8.9
United States	6.5	7.1	6.2

Table B illustrates four measures of rigidities in the labor market that might account for high European unemployment. The employment protection and labor standards indexes are measures of the legal protection afforded to workers in matters of hiring and firing and in other aspects, such as union representation and minimum wage laws. The replacement rate shows the share of income paid in unemployment benefits; the benefit duration is the number of years for which benefits are received.

In a recent article in the *Journal of Economic Perspectives,* Stephen Nickel of Oxford University analyses the effect of the labor market rigidities reported in Table B on the un-

Table B	Employment Protection	Labor Standards	Benefit (Replacement Rate%)	Benefit Duration (Years)
France	14	6	57	3
Germany	15	6	63	4
Italy	20	7	20	0.5
Spain	19	7	70	3.5
United Kingdom	7	0	38	4
United States	1	0	50	0.5

employment rate. His main conclusions (based on this and other data) are that some labor market rigidities are more important than others in causing high unemployment.

High unemployment is associated with... 1) generous unemployment benefits that are allowed to run on indefinitely, combined with little or no pressure on the unemployed to obtain work...2) high unionization with wages bargained collectively and no coordination between either unions or employers in wage bargaining 3) high overall taxes impinging on labor... and 4) poor educational standards.

Labor market rigidities that do not....[raise unemployment]... are 1) strict employment protection legislation... 2) generous levels of unemployment benefits ... accompanied by pressure to take jobs and 3) high levels of unionization with a high degree of coordination in wage bargaining particularly among employers.

Stephen Nickel, "Unemployment and Labor Market Rigidities: Europe Versus North America,"*Journal of Economic Perspectives* 11, no. 3 (September 1997): 55–74.

countries have lowered trade barriers there is now a much greater degree of competition between low-skilled workers in the United States and low-skilled workers in developing countries. Because the average worker in the apparel industry in China makes just one-twentieth as much as the average worker in the apparel industry in the United States (even though they are sewing the very same garments) it seems possible that increased competition with low-skilled foreign labor has increased the wage dispersion in the United States.

But why has the wage gap between skilled and unskilled workers increased more in the United States than in Europe? One explanation is that the European labor market is considerably more rigid than the U.S. market. In the United States, workers have relatively little legal protection from losing their jobs, and unemployment benefits are less generous and last for a shorter period of time than in many European countries. In the United States, for example, an unemployed worker can expect to receive only 50% of his or her working wage in the form of unemployment benefits and, more importantly, can go on collecting for only six months. In Spain an unemployed worker receives 70% of his or her working wage and can collect for 3.5 years. Correspondingly, unemployment in Spain is around 19% of the labor force, a level that hasn't been seen in the United States since the Great Depression. It is likely that rigidities in the European labor market prevented the fall in the demand for unskilled labor from causing their wage to drop, and the result has been increased European unemployment.[5]

Policies to Alleviate Unemployment

The issue of what to do about unemployment is the subject of a great deal of discussion in policy circles. The answer must surely depend on what causes unemployment, but here there is no consensus. No one would argue that unemployment should be eliminated entirely, since some level of frictional unemployment is necessary in a dynamic labor market in which workers frequently change occupations to keep up with new technologies. Similarly, some fluctuations in the unemployment rate over the business cycle may also be tolerable.

There are two dimensions to the question of what the government should do about unemployment. The first is whether it should attempt to intervene during recessions when unemployment is temporarily above its natural rate. This question is itself a fuzzy one—some economists (particularly those from the real business cycle school) believe that most recessions are generated by fluctuations in the natural rate itself and that the mechanism that restores equilibrium is very fast. If this is true there is not much need to stabilize unemployment over the business cycle since most recessions are caused by the economy adapting to a new technology. One would think, in this case, that some increase in the unemployment rate during recessions is a healthy sign, as workers change jobs and learn new skills.

But although some increase in the unemployment rate during recessions should probably be tolerated, some business cycles are not caused by changes in technology. The Great Depression is one example of a recession in which the equilibrating mechanisms of the market system seem to have gone very badly wrong. If most recessions are like the Great Depression, perhaps the government should intervene actively to speed the process that restores unemployment to its natural rate. In order to better understand the arguments

5. For a very readable summary of the European unemployment problem, see "Europe hits a brick wall." *Economist* April 5, 1997, available on the Internet at http://www.enews.com/magazines/economist/archive/04/970405-009.html.

WEBWATCH 7.1   **Unemployment and the Minimum Wage**

A good source of articles on popular issues is the magazine *Jobs and Capital,* published by the Milken Institute in Santa Monica California and available at
http://www.mijcf.org/Policy/jobs_capital/index.html#IV.
In the summer of 1993, *Jobs and Capital* published an article by Alan Krueger, a leading proponent of the position that the minimum wage does not increase unemployment. Krueger's position can be found in the article "Have Increases in the Minimum Wage Reduced Employment?"
http://www.mijcf.org/Policy/jobs_capital/jc1996_4/frame7.html.
For an equally forceful statement of the opposite position see "The Cruelty of the Minimum Wage" by Finis Welch, who argues that the studies cited by Krueger are badly flawed. Welch's article can be found at
http://www.mijcf.org/Policy/jobs_capital/jc1996_4/frame7.html

---

for and against government intervention, we first need to understand how the complete economy functions, but we must defer this issue to later chapters.

The second dimension of unemployment policy is what government should do to lower the natural rate. We have already pointed out that several European countries have much higher unemployment rates than that of North America, and the issue of how to alleviate long-term structural unemployment is a central concern to policy makers in these countries. Some economists have argued that one of the major causes of high European unemployment is the fact that these countries have legislation to protect jobs that makes it difficult to hire and fire workers. Others point to minimum wage legislation that is thought by some to raise unemployment. But although economic theory clearly predicts that a high minimum wage will cause additional unemployment, the evidence on this issue is less clear. For a pair of arguments on each side of this issue, see the articles by Alan Krueger (who thinks that minimum wage legislation does not raise unemployment) and Finis Welch (who thinks that it does), listed in Webwatch 7.1.

CONCLUSION

In the modern view of unemployment there is a natural rate of unemployment that occurs as a consequence of flows into and out of the labor force. Keynesians believe that unemployment is typically different from this natural rate because the nominal wage is slow to adjust after a nominal shock, such as a change in the quantity of money. Output falls in response to a drop in the quantity of money because the nominal wage does not immediately fall to restore equilibrium. This failure of the nominal wage to fall causes the real wage to rise temporarily as the price level falls. As a consequence, firms reduce the number of workers that they employ.

Economists disagree over whether government policy should seek to stabilize unemployment over the business cycle. It seems likely that unemployment rates differ across countries because of different policies. Currently, there is an active debate over the best way to deal with this issue.

KEY TERMS

Efficiency wages   Nominal rigidity
Externality   Okun's law
Frictional unemployment   Private profits
Menu costs   Search theory
Natural rate of unemployment

PROBLEMS FOR REVIEW

1. Explain, in two paragraphs or less, the main differences between the Keynesian theory of aggregate supply and the classical theory of aggregate supply.

2. Suppose that all wages in the economy were automatically linked to a price index through a cost-of-living adjustment. How would this institutional change alter the Keynesian theory of aggregate supply?

3. Explain, in words, the difference between the real wage and the nominal wage. According to the Keynesian theory of aggregate supply, does the real wage rise or fall during a recession? Is this prediction consistent with evidence from the Great Depression?

4. Suppose that the economy's demand for labor is given by the equation

7.3
$$\frac{w}{P} = 10 - \frac{1}{2}L$$

and the production function is given by

7.4
$$Y = 10L - \frac{1}{4}L^2 - \frac{1}{12}\underline{L}^3$$

where L is the labor employed by a typical firm and $\underline{L}$ is the average labor employed by other firms in the economy. Assume that in equilibrium

7.5
$$L = \underline{L}$$

If the supply of labor to each firm is equal to 3, what is the natural rate of unemployment in this economy? (You need to read the appendix to answer this question.)

5. What is meant by Okun's Law? If the unemployment rate were to increase from 3% to 4%, how much would you predict that output would fall below trend?

6. Explain, in words, what is "natural" about the natural rate, according to the search theory of unemployment. Pay particular attention to the question: why doesn't the real wage fall to equate the demand and supply of labor?

7. In the Keynesian theory of aggregate supply, money is neutral in the long run. Explain what happens in the short run if the money supply increases. Also explain what happens to the price level, the nominal wage, unemployment, and GDP in the transition from the short run to the long run.

8. What are the main differences between the European labor market and the North American labor market? Explain what has happened to the differences between the wages of skilled and unskilled workers in North America over the past twenty years and outline two possible explanations for this phenomenon.

9. What does Stephen Nickel cite as the major labor market rigidities responsible for increasing unemployment? Some economists argue that changes in technology, which raised the gap between the wage paid to skilled and unskilled workers in North America, were responsible for increasing unemployment in Europe. Does Nickel agree with this argument? If not, why not? You will need to read Nickel's article in the *Journal of Economic Perspectives.*

10. Read the articles by Alan Krueger and Finis Welch (Webwatch 7.1). Compare and contrast the views of Krueger and Welch with regard to the minimum wage and its effect on unemployment.

APPENDIX: THE ALGEBRA OF THE NATURAL RATE

This appendix is advanced and it uses calculus. It is not essential to understanding the rest of the book, but if you are comfortable with calculus, it will help you to understand how the search theory works. We begin with an algebraic example of the natural rate of unemployment. The production function in our example is given by

7.6
$$Y = 3L - \frac{L^2}{2} - C$$

and the supply of labor is equal to 2 units per firm

7.7
$$L^S = 2$$

The firm solves the problem

7.8
$$\max 3L - \frac{L^2}{2} - L\frac{w}{P} - C$$

which leads to the labor demand curve

7.9
$$3 - L = \frac{w}{P}$$

The profit of the firm is equal to

7.10
$$\pi = 3L - \frac{L^2}{2} - L\frac{w}{P} - C$$

If we substitute for L from the labor demand curve we get

7.11
$$\pi = 3\left(3 - \frac{w}{P}\right) - \frac{\left(3 - \frac{w}{P}\right)^2}{2} - \left(3 - \frac{w}{P}\right)\frac{w}{P} - C$$

which is equal to

7.12
$$\pi = \underbrace{\frac{(3 - w/P)^2}{2}}_{\textbf{Private profit}} - \underbrace{C}_{\textbf{Search cost}}$$

The real wage must be greater than 0 and less than 3. (If it is greater than 3, the firm will demand 0 labor.) Notice that the profit of the firm increases as the real wage falls from 3 to 0. Firms are always better off when the real wage is lower. In the classical model the real wage will fall until the demand equals the supply of labor. Let's see how this works. If there were no search costs, $C = 0$, the real wage will be set to equate the demand and supply of labor:

7.13
$$L = 3 - \frac{w}{P} = 2 = L^S \qquad \text{or} \qquad \frac{w^E}{P} = 1$$

Each firm demands $(3 - w/P)$ workers, and the supply of workers per firm is 2, which implies that the equilibrium real wage in the classical model is equal to 1.

Now let's see what happens when there are search costs that depend on the labor hired by other firms, $\underline{L}$. The search costs are given by

7.14
$$C = \frac{\underline{L}^3}{3}$$

Notice that C depends on $\underline{L}$ and not on L, so the firm does not take this effect into account when it maximizes profit. The labor demand curve is exactly the same as in the classical model and so is the term we call *private profit*. The difference is that now the term C depends on the real wage. Since every other firm in the economy will demand labor in the same way, in equilibrium $\underline{L}$ will also depend on the real wage.

7.15
$$\pi = \underbrace{\frac{(3 - w/P)^2}{2}}_{\textbf{Private profit}} - \underbrace{\frac{(3 - w/P)^3}{3}}_{\textbf{Search cost}}$$

If we differentiate this expression with respect to w/P and set the derivative to zero, we find that profit is maximized when

7.16
$$\frac{\delta\pi}{\delta w/P} = -(3 - w/P) + (3 - w/P)^2 = 0$$

or

7.17
$$\left(\frac{w}{P}\right)^* = 2$$

In the search model each firm employs $(3 - w/P)$ workers. When $w/P = 2$, no firm will increase its profit if w/P either increases or falls; this is our definition of the natural real wage. Because the supply of labor per firm is equal to 2 workers and each firm employs $L^* = (3 - 2) = 1$ worker, the natural rate of unemployment in this economy is 50%.

CHAPTER 8

The Demand for Money

❶ INTRODUCTION

In the classical theory the only variable that shifts the aggregate demand curve is the quantity of money. But if we want to understand all of the reasons why unemployment might fluctuate over the business cycle, we need to expand on the classical theory. Some recessions may be caused by contractions in the quantity of money, but others may have different causes. The first reason, then, to study the Keynesian theory of aggregate demand is to aid in our understanding of the causes of business cycles.

The Keynesian theory of aggregate demand is essential to Keynes' idea of **demand management**. Demand management is the active intervention by government through fiscal policy (changing taxes) or monetary policy (changing the interest rate) in an attempt to maintain a steady growth rate of the economy without deep recessions or bouts of high inflation.

How does the Keynesian theory of aggregate demand differ from the classical theory? The classical theory of aggregate demand is based on the quantity theory of money and assumes that the quantity of money demanded by households is a constant fraction of their income. This assumption implies that the propensity to hold money, k, is constant. In practice, the propensity to hold money is a variable that depends on the rate of interest. Once we allow for the influence of interest rates on the propensity to hold money, we must study the way the interest rate is itself determined. The determination of the interest rate and the determination of aggregate demand are two separate pieces of a puzzle. When we put the

165

pieces together, in Chapter 10, we can show all of the forces that determine business cycles, and we will have an apparatus for studying how the government can influence aggregate demand through fiscal and monetary policy.

❷ THE OPPORTUNITY COST OF HOLDING MONEY

To understand the modern theory of the demand for money, we construct an idealized economy, in which the interest rate influences money demand by altering the allocation of savings between money and bonds.

Liquidity Preference

Some assets pay higher rates of interest than others, even when the two assets are equally risky. Assume that all of the assets in our ideal economy can be divided into two types: those that pay interest, called bonds, and those that are held even though they do not pay interest, called money. The theory of why private agents hold money when they could earn interest by holding bonds is called the theory of **liquidity preference.**

The theory of liquidity preference asserts that households hold money because money is commonly accepted in exchange for services or commodities. Assets that are useful because other agents will accept them in exchange are called **liquid assets.** Although our theory divides assets into just two categories, in the real world there is a spectrum of assets with differing degrees of liquidity. Assets that are more liquid pay a lower rate of return. An example of two similar assets that are both held, even though one pays a higher rate of interest than the other, are dollar bills and bank accounts. All of us carry dollar bills even though we could put our cash into a bank account that pays a positive rate of interest. We carry cash because it is useful to us. It is more liquid than a bank account because in some everyday situations we may wish to purchase a commodity and the vendor will accept cash but not a check.

In the real world there is a second reason why some assets pay a higher rate of return than others: They are riskier. Other things being equal, most individuals prefer a steady income to an income that fluctuates; economists call this **risk aversion.** As a consequence of risk aversion, securities with a less certain payment must on average pay a higher return. Risk aversion is secondary to our investigation so we assume that all assets are equally risky.

Balance Sheets of Firms and Households

We begin with a simplified description of the assets and liabilities held by households and firms.[1] One kind of asset held by households is the bonds issued by firms. We refer to these bonds as B and call them **corporate bonds** to distinguish them from government bonds. A corporate bond is a promise to make a fixed payment, called the **coupon,** on the bond every year forever. A bond of this kind is called a **perpetuity** and its price is denoted by P^B. Another asset held by households is money, M. The sum of the value of bonds and money held by households is called the household's net worth, also referred to as household **wealth**; we use W to represent wealth (not to be confused with w, the nominal wage).

---

1.   In our exposition, households own no real assets. In reality, households own houses and durable goods, and corporate liabilities include equity, stock options, and futures contracts.

FIGURE 8.1
The Balance Sheets of
Households and Firms
The household owns two types of financial
assets: money and corporate bonds.

Households	
Assets	Liabilities
Corporate bonds $P^B B$	
Money M	Net worth W
W	W

The firms own one real asset, the capital
stock, which is offset by financial liabilities in
the form of corporate bonds.

Firms	
Assets	Liabilities
Capital stock PK	
	Corporate bonds $P^B B$
PK	$P^B B$

In our model we assume that the only asset owned by firms is the **capital stock**. The value of this capital stock is equal to the price of commodities, P, times K, the physical quantity of capital goods.[2] On the liability side of their balance sheet, firms owe the value of corporate debt, $P^B B$, to households. The value of this corporate debt is equal to the number of bonds outstanding multiplied by the price of bonds, P^B. The balance sheets of households and firms are described in Figure 8.1.

Wealth and Income

The assets and liabilities of households and firms change over time as a consequence of production, consumption, and exchange. At the beginning of a typical week, households own stocks of money and bonds. The composition of their wealth is illustrated in Equation 8.1. The composition of household wealth affects household income because bonds earn a flow of interest payments but money does not.

8.1 $$W = M + P^B B$$

> Wealth must be held either as money or as bonds.

During the week households sell labor to firms, purchase consumption commodities, and receive income from ownership of firms in the form of interest on corporate bonds.

---

2.   In the real world, firms hold money for the same reason households do: to smooth the timing of their purchases and their sales. To keep our presentation simple, in this chapter we assume that all of the cash in the economy is in the household sector and that the only asset held by firms is the capital stock.

Households accumulate wealth by adding to their stocks of money and bonds. The accumulation of wealth through the decision not to consume is called **saving**. The relationship among saving, income, consumption, and wealth is illustrated in Equation 8.2. Additions to wealth, $\Delta W/P$, are equal to saving.

8.2
$$\frac{\Delta W}{P} = S = Y - C$$

> Saving by households is used to accumulate wealth (the triangle means "the change in"). Saving is equal to income, Y, minus consumption, C.

In addition to choosing how much of their income to save, households decide how to allocate their existing wealth between alternative assets. This is called **portfolio allocation**. Since the households in our model may hold only money or bonds, their portfolio allocation decision is relatively simple. Household wealth, W, must be divided between assets that bear interest (bonds), and assets that don't bear interest, (money).

To show how the household perceives the tradeoff between income and liquidity, we can develop the household's budget constraint. Equation 8.3 divides household income into two parts: the interest rate, i, times the real value of corporate bonds; (the income from wealth) and the real wage multiplied by labor hours supplied (labor income). If the household were to transfer all of its portfolio to interest-bearing bonds, it would maximize its income. This maximum possible income, Y^{MAX}, is defined by Equation 8.4. In general, the household does not want to earn Y^{MAX} because it would have to give up the convenience of using money in transactions.

8.3
$$Y = i\frac{P^B B}{P} + \frac{w}{P}L$$

> Income has two parts: income from owning bonds and income from labor.

8.4
$$Y^{MAX} = i\frac{W}{P} + \frac{w}{P}L$$

> If all wealth were held as bonds (and none as money) the household could earn the maximum possible income, Y^{MAX}.

8.5
$$Y = Y^{MAX} - i\frac{M}{P}$$

> When the household chooses to hold some of its wealth as money it loses income it could otherwise have earned. The lost income is equal to the interest rate times the value of the household's average money holding.

Equation 8.5 is an expression for the income earned by a household that decides to allocate some portion of its wealth to money. By holding money, it chooses to earn income Y, which is less than the maximum. The modern theory of the demand for money views Equation 8.5 as a constraint on household actions. According to this theory, households choose how much income to earn (bonds to hold) and how much money to hold. As individuals transfer their wealth from money to bonds, they increase their income but simultaneously decrease their liquidity.

❸ THE UTILITY THEORY OF MONEY

The **utility theory of money** explains how the representative household chooses a point on its budget constraint. To describe the reason for holding money, we assume that money yields utility, which we model with a utility function. The utility function describes the utility attained by the household for alternative combinations of money and income. Income yields utility because it can be used to purchase commodities. Money yields utility because of its liquidity, which facilitates exchange.

Two Properties of the Utility of Money

The utility theory of money captures the idea that money is useful in exchange by modeling it as a durable good, like a refrigerator or a television set. Just as a television set yields a flow of entertainment services, so money yields a flow of liquidity services. Unlike the utility of consuming a meal or going to the movies, however, the utility of using money is indirect. Cash enables us to take advantage of opportunities as they arise without having to go to the trouble of first liquidating other assets.

The fact that the utility gained by holding money is indirect suggests that it is different from the utility yielded by other commodities. What units should we use to measure the way that money influences utility? One possible answer is to measure money by the number of dollars that we hold, just as we would measure apples by the number of apples and oranges by the number of oranges. This answer, however, fails to capture the idea that money is not useful for its own sake; it is useful only because we can exchange it for other commodities.

If a person carries twice as much money around one week as the week before, he or she will be able to buy and sell twice as many commodities. Similarly, if a person carries exactly the same quantity of cash, but the prices of all of the goods are cut in half, he or she will, once again, be able to buy and sell twice as many commodities. Money is useful because we use it to trade commodities, which suggests that we should measure money in units of commodities. The value of money measured in units of commodities is called **real money balances**. To measure real balances we divide the nominal quantity of money by an index of the general level of prices. This argument can be used to formulate the first property of a utility function for money.

Property 1: *When households hold more real balances their utility increases.*

Money makes it easier to buy and sell goods. The more transactions a household carries out, the more utility it will gain by holding money. Because households with higher incomes are likely to need to carry out more transactions, the utility theory of money uses income as a measure of transactions. Additional income indirectly increases the benefit of holding money. This leads to the second property of a utility function for money.

Property 2: *When households have more income their utility increases.*

Using mathematical notation we can write an expression for the utility function of money that takes the form

8.6

$$U = U\left(Y, \frac{M}{P}\right)$$

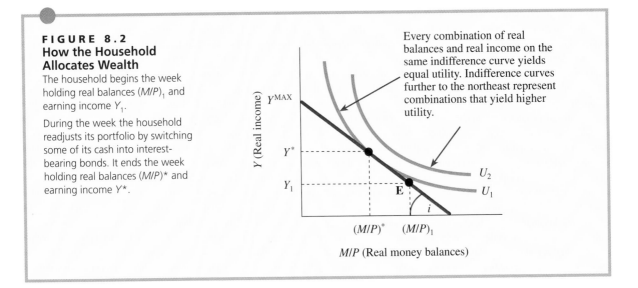

FIGURE 8.2
How the Household Allocates Wealth

The household begins the week holding real balances $(M/P)_1$ and earning income Y_1.

During the week the household readjusts its portfolio by switching some of its cash into interest-bearing bonds. It ends the week holding real balances $(M/P)^*$ and earning income Y^*.

Every combination of real balances and real income on the same indifference curve yields equal utility. Indifference curves further to the northeast represent combinations that yield higher utility.

U is the utility derived by a household that earns income Y and holds real balances equal to M/P.

Properties 1 and 2 imply that the function $U(Y, M/P)$ is increasing in Y and M/P. This means that utility always grows if either Y or M/P increases. By specifying different functional forms for U we can derive specific predictions about the way the household responds when income and the rate of interest change.

Allocating Wealth

The utility theory of money argues that money is held up to the point at which its marginal benefit equals its marginal cost. Figure 8.2 illustrates the solution to the household's portfolio allocation problem.

Points on or below the household's budget constraint (the purple line) represent feasible combinations of liquidity services, measured by M/P, and income Y. The vertical intercept of the budget constraint shows how much income the family would have if it chose to allocate its entire wealth portfolio to bonds. The slope of the budget line is equal to minus the nominal interest rate. This slope represents the rate at which the household can trade liquidity services for more income.

Point **E** in Figure 8.2 represents the combination of real balances held and income earned at the beginning of a typical week. This is the household's initial position; if the household trades money for bonds at interest rate i it can move to any other point on the purple, downward-sloping budget line.

Which point will the household choose? Its preferences for liquidity are described by a set of indifference curves, U_1 and U_2. Points on the same indifference curve show combinations of liquidity services and income that yield equal utility to the household. Curves that are higher and to the right represent higher values of utility. The solution to the household's utility maximization problem is for it to choose the point on the highest indiffer-

FIGURE 8.3
How Equilibrium Is Established

The economy begins at point E_1 in which the households voluntarily choose to hold the same money stock and bonds at the end of each week as they started with at the beginning of each week.

The Federal Reserve increases the money stock from $(M^S/P)_1$ to $(M^S/P)_2$. The interest rate falls from i_1 to i_2 and the price of bonds rises, increasing the household's wealth (at the beginning of the week immediately following the Fed policy change) to point **A**. Given this wealth, the household voluntarily chooses to hold the increased money stock $(M^S/P)_2$.

The economy ends the week (after the Federal Reserve policy change) at the new equilibrium, E_2.

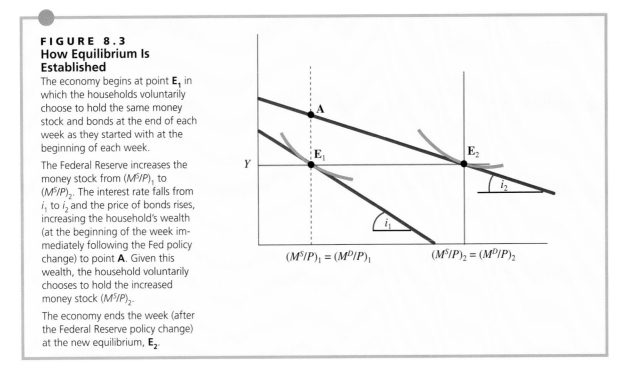

$(M^S/P)_1 = (M^D/P)_1$ $(M^S/P)_2 = (M^D/P)_2$

ence curve that is also on its budget constraint. The figure shows that, for the interest rate i, given the household's wealth, the point $\{(M/P)_1, Y_1\}$ is not an optimum. The household should choose to readjust its portfolio by converting some of its cash into interest-bearing bonds and, at the end of the week, end up at the point $\{(M/P)^*, Y^*\}$.[3]

Establishing Equilibrium

From the point of view of individual families in the economy, the purple budget line in Figure 8.2 is fixed by two factors: the interest rate i and the income and real balances available to the household at the beginning of a typical week, point **E.** From the point of view of the economy as a whole, the endowment point of the household is fixed by its income and the money supply, set by the Federal Reserve. The price of bonds and the interest rate must adjust in equilibrium so that the household chooses to end the week holding the same real balances and earning the same income from its bond portfolio as it did at the beginning of the week.

Figure 8.3 illustrates how an equilibrium is established. The household begins the week holding real balances $(M^S/P)_1$ and earning income Y (from the employment of labor and capital in production). At point E_1, when the money supply equals $(M^S/P)_1$, the economy is in equilibrium, because at the end of a typical week the household voluntarily chooses to hold the existing supply of money. This is illustrated in Figure 8.3 by the indifference curve through the point E_1 tangent to the budget line.

---

3.   See the appendix to this chapter for a mathematical solution to this problem.

Now suppose that the Federal Reserve chooses to increase the money supply from $(M^S/P)_1$ to $(M^S/P)_2$. The household begins the week holding money supply $(M^S/P)_1$, but it must choose to end the week holding money supply $(M^S/P)_2$. The only way that this can happen is if the household's wealth is increased by a change in the price of outstanding bonds. As the price of outstanding bonds rises, the household's initial position moves from point $\mathbf{E_1}$ to point $\mathbf{A}$. At the same time, the interest rate falls from i_1 to i_2. When the household begins the week with initial position $\mathbf{A}$, and when it can trade at the interest rate i_2, it will choose to end the week holding money supply $(M^S/P)_2$ and earning income Y from its portfolio. Equilibrium is established through a change in the price of bonds and a change in the rate of interest that causes the household to choose, voluntarily, to hold the quantity of money supplied.[4]

④ USING THE THEORY OF MONEY DEMAND

The classical theory assumes that the propensity to hold money is a constant, but in the real world the propensity to hold money has fluctuated in a systematic way over a hundred years of data. The modern theory is able to explain why these fluctuations have occurred.

The Mathematics of the Utility Theory of Money

In general, the solution to the household's money demand problem depends on the shape of its indifference curves. One special case is given by the formula for the utility of money

8.7
$$U = \frac{1}{1 + h} \ln (Y) + \frac{h}{1 + h} \ln \left(\frac{M}{P}\right)$$

where the parameter h measures the relative importance of liquidity to the household.[5] This special case leads to a formula for the demand for money that is easy to compare with the classical model. We can show that a family with this utility function will choose to hold a fraction, h/i, of its income as cash in every period. (Because the proof of this statement uses calculus, we have left it for the appendix.) Unlike the classical demand for money, in the modern theory the propensity to hold money is equal to a constant parameter h, divided by the interest rate, i:

8.8

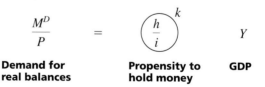

$$\frac{M^D}{P} \qquad = \qquad \left(\frac{h}{i}\right)^k \qquad Y$$

Demand for   Propensity to   GDP
real balances   hold money

Equation 8.8 can be used to compare the classical theory of the demand for money with the modern theory of the demand for money as formulated in the utility theory of money.

---

4.   Firms are financed not only by debt, but also by equity. A change that makes the profitability of the firm go up or down is reflected in the value of corporate equity and in the income earned by the typical household that owns this equity. The mechanism described here explains why the value of the stock market typically rises when the Federal Reserve increases the money supply and lowers the interest rate.

5.   The symbol ln means "natural logarithm"; some of the properties of logarithms are reviewed in Appendix B.

Like the classical theory, the modern theory predicts that the quantity of money demanded, measured in units of commodities, is equal to the propensity to hold money, k, multiplied by GDP. Unlike the classical theory, in modern theory k is not a constant. It is equal to the parameter h divided by the interest rate.

Evidence for the Modern Theory

To compare the classical and modern theories we introduce time series observations from 1890 to 1997 of the rate of interest, i, and of a variable called the **velocity of circulation,** for which we use the symbol v. The velocity of circulation is the number of times per year that the average dollar bill circulates in the economy, measured in units of 1/years. The propensity to hold money is the fraction of a year's income that is held on average as a stock of money. It is the inverse of the propensity to hold money, k. In 1993, for example, k was equal to 1/6 years, reflecting the fact that the stock of money was equal to two months (one-sixth of a year) of income. The velocity of circulation in the same year was equal to 6, meaning that the average dollar circulated six times during the year.

8.9 $$v \equiv \frac{1}{k}$$

The velocity of circulation measured in units of 1/years · · · · · · · · · · · · · · **The propensity to hold money measured in units of years**

We have chosen to present evidence of the movement of v rather than k because the connection between i and v (two variables that move in the same direction) is more apparent in a graph than the relationship between i and k (two variables that move in opposite directions).

There are many concepts of money. In panel A of Box 8.1, the purple line represents the velocity of circulation for the most frequently used concept (called $M1$), which includes cash and currency, checking accounts, and a few smaller items. The velocity of circulation is plotted on the left-hand scale of the figure. Notice that it is far from a constant, in contradiction to the classical theory of money demand. In 1942 the velocity of circulation fell to 2 and in 1981 it exceeded 7. But although the velocity of circulation is not a constant, it has closely paralleled the interest rate, as predicted by the modern theory of the demand for money. The red line represents the rate of interest on six-month commercial loans, measured on the right-hand scale in percent per year. Notice that although the velocity of circulation has moved substantially over the century, its movements have always been accompanied by movements in the rate of interest.

During the Great Depression, beginning in 1930, the velocity of circulation fell from 4 to 3 in the space of a few months. This drop was accompanied by a steep fall in the rate of interest from 5% to 2.5%. At the end of World War II the rate of interest began to climb, and so did the velocity of circulation. According to the modern theory of the demand for money, these changes in velocity were caused by the associated increase in the rate of interest. As the opportunity cost of holding money increased after the war, people reduced the amount of cash that they kept on hand by passing it from one person to another more quickly; that is, the velocity of circulation increased. This increasing velocity continued

BOX 8.1
FOCUS ON THE FACTS:
Comparing the Quantity Theory of
Money and the Modern Theory of
the Demand for Money
According to the quantity theory of money, the propensity to hold money, k, is a constant. The modern theory of the demand for money predicts instead that k depends on the nominal interest rate. To see this we study the behavior of the velocity of circulation (the inverse of k) and the interest rate over the past century. Notice that velocity has not been constant. However, the low-frequency movements in velocity mirror the low-frequency movements in the interest rate.

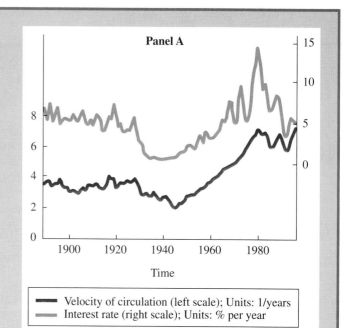

Velocity of circulation (left scale); Units: 1/years
Interest rate (right scale); Units: % per year

Panel B presents the same information as a scatter plot. The purple line is the best straight line through the points. The correlation coefficient between the velocity of circulation and the interest rate is 0.75.

We can infer from this data that the modern theory of the demand for money is a better description of the data than the quantity theory of money.

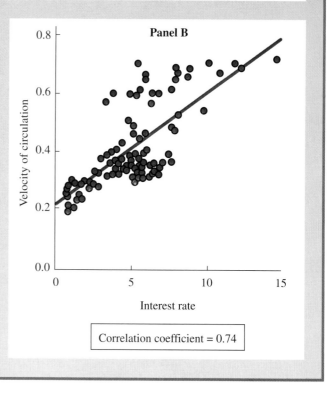

Correlation coefficient = 0.74

WEBWATCH 8.1   **Electronic Money**

The Federal Reserve Bank of Chicago maintains a Web site at
http://www.frbchi.org.
One of the features of this site is a section on economic education, where you can find a
range of articles on all aspects of monetary economics.

Economists have found that the relationship between the velocity of circulation and the
interest rate has shifted in recent years. Velocity is higher today than one would have predicted
based purely on the historical relationship between money, income, and the interest rate. Some
economists have speculated that the demand for money function is shifting as technological
changes make new forms of money more attractive and there is less need for paper money.

These new forms of money include ATM cards, "smart" cards, and electronic funds
transfers, all of which are growing rapidly as the Internet and other electronic communications grow in importance. For an excellent summary of these new technologies and assessment of their likely impact on our lives, check out the piece on electronic money and the future of the payments system by Keith Feiler (edited by Tim Schilling) at
http://www.frbchi.org/pubs-speech/publications/booklets/emoney.pdf.

---

right up to 1981, when the interest rate peaked at 14%. After 1981 interest rates began to
drop again, and once more this drop was accompanied by a fall in velocity, just as it had
been in the 1930s.

❺ THE LM CURVE

The rate of interest can be influenced by the Federal Reserve System through changes in
the supply of money. Manipulation of the money supply in an attempt to influence endogenous variables, such as the interest rate or the level of income, is called **monetary policy.**

To illustrate the effects of monetary policy on the rate of interest, we develop an equation
that explains the relationship between the rate of interest and GDP when the quantities of
money demanded and supplied are equal. The graph of this equation is called the **LM curve.**[6]

The Supply of Money

In developing the LM curve we assume that the entire money supply is an exogenous variable directly under the control of the Federal Reserve Board. The assumption that money
is exogenous is represented by Equation 8.10, in which we place a bar over the symbol M
to represent a fixed number that is picked each period as an instrument of policy.

8.10 $$M^S \qquad = \qquad \overline{M}$$

Supply of money   **Exogenous money supply**

The assumption that the money supply is exogenous is an oversimplification, since,
strictly speaking, the Federal Reserve Board can directly control only a small part of the

---

6.   The name LM curve comes from <u>L</u>iquidity preference equals the supply of <u>M</u>oney ($L = M$).

stock of money. The rest of the money supply moves closely with the part that the Federal Reserve Board controls, so the assumption that the Federal Reserve Board controls the entire money supply is a good one that will greatly simplify exposition of the theory.

The Price Level

The theory of the demand for money deals with how the real value of money depends on income and the interest rate, but the theory of the money supply is a theory of how the *nominal* quantity of money is controlled by the Federal Reserve Board. The real supply of money depends not only on the behavior of the Federal Reserve Board, it also depends on the price level. To complete our development of the LM curve, we assume that the price level is exogenous, or fixed.

8.11 $$P \qquad = \qquad \bar{P}$$

                        Price level   **Exogenous price level**

To derive a relationship between the interest rate and GDP (the LM curve), we might suppose that the price is equal to 100. If the price level changes to some other value, say 200, we will have to draw a new LM curve that has a different position. We return to this idea in Chapter 10, when we develop the Keynesian theory of aggregate demand.

Deriving the LM Curve

Figure 8.4 shows how to derive the LM curve. Both panels plot the nominal interest rate on the vertical axis; the horizontal axes measure different variables: Panel A plots the nominal interest rate against income, and panel B plots the nominal interest rate against the quantity of money demanded and the quantity of money supplied.

We know that the quantity of money demanded, measured in commodity units, is a function of the nominal interest rate. Because there is a different demand for money function for every level of income, we use the symbol $L(Y)$ to represent the demand for money schedule that would apply if the level of income were equal to Y. Panel B draws two such schedules, $L(Y_1)$ and $L(Y_2)$, one for each of two levels of income. $L(Y_2)$ is to the right of $L(Y_1)$ because Y_2 is greater than Y_1. For every value of the rate of interest, the demand for money will be greater, and with it the value of income will also be greater. The vertical line in panel B depicts the supply of money, measured in commodity units. Notice from this graph that the curves $L(Y_1)$ and $L(Y_2)$ intersect the line M^S/P at different points.

The LM curve is derived by moving back and forth between the two panels. Begin in panel A and pick a particular value for GDP, say Y_1. Now move to panel B and draw the demand for money as a function of the interest rate, given that income is equal to Y_1. For this demand for money schedule the equilibrium interest rate, that is, the interest rate at which the quantity of money supplied equals the quantity of money demanded, is equal to i_1. Translate this interest rate, i_1, back to panel A to find point **A** on the LM curve. By repeating this process for the level of income Y_2, you can find a second point on the LM curve, point **B**. At a higher level of income the equilibrium interest rate must also be higher, so point **B** is above and to the right of point **A**. In other words, the LM curve slopes up.

In Figure 8.4 the natural rate of output is Y^*. It is tempting to think that the nominal interest rate will be determined at the point where Y^* intersects the LM curve, but there is

FIGURE 8.4
Deriving the LM Curve
This figure shows how to derive the graph of the LM curve. Panel A shows that there is a different demand for money curve for different values of income. Panel B plots the graph of the LM curve. At every point on the LM curve the quantity of money demanded is equal to the quantity supplied.

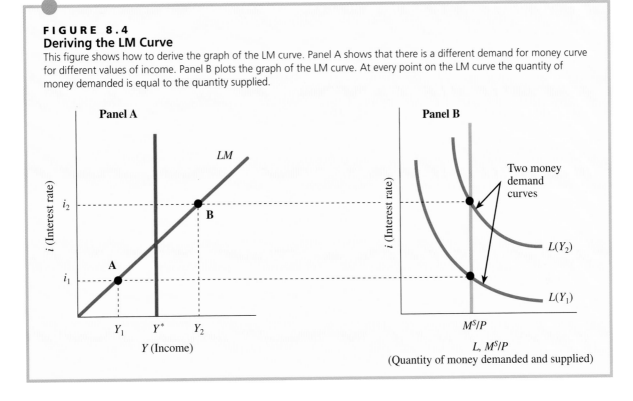

no reason why this should be so, since in the short run income can differ from its natural rate. There must be a relationship between the nominal interest rate and income such that the quantity of money demanded is equal to the quantity supplied, but we cannot say which combination of income and the interest rate will be determined in equilibrium. We examine this issue in Chapter 10.

The Importance of the LM Curve

Why are combinations of income and the nominal interest rate that lie on the LM curve any different from those that do not? The answer is that the combinations of Y and i that lie on the LM curve are the only Y and i combinations for which the quantity of money in circulation is willingly held. Another way of saying this is that on the LM curve the quantity of money demanded is equal to the quantity supplied.

What would happen if, at a given level of income, the interest rate were too high or too low? Suppose first that the interest rate was above the LM curve. In this case households would find that they were holding more money than they would like, and they would try to convert some of their cash into bonds. But because there is a finite supply of bonds on the market, the sellers of bonds (firms that are borrowing money) would be able to offer lower interest rates and still find lenders. This process of converting money to bonds would end at the point when the interest rate went back to the LM curve, since only at this point is the stock of money willingly held. Now suppose that the opposite situation occurred and the interest rate dropped below the LM curve. In this case, households would find that they did not have enough liquidity and they would sell some of their bonds in an attempt to hold more cash to meet their daily transaction needs. But as households sell bonds, some firms would not be able to borrow all of the money that they needed for investment purposes and they would bid up the interest rate to attract funds back into the capital market. This process of bidding up the interest rate would stop only when the nominal interest rate went back to the LM curve. To summarize, the LM curve represents points for which the existing stock of money in circulation is willingly held.

The LM curve balances two opposing forces. Consider a point on this curve. When income increases, holding the interest rate fixed, the quantity of money demanded will increase because households need more liquidity to finance extra transactions. But the money supply is fixed by the Federal Reserve Board. If income remains higher, the quantity of money demanded would exceed the quantity supplied. Equality can be restored by increasing the interest rate and making bonds more attractive, thereby inducing households to switch back to their original money-demand decision. Higher levels of income are compensated by a higher rate of interest because these variables pull the quantity of money demanded in different directions. This is why the LM curve slopes up.

The Algebra of the LM Curve*

This section is optional and is provided for those who find equations easier to understand than graphs. In Equations 8.12–8.15 we make a special assumption about the utility function in order to derive an equation for the LM curve using algebra. This assumption is that the utility function is equal to a weighted sum of the logarithms of income and real balances (the assumption we used to derive Equation 8.8). Different assumptions about the shapes of the indifference curves for liquidity and income lead to different predictions about the exact function that describes the demand for money.

DERIVING THE LM CURVE

8.12 $$M^S = M^D$$

> *Step 1*: Quantity of money demanded equals quantity of money supplied.

8.13 $$M^S = \bar{M}$$

> *Step 2*: Replace quantity of money supplied in Step 1 by exogenous quantity (determined by the Federal Reserve Board).

8.14 $$\frac{M^D}{P} = \frac{h}{i}\,Y$$

> *Step 3*: Replace quantity of money demanded in Step 1 by money demand function from modern theory of the demand for money.

8.15 $$i = \frac{hP}{M}\,Y$$

> *Step 4*: Rearrange terms to find the equation of the LM curve.

Equations 8.12–8.15 derive the LM curve in four steps. Step 1 sets the quantity of money demanded equal to the quantity of money supplied. If households are holding too much money, they can plan to spend more than their income either by buying goods and services or by buying bonds. Similarly, if families are holding too little money, they can plan to spend less than their income either by cutting back on expenditure or by selling some of their bonds in the financial markets. Step 2 is the assumption that the quantity of money supplied is chosen by the Federal Reserve Board. Step 3 is the formula for the quantity of money demanded as a function of income and the interest rate. Finally, Step 4 puts together demand and supply to generate an equation that characterizes the values of the rate of interest and the level of GDP for which the demand equals the supply of money. This equation is the LM curve.

Monetary Policy and the LM Curve

In Chapter 10 we put the LM curve together with a second equilibrium relationship, the IS curve, and show how the two curves are used to analyze the effects of monetary and fiscal policy on the equilibrium of the whole economy. To understand how changes in the money supply affect the economy we must first understand how the position of the LM curve changes in response to changes in monetary policy.

The slope and position of the LM curve are determined only by the real value of the supply of money. This important property follows from the fact that money is held only for its ability to buy goods and not for its own sake. It follows that changes in the real value of the money supply can come about either as a result of an increase in the nominal quantity of money, M, or as a result of a fall in the price of commodities, P. In either case the real value of the supply of money goes up. Let's trace the effect on households of an increase in the real value of the supply of money.

As the real money supply increases, households find that they are holding more money than they require for their daily transactions. Some households try to eliminate the excess cash by lending it to firms. But that results in more lenders than borrowers at the current interest rate, and firms become able to attract funds at a lower nominal interest rate. The net effect, then, of an increase in the quantity of money is to cause the nominal interest rate to fall. In Figure 8.5 this shows up as a rightward shift in the LM curve—a lower equilibrium interest rate for every value of income.

The graphs in Figure 8.5 show why an increase in the quantity of money supplied causes a shift of the LM curve. The two LM curves in panel A are drawn for two values of the supply of money. Point **A** is on the LM curve associated with a money supply of M_1, and point **B** is on the LM curve associated with the supply of money M_2. Notice that when the quantity of money supplied is greater, the equilibrium interest rate that causes the quantity of money demanded to equal the quantity supplied is lower at every level of income. This is illustrated in the figure by the point at which the demand for money curve $L(Y_1)$ that applies when the level of income is Y_1 crosses the money supply curve for each of two values of the money supply, M_1 and M_2.

CONCLUSION

Assets have different degrees of liquidity depending on how useful they are in exchange. Less liquid assets pay a higher interest rate to induce us to hold them. We model this

FIGURE 8.5
How an Increase in the Money Supply Shifts the LM Curve

This figure shows how changes in the money supply affect the LM curve. Panel A shows how the rate of interest changes when the stock of money increases. Panel B shows how the LM curve shifts in response.

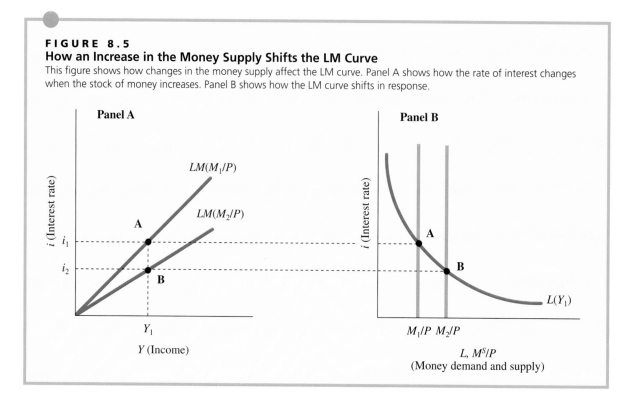

by assuming that there are two kinds of assets; bonds that pay interest and money that does not.

To explain why households use money, we assume that the real value of money yields utility. Holding money is costly because more income could be earned by holding bonds; this income could be used to purchase commodities. Households balance the marginal utility of real money against the interest lost from holding it. The resulting money demand function generalizes the quantity theory of money by allowing the velocity of circulation (the inverse of the propensity to hold money) to depend on the interest rate. The data support the utility theory of money over the quantity theory of money that sets the velocity of circulation constant. In a century of data, the velocity of circulation has not been constant; it varies directly with the interest rate.

In equilibrium, the quantity of money demanded equals the quantity supplied. Higher income causes the quantity of money demanded to increase; households hold additional cash to finance additional transactions. A higher interest rate causes the quantity of money demanded to fall as holding cash becomes more costly in terms of income foregone. There is an upward-sloping locus of points on a graph of income against the interest rate; this graph; called the LM curve, describes combinations of income and the interest rate for which the quantity of money demanded equals the quantity supplied.

KEY TERMS

Capital stock	Perpetuity
Corporate bonds	Portfolio allocation
Coupon	Real money balances
Demand management	Risk aversion
Liquid assets	Saving
Liquidity preference	Utility theory of money
LM curve	Velocity of circulation
Monetary policy	Wealth

PROBLEMS FOR REVIEW

1. Analyze the effect on the balance sheet of a commercial bank when one of its customers uses a credit card. Using your analysis, discuss the relationship of credit cards to money. Your answer should specifically address the question, are credit cards money?

2. How does the variable Y^{MAX} change when the price of bonds increases? Why? How does this change shift the budget constraint of the household?

3. Draw the indifference curves for the utility function

$$U = \min\{Y, M/P\}$$

How would a household with these preferences respond to changes in the rate of interest? How is your answer related to the classical theory of the demand for money?

4. Draw the indifference curves for the utility function

$$U = Y + M/P$$

How would a household with these preferences respond to changes in the rate of interest?

5. Explain the relationship of the propensity to hold money to the velocity of circulation. What are the units of velocity?

6. Explain in words why the LM curve slopes up.

7. Find the equation of the LM curve when the utility of money is given by the expression

$$U = \frac{\left(\dfrac{M}{P}\right)^{1-\lambda} + \theta Y^{1-\lambda}}{1 - \lambda}$$

8. Suppose that the introduction of automatic teller machines reduces the demand for money for every value of the level of income and the rate of interest (the parameter h falls). Analyze the effect of this innovation on the LM curve.

9. Suppose that the supply of money and the price level both increase by 25%. What effect will these changes have on the LM curve?

10. Write a short essay that compares and contrasts the classical theory of the demand for money with the utility theory of the demand for money. Which theory fits the data better? Why?

11. Read the article on electronic money at
http://www.frbchi.org/pubs-speech/publications/booklets/emoney.pdf
and answer the questions at
http://www.frbchi.org/educator/emoney_q&a.html.

APPENDIX: THE ALGEBRA OF THE DEMAND FOR MONEY

There are many possible mathematical functions that we could use to capture the properties of a demand for money function in a mathematical formula. Different equations lead to different quantitative predictions. All of the formulations of the utility theory of money, however, give the same qualitative prediction: that an increase in the opportunity cost of holding money causes households to switch their portfolios from money to bonds.

Equation 8.16 expresses the utility U that would be gained by using money to facilitate exchange when the household earns income Y, when it holds M dollars, and when the average price of commodities equals P. Utility for this example is a weighted sum of the logarithms of income and real balances with weights $h/1(1 + h)$ and $1/(1 + h)$. This particular utility function leads to a simple formula for the demand for money.

8.16
$$U = \frac{1}{1 + h} \log(Y) + \frac{h}{1 + h} \log\left(\frac{M}{P}\right)$$

The problem of allocating wealth between money and bonds is expressed as a special case of the problem of maximizing utility subject to a budget constraint. The household maximizes Equation 8.16 subject to the constraint

8.17
$$Y + i\frac{M}{P} = i\frac{W}{P} + \frac{w}{P}L$$

To solve a problem of this kind, find the indifference curve that is tangent to the budget constraint. Equation 8.18 shows how to do this using calculus.

8.18
$$\frac{\partial U/\partial(M/P)}{\partial U/\partial U} = \frac{hY}{(M/P)} = i$$

In general, to find the slope of the indifference curve we differentiate the utility function with respect to income and real balances, and take the ratio of the two partial derivatives. This procedure gives the general expression for the slope of the indifference curve, the first term in Equation 8.18. In the special example that we are studying this procedure leads to the expression given in the middle term of Equation 8.18. The slope of the indifference curve is proportional to the ratio of GDP to real balances. This method represents the algebraic expression of the idea that the family will equate the marginal benefit of holding money to its marginal cost.

The formula for the demand for money that comes out of the monetary utility problem is given in Equation 8.19:

8.19
$$\frac{M}{P} = \frac{h}{i} Y$$

In our special example, the representative family will choose to hold a fraction h/i of its income as cash in every period.

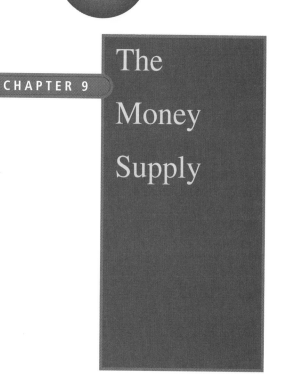

CHAPTER 9

The Money Supply

❶ INTRODUCTION

Money comes in different forms. Some societies use commodities like gold or silver as money, others use paper or even electronic money. The modern banking system has evolved to facilitate exchange by developing new liquid assets like bank accounts and credit cards.

How is the stock of liquid assets controlled in a modern society? The Federal Reserve Board cannot directly decide on the liquidity of the economy because private banks can create money. By setting the stock of cash and coins in circulation and by restricting private bank deposits with the Central Bank, however, the Federal Reserve Board can indirectly control the money supply. This chapter explains how this process works.

❷ A SHORT HISTORY OF MONEY

The model we developed in Chapter 8 distinguished only two kinds of financial assets, money and bonds. In reality there are many kinds of financial assets, all with differing degrees of liquidity. One of the roles of the banking system is to convert assets that are relatively illiquid into those that are more readily accepted in exchange. Banks create liquidity by substituting their own liabilities for the liabilities of other agents in the economy. An example of liquidity creation is the process through which a bank makes a loan to a firm. The firm takes the loan and buys capital. The bank creates a liability in the form of a deposit that the firm may write checks on. Through this process the banking system substitutes liabilities that are acceptable in exchange (bank accounts with checking privileges) for liabilities that are not (loans to corporations).

How Banks Create Money

All societies that engage in trade use money of one form or another. The earliest forms of money were commodities that were easily transported, divisible, and durable, and in many societies these commodity moneys took the form of one or more of the precious metals. In Europe gold and silver have been used as a means of exchange since Roman times, although the relative importance of these two metals has varied from one century to the next. As trade developed in the Middle Ages, merchants began to store their wealth with goldsmiths for safekeeping. It became possible to buy or sell a commodity without ever physically moving the gold itself; instead, one could write a note to the goldsmith asking him to transfer ownership of the gold to another person. This practice eventually developed into the institution of modern banking. Today, in a good part of the world, the money stock is in the form of accounts at banks, rather than in the form of notes and coins. The practice of writing a check on an account is the modern equivalent of the medieval practice of writing a note to the goldsmith.

Banks keep some of their customer's deposits in their vaults. These are called **reserves**. Historically, bankers found that they needed to keep only a small fraction of their deposits in the form of reserves, and they took advantage of this fact by lending out their customer's money, at interest, thereby realizing a profit. The process of a commercial bank lending money results in the creation of new money because it creates an asset (the loan to a new customer) and a liability (a new deposit). Since this deposit is a medium of exchange (the customer can write checks on the new account), the bank has created money.

Consider an example, described in Table 9.1, of how money creation operates in practice. A new bank might begin with customer deposits of $2 million in currency (coins and paper money). This bank now has reserves of $2 million in currency and deposits of $2 million in the form of customer accounts. This is the situation depicted in panel A. Since a bank's depositors do not require access to their funds on a daily basis, it is not necessary for the bank to keep reserves on hand equal to 100% of its deposits. The fact that customers do not continually withdraw funds is due, in part, to the service offered by the banking system. Instead of withdrawing currency and physically transferring it to another location, the bank transfers money from one account to another on paper. If the account to which the funds are paid is at the same bank, this process does not require any action other than a bookkeeping entry on the two customer accounts. If the account is at another bank, the banknotes and coins can be transferred from the vaults of one bank to the other without the money ever leaving the banking system as a whole.

Suppose that the bank finds that, on average, it needs to keep an amount equal to 20% of its deposits on hand in the form of cash reserves. It may create new deposits by lending money to businesses, in the form of new accounts, up to the point at which the total deposits of the bank are equal to five times (the inverse of 20%) its reserves. In our example this would imply that the bank can create new deposits of $8 million, giving the bank total

TABLE 9.1
The Creation of Money by a Commercial Bank

(Panel A) Commercial bank balance sheet before making a loan			(Panel B) Commercial bank balance sheet after making a loan		
Assets		Liabilities	Assets		Liabilities
Loans 0			Loans 8		
Reserves 2	Deposits	2	Reserves 2	Deposits	10
	2	2		10	10

All figures are in millions of dollars.

liabilities of $10 million, total deposits of $10 million and reserves of $2 million. This is the situation depicted in panel B. The feature that prevents the bank from making more than $8 million in loans is that, if it were to expand further, its reserves would fall to less than 20% of its deposits and it would have insufficient reserves to meet the day-to-day requirements of its customers.

It might seem that banking is profitable because the owners of banks can create money at will, but competition keeps banks from generating excess profits. If individual banks make large profits, new banks will enter the industry and try to attract customers by offering to pay interest on deposits. The process of competing for customers bids up the interest rate on deposits and bids down the interest rate on loans. The equilibrium of the competitive process keeps the banking system as a whole earning enough interest on its loans to pay interest to its customers in the form of interest on their deposits.[1]

In the United States bank reserves are regulated by the government, and the Federal Reserve System requires commercial banks to keep a minimum ratio of reserves to deposits. This ratio is adjusted periodically as part of Federal Reserve policy.

The Development of Fiat Money

Although monetary systems were originally based on commodities, there has been a steady move throughout the world away from commodity money and toward a system of **fiat money**. Fiat money does not represent a claim to any physical commodity but instead is backed by laws that require money to be accepted in all legal transactions. Even during the period of commodity money, there were typically more claims to gold circulating, in the form of banknotes, than there was gold in existence. In effect these banknotes were fiat money, because if all of the note-holders were to have demanded repayment at once, the world stock of gold would not have been great enough to meet the demand. The sys-

---

1.   Putting aside the bank's operating expenses, the relationships among the loan rate, the deposit rate, and reserves are simple. If the bank holds reserves of 20% of its deposits, for example, it must charge an interest rate on its loans that is 20% higher than the interest rate that it receives on its deposits, just to stay in business. If the bank also must cover operating expenses, this spread must be even greater.

tem of notes that were partially backed by gold was the origin of our modern system of payments, in which money is 100% fiat.

The medieval practice of leaving gold with goldsmiths for safekeeping was also the origin of paper money, which originally represented a claim to gold that was held on deposit at the goldsmith's place of business. A **banknote** is like a check, except that it is transferable from one person to another. There is no reason why commercial banks should not issue banknotes, and there have been periods of history when private notes *did* circulate. In most societies, however, the power to issue banknotes has been claimed as a monopoly right by the government. Issuing money is a revenue-generating activity. In some societies money creation is almost the only source of revenue, because the government's power to tax is severely limited by the absence of an organized and efficient system of tax collection.[2]

Until the 1930s all money, throughout the world, was at least partially backed by commodities, and for a considerable period of time, beginning in the nineteenth century, the dominant commodity was gold. During this period the money that circulated was partly in the form of gold coins, but for the most part it consisted of paper money that represented a claim on gold. A national currency convertible to gold is said to operate on a **gold standard**. During the time when the gold standard prevailed, most nations guaranteed to convert their currencies to gold at a fixed price. At the end of the World War II most nations agreed to maintain a fixed exchange rate against gold, but there was some flexibility built into the system that allowed countries to change their exchange rates periodically in response to domestic shortages of foreign exchange. In 1973 the world moved to a system of **flexible exchange rates,** and since then nothing has backed the value of the U.S. dollar other than the credibility of the U.S. government.

As long as governments maintained convertibility of paper money to gold they were limited in their ability to create more money. Central banks had to keep a certain reserve of gold to meet the public demand, just as private banks today are limited in their ability to create deposits by the need to keep reserves of cash. During the 1930s the gold standard collapsed irrevocably, and one by one, all the countries in the world lost their ability to convert their currencies, thereby removing the limit that the gold standard had placed on their ability to create money. The world monetary system has, for the past sixty years, moved steadily closer to a pure fiat money system. With the move to a flexible exchange rate system in 1973 there is now no limit on the quantity of each currency in circulation, other than the choices of national governments.

❸ THE ROLE OF THE CENTRAL BANK

The stock of money in circulation at any point in time is fixed. Because trade involves passing money from one person to another, it is not possible for all individuals to reduce their holding of money at the same time. Therefore the demand-for-money must be identically equal to its supply. But although the stock of money at a point in time is fixed, this stock can vary from one week to the next. This section is about how this happens.

---

2.   In Argentina and Bolivia the fact that the revenue from money creation is an important component of government finance is responsible for the very high and recurrent inflations in their economies in recent years.

The Federal Reserve System

Most countries in the world have a **central bank**, which is usually a branch of government. In the United States the central bank consists of not one, but a system of 12 districts, each with its own **Federal Reserve Bank** (see Figure 9.1). The **Federal Reserve System** was created in 1913 to regulate the nation's money supply and to operate as a banker to the commercial banks. At that time, there was a general concern over fluctuations in interest rates, which moved not only with the business cycle but also with the seasons. One of the original intentions of the politicians who created the Federal Reserve System was that it would act to stabilize these interest rate fluctuations by actively intervening in the credit markets to borrow and lend. The nineteenth century had also witnessed a number of banking panics, in which depositors at commercial banks all tried to withdraw their money at once, resulting in a collapse of the banks involved. By acting in a timely fashion to provide reserves to the system in times of crisis, the Federal Reserve System would, it was thought, be able to prevent such events from reoccurring.

In some countries, monetary policy is decided by elected officials, and the central bank has little independence from the government. For example, in the United Kingdom, until very recently, the central bank had little independence.

In the United States, monetary policy is conducted by a committee, the **Federal Open Market Committee** (FOMC) of the Federal Reserve System. The Federal Reserve System itself is run by the **Board of Governors of the Federal Reserve System**. The Board of Governors has seven members, appointed by the president and confirmed by the Senate, and each governor serves a nonrenewable 14-year term. The chairman is chosen from the seven board members and serves a four-year term.

The FOMC meets eight times a year and is responsible for the day-to-day running of monetary policy. The voting members of the committee consist of the seven members of the Board of Governors, the president of the Federal Reserve Bank of New York, and presidents of four other Federal Reserve Banks. These four voting members rotate among the other 11 Federal Reserve Banks. Although only five of the Federal Reserve presidents get to vote at any one time, all of them are present at FOMC meetings and can, therefore, influence policy. The design of the American system, which is unusual in that most countries have a single central bank, was designed to spread the power to regulate the money supply both regionally and among diverse interest groups. Americans, in 1913, were deeply distrustful of the power of East Coast financial interests, and two earlier attempts to set up a central bank had already failed.[3]

How the Federal Reserve System Operates

The money supply in the United States consists of currency and coins in the hands of the public plus items such as checking accounts at commercial banks. As commercial banks go about their day-to-day operations of borrowing and lending, they expand and contract the volume of bank deposits. For example, when a commercial bank makes a loan to a customer, it simultaneously creates a deposit. The key to understanding the operation of a central bank is the fact that the creation of deposits by private banks is not unlimited. Private banks can only create deposits to the extent that they have reserves of cash and cur-

---

3.   The First Bank of the United States was disbanded in 1811, and the Second Bank of the United States was abolished in 1836.

FIGURE 9.1
The Twelve Federal Reserve Districts

The Federal Reserve System is divided into 12 districts, each with its own Federal Reserve Bank. These banks serve as lenders to commercial banks in their district and issue federal reserve notes. Most districts also have one to five Federal Reserve branch banks under the direction of the main federal reserve bank in that district. There are 25 branch banks nationwide.

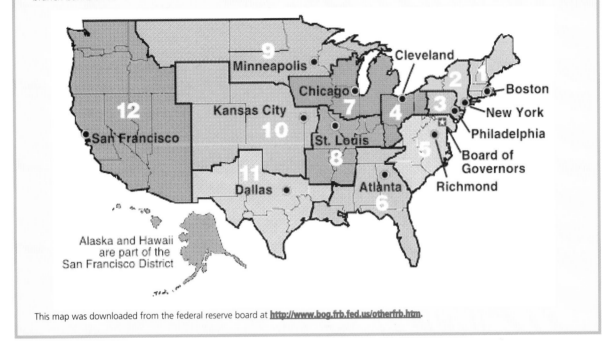

This map was downloaded from the federal reserve board at http://www.bog.frb.fed.us/otherfrb.htm.

rency. By expanding and contracting the availability of reserves, the FOMC can effectively control the money supply of the entire country.

One's definition of money can include only checking accounts or all kinds of deposits with financial institutions. In the United States the different definitions of money are ordered in terms of increasing broadness. The most commonly used definition, called M1, consists of cash and currency in the hands of the public, checkable deposits at commercial banks, and a few smaller items. Another definition, M2, includes savings deposits, and M3 is broader still. All of the items included in M1 are also in M2, and all of the items in M2 are in M3. All of these concepts of the money supply can be controlled, to a greater or lesser extent, by manipulating the reserves of the banking system.

There are three ways that the Federal Reserve System controls the reserves of the banking system. First, the FOMC mandates that commercial banks must keep on hand a minimum percentage of their deposits in the form of liquid reserves of cash and currency.[4] This minimum is called the **required reserve ratio**. By changing the required reserve ratio from time to time, the FOMC controls the ability of commercial banks to create money. Second, the Federal Reserve System acts as a **lender of last resort**. This means

4.   These reserves may also be in the form of accounts held by private banks within the Federal Reserve System.

WEBWATCH 9.1   **Check out the Board of Governors on the Internet**

The Federal Reserve Board building in Washington, D.C. The following information is from the Board of Governor's home page, available at http://www.bog.frb.fed.us/aboutfrs.htm.

The Federal Reserve System is the central bank of the United States. It was founded by Congress in 1913 to provide the nation with a safer, more flexible, and more stable monetary and financial system; over the years, its role in banking and the economy has expanded.

Today, the Federal Reserve's duties fall into four general areas:

1. Conducting the nation's monetary policy by influencing the money and credit conditions in the economy in pursuit of full employment and stable prices
2. Supervising and regulating banking institutions to ensure the safety and soundness of the nation's banking and financial system and to protect the credit rights of consumers (Federal Reserve Regulations)
3. Maintaining the stability of the financial system and containing systemic risk that may arise in financial markets
4. Providing certain financial services to the U.S. government, to the public, to financial institutions, and to foreign official institutions, including playing a major role in operating the nation's payments system.

---

that if a commercial bank is short of reserves the Federal Reserve will lend money to bail them out. The rate at which the Federal Reserve System lends to the commercial banks is called the **discount rate.** Since World War II, the Federal Reserve Board has actively discouraged banks from using this facility. The third way that the Federal Reserve System controls reserves is through a technique called **open market operations**. This has been the principal mode of operation of the system in recent years.

Open Market Operations

Whenever the Federal Reserve System buys an asset, that asset is turned into money. This ability of the FOMC to create or destroy money by selling or buying financial assets on the open market explains how the Federal Reserve System is able to expand or contract the nation's money supply.

The daily financial operations of the government are conducted by the Treasury Department, which collects tax revenues and finances government expenditures and transfer payments. In any period of time the Treasury may plan to make expenditures that are either greater or less than its revenues from taxation. An expenditure plan that exceeds revenues results in a **deficit**; an expenditure plan that is less than revenues results in a **surplus**. In order to finance a deficit or a surplus, the Treasury will sell or buy bonds in the capital markets. At any point in time there will be a given quantity of government debt in existence, B^T, which is owned in part by private agents, B^P, and in part by the central bank, B^F.

9.1
$$B^T \quad = \quad B^F \quad + \quad B^P$$

Total government debt		**Government debt held by the Federal Reserve System**		**Government debt held by the public**

When the Federal Reserve buys an asset, any asset, an equal quantity of money is created and placed in the hands of the public. The assets of the Federal Reserve System consist mainly of government debt, although there are also other items such as gold reserves and holdings of foreign currencies. The liabilities of the Federal Reserve System consist of Federal Reserve notes and the deposits of commercial banks. If we lay aside the complications that arise from the existence of the commercial banking system, we can envisage a world in which the *only* form of money is banknotes. In this simple world, the central bank would print notes and give them to the Treasury in return for its debt. The Treasury would use these banknotes to purchase commodities from the public.

9.2

$$B^F = M$$

Loans to the Treasury   **Monetary Base**

> The assets of the Federal Reserve System consist of loans made to the treasury. These loans consist of Federal Reserve holdings of government debt. In a world with no commercial banks, the liabilities of the Federal Reserve would equal the supply of money. In the real world, these liabilities are equal to the monetary base on which broader concepts of money are built.

Equation 9.2 illustrates the relationship between government debt and money in a world with no commercial banking system. In this world there would be a single concept of money, equal to the liabilities of the Federal Reserve System. These liabilities would consist solely of banknotes that would circulate among the members of the public.

In the real world the liabilities of the Federal Reserve System are called the **monetary base**. Firms and households hold a fraction of the Federal Reserve notes in circulation; the remainder of these notes make up the reserves of the commercial banking system. Private banks create new deposits by making loans to firms and households based on their holdings of reserves. To the extent that private agents can write checks on their deposits, the commercial banking system creates additional money. Because the ratio of deposits to the monetary base is, in practice, stable, the central bank can control the money supply (including commercial bank deposits) by manipulating the monetary base.

❹ THE MONETARY BASE AND THE MONEY MULTIPLIER

The liabilities of the Federal Reserve System create a base for the entire commercial banking system by providing reserves on which commercial banks build additional liquid assets.

We have already described a world in which the liabilities of the Federal Reserve System consisted entirely of banknotes. In the real world there is an additional important component of the Federal Reserve's liabilities: reserves of the commercial banks held as accounts by the Federal Reserve System. These accounts are assets to the commercial banking system and a liability to the Federal Reserve System in the same way that a private bank account is an asset to its owner and a liability to the bank at which it is held. We use the symbol R (for reserves) to refer to these deposits. It makes no difference whether these reserves exist as bookkeeping entries at Federal Reserve Banks or in the form of banknotes held in the vaults of the commercial banks. In either case, the commercial banks can access them at short notice to provide banknotes to their customers.

Who Holds the Monetary Base

Equation 9.3 asserts the equality between the assets and liabilities of the Federal Reserve System in a model that allows for commercial banks. We again assume that the Federal Reserve System holds only government bonds, B^F, in its asset portfolio. The liabilities side of the Federal Reserve balance sheet is, however, no longer identical to the money supply, because the money supply consists not only of circulating currency but also of checkable deposits with commercial banks. In this more realistic environment, the liabilities of the Federal Reserve System are referred to as the monetary base. Equation 9.4 divides the monetary base into two components: circulating currency, CU (Federal Reserve bank-notes), and the reserves of the commercial bank, R. These reserves are held partly as cash in vaults of commercial banks and partly as accounts at the Federal Reserve System. Equation 9.5 defines the money supply, M, as the sum of currency in the hands of the public, CU, and checkable deposits with the commercial bank, D.

9.3	$$MB = B^F$$	The liabilities of the Federal Reserve System are called the monetary base, MB. The assets consist of liabilities of the Treasury, B^F (that part of the government debt that is held by the Federal Reserve System).
9.4	$$MB = R + CU$$	The monetary base is held partly as the reserves, R, of the banking system and partly as currency, CU, in the hands of the public.
9.5	$$M = D + CU$$	The money supply, M, consists of the deposits of customers with commercial banks, D, plus currency in the hands of the public, CU.

The Money Supply and the Monetary Base

The money supply can be described as a multiple of the monetary base, called the **money supply multiplier**. The idea behind the money supply multiplier is that the ratio of currency to deposits and the ratio of reserves to deposits are relatively stable. If we view these ratios as constants, the money supply multiplier is a constant and the money supply is exogenously controlled by the Federal Reserve System.

To derive the money supply multiplier we begin with two definitions. Let cu be the ratio of currency to deposits, and let rd be the ratio of reserves to deposits.

$$cu = \frac{CU}{D} \qquad rd = \frac{R}{D}$$

It follows from the definition of the money supply (Equation 9.5) and the definition of the division of the monetary base (Equation 9.4) that the money supply is a fixed multiple of the monetary base.

TABLE 9.2
Deriving the Money Multiplier

9.6	$\dfrac{MB}{D} = \dfrac{R}{D} + \dfrac{CU}{D}$	*Step 1:* Divide the definition of the monetary base by deposits.
9.7	$\dfrac{M}{D} = \dfrac{D}{D} + \dfrac{CU}{D}$	*Step 2:* Divide the definition of the money supply by deposits.
9.8	$M = \left(\dfrac{1 + cu}{rd + cu}\right)MB$	*Step 3:* Take the ratio of step 2 to step 1 and substitute the definition of *cu* and *rd*.
9.9	$m = \left(\dfrac{1 + cu}{rd + cu}\right)$	*Step 4:* This leads to *m*, the definition of money supply multiplier.

Table 9.2 shows how the money supply is related to the monetary base. In step 1 we divide through the definition of the monetary base by *D*. In step 2 we divide the definition of the money supply by *D*. In step 3 we take the ratio of steps 1 and 2 and substitute the definitions of *rd* and *cu* for the ratios *R/D* and *CU/D*. The final equation defines the money supply—currency held by the public plus checkable deposits at commercial banks—as a multiple *m* of the monetary base. Because the Federal Reserve System can control the monetary base through open market operations, it can also control the entire money supply, as long as the money multiplier remains stable.[5]

CONCLUSION

Commercial banks developed from the practice of depositing gold and silver coins with goldsmiths for safekeeping. Since their customers did not typically demand access to their coins at the same time, the goldsmiths could lend them at interest to other traders, creating deposits that themselves began to circulate in the form of promissory notes. Our modern banking system mirrors this medieval system, with the difference that coins and paper money have replaced gold as the ultimate means of payment.

The Federal Reserve System controls the money supply by setting the discount rate and choosing reserve requirements; but its major tool is open market operations, the purchase and sale of government bonds on the open market. Open market operations result in changes in outstanding liabilities of the Federal Reserve. The Federal Reserve System's own liabilities, called the monetary base, are partly held by commercial banks and partly

---

5.   In practice, the currency deposit ratio, *cu*, and the reserve deposit ratio, *rd*, are not constants—they vary with the rate of interest. But because *cu* and *rd* vary in a predictable way, the Federal Reserve is still able to control the money supply.

by the public as circulating banknotes. The money supply consists of circulating currency in the hands of the public plus the deposits of households and firms with commercial banks. Although the Federal Reserve Board cannot control the money supply directly, it *can* control the monetary base and, because the money supply is a multiple of the monetary base, the Federal Reserve can indirectly control M1.

KEY TERMS

Banknote

Board of Governors of the
    Federal Reserve System

Central bank

Deficit

Discount rate

Federal Open Market Committee (FOMC)

Federal Reserve Bank

Federal Reserve System

Fiat money

Flexible exchange rates

Gold standard

Lender of last resort

Monetary base

Money supply multiplier

Open market operations

Required reserve ratio

Reserves

Surplus

PROBLEMS FOR REVIEW

1. Suppose that the Federal Reserve Board sells Japanese yen on the open market. Explain how this transaction would affect the position of the LM curve.

2. Suppose that the required reserve ratio is equal to 10% and commercial banks hold only required reserves. If the currency deposit ratio is fixed at 20%, what is the size of the money multiplier?

3. Consider the balance sheet of a financial institution that issues a credit card with a limit of $5,000. Analyze the asset and liability side of the institution's balance sheet as the household uses its credit card to make a $4,000 purchase. Is the credit card money? Is the unused portion of the credit limit ($1,000) money?

4. What is meant by "the gold standard"? What are the potential advantages of this system? What are the potential disadvantages?

5. What is the FOMC? Who votes on the FOMC? How often does it meet?

6. Suppose that the money supply multiplier, $m(i)$, is a function that increases when the interest rate increases. Suppose that the Federal Reserve System controls the monetary base. (*Hint*: In this specification the money supply is endogenous.)

   a. How would this modification affect the slope of the LM curve? Would it become flatter or steeper? Why?

   b. In the real world the money supply is positively correlated with the interest rate. Can you explain why this is so?

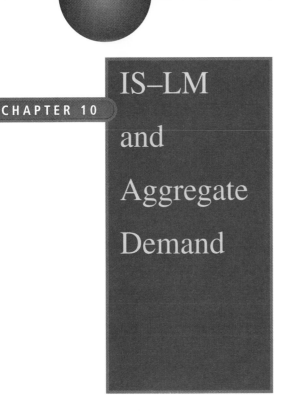

CHAPTER 10

IS–LM and Aggregate Demand

❶ INTRODUCTION

In Keynesian theory, aggregate demand depends not only on the money supply, as in classical theory, but also on fiscal policy and on the expectations of households and firms. The Keynesian theory of aggregate demand is constructed on two assumptions. First, the quantity of savings supplied equals the quantity of investment demanded; in other words, the capital market is in equilibrium. Second, the quantity of money demanded is equal to the quantity of money supplied; in other words, the existing stock of money in circulation is willingly held. This sounds a lot like the classical analysis that we studied in Chapter 6 (equilibrium in the capital market) and Chapter 5 (equality of the demand and supply of money). What is different, in the Keynesian theory, is that we have equilibrium in these two markets *at the same time*.

The classical model is relatively simple to explain because classical economists made assumptions that let us put the pieces of the economy together in a sequence of independent steps. The most important of their assumptions were that income is always determined with full employment in the labor market and that the quantity of money demanded is independent of the interest rate. But the real world is more complicated than the classical model. Employment may fluctuate around the natural rate, and the interest rate is not determined independently of the equilibrium that prevails in the labor market. Once we drop the classical assumptions, we need to go back and reformulate the theory of aggregate demand.

❷ EQUILIBRIUM IN THE CAPITAL MARKET

According to the classical theory of the capital market, the real interest rate is determined at a point where the demand for investment by firms is equal to the supply of savings by households. The classical economists were able to determine savings without mentioning income because, in the classical model, there was only one relevant level of income, full employment income, the level that is determined when the quantity of labor demanded is equal to the quantity supplied. But in the Keynesian view, there is no unique level of employment and hence no unique level of income. We take account of the fact that income may vary over the business cycle by constructing a more complete theory of the capital market. In our revised theory there is a different equilibrium interest rate for every level of income. We can derive a graph in which we plot pairs of values of the interest rate and the level of income for which the capital market is in equilibrium. This curve is called the IS curve.

The Real Interest Rate and the Nominal Interest Rate

In Chapter 6 we distinguished between the *real interest rate* and the *nominal interest rate*. The real rate is the nominal rate adjusted for changes in the purchasing power of money, and it is the real rate that influences saving and investment decisions. But although equilibrium in the capital market determines the real interest rate, it is the nominal interest rate that we observe directly. A given nominal rate will translate into a lower real rate in an economy in which savers and investors expect high inflation than in an economy where they expect low inflation.

We have already met one definition of the real interest rate. Now we introduce a second. We need two definitions of the real interest rate because households and firms do not know what the inflation rate will be when they enter into borrowing and lending agreements. We distinguish the real interest rate that agents expect to occur from the one that actually occurs by defining them as **ex ante** and **ex post** real interest rates, respectively.

Recall that, in Chapter 6, we defined the real interest rate as

10.1 $r = i - \Delta P/P$

> This equation defines the **ex post** real interest rate.

where i is the nominal interest rate and $\Delta P/P$ is the inflation rate that will hold over the life of a loan. This version of the real rate, found by subtracting the actual inflation rate from the nominal interest rate, is called the ex post real interest rate. *Ex post* means "after the fact" to represent the fact that the ex post real interest rate will not be known until the loan is repaid.

Because the inflation rate is unknown at the time that borrowers and lenders enter into commitments in the capital markets, households and firms must form an expectation of the future inflation rate. This observation leads to a second definition of the real interest rate, called the *ex ante* real rate, that is defined as the difference between the nominal interest rate and the expected inflation rate.

BOX 10.1
How to Buy a House: A Case Study of Interest Rates and Inflation

Expected inflation is reflected in interest rates because if lenders expect inflation they will demand a higher nominal interest rate to compensate them for the loss in purchasing power of the money with which the loan is repaid. It is possible to gauge how much inflation is expected by market participants over different horizons by looking at the differences between long-term interest rates and short-term interest rates.

One decision that you may face at some point in your life is how to finance the purchase of a house. Typically you will have two options: to borrow money over a long-term horizon, or to borrow money over a series of short-time horizons. The following graph shows how much you would have paid for these loans each month, beginning in January of 1980.

Short-term mortgages are typically indexed at 1 or 2 percentage points above a short-term rate, such as the rate paid on three-month Treasury Bills by the government. The three-month T-bill rate is graphed in this figure, along with the rate on thirty-year loans. If you had taken out a thirty-year loan in January of 1993, you would have locked in a rate of 4% for the life of the loan.

In September of 1981 the interest rate was very high. A family that bought a house faced two options. They could take out a thirty-year fixed-rate mortgage at 18%, or they could take out a series of one-year mortgages. Over a five-year horizon the sequence of short mortgages would have resulted in substantial savings, because interest rates fell substantially from 1981 through 1986.

In February of 1986 the situation was very different. Thirty-year mortgages were available at 6%, but over a five-year horizon the short rate climbed as high as 9%. On a $100,000 mortgage, a three-percentage-point interest rate rise would result in increased monthly payments of $250, a substantial increase for a young family on a tight budget. A fixed-rate mortgage was a better bet.

Unfortunately there is no hard-and-fast rule as to when it is a good idea to borrow long term and when it is better to borrow short term. It all depends on whether you are better at guessing what future inflation will be than other players in the market.

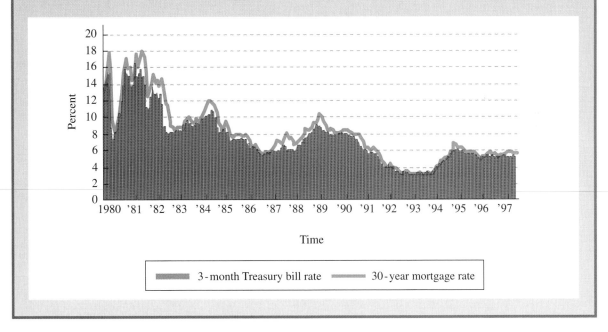

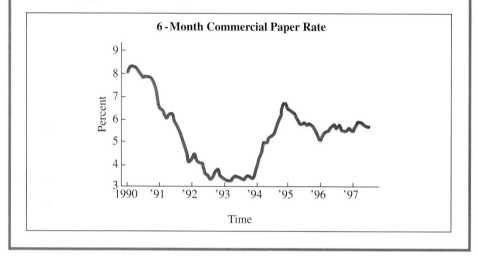

10.2 $r^E = i - \Delta P^E/P$

> This equation defines the ex ante real interest rate, r^E. The superscript E on the terms r^E and $\Delta P^E/P$ stand for expected.

The ex ante real interest rate would be the same as the ex post real interest rate if households and firms could perfectly predict the future price level, but this is not usually the case. In times of rapid, unexpected inflation, the ex post real interest rate and the ex ante real interest rate may be very different from each other. For example, during the period immediately following the oil price shocks in 1973 and 1979, inflation rose very rapidly in a way that no one had expected, and many individuals who entered into borrowing and lending contracts were surprised. Lenders were hurt because the value of the interest that they received was lower (in terms of the commodities that it could purchase) than they had anticipated when they lent their money. On the other hand, many borrowers were very pleasantly surprised. An example would be a family that borrowed money to buy a home by taking out a thirty-year fixed-rate mortgage. In 1970 the mortgage interest rate was less than 8%, but by 1980 it had climbed close to 15%. Families with fixed-rate mortgages found that inflation increased the value of their homes whereas the cost of their debts was fixed in nominal terms, and many borrowers became quite rich in a relatively short period of time.

The IS Curve

In the classical theory, income is determined by the assumption that there is no unemployment. Given this assumption, the determination of the real interest rate is relatively straightforward: once they had determined full employment output, the classical economists were able to represent saving by an upward-sloping supply schedule. The equilibrium real interest rate was thus the rate at which the quantity of saving supplied equaled the quantity of investment demanded.

In the Keynesian model there is no unique level of income. Instead, income may be at the natural rate, above the natural rate, or below the natural rate. The fact that income may fluctuate over the business cycle affects the interest rate, because households are willing to save more if they are rich than if they are poor. When income is high (unemployment is low), there will be a relatively high supply of savings in the capital market. Firms will not need to offer a high rate of interest to attract lenders, so a high value of income will be associated with a low equilibrium interest rate. If, instead, income is low (unemployment is high), investors will compete with each other to borrow a small pool of savings, and they will bid up the rate of interest. A low value of income will be associated with a high equilibrium interest rate. In the Keynesian model we summarize this idea by deriving a schedule, the **IS curve**, that plots the nominal interest rate on the vertical axis and the level of income on the horizontal axis. At every point on the IS curve the capital market is in equilibrium.[1]

Investment, Saving, and the Nominal Interest Rate

The IS curve plots values of the nominal interest rate against income for which the capital market is in equilibrium. But the saving and investment schedules that we derived in Chapter 6 depend on the real interest rate, not the nominal rate. To derive the IS curve we need to recognize that saving may depend not only on the real interest rate, but also on income. Second, we must recognize that the real interest rate is equal to the nominal rate minus expected inflation. The saving function, accounting for these amendments, can be written as $S(Y, i - \Delta P^E/P)$, and the investment function can be written as $I(i - \Delta P^E/P)$, where the terms Y and $i - \Delta P^E/P$ remind us that saving and investment depend on these two variables. We use the ex ante real interest rate, not the ex post rate, because at the time that saving and investment decisions are made, the future price level is unknown.

To show how the nominal interest rate is determined, we can develop a diagram, shown in Figure 10.1, that plots the nominal interest rate against the quantity of investment demanded and the quantity of savings supplied. We have drawn two saving schedules and two investment schedules. Consider first the schedule labeled S_1, which plots the quantity of savings supplied on the horizontal axis, against the nominal interest rate on the vertical axis, given that the household earns income Y^* and expects inflation of $\Delta P^E/P_1$. Now consider the investment schedule labeled I_1. This schedule plots the quantity of investment demanded on the horizontal axis, against the nominal interest rate on the vertical axis, given that the firm expects that the inflation rate equals $\Delta P^E/P_1$. For this common level of expected inflation, the nominal interest rate that equates the quantity of savings supplied to the quantity of investment demanded equals i_1^*.

1.   The term *IS curve* comes from the fact that, in a closed economy model with no government, at every point on this curve investment equals saving.

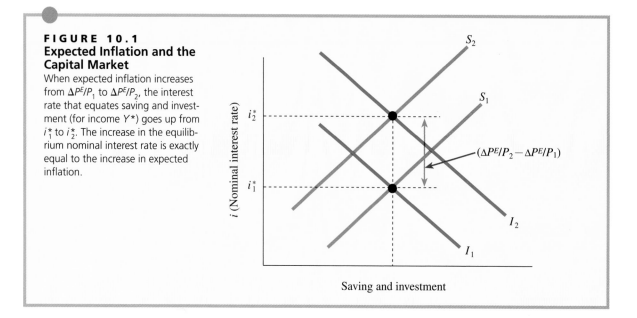

FIGURE 10.1
Expected Inflation and the Capital Market
When expected inflation increases from $\Delta P^E/P_1$ to $\Delta P^E/P_2$, the interest rate that equates saving and investment (for income Y^*) goes up from i_1^* to i_2^*. The increase in the equilibrium nominal interest rate is exactly equal to the increase in expected inflation.

What happens in the capital market when both firms and workers revise their expectation of inflation from $\Delta P^E/P_1$ to some higher level $\Delta P^E/P_2$?[2] In this case, we draw a new saving schedule, S_2, and a new investment schedule I_2. Notice that the saving schedule S_2 is shifted up from the saving schedule S_1 by exactly the increase in expected inflation $(\Delta P^E/P_2 - \Delta P^E/P_1)$. Similarly, the new investment schedule translates up from the old one by the same distance. This happens because investment and saving depend on the real interest rate, and when the nominal interest rate goes up by the amount of the additional expected inflation, households supply the same savings and demand the same investment as before the increase. Because i_1^* was an equilibrium before inflation increased, $i_2^* = i_1^* + (\Delta P^E/P_2 - \Delta P^E/P_1)$ must be an equilibrium afterwards.

❸ DERIVING THE IS CURVE

We can use the capital market diagram to illustrate how the interest rate that clears the capital market is different for different values of income. Our ultimate goal is to show that there is a unique interest rate and a unique level of income for which the capital market is in equilibrium *and* the quantity of money in the economy is willingly held.

---

2.   We could also analyze what happens when firms and households have *different* expectations of inflation. There is no good reason to suppose that expectations between firms and households should be asymmetrical, so we typically assume that expectations are held in common by all participants in the market.

FIGURE 10.2
Investment, Saving, and the IS Curve
Panel A represents equilibrium in the capital market for three levels of income. When income is equal to Y_1, households are willing to save an amount represented by S_1. Similarly, when income is Y^* or when it equals Y_2 the corresponding saving schedules are S^* and S_2. Panel B shows the IS curve. At every point on this curve the quantity of investment demanded equals the quantity of savings supplied. For higher levels of income the equilibrium interest rate is lower because households are willing to save more at every value of the interest rate. At every point on the IS curve investment equals savings.

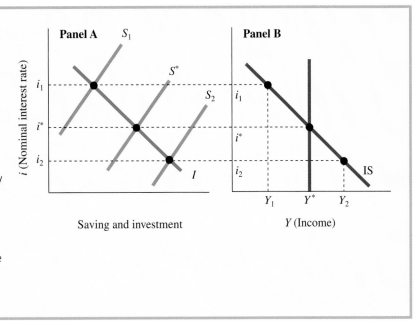

The IS Curve in a Graph

In Figure 10.2 we derive a graph of the IS curve. On panel A we plot the nominal interest rate on the vertical axis; on the horizontal axis we plot the quantity of savings supplied and the quantity of investment demanded. On panel B we plot the nominal interest rate on the vertical axis and the level of income on the horizontal axis. Both schedules are drawn for a given expectation of inflation.

Unlike the classical model, the Keynesian model admits the possibility that saving may depend, not just on the interest rate, but also on income. When households have high income they save more than when they have low income. Beginning with panel B, suppose that income is at the natural rate, Y^*. To represent the way that saving depends on income we must draw a different saving schedule for each value of income. Given the saving schedule S^*, we see from panel A that, when income equals Y^*, i^* is the interest rate that equates the supply of savings to the demand for investment. We can translate this interest rate across to panel B and plot a point on the IS curve at $\{Y^*, i^*\}$.

What about different values of income? Suppose instead of $Y = Y^*$, we ask what interest rate will clear the capital market when Y is lower or higher than Y^*. In Figure 10.2 we have derived two other points on the IS curve, one when output is at Y_1, a level that is lower than the natural rate Y^*, and one at Y_2, a level that is higher than the natural rate Y^*. When $Y = Y_1$, the quantity of savings supplied is lower for every interest rate than when $Y = Y^*$. We represent this by the saving schedule S_1, a saving schedule that is everywhere to the left of the schedule S^*. At Y_1, households have lower income than Y^* and are less willing to supply savings to the capital market. Because the investment schedule slopes down, the interest rate i_1 that equates saving and investment when $Y = Y_1$ is *higher* than i^*. We can translate this equilibrium interest rate across to panel B to plot a second point on the IS curve at $\{Y_1, i_1\}$. Finally, we may repeat the argument when income is equal to Y_2, a level that is higher than the natural rate Y^*. A similar argument shows that in this case the equilibrium interest rate i_2 is *lower* than i^*, and we may translate this rate across to panel B to find a third point on the IS curve at $\{Y_2, i_2\}$.

The vertical line on panel B represents the level of income that corresponds to the natural rate of unemployment. We call this the **natural rate of output.** In the classical model, the economy is always at full employment, but in the Keynesian approach output may be above, at, or below Y^*. What are the factors that would cause the economy to operate at a point other than Y^*? The demand and supply of money can be combined with the analysis of the IS curve to determine a level of demand other than Y^*. But before we study the interaction of money with the real economy, we need to explore the factors that are responsible for shifts in the IS curve. This can help us understand how government policies that change taxes and government expenditure interact with the private economy to influence employment and GDP.

Variables that Shift the IS Curve

Various exogenous variables influence the economy through their effect on the IS curve. In studying a closed economy,[3] we can use the IS curve to show the effect of fiscal policy on the capital market.

Suppose, for example, that the government plans to run a budget deficit. Government deficits influence the equilibrium interest rate because the government competes with investors for private savings. Deficits also influence the capital market equilibrium by shifting the saving schedule—households have less **disposable income** when the government takes away part of private income in taxes net of transfers. We may take into account the impact of the government on the capital market by amending the capital market equilibrium equation in the following way:

10.3
$$I(i - \Delta P^E/P) + D = S(Y, T - TR, i - \Delta P^E/P)$$

The left side of Equation 10.3 is the total demand for borrowing by firms and government. This consists of the demand for investment, $I(i - \Delta P^E/P)$, which firms finance by borrowing in the capital market, plus D, the government budget deficit, which the government must finance by borrowing in the capital market. The notation $S(Y, T - TR, i - \Delta P^E/P)$ indicates that saving depends on income Y, net taxes $(T - TR)$, and the expected real interest rate, $i - \Delta P^E/P$.

Government Purchases and the IS Curve

What happens if the deficit goes up? This depends in part on whether government purchases of goods and services goes up or net taxes go down. Let's take the case in which

---

3. In Chapter 11 we show that in an open economy this analysis must be amended to allow for the fact that countries may borrow from abroad.

FIGURE 10.3
Government Purchases and the IS Curve

The green arrows indicate the shifts in the $I + D$ curve and in the IS curve that occur when government purchases increase from G_1 to G_2.

Panel A illustrates equilibrium in the capital market for two values of the government budget deficit, $D(G_1)$ and $D(G_2)$. The supply of savings is drawn for the case in which $Y = Y^*$. By assumption, $D(G_2)$ is bigger than $D(G_1)$. The deficit increases in this picture because government spending has increased from G_1 to G_2. As the government deficit increases, the government competes with firms for private savings and drives up the interest rate from i_1^* to i_2^*. This is illustrated as a shift in the curve $I + D$.

Panel B shows that the effect of this increase in government expenditure is to shift the IS curve to the right.

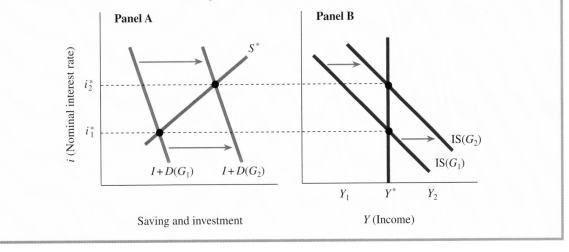

government purchases go up and assume that government goods and services cannot easily be substituted for private consumption goods. This is often, although not always, a reasonable assumption. Some government purchases *are* good substitutes for private purchases, such as education. If the government increases expenditure on education, private saving is likely to increase because some households will choose to send their children to public schools instead of to private schools, and they will save part of the income they would have spent on tuition. But for now we assume that the private saving schedule is unaffected by an increase in government purchases. The effect of an increase in government purchases is illustrated on Figure 10.3.

On panel A of Figure 10.3 we have drawn the demand for investment plus the demand for funds by the government for two different values of government purchases. This combined demand for funds in the capital market is the locus $I + D$, which is drawn under the assumption that government purchases equal G_1 and again when government purchases are at the higher level G_2. The notation $D(G_1)$ refers to the government budget deficit when government expenditure equals G_1. Similarly, $D(G_2)$ refers to the government budget deficit when government expenditure equals G_2. To find what happens to the IS curve at different values of government purchases, we must first pick a level of income so that we may draw the appropriate saving schedule. Let's choose the natural rate Y^*. Because we are not explicitly considering changes in taxes and transfers in this diagram, we have suppressed the fact that saving depends on net taxes. We have written the savings schedule, when $Y = Y^*$, as S^*.

When income is equal to Y^*, what nominal interest rate is consistent with equilibrium in the capital market? If government purchases equal G_1, the equilibrium interest rate when $Y = Y^*$ is i_1^* because this is the interest rate for which the quantity of funds demanded by government plus the quantity of investment demanded by firms equal the quantity of savings supplied by households. But if government purchases increase to G_2, the equilibrium interest rate when $Y = Y^*$ increases to i_2^*. This second interest rate is higher than the first because the government competes with firms for the funds of private savers and drives up the interest rate in a capital market equilibrium.

Taxes, Transfers, and the IS Curve

To analyze the effect of a change in net taxes on the IS curve, assume that taxes are levied as a lump sum on households and firms, ignoring the fact that tax revenues rise when income increases. This is the simplest case to analyze because it allows us to ignore the effects of changes in tax rates on labor supply.[4] Assume as well that net taxes affect saving only through their effect on disposable income. Figure 10.4 illustrates the way that the IS curve shifts when net taxes go up, under these two assumptions.

Figure 10.4 plots the same two graphs that we used to analyze how government purchases shift the IS curve. For the case of a change in net taxes we need to consider two effects of an increase in taxes on the capital market. First, a direct effect follows from the fact that when net taxes increase, the government demands less funds in the capital market. This direct effect shifts the $I + D$ schedule to the left. Second, an indirect effect follows from the fact that when net taxes increase, households have less disposable income and their supply of savings fall. Let's consider these two effects and how they influence capital market equilibrium.

Beginning with panel B, we ask the question, what is the interest rate for which the capital market is in equilibrium when income is at the natural rate Y^*? We analyze the direct effect of a tax increase first. From panel A we see that when taxes are equal to T_1, the demand for funds by firms and government is given by the curve $I + D(T_1)$, where the notation $D(T_1)$ means the deficit when tax revenues equal T_1. When taxes increase to T_2 the government borrows less money in the capital market, and this reduced demand is represented by a leftward shift of the $I + D$ schedule from $I + D(T_1)$ to $I + D(T_2)$. $D(T_2)$ is smaller than $D(T_1)$ for every value of the interest rate because the government borrows less when tax revenues are higher.

Now consider the indirect effect of an increase in net taxes. Consider first the supply of savings schedule when taxes equal T_1 as S_1^*. Now let taxes increase to T_2. The effect of this increase is to shift the supply of savings schedule to the left, back to S_2^*, because households have less disposable income available for saving. Which of these effects is greater, the direct effect or the indirect effect? Because households typically save only a fraction of their disposable income, it seems reasonable to assume that the direct effect will dominate the indirect effect, and the $I + D$ schedule will shift to the left by more than

---

4.   We leave the more realistic case of proportional income taxes for you to work out as an exercise.

FIGURE 10.4
Taxes and the IS Curve

The green arrows indicate the shifts in the $I + D$ curve and in the IS curve that occur when tax revenues increase from T_1 to T_2.

Panel A illustrates equilibrium in the capital market for two values of the government budget deficit, $D(T_1)$ and $D(T_2)$. By assumption, $D(T_2)$ is smaller than $D(T_1)$. The deficit falls in this picture because tax revenues have increased from T_1 to T_2. As the government deficit falls, competition with firms for private savings decreases, which tends to lower the real interest rate. The effect on the demand for funds by borrowers (both private firms and government) is illustrated as a leftward shift in the curve $I + D$. Another offsetting effect as taxes increase is that households are less willing to supply savings to the capital market because they have less disposable income. This effect is illustrated as a leftward shift of the supply of saving schedule from S_1^* to S_2^*. The net effect is to lower the equilibrium interest rate from i_1^* to i_2^*, but not by as much as when the deficit fell because of a drop in government purchases.

The supply of saving schedule in panel A is drawn for the case in which $Y = Y^*$. When tax revenues increase, the equilibrium interest rate (for the level of income Y^*) goes down from i_1^* to i_2^*. Panel B shows that the effect of this increase in tax revenues is to shift the IS curve to the left.

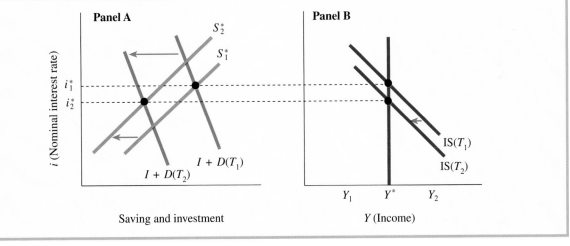

the savings schedule.[5] Because the $I + D$ schedule shifts by more than the savings schedule, the net effect of increase in net taxes is to shift the IS curve to the left. The leftward shift of the IS curve when taxes increase is smaller than the rightward shift when government purchases increase, because, in the case of taxes, the saving curve shifts to partially offset the change in the demand for funds by government.

Shifts in the Investment Schedule and the IS Curve

A third variable that can shift the IS curve has nothing to do with government. Shifts may occur as a result of private behavior. In Chapter 6 we identified two factors that might shift the investment schedule: a change in productivity due to a new invention or a change in beliefs about future rates of return. Both of these events cause shifts in the IS curve.

Figure 10.5 illustrates the effect of a shift in the investment schedule on the IS curve. The investment schedule can shift to the right for one of two reasons. It might be that firms

5.   Robert Barro has argued that the shift in the saving schedule in this case equals the shift in the $I + D$ schedule and the IS curve does not move at all. Barro's argument, called Ricardian Equivalence, is discussed in Chapter 12.

FIGURE 10.5
Shifts in Investment and the IS Curve
The green arrows indicate the shifts in the *I* + *D* curve and in the IS curve that occur when investors forecast that productivity will increase or that there will be higher inflation in the future.

Panel A illustrates equilibrium in the capital market for two values of the investment schedule, I_1 and I_2. The supply of savings is drawn for the case in which $Y = Y^*$. By assumption, I_2 is bigger than I_1. As investment increases, firms compete harder for private savings and drive up the interest rate from i_1^* to i_2^*. This is illustrated as a shift in the curve *I* + *D*.

Panel B shows that the effect of this investment increase is to shift the IS curve to the right.

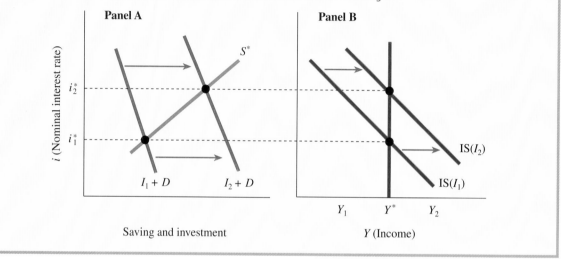

expect a new technology will increase profitability, but in order to exploit this technology they must build new kinds of capital equipment. The growth of the computer industry in the 1980s or biotechnology in the 1990s are examples of investment demand shocks that shift the IS curve to the right in this way. The IS curve might also shift if firms and households expect increased inflation and the current nominal rate seems low in terms of the commodities that will be produced in the future. An increase in expected inflation shifts the IS curve to the right because it lowers the expected real cost of borrowing.

❹ IS–LM AND THE KEYNESIAN THEORY OF AGGREGATE DEMAND

We are now ready to put together the two parts of the Keynesian theory of aggregate demand: the IS and LM curves. At every point on the LM curve the quantity of money demanded equals the quantity supplied. At every point on the IS curve the capital market is in equilibrium. We can show that the aggregate demand for commodities is determined at the point where IS and LM intersect.

Constructing the IS–LM model is similar to the derivation of the aggregate demand curve in the classical model. In order to draw the LM curve in Chapter 8, we assumed that the price level is fixed at the level *P*. To construct the IS–LM model, we make the same assumption. When we put together the IS and LM curves we can describe the simultaneous determination of the nominal interest rate and income in an **IS–LM equilibrium**. We can also go beyond the IS–LM analysis by showing that there is a different IS–LM equilibrium for every value of the price level. The relationship between the price level and the equilibrium value of income in the IS–LM model is called the **Keynesian aggregate demand curve.**

Rational Expectations: Which Variables Are Exogenous?

Before we explain the determination of aggregate demand in the Keynesian model, let's be precise about what, in our analysis, is fixed and what is not. Recall that variables held fixed are called exogenous and those determined inside the model are called endogenous. This is an important distinction in modern policy analysis because of a concept called **rational expectations,** the idea that households' and firms' beliefs of future prices and the future value of their incomes must be modeled endogenously.

In this chapter we do not model expectations endogenously. Instead, the predictions of the model must be taken as conditional, based on the assumption that expectations will not be altered in response to specific policy changes. For example, we assume that an increase in the money supply is not expected to alter the future course of inflation. In Chapter 16 we modify this assumption.

For now we assume that the Federal Reserve Board fixes the supply of money, M. For every possible value of M there will be a different LM curve. We can show how changes in monetary policy alter the position of the LM curve and demonstrate that changes in M can be used to influence the interest rate, income, and employment. We also assume that the government fixes government purchases, G, transfer payments, TR, and taxes, T. We can show that there is a different IS curve for every value of T, TR, or G and use our knowledge of how fiscal policy shifts the IS curve to predict the effects of different policies on the interest rate, income, and employment.

We deal with the price level in two steps. When we build the IS–LM model we take P as fixed; later, when we combine aggregate demand and supply, we show how P is determined in the complete model. The effect of expectations on equilibrium is much more controversial. Modern macroeconomists argue that this assumption is, at best, a first approximation and, at worst, can invalidate much of the analysis of the Keynesian theory. To fully describe an IS–LM equilibrium in a rational expectations model, we need to describe policies as rules that enable households to forecast their future impact. We treat this idea in Chapter 16, after we deal more carefully with dynamic economics.

IS–LM Equilibrium

In Figure 10.6 we combine the LM curve from Chapter 8 with the IS curve that we developed in this chapter. The notation LM(M/P) reminds us that that there is a different LM curve for every value of the real money supply. Similarly, the notation IS($G,T - TR, \Delta P^E/P$) reminds us that there is a different IS curve for every value of government purchases, G, net taxes, $T - TR$, and expected inflation. Recall that the LM curve is special because it denotes values of the interest rate and income for which the quantity of money is willingly held. Alternatively, we can say that the quantity of money demanded is equal to the quantity supplied. Similarly, the IS curve is special because it represents values of the interest rate and income for which the capital market is in equilibrium.

FIGURE 10.6
The Complete IS–LM Model
The equilibrium of the IS–LM model is determined at the point of intersection of the IS and LM curves. At every point on the LM curve the quantity of money demanded is equal to the quantity of money supplied. At every point on the IS curve the capital market is in equilibrium. Only at the point of intersection of IS and LM are both markets in equilibrium simultaneously. Notice that IS–LM equilibrium does not necessarily occur at the natural rate of output, Y^*.

The red arrows indicate possible adjustment paths back to equilibrium.

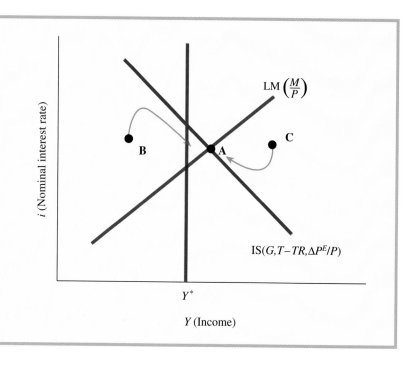

The equilibrium of the IS–LM model occurs at point **A,** in Figure 10.6, where the IS and LM curves intersect. This is the only point at which the capital market is in equilibrium and, simultaneously, the quantity of money in circulation is willingly held. Could the economy be at a point *other* than point **A**? There are two forces pulling the economy back to the point of intersection of IS and LM curves. First, suppose that the economy is at a point below the IS curve: Pick a point on the IS curve and lower the interest rate holding income fixed. As the interest rate falls, investment increases and saving falls; hence points below the IS curve are points for which investment exceeds saving. Investors bid up the interest rate in an attempt to secure funds and the interest rate rises. A similar argument establishes that points above the IS curve are points for which saving exceeds investment. Investors can offer lower interest rates because there is an excess of savers in the market.

What about points that are off the LM curve? At any point to the left of the LM curve, income is lower but with the same interest rate. Because income is lower, the quantity of money demanded must also be lower. It follows that points to the left of the LM curve are points for which there is an excess supply of money. Households are holding more money than they need to finance their daily transactions and will try to spend this money by demanding more commodities; thus the aggregate demand for goods and services will increase. As demand increases, firms hire more workers, and employment and income rise until the economy is back on the LM curve. A similar argument establishes that if the economy is to the right of the LM curve, there is an excess demand for money. Households buy fewer commodities and aggregate demand falls. As demand falls, firms lay off workers, and employment and income fall until the economy is back on the LM curve. Point **A** is special because of the forces that move the economy toward it. Point **A** is the IS–LM equilibrium.

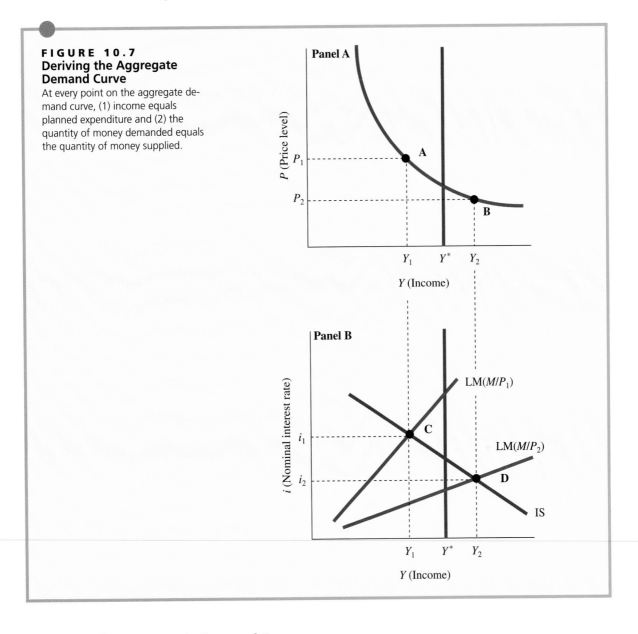

FIGURE 10.7
Deriving the Aggregate Demand Curve
At every point on the aggregate demand curve, (1) income equals planned expenditure and (2) the quantity of money demanded equals the quantity of money supplied.

The Keynesian Aggregate Demand Curve

We are now ready to put together the complete Keynesian theory of aggregate demand by dropping the assumption that the price level is fixed and asking how equilibrium income in the IS–LM model differs for different values of the price level. We derive a graph, called the aggregate demand curve, that links the price level to the aggregate quantity of commodities demanded.

Figure 10.7 derives the aggregate demand curve on a diagram with two panels. On panel A we plot the price level against GDP. Notice that on this panel we have drawn a downward-sloping curve. This curve resembles the aggregate demand curve from the classical model that we studied in Chapter 5. It is different from that model because, in the Keynesian theory, the position of the aggregate demand curve depends not only on the money supply, but also on fiscal policy and on expectations. We can show how this curve is derived by relating it to the IS–LM model, plotted on panel B of the same figure.

Begin with panel A and choose a price level, P_1. We want to know, at the price level P_1, what level of aggregate demand for goods and services is consistent with IS–LM equilibrium, so we turn to the IS–LM diagram. We must know the price level to construct this diagram, because the real value of the supply of money depends on it. Given the price level P_1, the LM curve is LM(M/P_1) and the IS–LM equilibrium is at **C** on panel B. Tracing equilibrium income up to panel A gives a point, **A**, on the Keynesian aggregate demand curve. At point **A** it is simultaneously true that the quantity of money demanded equals the quantity supplied and the capital market is in equilibrium.

To find a second point on the AD curve, let the price level drop from P_1 to P_2. As the price level falls, the LM curve shifts to LM(M/P_2) and the equilibrium level of income increases to Y_2. The new IS–LM equilibrium is at **D**. Tracing equilibrium income Y_2 back to panel A, we can plot a second point, **B**, on the aggregate demand curve. Because a fall in the price level shifts the LM curve to the right, the aggregate demand curve slopes down.

Fiscal Policy and the Aggregate Demand Curve

The Keynesian theory of aggregate demand provides a more complete account, than the classical theory, of the causes of business fluctuations. This idea can be put into practice by studying the changes in the aggregate demand curve that occur in response to changes in monetary and fiscal policy. We begin by studying the way that changes in fiscal policy alter aggregate demand.

Suppose that government purchases of goods and services increase from some level G_1 to a higher level, G_2. Figure 10.8 graphs the effect of this increase. On panel B of the figure, we have drawn two IS curves and one LM curve. The LM curve is drawn under the assumption that the price level is equal to P_1. We can show that the IS–LM equilibrium occurs at a higher level of income when government purchases equal G_2 than when they equal G_1 by drawing two IS curves, one for each level of government expenditure. The effect of increasing government expenditure, at a given price level, is to increase equilibrium income from point **C** to point **D**. By tracing the old and new equilibrium levels of income to panel A, we can plot points on two aggregate demand curves, both at the same price level, P_1. Point **A** is associated with the level of spending G_1 and point **B** with G_2.

Monetary Policy and the Aggregate Demand Curve

Figure 10.9 analyzes monetary expansion. Panel B of this figure depicts one IS curve and two LM curves. Both LM curves are drawn on the assumption that the price level is equal to P_1; for one LM curve the nominal money supply is M_1 and for the other it is at the higher level, M_2.

Suppose first that the money supply is equal to M_1. When the price level equals P_1, at what level of income will the capital markets be in equilibrium and, simultaneously, the quantity of money demanded equal the quantity supplied? To answer this question we must draw the LM curve on panel B that corresponds to the nominal money supply M_1 and

FIGURE 10.8
How Fiscal Policy Shifts the Aggregate Demand Curve
As G increases from G_1 to G_2, the IS curve shifts out from $IS(G_1)$ to $IS(G_2)$. When the price is P_1, the LM curve is $LM(M/P_1)$. Given this price level, the points **C** and **D** represent equilibrium points of the IS–LM model.

When $P = P_1$, **A** is a point on the aggregate demand curve for the fiscal policy $G = G_1$. **B** is a point on the aggregate demand curve for the fiscal policy $G = G_2$. The aggregate demand curve when $G = G_1$ is given by $AD(G_1)$, and when $G = G_2$ it is given by $AD(G_2)$.

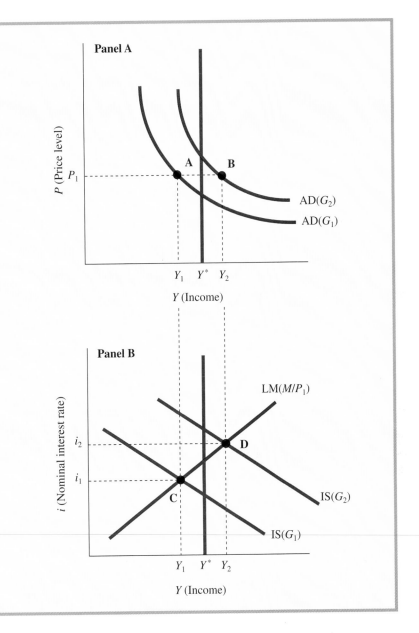

the price level P_1: $LM(M_1/P_1)$. The LM curve $LM(M_1/P_1)$ crosses the IS curve at point **C** and results in an IS–LM equilibrium with income Y_1. Now trace this level of income up to panel A to find a point on the aggregate demand curve, $AD(M_1)$. To find additional points on the same aggregate demand curve, we repeat the exercise for different price levels but for the same nominal money supply, M_1.

At a higher quantity of money, M_2, there is a different aggregate demand curve, $AD(M_2)$, which is everywhere to the right of the curve $AD(M_1)$. To find a point on this curve we must

FIGURE 10.9
How Monetary Policy Shifts the Aggregate Demand Curve

As M increases from M_1 to M_2, the LM curve rotates from LM(M_1/P_1) to LM(M_2/P_1). Given the fixed IS curve, the points **C** and **D** represent equilibrium points of the IS–LM model. For the price level P_1, the point **A** is on the aggregate demand curve associated with the policy $M = M_1$. The point **B** is on the aggregate demand curve associated with the policy $M = M_2$. The aggregate demand curve when $M = M_1$ is given by AD(M_1). When $M = M_2$ it is given by AD(M_2).

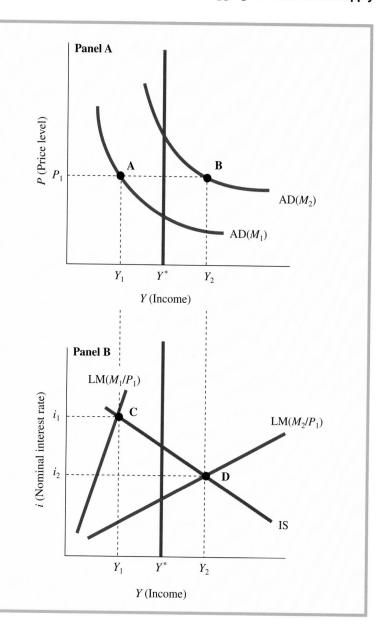

conduct a similar exercise. Once again we begin on panel A with the price level P_1, but the LM curve on panel B when the money supply equals M_2 is now given by LM(M_2/P_1). This LM curve is further to the right of the LM curve LM(M_1/P_1) because the nominal quantity of money is higher. It follows that the IS–LM equilibrium, when the money supply is M_2, is at point **D** with income Y_2, a higher level of income than the equilibrium when the money supply is M_1. Tracing Y_2 up to panel A, we can find point **B** on the curve AD(M_2).

We could analyze the effects of any of the other variables that shift the IS or LM curves in a similar way. For example, if taxes fall, the effect would once again be to shift the ag-

TABLE 10.1
Factors That Shift the Aggregate Demand Curve

	Variables	*Direction of Shift*
$\Delta P^E/P$	Expected inflation	Right
G	Government expenditure	Right
I	Investment (productivity)	Right
TR	Transfers	Right
T	Taxes	Left
M	Money supply	Right

gregate demand curve to the right, since for any given price level the equilibrium value of income on the IS–LM diagram will be greater. Table 10.1 summarizes the effect of changes in the exogenous variables in the IS–LM model on aggregate demand. With the exception of the price of commodities, the variables that shift the aggregate demand curve are the same variables that shift the IS and LM curves. If government purchases increase, if taxes fall, or if expectations of inflation increase, the IS curve will shift to the right. Because a rightward shift of the IS curve causes the level of income to go up, for every possible value of the price of commodities, the variables that shift the IS curve to the right will also shift the aggregate demand curve to the right. A similar argument applies to an increase in the quantity of money. If the Federal Reserve increases the money supply, the LM curve will shift right. Because the quantity of commodities demanded will be higher for any price level, it follows once again that the aggregate demand curve will shift to the right.

There is one exception to the statement that the variables that shift the IS and LM curves will also shift the aggregate demand curve; that exception is the price level itself. Because the aggregate demand diagram has the price level on the vertical axis, the effect of a change in the price level on aggregate demand is captured by a movement *along* the curve, not by a shift *of* the aggregate demand curve.

❺ AGGREGATE DEMAND AND SUPPLY

We are now ready for a more complete theory of business cycles than the theory developed by the classical economists.

What Causes Business Cycles?

In Figure 10.10 the aggregate demand curve is combined with the short-run and long-run aggregate supply curves from Chapter 7. This figure examines the predictions of the Keynesian model and compares those predictions with data from two historical episodes. The

FIGURE 10.10
Demand and Supply Shocks

Panel A illustrates the effect of demand shocks in the complete Keynesian model. If most shocks are due to shifts in demand, we would expect to see, in the data, that most observations lie on an upward-sloping supply curve.

Panel B illustrates that this is indeed what we observed in the period from 1921 through 1939.

Panel C shows that temporary supply shocks also cause fluctuations in output. If most shocks in a given period are due to shifts in aggregate supply, we would expect to see that most observations in the data lie on a downward-sloping aggregate demand curve.

Panel D illustrates that this is what we saw in the period from 1970 to 1989. An example of a supply shock was the 1973 increase in the price of oil. Because oil is highly complementary with other factors, the aggregate production function shifted down as oil became scarce and it became more difficult to produce a given quantity of output from U.S. labor and capital. If business cycles are caused by demand shocks, prices should be procyclical; if they are caused by supply shocks, prices should be countercyclical.

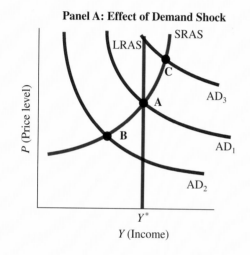

Panel A: Effect of Demand Shock

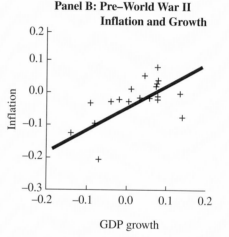

Panel B: Pre–World War II Inflation and Growth

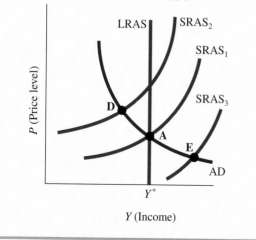

Panel C: Effect of Supply Shock

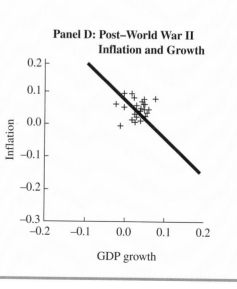

Panel D: Post–World War II Inflation and Growth

BOX 10.2
Could the Great Depression Happen Again?

In October of 1987 the Dow Jones Index, a leading measure of stock market values, fell by 20% in a single day. This drop in value was comparable to the stock market crash in 1929 that preceded the Great Depression, and it left many analysts wondering whether the Great Depression could happen again.

In 1987, a major drop in the stock market was *not* followed by a major recession. What was different about 1987?

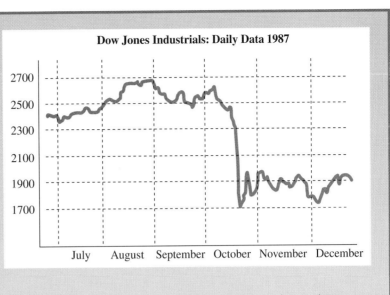

Dow Jones Industrials: Daily Data 1987

Gary H. Stern, president of the Federal Reserve Bank of Minneapolis, identifies four policy management lessons from the 1929 experience that may have contributed to our successful management of the 1987 episode:

1. maintain the stability of the banking system;
2. support normal credit extension practices and smoothly functioning financial markets;
3. assure adequate growth of the money supply; and
4. sustain and enhance international trade.

You can read Gary Stern's article, "Achieving Economic Stability: Lessons from the Crash of 1929" at
http://woodrow.mpls.frb.fed.us/pubs/ar/ar1987.html. As president of one of the twelve regional Federal Reserve Banks, Stern actively participates in the creation of U.S. monetary policy, and his views on the role of demand management are guided by practical experience.

first, 1921 through 1939, is a period when most economists agree that business cycles were caused by fluctuations in aggregate demand. The second, 1970 through 1989, is a period when business cycles were caused by fluctuations in aggregate supply.

Panel A of Figure 10.10 plots two aggregate demand curves and a short- and long-run aggregate supply curve. Suppose that there is a big movement in the aggregate demand curve that causes it to move from AD_1 to AD_2. Many economists believe that this is what happened in the Great Depression, although they disagree about what caused the movement in aggregate demand. Keynes thought that the causal factor was a collapse in the confidence of investors, which reduced demand for investment goods.[6] If aggregate demand drops, but

6.   Milton Friedman, a leading proponent of monetarism, believes that the Federal Reserve System is at fault for failing to increase the money supply during the period immediately preceding the Great Depression. During the period from 1921 to 1929, there was a big increase in investment and a surge in GDP growth, leading to an increase in the demand for liquidity. Friedman argues that the effect of failing to increase the money supply in a fast-growing economy is the same as lowering the money supply in an economy that is not growing. Friedman's explanation would go like this. Beginning at a point like **A** on panel A, suppose that Y^* shifts to the right. Now the short-run equilibrium is at a point at which short-run aggregate supply intersects aggregate demand, but it is to the left of long-run aggregate supply. You might like to draw this for yourself and show that the effect on unemployment is similar to the Keynesian explanation.

the nominal wage is slow to adjust downward, the economy will move down the short-run aggregate supply curve to a point like **B**. At **B**, the real wage has risen, firms hire fewer workers, the price level has fallen, and unemployment is above the natural rate. Now suppose that aggregate demand increases again rapidly, as it did when the United States entered World War II. The aggregate demand curve shifts to the right to AD_3 and the equilibrium of the economy shifts to point **C** in panel A. At **C**, the real wage has fallen, firms hire more workers, the price level has increased, and unemployment is below the natural rate. If business cycles are caused by random, unpredictable movements in aggregate demand, we would expect to see that prices and output are procyclical because the economy is swinging backward and forward, up and down a short-run aggregate supply curve.

Panel C of Figure 10.10 shows what happens if the economy experiences shocks to aggregate supply. When these shocks are temporary, the short-run aggregate supply curve, (SRAS), shifts back and forth from $SRAS_1$ to $SRAS_2$, causing a recession, and to $SRAS_3$, causing a boom. Notice that if business cycles are mainly caused by supply shocks, the price level should be *countercyclical,* because the economy is swinging back and forth along a downward-sloping aggregate supply curve.

Panels B and D of Figure 10.10 illustrate the U.S. data in the pre– and post–World War II eras. Notice that from 1921 to 1939 most business cycles were due to demand swings, but in the postwar period supply moved more. The major recessions in the period from 1970 to 1989 were caused by the oil price shocks in 1973 and 1979. A sharp increase on the price of oil caused the aggregate technology to become less productive for a given input of labor, because oil is an essential input to factories, machines, and basic transportation.

Could the Great Depression Happen Again?

If we accept this view of business cycles, it seems apparent that government can intervene to reduce the magnitude of economic fluctuations. Indeed, a major theme of Keynes' book *The General Theory of Employment, Interest and Money* was that that government can and should manage aggregate demand to prevent major recessions. The idea that government is responsible for maintaining a high and stable level of employment is directly attributable to Keynes, and it became the dominant theme of postwar economic policy. How successful was this idea?

A close comparison of panels B and D in Figure 10.10 reveals an interesting fact: The magnitude of business cycles has been much lower in the postwar period than in the period between the wars. One optimistic explanation for this is that we are doing a better job of managing the economy in the postwar period as a direct result of the influence of Keynesian demand management. The Federal Reserve learned important lessons from the Great Depression, and it is unlikely to allow the banking system to collapse as it did in the early 1930s. For a summary of the view that policy has improved, look at Box 10.2 and the article by Gary Stern, president of the Federal Reserve Bank of Minnesota.

A second, less optimistic view of the stability of the postwar period has been put forth by Christina Romer of the University of California at Berkeley.[7] By reconstructing the

---

7.   Christina Romer, "The Prewar Business Cycle Reconsidered: New Estimates of Gross National Product, 1869–1908," *Journal of Political Economy* 97, No. 1 (February 1989), pp. 1–37.

postwar data using the prewar methods, Romer produced a comparable data series for the entire period. Using these data, she argues that part of the apparent improvement in stability is an illusion created by more accurate data-measuring methods.

The Government Role in Stabilizing Business Cycles

It seems clear that the government can intervene in the economy by changing fiscal and monetary policies. Whether interventions reduce, rather than exacerbate, economic fluctuations is a much more contentious issue. How would economic stabilization work? First, the government must recognize that the economy is in recession. Because economic statistics are collected and compiled over a relatively long time, this in itself is no easy task. Preliminary estimates of GDP in a given quarter are, at best, guesses, and they are often still being revised as much as three or four years after the date for which they were made. Once it has been decided that the economy really is in recession, the government must then act to stimulate aggregate demand. Changing expenditures or taxes could take a year or more to get through the legislature. If the Federal Reserve System stimulates demand by increasing the money supply and lowering the interest rate, there may again be a long and variable lag before the private sector responds. Advocates of stabilization policy argue that these lags are unimportant and that the government can and should act to maintain a high and stable level of aggregate demand. Critics argue that trying to stabilize the economy is a hopeless task, and the best thing the government can do is refrain from adding additional noise to the economic system by constantly changing economic policy.

A second argument against active economic stabilization is more subtle. This second argument is based on the idea that expectations are not exogenous, as we assumed in this chapter. In modern equilibrium theories, expectations are determined rationally, as part of the behavior of households and firms in an economic equilibrium. Whereas the models that we have studied so far are static, rational expectations theories are explicitly dynamic; that is, they explicitly account for the passage of time. Rational expectations theories lead to different conclusions from the classical or Keynesian models because households and firms may take actions today that depend on beliefs about the future. The fact that beliefs enter into economic decisions in nontrivial ways has many implications that we are only now beginning to understand. In Part C we study the theory of rational expectations and how intertemporal equilibrium theory has influenced the debates over the role of government and over the best way to manage the economy.

CONCLUSION

The real interest rate is equal to the nominal interest rate minus expected inflation. Investment depends on the real interest rate; saving depends on the real interest rate and on income. The interest rate that equates saving and investment is different for different levels of income, and the schedule of values of income and the interest rate for which saving equals investment is called the IS curve. The IS curve slopes down because when the interest rate falls, firms want to invest more. To restore equilibrium in the capital market, income must also be increased so that saving and investment are once more equal. The position of the IS curve is shifted by expected inflation, government purchases, taxes, and transfer payments. If government purchases or transfers increase, if taxes fall, or if expected inflation increases, the IS curve shifts to the right.

An IS–LM equilibrium is a level of income and an interest rate for which the capital market is in equilibrium and the quantity of money demanded equals the quantity supplied. It occurs at the point at which the IS and LM curves intersect. Because the position of the LM curve depends on the price level, there is a different IS–LM equilibrium for every value of P. As the price level falls, the LM curve shifts to the right and equilibrium income increases. The schedule of all pairs of price levels and equilibrium income levels is the Keynesian aggregate demand curve. The position of the Keynesian aggregate demand curve depends on government purchases, transfers, taxes, expected inflation, and the nominal money supply.

The complete Keynesian theory explains changes in income and the price level by shifts in aggregate demand and supply. If most business cycles are caused by aggregate demand movements, then the price level should be procyclical. This is what happened in the prewar period. If most business cycles are caused by supply shocks, then the price level should be countercyclical. This is what happened in the postwar period. Economists disagree over whether business cycles can or should be stabilized through active government intervention.

KEY TERMS

Disposable income

Ex ante real interest rate

Ex post real interest rate

IS curve

IS–LM equilibrium

Keynesian aggregate demand curve

Natural rate output

Rational expectations

PROBLEMS FOR REVIEW

1. Explain the difference between the ex ante real interest rate and the ex post real interest rate. Which is relevant for economic decisions? Which is easier to measure?

2. Using Ted Bos's chart-maker at http://bos.business.uab.edu/, construct graphs of five different interest rate series from 1990 to 1997. You may choose any five series you like. Write down any difference you see between the series. Can you rank them? Is one always higher than the others? Is one more volatile than the others? Try to explain the differences you see.

3. If firms expect higher inflation, but households do not, will the IS curve shift to the right or the left? Explain your answer.

4. List as many factors as you can think of that will shift the IS curve to the left.

5. Explain, in words, why the AD curve slopes down. Why does an increase in the money supply shift the AD curve? Trace out the economic mechanism that causes this shift.

6. Show that in the IS–LM model, fiscal policy cannot affect output if the LM curve is vertical. Explain how this fact affects the way that fiscal policy alters aggregate demand in the complete Keynesian model. How is your answer related to the classical theory of aggregate demand?

7. In the IS–LM model, the position of the LM curve depends on the price level as well as on the stock of money. Why doesn't the position of the AD curve depend on the price level?

8. What factors affect the slope of the aggregate demand curve? Explain in particular how the slope of the aggregate demand curve would change if investment became more sensitive to the interest rate. Contrast two cases, one in which a 1% increase in the interest rate leads to a 1% drop in investment (all other things held constant), and a second case in which a 1% increase in the interest rate leads to a 2% drop.

9. The following data is drawn from the economy of Legunia.

Year	Price level	Interest rate	GDP
1897	80	5	70
1898	65	4	60
1899	70	7	68
1900	100	7.5	75
1901	20	3	40

The president of Legonia is given conflicting advice. One advisor tells him that business cycles are being caused by supply shocks. A second advisor says that the problem is due to random shocks to the money supply. The third agrees that the problem is on the demand side, but he argues that random shocks to investment spending are causing the cycle. Which advisor do you think is right? Why?

10. Read the article by Gary Stern at **http://woodrow.mpls.frb.fed.us/pubs/ar/ar1987.html** and write a short essay summarizing his main arguments.

MATHEMATICAL APPENDIX:
THE ALGEBRA OF THE KEYNESIAN THEORY OF AGGREGATE DEMAND

This appendix is optional and is intended for those readers who are more comfortable with algebra than with graphs. We derive the equation of the IS curve and the aggregate demand curve under some simple assumptions about saving and investment. Assume that the saving function can be represented by the equation

10.4
$$S = s(Y + TR - T)$$

The notation $s(Y + TR - T)$ means s (a number between zero and one) multiplied by disposable income. This way of writing the saving schedule assumes that saving is a constant fraction of disposable income, $(Y + TR - T)$ and that it does not depend on the interest rate. The way that saving depends on disposable income is captured by the single parameter s. We call this parameter the *marginal propensity to save*. The assumption that saving does not depend on the interest rate means that the graph of the saving function, in this case, would be a vertical line.

The saving function represents the money that households are willing to lend to borrowers when the real interest rate is $i - \Delta P^E/P$. The other side of the capital market is represented by the investment schedule plus the demand for funds by government; an amount that is equal to the budget deficit. We refer to the net demand for funds by firms and government as the $I + D$ schedule, and we model the $I + D$ schedule with the equation

10.5
$$I + D = [\bar{I} - e(i - \Delta P^E/P)] + (G + TR - T)$$

Here we assume that the investment function $I(i - \Delta P^E/P)$ depends on two parameters, $\bar{I}$ and e. The parameter $\bar{I}$ is the amount of investment that is independent of the interest rate, and the parameter e is the slope of the investment function.

To derive the equation of the IS curve we must find the interest rate for which the capital market is in equilibrium for each value of income. The algebra of the IS curve comes from solving the equation

10.6
$$s(Y + TR - T) = \left[\bar{I} - \left(e\,i - \frac{\Delta P^E}{P}\right)\right] + (G + TR - T)$$

to find i in terms of Y. The left side of Equation 10.6 is saving and the right side is investment plus government borrowing. The expression we seek is then

10.7
$$i = \frac{\Delta P^E}{P} + \frac{1}{e}[\bar{I} + G + (TR - T)(1 - s)] - \frac{s}{e}Y$$

The slope of the IS curve is represented by the ratio of the parameters $-(s/e)$. This slope will be flat if e is high or if s is small. The intercept of the IS curve with the vertical axis is given by the parameters

$$\frac{\Delta P^E}{P} + \frac{1}{e}[\bar{I} + G + (TR - T)(1 - s)]$$

and the curve will shift if any of these variables (or parameters) changes.

Now let's turn to the aggregate demand curve. Recall that in Chapter 8 we found the equation of the LM curve

10.8
$$i = \frac{hP}{M} Y$$

Putting together Equations 10.7 and 10.8 and arranging terms, we can find an expression for the aggregate demand curve

10.9
$$P = \frac{M}{h}\left\{ \frac{(\Delta P^E/P) + \frac{1}{e}[\bar{I} + G + (TR - T)(1 - s)]}{Y} - \frac{s}{e} \right\}$$

The graph of this equation is a downward-sloping line that approaches $P = \infty$ at $Y = 0$ and that cuts the horizontal axis at

$$Y = \frac{e}{s}\left\{ \frac{\Delta P^E}{P} + \frac{1}{e}[\bar{I} + G + (TR - T)(1 - s)] \right\}$$

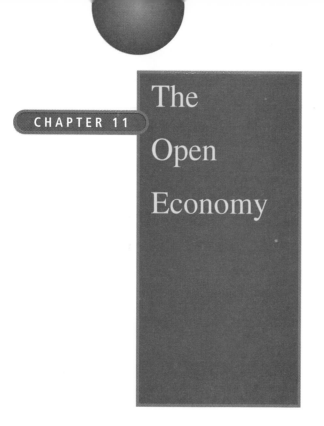

CHAPTER 11

The

Open

Economy

❶ INTRODUCTION

Monetary policy in the world economy has operated under two systems: fixed and floating exchange rates. Under a fixed-rate system, the rate at which the currency of each country can be exchanged with every other currency is fixed. This is the system that operated from 1948 through 1973, when the world switched to a floating exchange rate regime. Under floating exchange rates, the system currently in place, the relative price of the money of one country for the money of another fluctuates on a daily basis.

❷ FIXED AND FLEXIBLE EXCHANGE RATES

Exchange Rate Regimes

Money is a commodity that is widely accepted in exchange; if there were a single world money, the topic of international trade would be relatively easy. However, every country in the world uses different currency and the relative prices of international currencies change from one day to the next. The rate at which one currency trades for another is called an **exchange rate.**

TABLE 11.1
Exchange Rates
on June 1,1992
in Currency Units
per U.S. Dollar

Country	Exchange Rate
Canadian dollar	1.20470
German Deutschemark	1.6
French franc	5.3735
Italian lira	1,206.06
Japanese yen	126.85
U.K. pound sterling	0.546001

Table 11.1 lists the exchange rates for six countries on June 1, 1992. On that day, one dollar would buy 1,206.06 Italian lira, but it would only buy 1.6 Deutschemarks.

Before World War II most currencies were convertible to gold, and therefore to each other, at a fixed rate. In 1944, at an important international conference held at **Bretton Woods,** New Hampshire, representatives from the leading countries of the world met to discuss the post-war international economic order. The Bretton Woods conference set up a new system in which the United States fixed the price of the dollar in terms of gold and guaranteed to buy or sell dollars at this fixed rate. All other countries in the world fixed their exchange rates to the U.S. dollar. Under Bretton Woods, the rates at which world currencies could be exchanged for dollars could be altered periodically. This system, called the gold exchange standard, resulted in a twenty-year period of relatively stable exchange rates. At the same conference, the **International Monetary Fund** (IMF) was created to monitor the arrangement and to act as a kind of world central bank. The period from 1948 to 1973 was a period of **fixed exchange rates** because it was possible, during this period, to trade international currencies with a fair degree of predictability of their future value.

The fixed exchange-rate system worked through active intervention of the central banks of the participating nations. Each central bank would guarantee to buy or sell its own domestic currency at a fixed rate. In order to intervene in the markets this way, the central banks held reserves of foreign exchange, and they sold these reserves if, in the private markets, there was an excess supply of the domestic currency. If there was an excess demand for the domestic currency the central bank would buy foreign exchange, thereby increasing its reserves. For this system to operate effectively, the demands and supplies of the private market had to average out to zero over time. In practice, however, some countries found that their reserves of foreign exchange became seriously depleted, and they no

WEBWATCH 11.1   **Exchange Rates on the Web**

How many Canadian dollars can you buy today in exchange for $100 U.S.? How many Saudi Arabian riyals? On Saturday December 13, 1997, $100 would buy 374.99 Saudi Arabian riyals. You can check out rates yourself on any given day at the Universal Currency Converter on the web at http://www.xe.net/cgi-bin/ucc/convert.

TABLE 11.2
Terms Used to Discuss Exchange Rates

Concept		Fixed Rate Regime	Flexible Rate Regime
Definition: *e* is the number of foreign currency units per dollar	*e* increases	Foreign currency **devalued**	Foreign currency **depreciates**
	e falls	Foreign currency **revalued**	Foreign currency **appreciates**

longer had enough foreign currency to maintain the official exchange rate. These countries engaged in **devaluation** of their currencies; that is, they increased the domestic currency price of foreign exchange (lowering the foreign price of the currency), thereby making it cheaper for foreigners to buy domestic goods and increasing the demand for the domestic currency.

The fixed exchange-rate system became increasingly unworkable as different countries pursued different monetary policies. Some countries, France and the United Kingdom for example, expanded their domestic money supplies relatively rapidly, and other countries, such as Germany and Japan, kept strict control over monetary growth. Because the exchange rate is nothing other than the rate at which one money exchanges for another, other things being equal, a big expansion in the quantity of one money over another makes it relatively less scarce and its market price falls. This is what happened to the currencies of France and the United Kingdom, both of which were forced to devalue their currencies (France in 1956 and the United Kingdom in 1965). Eventually, the attempts of different countries to follow different monetary policies led to the collapse of the system. In 1973 the fixed exchange-rate system was finally abandoned in favor of a system of **floating exchange rates,** in which the rate at which one currency trades for another is determined by the demands and supplies of each currency in the free market.

Because the U.S. dollar is widely used as an international medium of exchange, it is common to quote prices in terms of the dollar. In the United States we quote exchange rates in terms of the number of foreign currency units that can be bought for a dollar. Using *e* to mean the number of foreign currency units per dollar, we can discuss exchange rate movements four ways. In a fixed exchange-rate system, movements in the exchange rate were relatively infrequent. If *e* increased in this system, the movement was called a *devaluation* of the foreign currency (devaluation because the dollar would buy more foreign currency, so the currency was relatively less expensive). Similarly if, under the fixed-rate system, a country were to reduce *e*, this was called a **revaluation,** because Americans would be able to buy less of the foreign currency for a dollar, implying that the foreign currency had become more expensive. Under a floating exchange rate regime, currency movements occur on a daily basis. In this case, if *e* increases it is called a **depreciation** of the currency, and if *e* falls it is called an **appreciation.** These terms are summarized in Table 11.2.

Figure 11.1 illustrates the effect of the move from fixed to flexible exchange rates. It plots the exchange rates of the **Group of Seven** (abbreviated G7) industrialized nations.

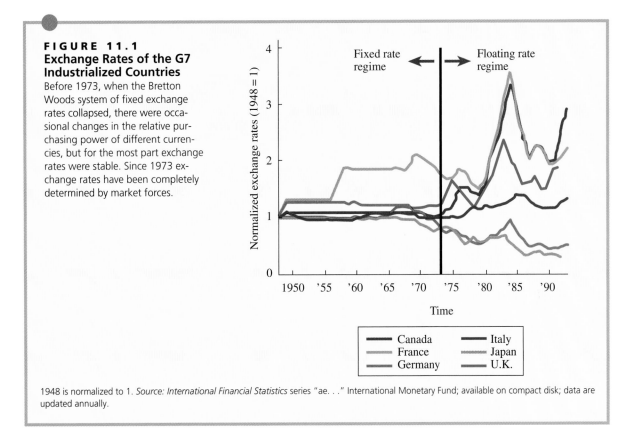

FIGURE 11.1
Exchange Rates of the G7 Industrialized Countries
Before 1973, when the Bretton Woods system of fixed exchange rates collapsed, there were occasional changes in the relative purchasing power of different currencies, but for the most part exchange rates were stable. Since 1973 exchange rates have been completely determined by market forces.

1948 is normalized to 1. *Source: International Financial Statistics* series "ae. . ." International Monetary Fund; available on compact disk; data are updated annually.

The G7 nations are Canada, France, Germany, Italy, Japan, the United Kingdom, and the United States. In Figure 11.1, the exchange rates have been normalized to 1 in 1948. Notice how much more variability there has been in the period of floating rates, since 1973, than in the period of fixed rates, from 1948 to 1973.

Real Exchange Rates and Purchasing Power Parity

One way of enriching the theory of demand and supply to take account of international trade is to think of the goods produced in the world as location specific. For example, a German automobile in New York is a different good from a German automobile in Munich. A simple extension of a model with a single commodity would treat the output of each country as a distinct commodity with its own price.

According to this way of analyzing trade, Americans do not just produce and consume one commodity, they consume American commodities, Japanese commodities, Mexican commodities, and so on. When the relative price of a foreign commodity changes, the amount of the commodity that Americans purchase also changes. The relative price of a basket of foreign goods, valued in terms of a basket of American goods, is called the **real exchange rate.** Changes in the real exchange rate shift the demand for domestic commodities as Americans substitute into or out of imported goods. When foreign goods are

FIGURE 11.2
Real Exchange Rates Against the Real U.S. Dollar for the G7 Countries

These graphs compare the relative purchasing power of a given bundle of commodities with an equivalent bundle of commodities in the United States for each of six countries. The figure shows that relative prices across countries change dramatically over long periods of time. For example, Italian goods are relatively less expensive in 1993 than they were in 1950, but goods in Japan are much more expensive. When real exchange rates change like this over long periods of time, economists say there is a failure of purchasing power parity.

Vertical axes measure the amount of one unit of a basket of real foreign consumption goods that can be purchased by one unit of a basket of real U.S. consumption goods. 1990 is normalized to 1 for all countries.

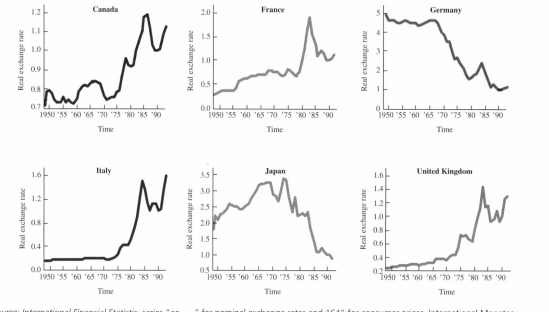

Source: International Financial Statistic, series "ae . . ." for nominal exchange rates and "64" for consumer prices. International Monetary Fund, available on compact disk; data are updated annually.

substituted for American goods, a fall in the price of foreign goods leads to an increase in the percentage of GDP going to imports. If, on the other hand, they complement American goods, a fall in the price of the foreign good could lead to a drop in the share of domestic spending devoted to imports.

Figure 11.2 shows what happened to real exchange rates for the G7 countries over the post-war period. Each graph shows the cost of a basket of foreign goods relative to the cost of an American basket. The particular basket of goods in each case is the one that makes up the consumer price index in each country. Because these goods may be different, it doesn't make much sense to compare the values of the real exchange rate in an absolute sense; however, it does make sense to see how these bundles of goods have become relatively more or less expensive over time. The most dramatic feature of Figure 11.2 is the big swings in the relative costs of the goods available in different countries. An American tourist in Tokyo, for example, could buy three and a half times as much of the average

Japanese consumer basket in 1975 than in 1990; Japan is a lot more expensive for an American tourist than it used to be. Italy, on the other hand, is four times cheaper.

The definition of the real exchange rate is given in Equation 11.1. The units of the domestic price index are dollars per basket of U.S. goods, where the basket of U.S. goods is the bundle that goes into the formation of the consumer price index. The units of P^f, the foreign price index, are foreign currency units per basket of foreign goods. Finally, the nominal exchange rate is measured in foreign currency units per U.S. dollar. Putting all of this together gives us a real exchange rate that measures the number of units of the basket of foreign goods per basket of U.S. goods.

11.1
$$re = e \times \frac{P}{P^f}$$

| **Real exchange rate** | **Nominal exchange rate** | **Ratio of the domestic price index to the foreign price index** |

Sometimes you see the term **purchasing power parity** mentioned in newspapers or magazines. Purchasing power parity is the idea that the real exchange rate should be equal to 1 because, so the argument goes, free trade should lead to real prices being equalized everywhere. In its weaker form, people sometimes refer to **relative purchasing power parity,** which means that the relative value of the GDP deflator between different countries should not change systematically over time. Relative purchasing power parity would mean that the real exchange rate of each country should show no systematic tendency to rise or fall. It is clear from Figure 11.2 that in the real world, real exchange rates move considerably over time. This does not contradict economic theory because there is no reason why different goods should sell at the same price; commodities in different locations are simply different commodities. The fact that a haircut in Lima, Peru is cheaper than a haircut in New York City is of little consolation to a New Yorker, since the haircut in Lima cannot be transported to New York. Even relatively homogenous goods that are easily transported may acquire trademarks that depend on country of origin. For example, a German automobile may become a prestige item even if a comparable American car is just as good. There is also no reason to expect that the relative prices of different countries' goods should remain stationary through time. In short, purchasing power parity is a useful theoretical concept mainly as a benchmark.

Nominal Exchange Rates and Interest Rate Parity

Although purchasing power parity does not hold in the data, there is a second relationship called *uncovered interest rate parity* that fares somewhat better.[1] Uncovered interest rate parity refers to the idea that the rates of return on comparable assets should be equalized throughout the world. If the interest rate in Germany is twice as high as the interest rate in

1.   It is possible to conduct statistical tests of the proposition of uncovered interest rate parity, and the strict test of the proposition in fact fails these formal tests. Economists are not *too* concerned about these failures since the strict form of the proposition does not allow for the fact that most investors are *risk averse,* in other words, the foreign interest rate can be a little higher than the domestic interest rate when the investment is very risky. An excellent summary of the empirical work on interest rate parity is contained in the article by Kenneth Froot and Richard Thaler, *Journal of Economic Perspectives,* Summer 1990.

FIGURE 11.3
Interest Rate Differentials with the United States
This figure shows the difference between the foreign interest rate and the U.S. interest rate for each of six countries each year from 1960 through 1993. In some years this difference has been greater than 10%. Why do people buy U.S. bonds when they could earn a higher rate of interest in a foreign country? The answer is related to changes in the exchange rate.

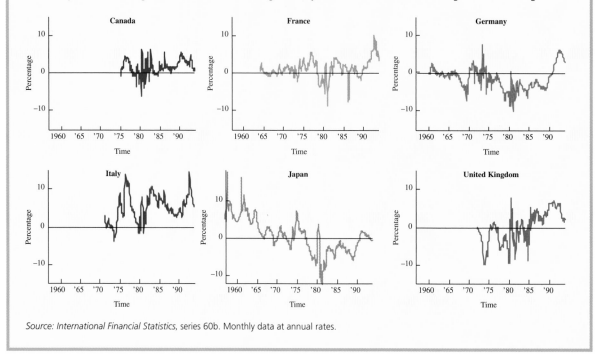

Source: International Financial Statistics, series 60b. Monthly data at annual rates.

the United States then we might expect Americans to move their money abroad in search of the higher rate of return.

Looking at Figure 11.3 you might think you should invest your money abroad. The graphs show the differences between the average monthly interest rates on overnight loans in each of the six G7 countries and interest rates in the United States. Italy, for example, looks like a relatively good place to invest your money: An investment in Italy has paid 6 percent more, on average, than a comparable investment in the United States since 1973. If you had invested in Italy, however, you might have been disappointed, because this analysis misses one significant factor: the possibility that the exchange rate might change. Consider the following two strategies for investing assets.

1. Take $1,000, buy U.S. government bonds on January 1, 1990, and cash them in, with interest, on January 1, 1991. The return from this strategy is equal to the U.S. interest rate, i.
2. Take $1,000 and buy Italian lira on January 1, 1990. Use lira to buy government of Italy bonds. Cash the bonds in on January 1, 1991. Convert the lira with interest, back

into U.S. dollars. The return from this strategy is equal to $i^f - \Delta e/e$, where i^f is the Italian interest rate and $\Delta e/e$ is the change in the exchange rate between 1990 and 1991.

In order to assess which strategy is better, we must form an opinion about the chances that the Italian lira will increase or decrease in value. On average it should be true that the interest rate in the domestic country equals the interest rate in the foreign country minus the expected proportional change in the exchange rate; this statement is called **uncovered interest rate parity.**[2] Equation 11.2 defines uncovered interest rate parity for two countries.

11.2
$$i \quad = \quad i^f \quad - \quad \frac{\Delta e}{e}$$

| **Domestic Interest rate** | **Foreign interest rate** | **Proportional change in the exchange rate** |

The idea behind uncovered interest rate parity is a powerful concept called the **absence of arbitrage.** Absence of arbitrage means that economists don't expect to see big opportunities available in the real world for individuals to get something for nothing. If such an opportunity existed, people would rush in and exploit the opportunity, thus causing the opportunity to disappear. In the case of international currency trades, if the rate of interest is much higher in another country and if exchange rates are stable, investors will put their money overseas, thereby bidding up the domestic interest rate and bidding down the foreign interest rate until the two rates are equalized.

Uncovered interest rate parity implies that the difference between interest rates on comparable assets, adjusted for exchange rate changes, should be equal to zero on average. Figure 11.4 illustrates these adjusted differentials for the same six G7 countries. Notice that there is no obvious tendency for the adjusted interest rate differentials to be either positive or negative over time. Notice that the scale of interest rate differentials between countries, adjusted for exchange rate changes, runs from +100% to −100%. Interest rate differentials are only of the order of 5% to 10% after 1973, because the raw interest rate differentials are dwarfed by exchange rate fluctuations. For example, although Italy paid 6% more than the United States on average, currency risk for holding Italian assets can amount to +/−80 to 100%.

The data for Figure 11.4 is only really meaningful for the floating rate period since 1973.[3] For example, Japan looks like a good investment over the fixed-rate period, because it paid a higher interest rate than the United States, and the dollar–yen exchange rate did not change. However, the market for the Japanese yen was not free during this period, and the Japanese government restricted the amount of yen that could be purchased by foreigners

2.   It is possible to earn interest in Italy without *any* exposure to exchange rate risk by arranging the sale of foreign exchange at a future date at a guaranteed price. The market for the sale of foreign currencies at future dates is very well developed, and international companies trade in this market frequently as a way of removing the risk of currency fluctuations. Not surprisingly, there are no differences in international interest rates when currencies are converted using the futures market, and this fact is called *covered interest rate parity.* The proposition stated in Equation 11.2 is called *uncovered interest rate parity,* to distinguish it from the covered case.

3.   The interest rates used to compute these graphs are for overnight funds in the money market. In the United States this interest rate is called the *federal funds rate,* and the major borrowers and lenders in this market are commercial banks, some of which need to borrow to meet their reserve requirements. Prior to 1973 the international money market was much less well developed, and in some countries no such market existed.

FIGURE 11.4
Interest Rate Differentials Adjusted for Exchange Rate Changes
Compare the difference in the scale used on the vertical axis of this figure with that of Figure 11.3. The magnitude of the potential gain (or loss) from speculation in foreign currencies is ten times greater than the differences between foreign and domestic interest rates. Investing in foreign bonds can be *very* risky.

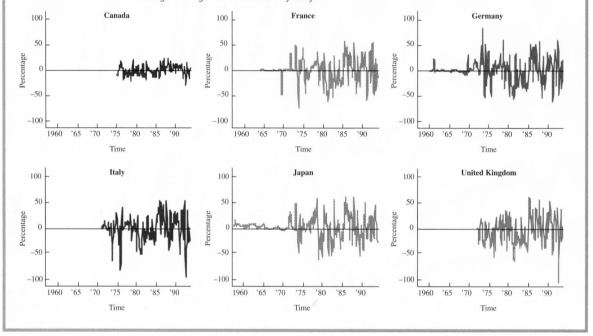

and prevented investors from repatriating profits from their Japanese investments. In other words, although there was a potential arbitrage opportunity in the yen, trade restrictions prevented anyone from exploiting this opportunity.

❸ MANAGING AN OPEN ECONOMY

In 1973 the world economy moved to a flexible exchange-rate system. Before 1973 most countries in the world pegged their exchange rates to the U.S. dollar. Because different countries tried to follow conflicting policy objectives, this system proved to be unworkable.

The Capital Markets and the Exchange Rate

In the period immediately following the Bretton Woods agreement, the international capital markets were approximately in equilibrium. Each country's exchange rate was chosen to maintain balance in its borrowing requirements. The relationship between a country's real exchange rate and its net borrowing from abroad is illustrated in Figure 11.5.

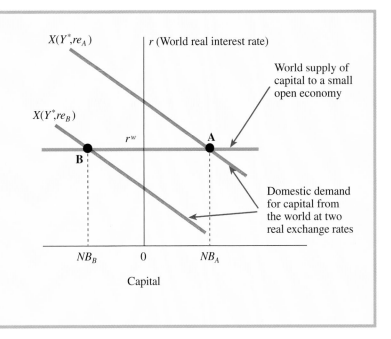

FIGURE 11.5
Devaluation and the
Balance of Payments
The net demand for capital from the rest of the world depends on the real exchange rate and on U.S. GDP. When the real exchange rate equals re_A, the U.S. demand for borrowing from the world is represented by the curve $X(Y^*,re_A)$. When the U.S. dollar is devalued (a move in the real exchange rate from re_A to re_B), the U.S. demand for borrowing from abroad is represented by the curve $X(Y^*,re_B)$. The curve $X(Y^*,re_B)$ is everywhere to the left of the curve $X(Y^*,re_A)$ because when U.S. goods are worth less (relative to foreign goods), U.S. borrowing (denominated in units of U.S. goods) is smaller.

Figure 11.5 is the diagram that we developed in Chapter 6 (Figure 6.9), modified to show that domestic borrowing from the world depends on both GDP and on the real exchange rate. The horizontal line at the real interest rate r^W is the world supply of capital to the domestic economy. The fact that this curve is horizontal reflects the assumption the country we are studying is small relative to the world economy[4] and can borrow and lend any amount at the world real interest rate, r^W. We have drawn two downward sloping demand curves. The curve $X(Y^*,re_A)$ represents the domestic economy's net demand for borrowing from the rest of the world when the domestic economy is at full employment ($Y = Y^*$) and when the real exchange rate equals re_A. The curve $X(Y^*,re_B)$ represents the economy's demand for capital from the world market when the domestic exchange rate depreciates from re_A to re_B.

Why does a change in the real exchange rate shift the demand for borrowing? The reason is that the domestic demand for capital is denominated in units of the domestic currency. To make the example concrete, let's suppose that the country we are studying is Italy. Figure 11.2 shows that in 1975 the real exchange rate of the lire against the dollar was 0.4, but by 1990 it had climbed to 1.6. Over this period, the basket of Italian commodities depreciated by a factor of 4, because in 1990 Americans could buy four times as many Italian goods with the income they earned in the United States. This depreciation reduced the need for Italians to borrow from the United States because the average Italian company would be able to finance the purchase of new factories by borrowing only a quarter of the basket of U.S. goods. This shows up on Figure 11.5 as a leftward shift of the

4.   When the economy is large, this line is upward sloping, but the rest of the analysis is the same as the case that we study here.

FIGURE 11.6
Long-Run Equilibrium in a Small Open Economy with a Fixed Exchange Rate
This figure depicts the capital and money market equilibrium, in the long run, in the foreign economy. The long-run equilibrium occurs when the LM curve intersects the IS curve at full employment.

The IS curve, in a small open economy, is horizontal, because the domestic interest rate is determined by the world rate, i^W, plus the expected appreciation of the exchange rate. In a fixed exchange rate world, the term $\Delta e/e$ is zero.

In the long run, foreign inflation, $\Delta P^f/P^f$, equals the foreign rate of monetary expansion, $\Delta M^f/M^f$.

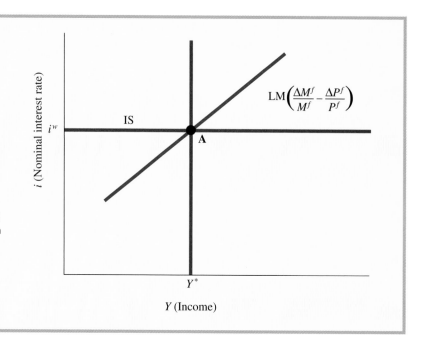

domestic demand for capital curve from $X(Y^*, re_A)$ to $X(Y^*, re_B)$. Before the devaluation, Italy was a net borrower on the world capital market; it demanded the funds NB_A each year. After the devaluation, it became a net lender; it supplied the funds NB_B.

In 1948, it was widely believed that a fixed exchange rate system would bring stability to the world capital markets. An attempt was made to peg exchange rates in 1948 so that each country would be able to maintain the exchange rate without a need for the central government to either accumulate or decumulate reserves of foreign exchange. In order to do this, the central bank of each country in the world kept reserves of foreign exchange. If there was an excess demand for the domestic currency at the pegged exchange rate, the central bank would supply the domestic currency in exchange for dollars. If there was an excess supply, the domestic central bank would supply dollars, drawing on its foreign currency reserves, and buy back the domestic currency. As long as there are as many periods of excess demand as there are of excess supply, this strategy should have been feasible. In some years, the central bank's reserves would increase, in others they would decrease. In practice this is not what happened.

Long-Run Equilibrium in a Fixed Exchange-Rate System

Figure 11.6 analyses the long-run equilibrium of the economy. The vertical line at the level of GDP Y^* represents the output that would be produced if the economy operated at the natural rate of unemployment. The horizontal line is the IS curve in a small open economy. This line is horizontal because it is assumed that the economy can borrow or lend freely at the world rate of interest i^W.

We have drawn an upward-sloping LM curve that passes through the IS curve (the i^W line) at full employment. This reflects the fact that, in the long run, the foreign inflation rate will adjust so that the economy is at the natural rate of unemployment. This occurs at the point where the foreign inflation rate equals the foreign rate of money growth.

The IS–LM model in the case of fixed exchange rates behaves very much like the closed economy model that we studied in Chapter 10, except that, if the exchange rate truly is fixed, there is no room for the central bank to influence the interest rate. The central bank controls the interest rate in a closed economy by altering the supply of domestic bonds available to lenders. But in an open economy, with a truly fixed exchange rate, borrowers and lenders can turn to the world capital markets with no fear of exchange-rate risk. If the central bank tried to peg an interest rate that is lower than the world rate, domestic lenders would put all of their money in foreign bonds. If the bank tried to raise the rate above the world rate, borrowers would turn to the world capital markets. The central bank can intervene in the market by pegging the exchange rate, but it cannot simultaneously pick the rate of interest.

There is one important exception to the freedom of central banks to choose the rate of interest, and it is an important one. Under the Bretton Woods agreement, exchange rates were pegged, not to gold, but to the U.S. dollar. This arrangement gave the United States the ability to pursue an independent monetary policy, since it could rely on other countries to maintain the exchange-rate agreement. In a fixed exchange-rate system, one country can pursue an independent interest rate policy, and in the postwar world from 1944 through 1973, that country was the United States.

The **balance of payments** in a fixed exchange-rate world is the change in the central bank's reserves as a consequence of its interventions in the foreign exchange markets to maintain the value of the currency. Under the Bretton Woods system, domestic monetary policies conflicted with the balance of payments of many countries in the world. This conflict arose because countries agreed to peg their exchange rates under Bretton Woods, but they did not agree to coordinate their monetary policies. Some countries, such as Japan and Germany, expanded their money supplies relatively slowly. Other countries, such as Italy and France, chose rapid monetary expansion in an effort to stimulate domestic employment. In the long run, forces that move the economy toward the natural rate of unemployment work by causing the rate of inflation to be equated to the rate of monetary expansion. It follows that rapid-money-growth countries were effectively choosing high inflation rates; low-money-growth countries were choosing low inflation rates.

The fact that countries chose different inflation rates would not, in a flexible exchange-rate world, be a problem. But in a fixed exchange-rate world changes in the purchasing power of different currencies are directly translated into changes in the real exchange rate.

11.3
$$\frac{\Delta re}{re} = \frac{\Delta e}{e} + \frac{\Delta P}{P} - \frac{\Delta P^f}{P^f}$$

| Proportional change in the real exchange rate | Proportional change in the nominal exchange rate | U.S. inflation rate | Foreign inflation rate |

Equation 11.3 defines the proportional change in the real exchange rate of the currency of a small open economy relative to the world medium of exchange (the U.S. dollar). It illustrates the idea that high foreign inflation causes the real exchange rate to appreciate (*re* falls) thereby making the goods of the small open economy more expensive on the world markets. Figure 11.1 shows that an appreciation of the currency (a move from r_B to r_A) will cause the country as a whole (government plus private citizens) to borrow more heavily from abroad. If private agents did not increase their borrowing on the world capital market, the central bank would be forced to borrow in order to prop up its foreign exchange reserves in an attempt to maintain the exchange rate.

In practice, countries like Germany and Japan that ran nonexpansionary monetary policies managed to amass large foreign exchange reserves, and there was pressure on their currencies to revalue. Countries like France and the United Kingdom that ran expansionary monetary policies were forced to borrow repeatedly to replenish their exchange reserves, and eventually they were forced to devalue their currencies. The culmination of this process was the collapse of the Bretton Woods agreement in 1973 and the move to a system of flexible exchange rates.

Long-Run Equilibrium in a Flexible Exchange-Rate System

In a flexible exchange-rate regime it becomes possible for each central bank to pursue an independent monetary policy without generating a balance of payments crisis. If a central bank chooses to give up control over the exchange rate, it *can* set the rate of interest. However, this possibility in itself opens up uncertainty to those businesses involved in international trade, because the monetary policy of each central bank will ultimately determine the exchange rate. For example, if the central bank of Italy decides to set a higher rate of interest than the central bank of the United Kingdom, the lira must depreciate, relative to the pound, over time. If this were not the case, world investors would invest in Italy. In the real world, currency movements in pursuit of perceived arbitrage opportunities are substantial and international investors are responsible for moving roughly $430 billion *per day* from one country to another, about twenty times the value of daily U.S. GDP![5]

Uncovered interest rate parity suggests that exchange rates should be determined by expectations of future policy changes. For example, suppose that you lived in a world with absolutely no uncertainty whatsoever and that you knew, for sure, that the interest rate in Italy would forever be 6% higher than the interest rate in the United States. This world would have an equilibrium in which the lira depreciated by 6% per year to compensate investors for the differences in international rates of interest. But what if you were unsure about future policy actions by the Italian central bank? If the Italian interest rate were to change, the exchange rate would have to change to reflect the new future path of depreciation. This uncertainty about the value of the currency is responsible for the wild swings in exchange rates that have occurred since the move to a flexible rate system.

Figure 11.7 depicts the long-run equilibrium in a small open economy under flexible exchange rates. This figure differs from the fixed exchange-rate case, Figure 11.6, because the interest rate is no longer equal to the world rate, i^W. Instead it is equal to the world rate *plus* the expected depreciation of the exchange rate. In a flexible exchange-rate system,

---

5. These figures are for 1989. "Foreign exchange," by Froot, Kenneth and Thaler, Richard, *Journal of Economic Perspectives* (Summer 1990).

FIGURE 11.7
Long-Run Equilibrium in a Small Open Economy with a Flexible Exchange Rate

This figure depicts the capital and money market equilibrium, in the long run, in the foreign economy with a flexible exchange rate. As in the fixed exchange rate case, the long-run equilibrium occurs when the LM curve intersects the IS curve at full employment.

The IS curve, in the flexible exchange rate case, occurs when the domestic rate of interest is equal to the world rate, i^W, plus the (expected) appreciation of the exchange rate. In the long run, the rate of exchange-rate appreciation is equal to the difference between the world inflation rate, $\Delta P/P$, and the inflation rate in the small open economy, $\Delta P^f/P^f$.

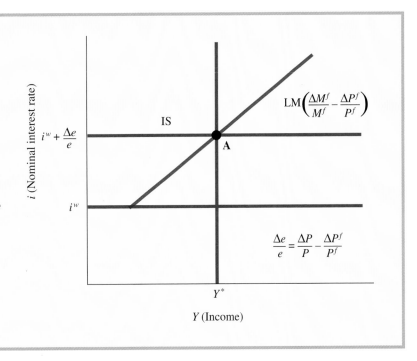

i (Nominal interest rate)

$i^w + \dfrac{\Delta e}{e}$

IS

$LM\left(\dfrac{\Delta M^f}{M^f} - \dfrac{\Delta P^f}{P^f}\right)$

A

i^w

$\dfrac{\Delta e}{e} = \dfrac{\Delta P}{P} - \dfrac{\Delta P^f}{P^f}$

Y^*

Y (Income)

domestic governments never experience balance of payments difficulties because the exchange rate is determined by the equality of demand and supply in the capital markets. Instead, the system may lead to wildly fluctuating exchange rates as private agents try to guess the behavior of central banks with respect to their future monetary policies.

❹ FIXED VERSUS FLEXIBLE RATES

Open Economy Macroeconomics

Our experiment with a flexible-rate regime is relatively new, and although we have some ideas about how a flexible-rate system works, in many ways we are still learning. The main things economists are fairly certain about concern the constraints on domestic policies that are implied by a fixed exchange-rate system.

LESSON NUMBER 1: THE CENTRAL BANK CANNOT CONTROL THE DOMESTIC INTEREST RATE IF IT WISHES TO MAINTAIN A FIXED EXCHANGE RATE

In an open economy with fixed exchange rates, the rate of interest must be the same in all countries. Since, by assumption, households and firms are free to invest abroad, and since, also by assumption, the exchange rate is effectively controlled by the central bank, the interest rate available in one country must equal the rate in every other country. If this were not the case, investors would shift their money to the country paying the highest rate of interest, thereby bidding down the high interest rate and bidding up the low one.

FIGURE 11.8
G7 Interest Rates (Government Bond Yields)

This figure depicts the nominal interest rate on government bonds of the G7 countries between 1948 and 1993.

Notice that during the fixed exchange-rate system (before 1973) these rates tended to move together. Under the flexible exchange-rate system (since 1973) there has been much greater divergence in nominal interest rates across countries.

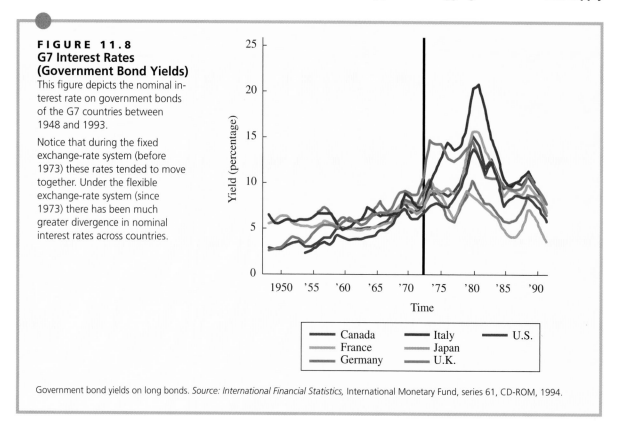

Government bond yields on long bonds. *Source: International Financial Statistics,* International Monetary Fund, series 61, CD-ROM, 1994.

There is an important qualification to this lesson. Although it is true that arbitrage will equalize interest rates across countries in a world of perfectly free international capital markets, during the Bretton Woods period, from 1948 through 1973, many governments tried to prevent this kind of arbitrage. Many national governments imposed strict **exchange controls,** that is, limits on the amount of currency that any one individual or firm could exchange at any one point in time.

Figure 11.8 graphs long-term rates of interest, the yields on long term bonds issued by national governments. These bonds represent similar kinds of assets, and in a fixed exchange-rate world with open capital markets we would expect to see their yields equalized. It is clear from the figure that, although bond yields were not exactly equalized over the fixed exchange-rate period, they did move much more closely together than in the period of flexible exchange rates, after 1973. The discrepancies between interest rates across countries in the fixed exchange-rate period were able to persist mainly due to the imposition of exchange controls. The fact that these rates did tend to move together in this period, however, suggests that the effectiveness of exchange controls was limited.

LESSON NUMBER 2: THE CENTRAL BANK CANNOT CONTROL THE MONEY SUPPLY IN A FIXED EXCHANGE-RATE SYSTEM

The idea that the interest rate is determined by world economic conditions has important implications for the ability of the central bank to influence its own stock of money.

The collapse of Bretton Woods was not inevitable. It followed from the attempts by each country to follow an independent monetary policy. Instead of borrowing to maintain the exchange rate, countries like France and the United Kingdom could instead have accepted lower rates of monetary expansion and hence lower inflation rates. These countries chose not to pursue these policies for reasons that we explain more fully in Chapter 16. Economists draw a distinction between the short run (the period over which prices are fixed and output is determined by the intersection of the IS and LM curves) and the long run (the period over which prices are flexible and output is determined by the vertical aggregate supply curve). The basic problem with a lower monetary growth rate is that, although it will result in lower inflation in the long run, in the short run slowing the rate of monetary growth leads to a recession.

LESSON NUMBER 3: THE CENTRAL BANK CANNOT, IN THE LONG RUN, CONTROL INFLATION IN A FIXED EXCHANGE-RATE SYSTEM

A third implication of a fixed-rate system is that, in the long run a country in a fixed exchange-rate system will not be able to control its own rate of inflation.

This result follows from the fact that in the long run, the inflation rate must equal the money growth rate. Since money growth rates are equalized in an open economy with fixed exchange rates, in the long run inflation rates must also be equalized. In a fixed-rate system the monetary policies of the countries are very closely tied together. Because any currency can be converted to any other currency at a fixed rate, there is essentially one world money. In a flexible exchange-rate system, on the other hand, monetary policies of each country become independent of each other.

Figure 11.9 graphs the effects of this difference on inflation rates across the G7 countries. In the fixed exchange-rate era, inflation rates moved quite closely, the one exception being France in 1956, which coincides with the devaluation of the franc. In the post-1973 world there was a much greater divergence of inflation rates as domestic monetary policies became decoupled from each other and exchange-rate movements absorbed the differences in policy.

Inflation and the Vietnam War

The three lessons from international economics are relatively simple, yet they have some important implications. For example, in the late 1970s and early 1980s most countries experienced a period of high inflation and high interest rates, which was very disruptive to financial markets. High inflation tends to be associated not just with increases in all prices, but also in increases in the volatility of relative prices; nominal prices for different commodities tend to rise in jumps, and these jumps do not all occur together. Economists do not fully understand why this relative price volatility occurs, but they do know that one of its consequences is disruptions in the functioning of the price system. One price system function is as a device for coordinating the flow of money from savers to investors. In a time of high inflation savers become less willing to lend, because the increased volatility of prices leads them to become uncertain about the real rate of return that they will earn.

Because the rate of inflation in the 1970s increased in almost every country in the world, it is natural to look for a common cause. The most likely cause of the world inflation is that the U.S. government began a dramatic expansion in borrowing in the late 1960s

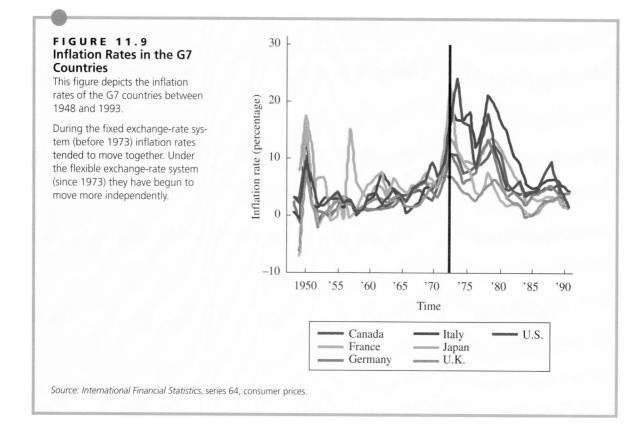

FIGURE 11.9
Inflation Rates in the G7 Countries

This figure depicts the inflation rates of the G7 countries between 1948 and 1993.

During the fixed exchange-rate system (before 1973) inflation rates tended to move together. Under the flexible exchange-rate system (since 1973) they have begun to move more independently.

Source: International Financial Statistics, series 64, consumer prices.

in order to pay for the Vietnam War. At the time, U.S. monetary policy was directed toward maintaining a low rate of interest. As the quantity of government debt expanded (to pay for the war), a good part of this debt was bought by the Federal Reserve. In other words, the increased government debt was converted into increases in the money supply. This expansion in the U.S. money supply was exported to the rest of the world through the fixed exchange-rate system. The unwillingness of foreign central banks to accept the continued monetary expansion implied by the fixed-rate system eventually led to the collapse of the fixed exchange-rate system in 1973. As is evident from Figure 11.9, the collapse of the fixed exchange-rate system came too late to prevent a burst of worldwide inflation that lasted for a decade or more.

The Problems of Monetary Union in Europe

The pros and cons of fixed versus flexible exchange rates are currently being debated by the countries of the European Economic Community (EEC). Some politicians within the EEC foresee Europe developing into a single federalist state, much along the lines of the United States, while other politicians would prefer a much looser federation with more powers held by the sovereign member states. As part of the integration process, there is already a European Parliament that has limited but growing powers to make laws for the community and to enforce common regulations. Many of the EEC countries also participate in the European Monetary System (EMS), which is a system of fixed exchange rates between the member countries of the EEC. The EMS was designed to lead to the adoption of a single currency, the Euro, in January 1999.

Within the EMS, all of the problems of the Bretton Woods system have reemerged on a smaller scale. In the Bretton Woods system, one country, the United States, had the ability to conduct an independent monetary policy. In the EMS, Germany has taken this role and all of the other countries were tied to accepting the monetary policies of the German central bank, the Bundesbank. The collapse of the Berlin wall in 1989 and the subsequent reunification of Germany placed unique demands on German fiscal policy, as the German government borrowed heavily to pay for reconstruction in the former East Germany. Unlike the U.S. experience of the 1970s, the Bundesbank was not prepared to finance reunification with monetary expansion; in other words, the Bundesbank did not monetize the growth in German government debt. The result was rising German interest rates as the private sector was forced to absorb the increased German borrowing. These rising interest rates were then transmitted to the rest of Europe through the EMS.

Just as the Bretton Woods system collapsed with increased U.S. borrowing triggered by the Vietnam war, so the EMS partially collapsed in 1991 when Italy and the United Kingdom devalued their currencies and withdrew from the system. The experience of the EMS and Bretton Woods system suggest one important lesson for the future of Europe: that for a system of fixed exchange rates (*a fortiori* for a common currency) to be effective the member states must run consistent fiscal policies.

International Economics: Europe Versus North America

The topic of open economy macroeconomics has traditionally received much less attention in the United States than in Europe. The reason for this is simple: in the postwar world order the United States was much less constrained by international considerations than were other countries. There are two reasons why, historically, the United States could afford to be less concerned about international issues than other countries. First, the United States is a relatively closed economy. Exports still account for only 15% of GDP and historically this figure was much smaller. Second, the United States was the lead country in the postwar monetary order, and the Federal Reserve was free to pursue an independent monetary policy without concern for the exchange rate. Both of these factors are eroding. We live in a world that is becoming increasingly integrated, and trade will inevitably grow as a proportion of GDP in every country in the world. Increasing trade allows increasing specialization. We are already seeing the effects of this in the world as manufacturing is increasingly shifted to low-wage countries, and high-wage countries such as the United States specialize in the service, information, and communications industries. As a consequence of increasing trade, we need to develop a trading system that ensures that businesses can buy and sell commodities overseas at prices that are not subject to huge fluctuations. At the moment, the world is experimenting with a system of flexible exchange rates, but it is likely that the number of world currencies will fall as blocks of countries that trade frequently with each other, such as the EEC, experiment with single currencies.

CONCLUSION

The exchange rate is defined as the number of foreign currency units that can be bought for a dollar. Given this definition, we learned how to define appreciation, depreciation, revaluation, and devaluation. When the exchange rate goes up, this movement is called a depreciation of the foreign currency; when the exchange rate goes down, it is called an appreciation. The same movements in exchange rates in a fixed exchange-rate regime are called devaluation or revaluation.

We also examined the meaning of the terms real exchange rate and absolute and relative purchasing power parity. In absolute purchasing parity, the real exchange rate is assumed to be the same across different countries. In relative purchasing power parity, real exchange rates are assumed to move in step. In the real world neither of these assumptions characterize the data because different countries produce different bundles of commodities and there have been big differences in relative prices over the past twenty-five years. The final concept we examined was uncovered interest rate parity. This concept holds that the rate of interest, adjusted for expected exchange-rate changes, should be the same across different countries.

The world economy behaves very differently under fixed and flexible exchange-rate regimes. The main modification that must be made to the domestic IS–LM model in the case of fixed exchange rates is that the interest rate is no longer under the control of the central bank because central bank policy must be directed towards supporting the exchange rate. If the exchange rate is set at the wrong level, there can be a conflict in the fixed exchange-rate world between domestic monetary policies and exchange rate targets. It is the existence of this tension between conflicting goals that led to the collapse of the fixed exchange-rate system in 1973. In the case of a flexible exchange-rate system, countries can follow independent monetary policies and world interest rates no longer need to move in step.

Along with introducing and defining some concepts that are important in international economics, this chapter contains one important lesson. For all countries but one, the functioning of domestic macroeconomic policy is very different in a world of fixed exchange rates from that in a world of flexible exchange rates. The main benefit of a fixed exchange-rate system is that it reduces the risk of investing abroad and thereby encourages trade. The main cost is that it removes the ability of a country to pursue independent monetary and fiscal policies. As long as we live in a world of nation states, the tension between the costs and benefits will remain and, in the absence of a coordinated system of world government, we are likely to see the retention of a system of many world currencies.

KEY TERMS

Absence of arbitrage	Depreciation
Appreciation	Devaluation
Balance of payments	Exchange controls
Bretton Woods	Exchange rate

Fixed exchange rates   Real exchange rate
Floating exchange rates   Relative purchasing power parity
Group of Seven (G7)   Revaluation
International Money Fund   Uncovered interest rate parity
Purchasing power parity

PROBLEMS FOR REVIEW

1. Consider a small open economy that begins in an income-expenditure equilibrium with a zero trade balance. Suppose that the central bank pegs the interest rate at 5%. Analyze the effects on the trade balance of the following events:

   a. An increase in government borrowing

   b. An increase in the world rate of interest

   c. A discovery of a new domestic technology that increases the domestic marginal product of capital

2. Briefly explain the difference between depreciation and devaluation. If the lira were to depreciate, would you get more lira for your dollar or less?

3. In a short paragraph, explain what is meant by the Bretton Woods system. When was it created, when did it end, and what was the main reason for its collapse?

4. What is meant by purchasing power parity? Does it hold in the real world? If not, why not?

5. What is meant by uncovered interest rate parity? Does the fact that interest rates are different mean that there are arbitrage opportunities? How does your answer depend on the exchange rate regime?

6. What main constraints on domestic policy are imposed by a fixed exchange-rate regime? What arguments can you give for moving to a fixed-rate system?

7. The following table gives some artificial data for the United States and an imaginary country called Lubania, which has a currency unit called the lotty. In 1951, Lubania left the Bretton Woods system and decided to pursue a separate, floating exchange rate.

Year	*U.S.*		*Lubania*		*(Lotties per $)*
	P dollars per U.S. basket	*i*	*P** lotties per Lubanian basket	*i**	*e*
1950	100	3	100	3	25
1951	102	3.5	51	3.5	25
1952	104	4	78	7	30
1953	108	4.5	108	9	60

   a. Calculate the real exchange rate for Lubania for each year from 1950 through 1953. What units is this measured in?

   b. Identify years in which depreciations, appreciations, devaluations, or revaluations of the lotty occurred.

   c. Calculate, for each year from 1950 through 1952, the interest differential between Lubanian and U.S. bonds.

   d. Calculate, for each year from 1950 through 1952, the interest differential adjusted for exchange-rate changes. Are there years in which you would have been better off investing in Lubania rather than in the United States?

   e. Would an American tourist be better off in Lubania in 1951 or in 1952?

   f. Does purchasing power parity hold between the United States and Lubania?

8. What problems will be encountered by a country that expands the money supply at a very rapid pace in a fixed exchange-rate system? Give examples of countries that encountered these problems during the Bretton Woods period. How did these countries resolve their problems?

9. After completing your degree, you decide to take a job in Europe as a financial reporter for CNN. In the year 2002, the British prime minister announces that Britain is going to join the European Monetary System and adopt the Euro as its currency. One of his critics points out that the European interest rate in 2002 is 14%. The prime minister responds that this is not a problem and that Britain will maintain an interest rate of 3% to protect British homeowners from high mortgage rates. Prepare a three-minute news story explaining to the CNN audience why the prime minister's plan is unlikely to succeed.

Dynamic Macroeconomics

Part 4 contains five chapters that are united by their concern with economic dynamics, an explicit theory of how the economy moves from one period to the next. Chapter 12 introduces the idea of a difference equation, the tool that we use to study the movement of economies through time. Chapters 13 and 14 use difference equations to understand economic growth and they are two of the most rewarding chapters in the book. They will bring you to the frontier of knowledge on the topic of economic growth.

In Chapters 15 and 16 you will learn how to extend the neoclassical model to a dynamic setting. Chapter 15 begins by introducing dynamics into the neoclassical model, and in Chapter 16 we will study the theory of *rational expectations*, a theory that underlies modern analyses of the role of monetary policy.

CHAPTER 12

Debt, Deficits, and Economic Dynamics

❶ INTRODUCTION

In previous chapters we analyzed how the economy behaves at a given point in time; this is called **static analysis**. This chapter introduces **dynamic analysis,** the study of how the economy behaves at different points in time. Although static analysis can go a long way toward answering questions that interest economists and policy makers, some issues in macroeconomics are explicitly dynamic. In this chapter we analyze one such issue, the economics of debt and deficits.

Following the publication of the *General Theory,* Keynesian economists advocated a policy of stabilization. They suggested that the government should raise government expenditure when unemployment is high and lower it when unemployment is low. The pursuit of policies of this kind made deficits grow, following World War II, as the government found it politically more expedient to increase spending than to raise taxes. Difference equations enable us to understand how these deficits accumulated and led to the recent crisis in which the government reduced expenditure to balance the budget.

❷ DEBT AND DEFICITS

The Relationship of the Debt to the Deficit

The government's budget equation is an example of a **difference equation,** an equation that shows how a variable changes from one period to the next. We can use this equation to study the connection between the national debt and the government budget deficit.

$$\textbf{12.1} \qquad B_t \quad = \quad B_{t-1} \quad \times \quad (1 + i) \quad + \quad D_t$$

Nominal value of new government debt	Nominal value of outstanding government debt	One plus the nominal interest rate	Primary government budget deficit

Equation 12.1 assumes that government debt is all of one-year maturity.[1] This means that the government issues bonds each year that it repays the following year at nominal interest rate i. Variables dated in the current year are denoted by the subscript t, and variables from the previous year are denoted by the subscript $t - 1$. For example, B_{t-1} represents the nominal value of existing government debt, carried over from year $t - 1$, and B_t is the new debt issued in year t. For simplicity we assume that the interest rate is the same every year.

The variable D_t is the **primary deficit.** This is equal to the value of government expenditures plus transfer payments, minus the value of government revenues. It is *not* the same as the deficit reported in the newspapers—the primary deficit excludes the value of interest payments on outstanding debt. Table 12.1 illustrates the relationship between the primary and reported deficits with data from 1995.

TABLE 12.1
Federal Expenditures and Receipts

Outlays (1995)	$ Billions	Receipts (1995)	$ Billions
Government purchases	454		
Transfer payments	713		
Other	235		
Total primary outlays	1,402	Total tax receipts	1,490
Primary Deficit			−88
Net interest	233		
Total outlays	1,635		
Reported deficit			+145

---

1. The maturity of a bond is the length of time before the principal must be repaid. The government issues debt of many different maturities. Because the complications introduced by allowing for different maturities do not add anything of substance to the problem, we treat the case in this chapter as though all bonds had one year maturity.

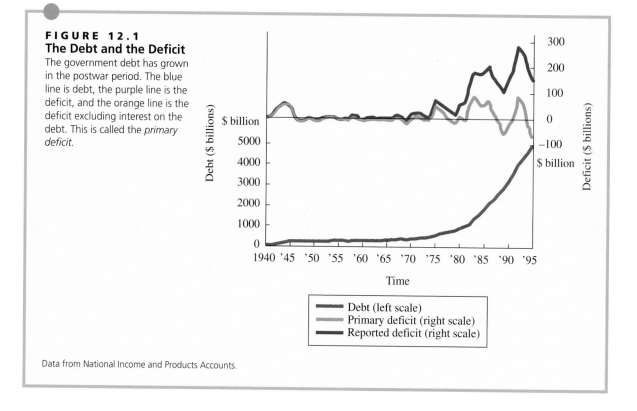

FIGURE 12.1
The Debt and the Deficit
The government debt has grown in the postwar period. The blue line is debt, the purple line is the deficit, and the orange line is the deficit excluding interest on the debt. This is called the *primary deficit*.

Data from National Income and Products Accounts.

Table 12.1 lists the values of the components of federal government expenditures and receipts in billions of dollars. The first column shows outlays, and the second, receipts from tax revenues. The primary deficit, D_t, was equal to −$88 billion in 1995. The fact that this number is negative means that receipts exceeded outlays; the primary budget was in surplus. But although the primary budget was in surplus, the **reported deficit** was equal to $145 billion. The reported deficit includes interest payments on the outstanding debt: in 1995 these interest payments amounted to $233 billion. Adding an outlay of $233 billion to a primary deficit of −$88 billion results in a reported deficit of +$145 billion. This is the reported deficit that you see in the newspapers, but the primary deficit is more useful to studying how the debt accumulates over time.

Figure 12.1 illustrates why policy makers have been concerned with the debt and the deficit in recent years. One obvious feature is that the national debt, represented by the solid blue line, grew dramatically in the 1980s. A related problem is that from 1940 through 1970 the government's budget was approximately balanced on average, but in the 1980s the deficit grew significantly, and there has been a reported deficit, the purple line, every year since 1970.

Although the growth of the debt is a problem, Figure 12.1 overstates how important this problem really is. To put the budget figures in a more appropriate light, Figure 12.2

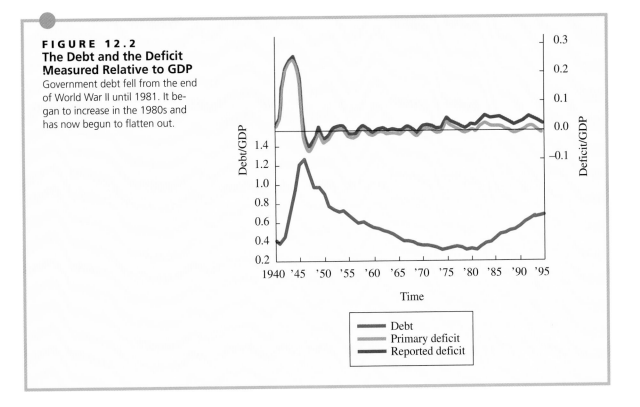

FIGURE 12.2
The Debt and the Deficit Measured Relative to GDP
Government debt fell from the end of World War II until 1981. It began to increase in the 1980s and has now begun to flatten out.

presents the same data measured as a percentage of GDP. To understand why it is appropriate to measure debt and deficits relative to GDP, consider an analogy in which a student leaves college with a credit-card bill of $100. Suppose she allows her credit-card bill to grow by 2% per year. Whether or not growing debt of this kind is a problem depends on whether her income increases at a sufficient rate to be able to pay the interest on the debt and eventually to repay the debt itself. As long as her income grows by more than 2% per year, the student's ratio of debt to income will actually be shrinking.

Just as the student's credit-card debt should be measured relative to her ability to repay it, so the national debt should be measured relative to the government's ability to repay. Because the ultimate source of the government's ability to repay is its ability to tax GDP, the appropriate measures of debt and the deficit of the United States are relative to GDP. Although government debt has grown every year in nominal terms, Figure 12.2 shows that it peaked relative to GDP in 1946 at a little over 1.2 GDPs. In 1946 the debt-to-GDP ratio was much higher than it is now, but for a good reason. The government had borrowed heavily to pay for World War II. Because the benefit of paying for a war accrues to future taxpayers as well as to contemporary taxpayers, the use of deficit financing in wartime makes good sense. The current situation is different: The government deficit has increased in peacetime.

❸ MODELING THE GROWTH OF GOVERNMENT DEBT

Now we are ready to write a mathematical model based on Equation 12.1 that shows how the national debt is related to the budget deficit. The government budget equation is a difference equation. The feature that distinguishes it from an ordinary algebraic equation is the variable B and its time subscript, t: that is, there is a different value of B for every value of t. The government budget equation tells us how the debt in any given year is related to that year's deficit, the interest rate, and the debt in the previous year. Once we know the deficit, the interest rate, and the initial level of debt, Equation 12.1 allows us to compute the stock of debt in every subsequent year. The process of finding the values of debt for each subsequent year, given an initial value of debt, involves solving the difference equation.

Using the GDP as a Unit of Measurement

Government debt measured in dollars has been growing almost every year since the United States began borrowing. But so have all of the other dollar-denominated variables in the U.S. economy. For this reason, Equation 12.1 is not a very useful tool: It cannot tell us whether debt is growing too fast relative to the government's ability to repay. A more useful method is transforming the government budget equation and measuring debt and deficits relative to GDP.

To make our task simpler, we assume that the growth rate of nominal GDP (n), the nominal interest rate (i), and the ratio of the primary deficit to GDP (d) are all constants. Nominal GDP grows because of real growth and inflation, both of which are included in the term n. The assumption that the deficit-to-GDP ratio is constant means that the government fixes the size of its primary deficit as a fraction of GDP. This fixed value equals d. Finally, we assume that the Federal Reserve Board fixes the interest rate at i by buying or selling debt in the open market.

12.2
$$b_t \quad = \quad d \quad + \quad \frac{(1+i)}{(1+n)} \quad \times \quad b_{t-1}$$

| **New debt as a fraction of GDP** | **Deficit as a fraction of GDP** | **Interest relative to the growth rate** | **Existing debt as a fraction of GDP** |

Equation 12.2 rewrites the budget constraint of the government using the GDP as a unit of measurement.[2] The variable b_t is the value of the debt this year as a fraction of this year's GDP, and b_{t-1} is the value of the debt last year relative to last year's GDP. The

---

2. **Mathematical Note:** Equation 12.2 is derived from Equation 12.1 by dividing both sides by nominal GDP at date t. Letting Y_t^n represent nominal GDP we get the expression

$$\frac{B_t}{Y_t^N} = \frac{D_t}{Y_t^N} + (1+i)\frac{B_{t-1}}{Y_{t-1}^N}\frac{Y_{t-1}^N}{Y_t^N}$$

We have multiplied and divided the second term on the RHS by Y_{t-1}^N because b_{t-1} is defined as B_{t-1}/Y_{t-1}^N. We get Equation 12.2 by recognizing that Y_t^N/Y_{t-1}^N is defined to be $(1+n)$ and D_t/Y_t^N is defined as d.

debt-to-GDP ratio grows for two reasons. First, the government must issue debt to cover a primary deficit; this is the term d, which measures the ratio of the deficit to GDP. Second, the government must pay interest on existing debt. This is captured by the coefficient $(1 + i)/(1 + n)$.

Suppose that the primary deficit is equal to zero; that is, the government raises exactly enough taxes to cover its expenditure, excluding interest. What will happen to the ratio of debt-to-GDP? The government must increase debt by a factor of $(1 + i)$ to pay the interest on existing debt. This factor makes the debt-to-GDP ratio increase. But nominal GDP is itself increasing at the rate $(1 + n)$, thereby expanding the capacity of the government to generate revenue through taxes. This factor makes the debt-to-GDP ratio decrease. The net effect of these two factors is captured by the ratio $(1 + i)/(1 + n)$. If i is greater than n, the debt-to-GDP ratio will grow. If it is smaller than n, the ratio will shrink.

Using Graphs to Analyze Difference Equations

A difference equation describes how a variable that changes over time (a **state variable**) depends on its own past value and on a number of parameters. The state variable in Equation 12.2 is the debt-to-GDP ratio, b, and the parameters are d, i, and n. The parameter d represents the intercept, and the compound parameter $(1 + i)/(1 + n)$ is the slope of a graph that plots the value of the debt-to-GDP ratio in year t against the debt-to-GDP ratio in year $t - 1$.

The solution to a difference equation is a list of values for the state variable, one for each date in the future. To compute the solution, we need to know the initial value of the debt-to-GDP ratio. We then iterate Equation 12.2 to generate successive future values of this variable. The solution tells us how big the government's debt-to-GDP ratio will be in every future year. By examining how the solution to the equation changes as we change the deficit or as the interest rate goes up or down, we can predict what changes in policy are necessary to bring the debt down to any particular level within a specified number of years. This is exactly the kind of question that is currently absorbing politicians. In order to answer questions of this kind, it is essential to be able to solve difference equations.

The solution to a difference equation can display very rich behavior. For example, the value of b_t could increase without bound. Alternatively, it could grow for a while and then settle down to a fixed value. Both kinds of behavior are possible, depending on the values of the parameters. A simple way of discovering how a difference equation behaves is to use a diagram that plots values of the state variable in successive periods on the two axes of a graph. A diagram of this kind for the government budget equation is given in Figure 12.3. The blue upward-sloping line is the graph of the difference equation $b_t = d + (1 + i)/(1 + n)b_{t-1}$; this is the government budget equation. The purple line at $45°$ to the axis is the steady state condition $b_t = b_{t-1}$, and the bold black line that zigzags back and forth is the solution to the budget equation if the initial debt equals b_0.

The point where the blue and purple lines intersect is called a **steady state solution.** A steady state solution is a value of the state variable that satisfies the government budget Equation 12.2 and that is independent of time. These two requirements are summarized in Equation 12.3, which reproduces Equation 12.2 without the subscript t on the variable b. Rearranging Equation 12.3 leads to an expression for the steady state solution in terms of the parameters d, i, and n; we refer to the steady state with the symbol $\bar{b}$ and solve for this

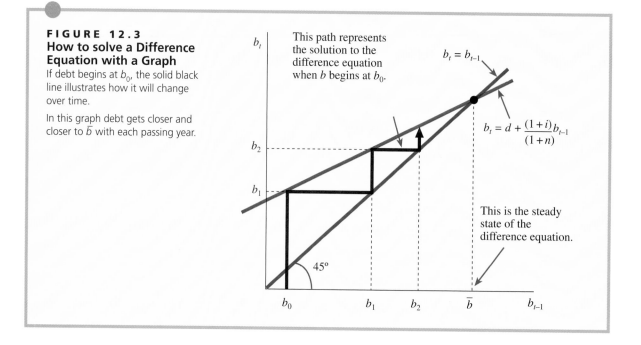

FIGURE 12.3
How to solve a Difference Equation with a Graph
If debt begins at b_0, the solid black line illustrates how it will change over time.

In this graph debt gets closer and closer to $\bar{b}$ with each passing year.

This path represents the solution to the difference equation when b begins at b_0.

$b_t = b_{t-1}$

$b_t = d + \dfrac{(1+i)}{(1+n)} b_{t-1}$

This is the steady state of the difference equation.

45°

steady state in Equation 12.4. The steady state solution is very special because if b ever becomes to equal $\bar{b}$, it will never change.

12.3
$$b = d + \frac{(1+i)}{(1+n)} b$$

The steady state of the difference equation solves this equation.

12.4
$$\bar{b} = \frac{(1+n)}{(n-i)} d$$

Collecting terms in b on one side of the equation leads to the formula for the steady state.

The stationary solution, in which b begins at $\bar{b}$ and stays there, is one possible solution to the difference equation. But what if the variable begins at a value less than $\bar{b}$, such as b_0? What will happen to subsequent values of b? The graph in Figure 12.3 can be used to answer this question.

In any given period, let the variable t stand for a specific number. Suppose, for example, that we let t equal 1. We may then plot b_0 on the horizontal axis of the graph and read off the value of b_1 as the point on line $b_1 = d + (1+i)/(1+n)b_0$ that is directly above b_0. This process can be repeated. If we now let t equal 2, we can plot the distance b_1 along the horizontal axis and read the value of b_2 from the line $b_2 = d + (1+i)/(1+n)b_1$ in the same way. The first step of the solution gives us b_1 as a point on the vertical axis of the graph. To plot this same distance along the horizontal axis, we can use the line $b_t = b_{t-1}$ (the 45° line) to translate the point b_1 from the vertical to the horizontal axis. Zigzagging between the blue line $b_t = d + (1+i)/(1+n)b_{t-1}$ and the purple 45° line, we can trace

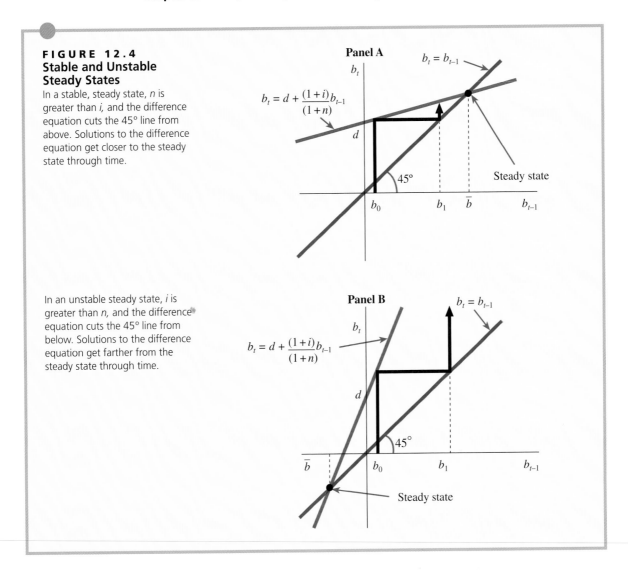

FIGURE 12.4
Stable and Unstable Steady States
In a stable, steady state, n is greater than i, and the difference equation cuts the 45° line from above. Solutions to the difference equation get closer to the steady state through time.

Panel A

$b_t = d + \dfrac{(1+i)}{(1+n)}b_{t-1}$

$b_t = b_{t-1}$

b_t

d

$45°$

b_0 b_1 $\bar{b}$ b_{t-1}

Steady state

In an unstable steady state, i is greater than n, and the difference equation cuts the 45° line from below. Solutions to the difference equation get farther from the steady state through time.

Panel B

$b_t = d + \dfrac{(1+i)}{(1+n)}b_{t-1}$

$b_t = b_{t-1}$

b_t

d

$45°$

$\bar{b}$ b_0 b_1 b_{t-1}

Steady state

the complete solution to the difference equation. This solution is represented on the figure as the black arrow.

Stable and Unstable Steady States

One property of steady states is called **stability.** If the steady state of the government budget equation is stable, the deficit is a much less pressing problem than if it is unstable.

Panels A and B of Figure 12.4 graph the solutions to two difference equations. Both are special cases of Equation 12.2. The slope of the difference equation in panel A is a positive number between zero and one: in panel B it is a positive number greater than one. For both figures the intercept of the difference equation is the same number, d.

The different values of the slopes of the equations causes the behavior of their solutions to differ. The steady state in case A is stable, and in case B it is unstable. To understand why, look at the path of the variable b_t that begins at some positive value b_0. This is represented in panel A as the zigzag arrow that gets closer and closer to the steady state. Contrast this to the situation in panel B, in which the zigzag arrow moves farther and farther away from the steady state as time progresses: b grows without bound. In panel B the steady state is unstable.

The fact that d is the same number in panels A and B of Figure 12.4 means that the government is running the same deficit-to-GDP ratio in both cases. The slope of the difference equation is the ratio of one-plus-the-interest-rate to one-plus-the-growth-rate of nominal GDP. In panel A this slope is less than 1.0, which corresponds to a situation in which the interest rate is less than the growth rate. In panel B it is greater than 1.0, which corresponds to a situation in which the interest rate is greater than the growth rate. Later, we return to this fact, as we analyze some economic consequences of stable versus unstable steady states.

Summarizing the Mathematics of Difference Equations

Let's recap. We have studied an equation of the form $b_t = d + (1 + i)/(1 + n)b_{t-1}$, where b is the state variable and d, i, and n are parameters. The solution is a list of values of b_t, one for each value of t, that satisfies the difference equation. To solve the equation, we need to provide the values of b_t at all future dates for some given value of b at an initial date.

There is a special kind of solution to the difference equation, called a steady state, that solves the equation and that is the same at every point in time. This solution is expressed algebraically by the formula

$$\bar{b} = \frac{(1 + n)\,d}{(n - i)}$$

If the state variable starts at a steady state, then it will stay there forever. Steady states can be either stable or unstable. If a steady state is stable, the state variable moves closer toward the steady state over time, wherever it starts from. If a steady state is unstable, the state variable moves farther away from the steady state for any starting point other than the steady state itself. The difference equation that we studied has a stable steady state if the interest rate is less than the growth rate of nominal GDP, and it has an unstable steady state if it is greater.

❹ THE SUSTAINABILITY OF THE BUDGET DEFICIT

Suppose that we live in an economy in which the nominal interest rate is less than the growth rate of nominal GDP. Later, we will look at the opposite case, in which the interest rate exceeds the growth rate. The behavior of the debt and the deficit are very different in the two situations.

Figure 12.5 presents data from the post-war U.S. economy. Notice that before 1979, the government was able to borrow at an interest rate that was less than the rate of nominal GDP growth. Although government debt increased every year, the government's income from tax revenues increased at an even faster rate, so the debt relative to GDP

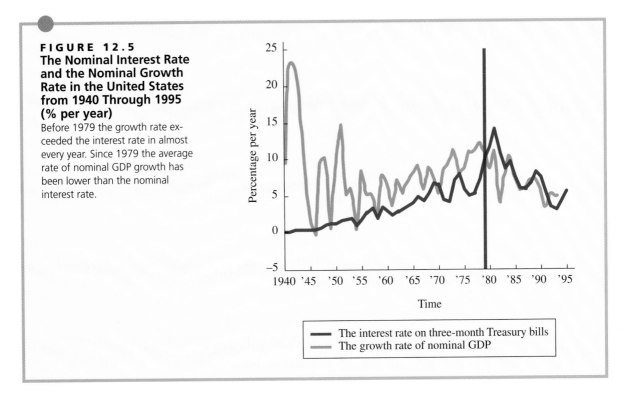

FIGURE 12.5
The Nominal Interest Rate and the Nominal Growth Rate in the United States from 1940 Through 1995 (% per year)
Before 1979 the growth rate exceeded the interest rate in almost every year. Since 1979 the average rate of nominal GDP growth has been lower than the nominal interest rate.

—— The interest rate on three-month Treasury bills
—— The growth rate of nominal GDP

decreased. In the 1980s the interest rate on short-term Treasury Bills often exceeded the rate of growth of nominal GDP. During this period, government debt grew at the rate of interest as the government borrowed to pay the principal and interest on existing debt. But its income did not grow as quickly, because tax revenues are proportional to GDP and, since 1980, the rate of nominal GDP growth has been lower than the interest rate.

Table 12.2 summarizes data on the deficit-to-GDP ratio, the interest rate, and the nominal growth rate before and after 1979, excluding the war years, during which the deficit was unusually high. In the earlier period, tax revenues were, on average, slightly higher than primary expenditures, and the average deficit was –0.6% of GDP. The average growth rate of nominal GDP was 7.5%, and the average interest rate on short-term government

TABLE 12.2
U.S. Data Before and After 1979

	Average Value 1950–1979	Average Value 1980–1995
d	–0.6%	+0.5%
n	7.5%	6.5%
i	3.8%	7.4%
$(1 + i)/(1 + n)$	0.965	1.008

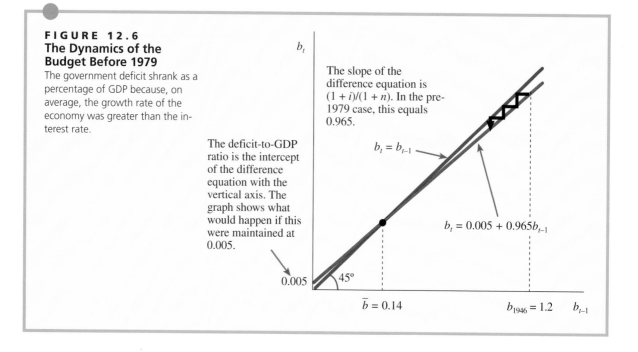

FIGURE 12.6
The Dynamics of the Budget Before 1979
The government deficit shrank as a percentage of GDP because, on average, the growth rate of the economy was greater than the interest rate.

The slope of the difference equation is $(1 + i)/(1 + n)$. In the pre-1979 case, this equals 0.965.

The deficit-to-GDP ratio is the intercept of the difference equation with the vertical axis. The graph shows what would happen if this were maintained at 0.005.

b_t

$b_t = b_{t-1}$

$b_t = 0.005 + 0.965b_{t-1}$

0.005

45°

$\bar{b} = 0.14$

$b_{1946} = 1.2$

b_{t-1}

debt was 3.8%. The average growth rate of nominal GDP exceeded the average rate of interest at which the government could borrow by 3.7 percentage points.

Contrast the situation in the pre-1979 period with the post-1979 situation. In 1981 the Reagan administration began a defense buildup, associated with a tax cut, that led to an increase in the primary deficit to nearly 2.5% of GDP by 1983. The average deficit over the period since 1979 was 0.5%, in contrast with the pre-1979 period, when it was negative. At the same time that the deficit increased, the interest rate on government debt rose from a pre-1979 average of 3.8% to a post-1979 average of 7.4%. The figures for d, n, and i are given in the first three rows of Table 12.2. The last row of the table calculates the slope of the difference equation in periods before and after 1979.

The Budget Equation Before 1979

At the end of World War II, debt was equal to 120% of GDP. For thirty years thereafter, the debt-to-GDP ratio fell steadily. The reduction occurred because the interest rate was lower than the growth rate. Using Equation 12.4, we can calculate that if the interest rate and the growth rate had remained unchanged, the economy would eventually have settled into a steady state.

Between 1947 and 1979, the slope of the government budget equation was 0.965, implying that the steady state of the budget equation was stable. During this period, debt declined slowly, and by 1979 it had fallen to 31% of GDP. Figure 12.6 illustrates how a difference equation can be used to describe the decline in debt that occurred during this period. In reality, the primary deficit fluctuated. Sometimes it was positive and sometimes it was negative, but it never exceeded 3% of GDP. The figure shows what would have hap-

FIGURE 12.7
The Dynamics of the Budget After 1979
The government deficit has been increasing as a percentage of GDP because, on average, the growth rate of the economy has been less than the interest rate.

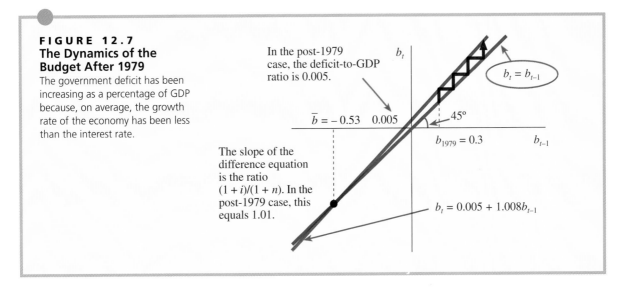

In the post-1979 case, the deficit-to-GDP ratio is 0.005.

$\bar{b} = -0.53$ 0.005

The slope of the difference equation is the ratio $(1 + i)/(1 + n)$. In the post-1979 case, this equals 1.01.

$b_t = b_{t-1}$

45°

$b_{1979} = 0.3$ b_{t-1}

$b_t = 0.005 + 1.008b_{t-1}$

pened to the debt if the interest rate had continued to remain less than the nominal GDP growth rate, and if the government had chosen to run a small deficit of 0.5% of GDP. Under this scenario, the debt would eventually have converged to a steady state level of 14% of GDP.[3] In the pre-1979 situation, a small positive primary deficit is sustainable forever. The government need not balance the budget because income growth always outstrips the growth of its debt.

If the growth rate of nominal GDP had continued to exceed the interest rate by 3.7 percentage points, and if the deficit-to-GDP ratio had remained constant, politicians would not be concerned in the 1990s with balancing the budget. However, in the 1980s nominal GDP growth slowed considerably, in part as a result of a slow-down in productivity growth and in part as a result of a reduction in inflation. At the same time, there was a big increase in the average interest rate. This led to a serious situation.

The Budget Equation After 1979

When the interest rate exceeds the growth of nominal GDP, the steady state of the budget equation must involve either a negative primary deficit or a negative debt.[4] This has important economic implications.

Figure 12.7 illustrates the situation since 1979. The debt-to-GDP ratio in 1979 was approximately 30%, but the interest rate was 1% *higher* than the growth rate of nominal

3.   The exact relationship of the steady debt ratio to the deficit is given by Equation 12.4. For the pre-1979 period, $(1 + n)/(n - i)$ is equal to $(1.075)/(0.075 - 0.038)$, which is approximately 29. If d equals 0.005 (half a percent), then $\bar{b}$ equals 0.005×29, or 0.14.
4.   **Mathematical Note:** Remember that the steady state is given by the expression

$$\bar{b} = \frac{(1 + n)^d}{(n - i)}$$

We know that $(1 + n)$ is positive. If i is bigger than n, the denominator of this expression is negative. If d is positive, then $\bar{b}$ must be negative. If d is negative, then $\bar{b}$ is positive.

GDP. The slope of the difference equation (the blue line) was equal to 1.008, *steeper* than the purple 45° line. Because nominal GDP was now growing at a rate smaller than the interest rate, a positive primary deficit was not sustainable. The figure illustrates that if the government were to try to maintain a positive primary deficit of 0.5% of GDP under the post-1979 conditions, the debt-to-GDP ratio would explode, and eventually the U.S. government would become bankrupt. The path of the debt-to-GDP ratio under these assumptions is represented by the bold zigzag line. Because the government's income cannot be bigger than GDP, bankruptcy will occur when the debt becomes so large that the entire U.S. GDP is unable to pay the interest. In practice, since the government's tax revenues are substantially less than GDP, bankruptcy will occur well before this point.

Figure 12.7 also illustrates that, when the interest rate exceeds the growth rate, the steady state debt is negative. A negative debt means that the government must lend to the private sector instead of borrowing from it. A policy of this kind is feasible and could be accomplished by increasing taxes above expenditures, using the revenues first to pay off the existing government debt, then to purchase financial assets from the private sector. Under the post-1979 configuration of interest rates and growth rates, the government would need to accumulate private sector assets equal to 53% of GDP in order to sustain a permanent budget deficit of 0.5% of GDP.

To accumulate enough assets to sustain a positive deficit, the government would need to run a large primary surplus for many years. An alternative policy, one that is more easily attainable, is to live with the existing level of debt but to raise enough revenue to service the interest on it. This policy is referred to as **balancing the budget.** There has been a lot of talk in political circles about requiring the government to balance its budget by passing a balanced budget amendment to the Constitution. Under a balanced budget policy, the government would try to set its reported deficit equal to zero. This policy prevents the debt-to-GDP ratio from exploding by raising enough revenue from taxation each period to pay the interest on outstanding debt. Because interest payments on the debt are positive, a zero reported deficit implies that the primary deficit would have to be negative.

Figure 12.8 illustrates the deficit policy that would be necessary if the government were to balance the budget immediately. In 1995, the debt-to-GDP ratio was 0.67. Assuming that the interest rate continues to exceed the growth rate by 1%, the government would need to maintain a primary deficit of –0.6% of GDP forever to stabilize the debt-to-GDP ratio at its 1995 level.[5]

Table 12.3 presents a finer breakdown of the government budget than that presented in Table 12.1. The table illustrates the magnitude of the problem. To reduce the reported deficit to zero, the government must run a primary deficit equal to the interest payment on its debt. In 1995, the primary deficit was –0.9% of GDP, but interest payments on the debt amounted to 3.2% of GDP. These interest payments are greater than the amount implied by our model, because some of the existing debt is of much longer maturity than one year and was issued at a time when the interest rate was much higher than it is today. Notice from the table that interest on the debt is almost as big as the entire national defense budget.

The Clinton administration has made some progress in reducing the deficit, but we still have some way to go. If you look closely at Figure 12.2 you will see that, in the last

5.   This figure follows from rearranging Equation 12.4. The deficit associated with any given steady state debt is equal to $(n - i)b/(1 + n)$. When $b = 0.67$, $n - i = -.01$, and $n = 0.065$, this formula implies that d must equal -0.006.

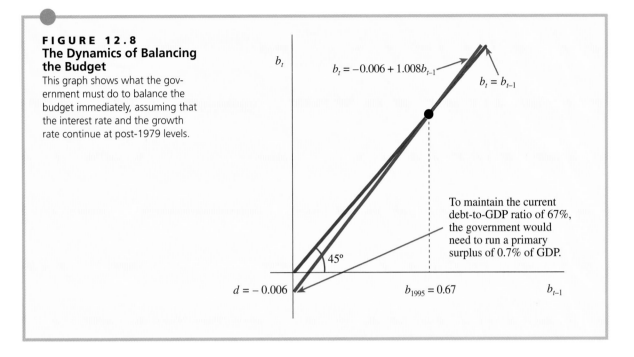

FIGURE 12.8
The Dynamics of Balancing the Budget
This graph shows what the government must do to balance the budget immediately, assuming that the interest rate and the growth rate continue at post-1979 levels.

$b_t = -0.006 + 1.008b_{t-1}$

$b_t = b_{t-1}$

To maintain the current debt-to-GDP ratio of 67%, the government would need to run a primary surplus of 0.7% of GDP.

45°

$d = -0.006$ $b_{1995} = 0.67$ b_{t-1}

TABLE 12.3
A Breakdown of the Budget Deficit in 1995

Outlays (1995)	% GDP	Receipts (1995)	% GDP
National defense	3.7%		
International affairs	0.2%		
Health	1.6%		
Medicare	2.1%	Individual income taxes	8.0%
Income security	3.0%	Corporate income taxes	2.1%
Social Security	4.6%	Social insurance	6.6%
Other	2.2%	Other	1.6%
Total primary outlays	17.4%	Total receipts	18.3%
Primary Deficit			**−0.9%**
Net interest	3.2%		
Total outlays	20.6%		
Reported deficit			**+2.5%**

Data are estimates of 1995 figures from the 1996 *Economic Report of the President,* table B-76, p. 369. These data are not fully consistent with Figure 12.1, which reports data from the National Income and Product Accounts.

WEBWATCH 12.1   **How to Balance the Budget**

An Internet site provided by UC-Berkeley's Center for Community Economic Research allows you to choose your own cuts in expenditure or increases in revenues in an effort to balance the budget. You can find the budget simulator at
http://garnet.berkeley.edu:3333/budget/budget.html. The following information is quoted from their budget simulator page.

Welcome to the National Budget Simulation!

This simple simulation should give you a better feel of the trade-offs which citizens and policy makers will need to make to balance the budget.

The National Budget Simulation is a project of UC-Berkeley's Center for Community Economic Research and was created by Anders Schneiderman and Nathan Newman.

You may also want to check out the Center's Web site: http://socrates.berkeley.edu:3333/.aboutccer.html, the Economic Democracy Information Network, which has a whole array of information on economic and policy issues.

This simulation asks you to cut the 1995 fiscal deficit in order to achieve a balanced budget. In order to make the choices we face in the budget clearer, we assume that you make the cuts all in one year. You may also want to increase spending in areas that you think are being shortchanged under present budget priorities.

---

few years, debt has almost stabilized as a percentage of GDP, and in that sense the problem is much less severe than it was a few years ago. But the magnitude of the interest payments on current debt is substantial, and we will face some difficult choices in the next few years if the budget is to be brought into balance.

❺ DIFFERENT PERSPECTIVES ON DEBT AND DEFICITS

Ricardian Equivalence

We have argued throughout this chapter that the increase in debt that occurred in the 1980s is a problem that needs to be addressed. One group of economists argues that this assumption is false and that high debt is not in itself a problem. The leading proponent of this view is Robert Barro of Harvard University; Barro's position is called **Ricardian Equivalence** after the English economist David Ricardo, to whom Barro traces his ideas.[6] Barro believes that the problems of the 1980s were caused by increased govern-

---

6.   A very readable source on these issues is the exchange between advocates and critics of Ricardian Equivalence in the *Journal of Economic Perspectives,* Spring 1989. See in particular the article by Robert J. Barro, "The Ricardian Approach to Budget Deficits," pp. 37–54, and the replies by B. Douglas Bernheim, "A Neoclassical Approach to Budget Deficits," pp. 55–72 and Robert Eisner, "Budget Deficits and Reality," pp. 73–94.

ment spending, and, to a first approximation, that it doesn't matter whether government spending is financed by debt or taxes. If government spending is financed by debt, according to Barro, households will choose to hold all of this increased debt without reducing the amount of saving that they devote to investment in new factories and machines. The reason that households would be willing to increase their saving in this way is that they anticipate that they will need to have extra wealth to pay increased taxes in the future. These households recognize that the government will eventually need to raise taxes in order to pay the principal and interest on its debt. Although the Ricardian view is not widely held by policy makers, it has been very influential among academics.

The Relationship Between the Budget and the Rate of Interest

The period after 1979 was qualitatively different from the period before 1979 for two reasons. First, the budget deficit has increased gradually as a fraction of GDP. Second, and more importantly, the interest rate has begun systematically to exceed the growth rate of nominal GDP. To keep our analysis simple, we have treated these two changes as independent of each other. In fact, this may not be the case. There are good reasons to think that the increase in the budget deficit in the United States may have *caused* the increase in the interest rate. However, before rushing to the conclusion that because the two events occurred together, one must have caused the other, we should consider some international evidence.

There are plausible reasons why an increase in U.S. government borrowing should drive up the U.S. interest rate. A simple economic model of borrowing and lending, of the kind that we studied in Chapter 6, suggests an effect of this kind. However, at the same time that the interest rate began to exceed the growth rate in the United States, a similar phenomenon occurred in all of the G7 nations. Figure 12.9 presents evidence from Canada, France, Japan, Italy, Germany, and the United Kingdom—the other six members of the Group of Seven. Notice that the pattern in these countries is comparable with the experience of the United States. In all cases, the interest rate before 1979 was less than the growth rate of nominal GDP in almost every year. After 1979, the situation was reversed.

All of this suggests that there was a common cause at work. Perhaps the increase in the U.S. budget deficit is responsible for the increase in the domestic interest rate. This is a possible explanation for the change in events—even in light of the international evidence—because the United States occupies a unique place in the international financial markets, and many currencies are in practice tied to the U.S. dollar even though in principle, in the era of floating exchange rates, there is no explicit link. The central banks of the G7 countries, other than the United States, often act to prevent dramatic changes in their exchange rates with the dollar. This international linkage implies that U.S. interest rate increases put pressure on nominal interest rates to increase throughout the world.

To sum up, the U.S. deficit is a worldwide problem because the interest rate and the growth rate have displayed similar patterns in many countries. It is possible that the problem originated in the United States because the government increased its primary deficit in the 1970s. This policy could have put pressure on the U.S. interest rate that was in turn transmitted to other countries. But this is not the only possible explanation, and to date there has been insufficient research on the issue to reach a definite conclusion.

FIGURE 12.9
The Interest Rate and the Growth Rate in the G7 Countries (Excluding the United States)

Why has the situation in the United States been so different since 1979? There are two possible explanations. One is that productivity growth has slowed down due to a change in the pace at which we are discovering new technologies. The second is that interest rates have increased as government borrowing increased. Whichever explanation is correct, these graphs illustrate that the phenomenon of slow growth and high interest rates is worldwide. Every country in the G7 group of industrialized nations has experienced similar difficulties. This could be because the underlying rate of productivity growth is common to all countries in the world. It could also be because world capital markets are linked, and a high deficit in the United States influenced the interest rate throughout the world.

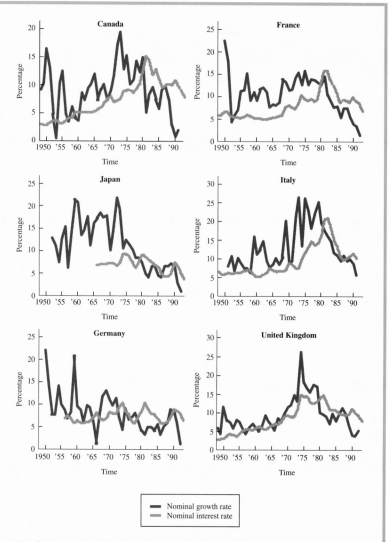

Data is from *International Financial Statistics,* International Monetary Fund. The interest rates are for comparable financial instruments across the six countries. The data is not available over the entire period for all six countries.

CONCLUSION

Difference equations are used to describe how a state variable changes over time. The solution to a difference equation is a list of numbers that describes the values of the state variable in successive periods. A steady state solution to a difference equation is a special kind of solution in which the state variable is the same in every period. Steady states can be stable or unstable. If a steady state is stable, the state variable converges towards it for any initial value; if it is unstable, the state variable diverges away from it.

The relationship of the government debt to the government budget deficit is described by a difference equation in which the debt-to-GDP ratio is the state variable. The behavior of this equation depends on the ratio of the interest rate to the growth rate. If the interest rate exceeds the growth rate, the steady state is unstable; if the interest rate is less than the growth rate, it is stable.

The U.S. debt-to-GDP ratio was described by a stable difference before 1979; since then it has been unstable. Before 1979 the government ran small budget deficits; these deficits did not cause the debt-to-GDP ratio to increase, because the economy grew more rapidly than the interest rate. After 1979 the interest rate exceeded the growth rate, and politicians were forced to reduce the deficit in order to balance the budget. The same phenomenon occurred throughout the world, and it may have a common cause. A likely candidate is the increase in the U.S. deficit that caused an increase in the interest rate. This increase was transmitted to the rest of the world through the international capital market.

KEY TERMS

Balancing the budget	Ricardian equivalence
Difference equation	Stability
Dynamic analysis	State variable
Primary deficit	Static analysis
Reported deficit	Steady state solution

PROBLEMS FOR REVIEW

1. For each of the following equations

   i. $x_t = 1.5 + (2/3)x_{t-1}$ iv. $x_t = 2 + 0.5x_{t-1}$

   ii. $x_t = 1.5\,x_{t-1}$ v. $x_t = 1 + x_{t-1}$

   iii. $x_t = 3 + 2x_{t-1}$

   a. Draw a graph of x_t against x_{t-1}.

   b. Find the value of the steady state.

   c. Say whether this steady state is stable or unstable.

2. Explain, in words, the difference between the government debt and the government budget deficit.

3. Explain, in words, the difference between the primary deficit and the reported deficit. Is one always bigger than the other? If so, why? If not, why not?

4. In many Western countries, population growth is falling. How do you think this will affect the budget deficit? Why?

5. You are hired by the editor of the *Wall Street Journal* to write a short article explaining why the government's debt, measured in dollars, is higher than at any time in U.S. history. Either take the view that the debt is a serious problem that needs to be immediately addressed *or* argue that the debt is not as serious as is often thought. In either case, your article should make use of the idea of debt measured as a fraction of GDP.

6. Explain, in words, the difference between a stable and an unstable steady state. Give an example of an economic issue for which this difference matters.

7. In Italy the government ran a budget deficit equal to 8% of GDP in 1995.

   a.   If the Italian interest rate is 5% and the growth rate of nominal GDP is 6%, calculate the steady state ratio of debt to GDP.

   b.   Suppose that the maximum the government can possibly raise in taxes is equal to 50% of GDP. Assuming that the interest rate equals 5% and the nominal growth rate of GDP equals 6%, at what value of the deficit will the interest payments on the steady state debt exceed the government's ability to finance these payments through taxes?

8. Using the national budget simulator at http://garnet.berkeley.edu:3333/budget/budget.html, create your own plan to balance the budget in one year.

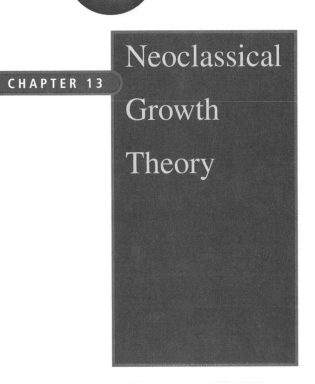

CHAPTER 13

Neoclassical Growth Theory

❶ INTRODUCTION

Growth theory is a tremendously active area of economic research. Until relatively recently, growth theorists concentrated on documenting the sources of growth. We know that per capita income in the United States has grown at 1.64% on average over the past century. How much of this 1.64% was due to increases in population, how much to increases in the capital stock, and how much to new discoveries and innovations? The major work on these issues was carried out in the 1950s, and the leading contributors were Robert Solow and T. W. Swan. Solow and Swan showed that investment in new capital and the growth of population cannot, in themselves, lead to continued growth in per capita income. Instead, they attributed growth to the continual invention of new technologies that made labor more productive. Since the source of these innovations was unexplained in the models of Solow and Swan,[1] their theory became known as the **exogenous growth theory.**

From the 1950s until the late 1980s, the theory of economic growth was a stagnant area for economic research. All of this changed for two reasons. First, a group of economists

---

1. T. W. Swan. "Economic growth and capital accumulation." *Economic Record* 32 (November, 1956): 334–361. Robert M. Solow. "A contribution to the theory of economic growth." *Quarterly Journal of Economics* 70 (February, 1953): 65–94.

WEBWATCH 13.1   Webwatch 13.1 Penn World Table Online

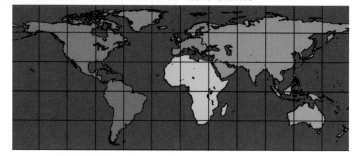

The Penn World Tables are available on the Internet at several sites. One of the most accessible is provided by the University of Toronto at **http://datacentre.epas.utoronto.ca:5680/**. The University of Toronto site provides an option that lets you plot graphs of any of the data series. These currently include data on 29 variables for 152 countries.

The graph in this panel was downloaded from the University of Toronto site. It represents investment as a share of GDP for the Peoples Republic of China for the period from 1960 through 1993.

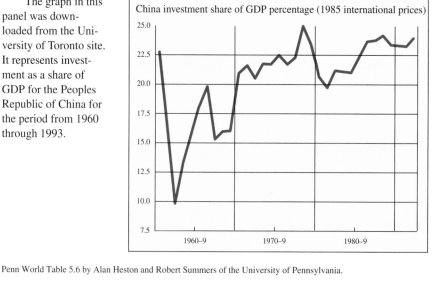

China investment share of GDP percentage (1985 international prices)

Penn World Table 5.6 by Alan Heston and Robert Summers of the University of Pennsylvania.

working at the University of Pennsylvania completed a project called the **Penn World Table.**[2] This is a comprehensive set of national income and product accounts for every country in the world beginning in 1950 or 1960 (depending on country). Originally the data ended in 1988 but it is now revised on a regular basis. The Penn World Table was innovative because it reports data that is comparable across countries, allowing for the fact that the GDP basket of goods differs from country to country. The Penn World Table records national income in every country in the world using the 1985 U.S. dollar as a common unit of measurement. The data shows that the world is changing in an unprecedented way. In the early 1800s a number of countries began to experience sustained growth in per

2.   Robert Summers and Alan Heston. "The penn world table." *Quarterly Journal of Economics* (May, 1991): 327–368.

capita income. The new data set shows that in the twentieth century, economic growth has become more and more common, and it allows us to compare growth rates for different countries and regions.

A second reason for the resurgence of growth theory in the 1980s is that a comprehensive source of data stimulated a whole new generation of research, as theorists now had a way of checking their conjectures about sources of growth. Two theoretical papers were instrumental in the resurgence of growth theory, one by Paul Romer of Stanford University and one by Robert E. Lucas, Jr. of the University of Chicago.[3] Lucas and Romer were not satisfied with the exogenous explanations of growth put forward by Swan and Solow. Instead, they searched for an explanation of the sources of technological progress. One of the main ideas pursued by the new growth theory is that innovations are accompanied by learning on the job, and this learning leads to the accumulation of knowledge. Economists refer to accumulated knowledge as **human capital.** Because the new growth theory accounts for the reasons that per capita income grows, rather than taking this growth as exogenous, it is referred to as the **endogenous growth theory.**

❷ THE SOURCES OF ECONOMIC GROWTH

Growth theory begins with the assumption that GDP is related to aggregate capital and labor through a production function. To keep things manageable, suppose that all of the output in the economy is produced from a single input.[4] Figure 13.1 presents data on output and input per person for the U.S. economy from 1929 through 1995. Output per person is GDP measured in thousands of 1987 dollars per capita. Input per person is an aggregate measure that is constructed by combining capital and labor in a way that we describe later in the chapter.

The data is unambiguous—more input leads to more output. The issue that separates exogenous growth theory from newer endogenous theories is how to interpret this data. Both theories agree that at a given point in time, with a given state of technology, output should be related to input through a production function. Exogenous growth theory insists, however, that the state of technology does not remain constant through time. The implication of this view is that each of the points in Figure 13.1 comes from a different production function.

Exogenous growth theory assumes that the production function satisfies a property called **constant returns to scale (CRS).** In the case of a production function with a single input, constant returns to scale means that the production function must be a straight line through the origin. Because the points in Figure 13.1 do not lie on a straight line through the origin, the slope of the production function must have changed from one year to the next. The figure presents two production functions, one for 1929 and one for 1990. Notice that the production function is steeper in 1990 than in 1929. According to exogenous growth theory, this slope is a measure of productivity. Increases in productivity are due to the discovery of new technologies and inventions. Because early work in growth theory did not try to explain the process of invention and innovation, productivity was left exogenous.

3.   Paul M. Romer. "Increasing returns and long-run growth." *Journal of Political Economy* 94 (October, 1986): 1002–1037. Robert E. Lucas, Jr. "On the mechanics of economic development." *Journal of Monetary Economics* 22 (July, 1988): 3–42.
4.   In reality there are many inputs. Even in macroeconomics, which is highly aggregated, we usually think of there being at least two: capital and labor. Introducing additional inputs complicates matters but does not change the main message of this section that exogenous and endogenous growth theorists disagree about the shape of the production function.

FIGURE 13.1
**Inputs and Outputs in the
United States, 1929–1995**

FIGURE 13.1
**Inputs and Outputs in the
United States, 1929–1995**
The production function in 1990
has a steeper slope than the pro-
duction function in 1929.

The increase in the slope of the
production function occurs because technological progress allows us to produce more output
for a given input.

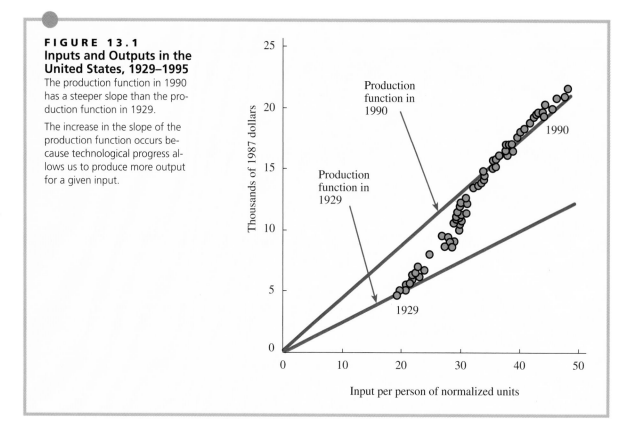

In contrast, endogenous growth theory rejects the assumption of constant returns to scale and allows for the possibility that the points in Figure 13.1 may all come from the same production function. We return to this idea in Chapter 14.

Production Functions and Returns to Scale

In applied work we usually specify a particular functional form for the production function. One function that is used frequently, because it can successfully account for a number of features of the data, is the **Cobb-Douglas function.** The Cobb-Douglas function is represented by Equation 13.1.

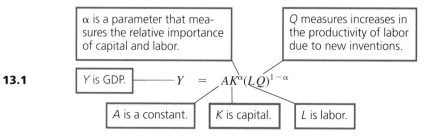

α is a parameter that measures the relative importance of capital and labor.

Q measures increases in the productivity of labor due to new inventions.

13.1

Y is GDP.

$$Y = AK^{\alpha}(LQ)^{1-\alpha}$$

A is a constant. K is capital. L is labor.

The symbols Y, K, and L stand for GDP, aggregate capital, and aggregate employment, respectively. Q is the efficiency of labor. Notice from the way that we have written the production function that there are two inputs, capital, K, and labor, L, multiplied by its efficiency, Q. We return to Q later.

The Cobb-Douglas production function contains two parameters that affect its shape. The constant A is a scale parameter that keeps the units of measurement consistent with each other. The parameter α (alpha), measures the relative importance of capital and labor in producing a unit of output. If the production function contains a complete description of all of the relevant inputs to the production process, this process should be reproducible at any scale. In other words, if all of the inputs to the production function are increased by a fixed multiple, then output should increase by the same multiple. This is the property of constant returns to scale. In the Cobb-Douglas production function, constant returns to scale means that the exponents on capital and labor add up to one.[5]

The Neoclassical Theory of Distribution

The **neoclassical theory of distribution** explains how the output of society is distributed to the owners of the factors of production, labor, and capital. The theory of distribution helps us to account for the importance of labor and capital as productive inputs. The theory asserts that factors are paid their **marginal products.** The marginal product of a factor is the amount of extra output that would be produced if the firm were to employ an extra unit of the factor. In other words, every hour of labor used by the firm earns the output that would be produced if an *extra* hour of labor were used to produce output. Similarly, every hour of capital earns the output that would be produced if an extra hour of capital were used in production. If factors of production are paid their marginal products, we can measure how much labor and capital contribute to growth by observing how much they are paid.

The Theory of Distribution and the Cobb-Douglas Function

Neoclassical distribution theory assumes that output is produced by a large number of competitive firms, each of which uses the same production function. If we assume that this production function is Cobb-Douglas, we can derive expressions for the profit maximizing rules of the firm. Using these expressions we can infer the magnitude of one of the key parameters of the production function from observing the share of national income that is paid to workers.

Because we assume that all firms use the same production function, the marginal product formula holds between aggregate variables. The profit-maximizing firm sets the marginal product of labor (MPL) equal to the real wage, w/P. If this is the case, the

---

5.   **Mathematical Note:** To check that the Cobb-Douglas function exhibits constant returns to scale, we need to multiply both capital and labor by a fixed number and see whether GDP is multiplied by the same number:

$$A(nK)^{\alpha}(nLQ)^{1-\alpha} = AK^{\alpha}(LQ)^{1-\alpha}\, n^{1-\alpha+\alpha} = nY$$

Multiplying capital by n causes GDP to be multiplied by n raised to the power α; multiplying labor by n multiplies GDP by n raised to the power $(1-\alpha)$. The total effect is the sum of these two effects: GDP multiplied by n raised to the power $\alpha + (1-\alpha) = 1$, or simply by n .

MPL, multiplied by employment and divided by income, should equal labor's share of income:

13.2 $$\text{MPL}\,\frac{L}{Y} = 1 - \alpha = \frac{wL}{PY}$$

> For the Cobb-Douglas function, labor's share of total income is a constant equal to $1 - \alpha$.

For most production functions the expression for MPL is a complicated function of capital and labor, but for the Cobb-Douglas function the marginal product of labor has a simple form.[6] For this function, the marginal product of labor multiplied by labor and divided by output is equal to $(1 - \alpha)$. This expression measures the percentage increase in output that will be gained by a given percentage increase in labor input; we call this the **labor elasticity** of the production function.[7]

We can also find an expression that describes the capital elasticity of the production function. The **capital elasticity** measures the percentage increase in output that will be produced by a given percentage increase in capital; for the Cobb-Douglas function this is α. It is important to know the labor and capital elasticities of the production function because they determine the relationship between the growth rate of output and the growth rates of factor inputs. Equation 13.2 is key because we can use it to estimate $(1 - \alpha)$. Once we know $(1 - \alpha)$, we also know α and can calculate how much of the growth in GDP per person is due to growth in labor and capital per person.

The right side of Equation 13.2 is the share of wages in income. The left side is the labor elasticity of production. In general there is no reason why this expression should be constant. For the Cobb-Douglas function however, this quantity is constant and is given by the expression $1 - \alpha$. This means we can directly measure the share of wages in income and use our measurement to estimate $(1 - \alpha)$, the labor elasticity of production.

Figure 13.2 presents data on labor's share of national income from 1929 through 1995. Labor's share has been approximately constant and equal to $\frac{2}{3}$. We can therefore set α equal to $\frac{1}{3}$ and $(1 - \alpha)$, to $\frac{2}{3}$ when we calculate the relationship of growth in capital and labor to the growth in GDP per person.

Growth Accounting

In Figure 13.1 we drew a graph of input per person against GDP per person. To construct a measure of input per person, we divided capital, employment, and real GDP by the population, N_t, to arrive at data in per capita terms. Now we explain this construction.

Equation 13.3 writes the Cobb-Douglas production function in per capita terms. Because we can infer (from national income accounts) that the exponent on capital is $\frac{1}{3}$ and the exponent on labor is $\frac{2}{3}$, we can combine labor and capital in a single measure of input per person. To construct this measure we raise capital per person to the $\frac{1}{3}$ power and em-

6.   **Mathematical Note:** The marginal product of labor is found by taking the derivative of the production function with respect to labor. For the Cobb-Douglas function, this is given by $\text{MPL} = (1 - \alpha)Y/L$.

7.   **Mathematical Note:** Another way of expressing the marginal product is $\Delta Y/\Delta L$ where Δ means "the change in." The labor elasticity, e_L, of the production function is the proportional change in Y for a given proportional change in L, that is

$$e_L = \frac{\Delta Y/Y}{\Delta L / L}$$

which can also be written as $\text{MPL}\frac{L}{Y}$.

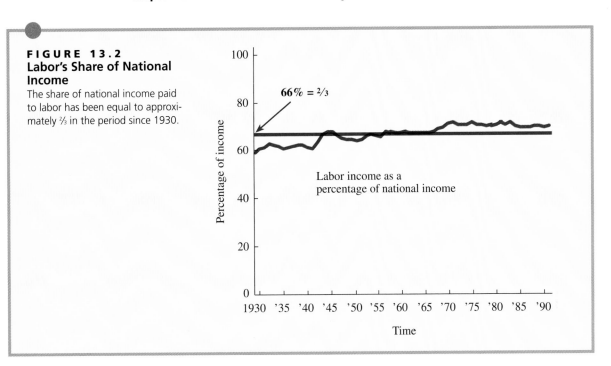

FIGURE 13.2
Labor's Share of National Income
The share of national income paid to labor has been equal to approximately ⅔ in the period since 1930.

ployment per person to the ⅔ power, and multiply them. This construction, illustrated in Equation 13.3, links output per person to input per person.

13.3

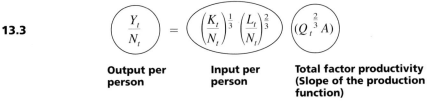

$$\left(\frac{Y_t}{N_t}\right) = \left(\left(\frac{K_t}{N_t}\right)^{\frac{1}{3}} \left(\frac{L_t}{N_t}\right)^{\frac{2}{3}}\right) \left(Q_t^{\frac{2}{3}} A\right)$$

Output per person   **Input per person**   **Total factor productivity (Slope of the production function)**

Output per person equals input per person multiplied by a term called **total factor productivity**.[8] If we construct the aggregate input in the way described in this equation, the graph of the production function is a straight line through the origin. On this graph, GDP per person is plotted against input per person, and total factor productivity corresponds to the slope of the production function. In Figure 13.1 we found that if we plot points on the production function for different years, these points do not lie on the same straight line through the origin. Solow took this as evidence of the fact that productivity has increased; that is, the slope of the production function has been increasing through time.

The fact that the slope of the production function has increased over time means that growth in labor and capital cannot on their own account for all of economic growth. Growth in labor and capital would be represented as a movement along the production function when the aggregate measure of input increases. In addition to this movement along the production function, part of growth in GDP per person must be due to changes in total factor productivity as measured by increases in the slope of the production

8.   Total factor productivity differs from labor productivity, which is the ratio of GDP to labor hours employed.

FIGURE 13.3
The Solow Residual in the United States

This graph plots the slope of the production function for every year from 1890 through 1995.

This slope is called the Solow Residual, after Robert Solow who invented the concept. It is a combined measure of the productivity of labor and capital.

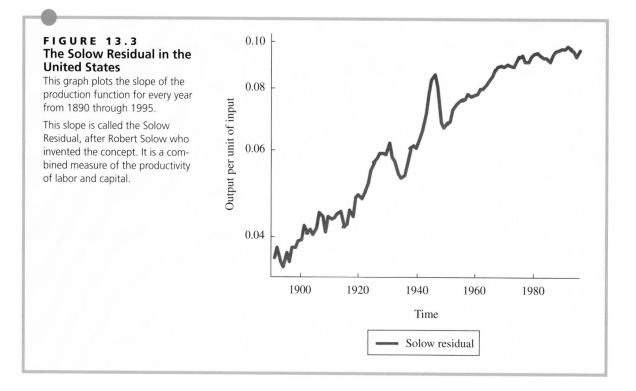

function. Economists call total factor productivity the **Solow Residual.**[9] The graph of the Solow residual, plotted against time, is presented in Figure 13.3.

The theory underlying the construction of the Solow residual is called **growth accounting,** because it allows us to account for the sources of growth by dividing the growth rate of GDP per person into its component parts. Figure 13.4 presents this division for the United States for the period from 1890 through 1995. On average, GDP per person grew by 1.64% per year, of which 0.55% was accounted for by growth in capital per person and 0.17% was accounted for by growth in employment per person. Because capital and employment growth add up to only 0.72%, the remaining 0.92% must be accounted for by increases in productivity.

Figure 13.4 reports averages of a century of data. Although century averages are useful, they can mask a considerable amount of year-to-year variation. For example, most of the growth in employment per person after World War II was a consequence of many more women entering the labor force. The main message of the figure is that although the economy has used larger quantities of the factors of production over the century, this is not the major source of increases in GDP per person. The largest contribution to growth in GDP per person came from increases in productivity.

9.   Robert Solow won the Nobel Prize in Economics in 1987 for his work in the theory of economic growth. His work was originally introduced in "A contribution to the theory of economic growth" in the *Quarterly Journal of Economics* (February 1956): 65–94. The formula used to construct the Solow residual is

$$SR_t = \frac{Y}{(K_t)^{\frac{1}{3}}(L_t)^{\frac{2}{3}}}$$

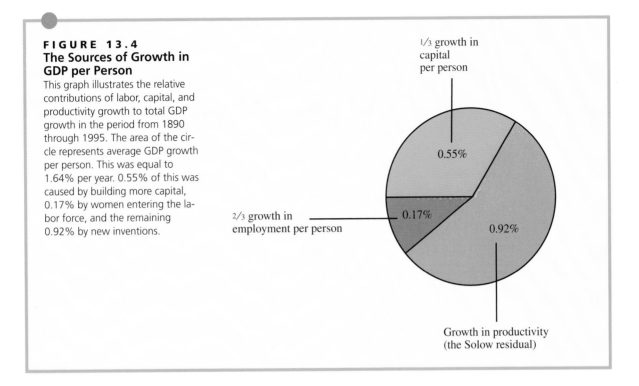

FIGURE 13.4
The Sources of Growth in GDP per Person
This graph illustrates the relative contributions of labor, capital, and productivity growth to total GDP growth in the period from 1890 through 1995. The area of the circle represents average GDP growth per person. This was equal to 1.64% per year. 0.55% of this was caused by building more capital, 0.17% by women entering the labor force, and the remaining 0.92% by new inventions.

⅓ growth in capital per person

0.55%

⅔ growth in employment per person

0.17%

0.92%

Growth in productivity (the Solow residual)

❸ THE NEOCLASSICAL GROWTH MODEL

We have described the factors that account for growth in GDP per person and measured the relative contributions of each factor in a century of data. One of these factors is the growth in capital per person, a variable that can be increased by increasing investment. This raises an obvious question: Can we increase growth by investing more as a nation? To answer this question we need to construct a model that spells out the link between investment and growth. This model, based on neoclassical assumptions about the theory of distribution, is called the **neoclassical growth model.**

Increases in productivity are necessary if a nation is to experience sustained growth in its standard of living. You might think that we could continue growing simply by building more and more factories and machines, but capital, on its own, cannot produce more output; it must be combined with labor. If an economy increases its investment rate, for a short period of time it will experience higher growth. But as more and more capital is added to a fixed quantity of labor, the incremental gains in output fall. The neoclassical growth model shows that an economy with a fixed production function subject to constant returns to scale cannot grow forever.

Three Stylized Facts

The neoclassical growth model begins with three "stylized facts" that characterize the U.S. data to a first approximation. The first is that GDP per person has grown at an average rate

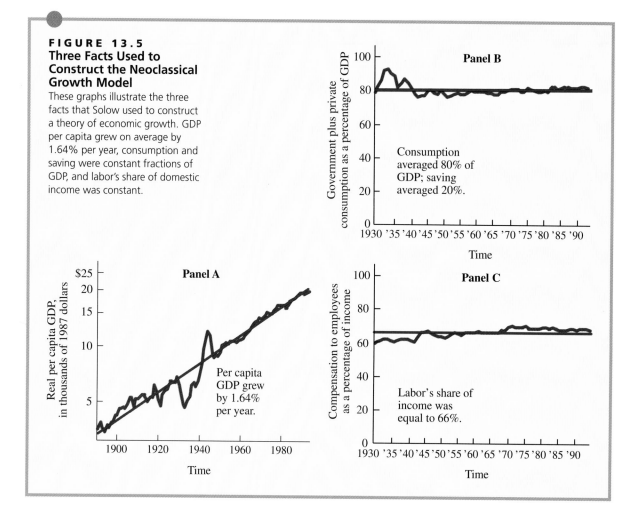

FIGURE 13.5
Three Facts Used to Construct the Neoclassical Growth Model
These graphs illustrate the three facts that Solow used to construct a theory of economic growth. GDP per capita grew on average by 1.64% per year, consumption and saving were constant fractions of GDP, and labor's share of domestic income was constant.

of 1.64% over the past century. The growth rate of GDP per person is captured by the slope of the line in panel A of Figure 13.5. The second and third stylized facts are that the share of consumption in GDP (panel B) and labor's share of income (panel C) have each remained approximately constant. The neoclassical growth model builds these constants into an economic model based on a competitive theory of production and distribution and uses this model to explain the GDP per capita growth rate.

Assumptions of the Neoclassical Growth Model

The growth model is described by a difference equation similar to the one we used in Chapter 12 in our study of the government budget. This difference equation is derived from Equations 13.4, 13.5, 13.6, and 13.7. Equations 13.4 and 13.5 are accounting identities and are true by definition. Equations 13.6 and 13.7 are more substantive. Equation 13.7

is the Cobb-Douglas production function. Equation 13.6 reflects an assumption about behavior.

13.4 $$S_t = I_t$$

> These two equations are accounting identities. They are true by definition.

13.5 $$K_{t+1} = K_t(1 - \delta) + I_t$$

13.6 $$\frac{S_t}{Y_t} = s$$

> This equation assumes that the savings rate is constant and is based on one of the three stylized facts.

13.7 $$Y_t = A\,(K_t)^{\frac{1}{3}}\,(Q_t L_t)^{\frac{2}{3}}$$

> This is the equation of the Cobb-Douglas production function. It combines the neoclassical theory of distribution and the stylized fact that labor's share of income is constant.

Equation 13.4 says that saving, S, equals investment, I. In the real world, saving by the United States could be used *either* for investment at home *or* for investment abroad. It is *not* strictly true that domestic saving equals domestic investment; the difference is made up by net exports. In practice, net exports are a relatively small fraction of GDP, and the assumption that they are zero is not too far from the truth.

Equation 13.5 defines the relationship between gross investment, I, and the stock of capital, K, at different points in time. It means that next year's capital stock is equal to the fraction of this year's capital stock that is left after depreciation plus any new investment in capital measured by gross investment, I. The δ (delta) represents the rate of depreciation, which we assume is 6%.

Equation 13.6 represents an important assumption about economic behavior. It asserts that the fraction of GDP that is saved, and therefore the fraction that is invested, is a constant denoted by s. This assumption fits one of the three stylized facts. For the U.S. economy, s is equal to 0.2 (80% of GDP is consumed by government or by private households and firms, and 20% is saved).

Equation 13.7 is the Cobb-Douglas production function parameterized with a value of α equal to $\frac{1}{3}$. This value of the output elasticity of capital is taken from the fact that labor's share of national income is equal to $\frac{2}{3}$. There are many assumptions involved in writing down this function and, as we discuss in Chapter 14, some are controversial. Given the neoclassical theory of distribution, however, the fact that the production function is Cobb-Douglas is implied by the fact that labor's share of income is constant.

Simplifying the Model

Equations 13.4–13.7 are all important components of the neoclassical growth model. Now we make three assumptions that are not strictly necessary, but that will help simplify the exposition.

Assumption 1 is that each person in the economy supplies exactly one unit of labor to the market. Using L to represent aggregate employment and N to represent the population of the economy, we represent this assumption with the formula $L/N = 1$. U.S. data shows some growth in employment per person over the century. However, the contribution of increases in employment per person to economic growth has been relatively small, and we lose little by neglecting it in our model.[10]

Assumption 2 is that population is constant: We represent the size of the population with the symbol N. Population growth is an obvious source of growth in GDP, although it cannot explain growth in GDP per person. Because we are interested in explaining growth in GDP per person, the variable that accounts for advances in our standard of living, we will ignore population growth for the time being.

Assumption 3 is that there are no changes in the efficiency of labor. We represent the constant efficiency of labor with the symbol Q. The case of fixed Q is easier to understand than the case in which technological change causes Q to grow, and using a fixed Q helps us to understand why technological change is so important to neoclassical theory.

Diminishing Marginal Product

Armed with our simplifying assumptions, we can show what happens to output per person if capital is increased and labor is fixed. To derive Equation 13.8, we divide both sides of the production function by population to arrive at the **per capita production function,** the relationship between output per person and capital per person.[11] We use lower-case letters to represent per capita variables: y for output per person and k for capital per person. The production function in per capita terms describes the technology that would be faced by a firm planning to add more capital to a fixed supply of labor.

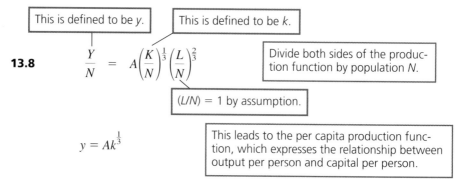

13.8
$$\frac{Y}{N} = A\left(\frac{K}{N}\right)^{\frac{1}{3}}\left(\frac{L}{N}\right)^{\frac{2}{3}}$$

This is defined to be y. | This is defined to be k. | Divide both sides of the production function by population N. | $(L/N) = 1$ by assumption.

$$y = Ak^{\frac{1}{3}}$$

This leads to the per capita production function, which expresses the relationship between output per person and capital per person.

The per capita production function is graphed in Figure 13.6. Notice that the curve gets flatter as k grows. This reflects the fact that the marginal product of capital gets smaller as more capital is added to the economy. Although the production function satisfies constant returns to scale, it displays a diminishing marginal product of capital. Do not confuse these concepts. Constant returns to scale implies that if capital and labor both change by a

10. It is now much more typical than it was twenty years ago for women to work in the marketplace rather than in the home. This shift in economic organization has resulted in an expansion of measured hours per person in employment. In practice, the contribution of an expansion in hours per person has had a relatively minor contribution to growth in GDP per person. Figure 13.4 shows that this effect accounted for 0.17% of the 1.64% per capita GDP growth over the century.
11. The constant returns to scale assumption lets us do this. Recall that if we multiply capital and labor by a fixed number, CRS means that we multiply GDP by the same number. We choose the number 1/N.

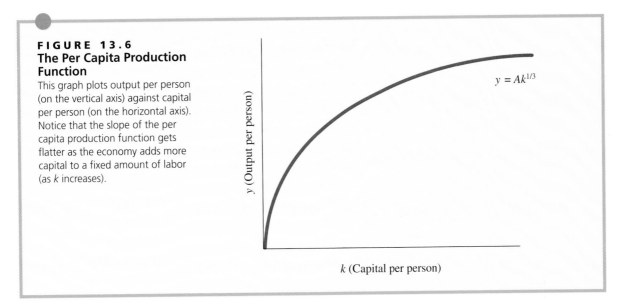

FIGURE 13.6
The Per Capita Production Function
This graph plots output per person (on the vertical axis) against capital per person (on the horizontal axis). Notice that the slope of the per capita production function gets flatter as the economy adds more capital to a fixed amount of labor (as k increases).

$$y = Ak^{1/3}$$

y (Output per person)

k (Capital per person)

fixed percentage, output will change by the same percentage. Diminishing marginal product of capital means that if capital changes by a fixed percentage, holding constant the input of labor, then output will change by a smaller percentage.

Three Steps to the Neoclassical Growth Equation

The **neoclassical growth equation,** a difference equation, describes the relationship between capital per person in any two successive years. In Chapter 12 we saw that difference equations can behave in different ways. For example, a variable that is modeled by a difference equation can grow without bound or it might converge to a steady state. The neoclassical growth equation has a stable steady state that the economy will converge to for any initial positive stock of capital per person. Because GDP per person depends only on capital per person, per capita GDP must also converge to a steady state. Because GDP per person converges to a steady state, the neoclassical growth model cannot, in the long run, explain growth. The following equations derive the neoclassical growth equation in three steps.

Step 1 $\qquad k_{t+1} = k_t(1 - \delta) + i_t$

> This is the investment identity. It defines how capital accumulates.

Step 2 $\qquad k_{t+1} = k_t(1 - \delta) + sy_t$

> This step assumes that investment (equal to saving) is proportional to output.

Step 3 $\qquad k_{t+1} = k_t(1 - \delta) + sAk_t^{\frac{1}{3}}$

> This step replaces output with the production function to generate the neoclassical growth equation.

13.9

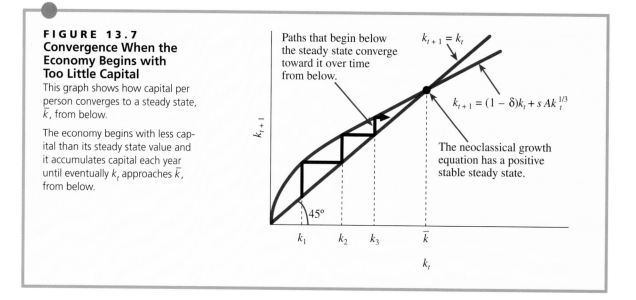

FIGURE 13.7
Convergence When the
Economy Begins with
Too Little Capital
This graph shows how capital per person converges to a steady state, $\bar{k}$, from below.

The economy begins with less capital than its steady state value and it accumulates capital each year until eventually k_t approaches $\bar{k}$, from below.

Paths that begin below the steady state converge toward it over time from below.

$k_{t+1} = k_t$

$k_{t+1} = (1 - \delta)k_t + s\,Ak_t^{1/3}$

The neoclassical growth equation has a positive stable steady state.

$45°$

$k_1 \quad k_2 \quad k_3 \quad \bar{k}$

k_t

k_{t+1}

The first step in deriving the neoclassical growth equation is to restate the capital identity in per capita form. In Step 1 capital per person next year, k_{t+1}, equals the capital per person this year that is left after subtracting depreciation, $k_t(1 - \delta)$, and adding new investment per person, i_t. Step 2 replaces investment per person by a constant fraction, s, of GDP per person, y_t. This uses the assumptions that investment and saving are equal and that saving is a constant fraction of GDP. Step 3 replaces GDP per person, y_t, with the per capita production function. The result is a difference equation in the single state variable, k, that is very similar to the equations we studied in Chapter 12. We can use Equation 13.9 to describe how capital and GDP per person change through time.

Graphing the Neoclassical Growth Equation

Figure 13.7 graphs the neoclassical growth equation. The blue curve is the graph of the neoclassical growth equation. The line at 45° to the horizontal axis represents the steady state condition for the difference equation; at every point on this line the capital stock per person in year $t + 1$ is equal to the capital stock per person in year t. The points where the neoclassical growth equation intersects the green 45° line are the steady states of the model: the steady state in which the economy has zero capital and a positive steady state labeled $\bar{k}$.

We can use the graph to study the path of the economy through time. Figure 13.7 illustrates what would happen to capital per person over time if the economy began with an initial stock of capital, k_1, less than the steady state stock $\bar{k}$. In the first period, as the economy begins with capital stock k_1, it produces output per person equal to $Ak_1^{1/3}$. If we save a fraction of this output and add it to the undepreciated capital, we increase the subsequent period's capital stock to a higher value, k_2. In this way, the economy will grow. But although the economy grows each period, the amount by which it grows gets smaller and

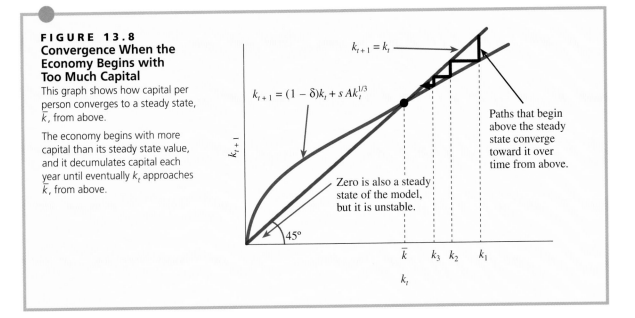

FIGURE 13.8
Convergence When the Economy Begins with Too Much Capital
This graph shows how capital per person converges to a steady state, $\bar{k}$, from above.

The economy begins with more capital than its steady state value, and it decumulates capital each year until eventually k_t approaches $\bar{k}$, from above.

$k_{t+1} = k_t$

$k_{t+1} = (1 - \delta)k_t + s\,Ak_t^{1/3}$

Paths that begin above the steady state converge toward it over time from above.

Zero is also a steady state of the model, but it is unstable.

$45°$

$\bar{k}$ k_3 k_2 k_1

k_t

smaller. This is because the economy is adding more capital to a fixed stock of labor. The additional GDP that can be produced in this way declines as diminishing returns to capital set in. The steady state to which the economy converges is a state in which the new investment each period is only just sufficient to replace the worn out capital due to depreciation. This steady state occurs at $\bar{k}$.

Figure 13.8 shows what will happen if the initial stock of capital, k_1, is greater than the steady state stock, $\bar{k}$. In this case, the level of capital is so high that the new investment is not sufficient to replace the capital that wears out from depreciation, and in the subsequent period the level of capital declines. Eventually the economy shrinks to the point where the constant fraction of GDP per person that is saved is just large enough to replace the depreciated capital; this is the steady state capital stock per person, $\bar{k}$.

The steady state is interesting from an economic point of view because it is stable. If the economy has been operating for a long time, we would expect it to have reached the steady state, and we should look for the features of the economy that tell us where it is located. Equation 13.10 gives the formula for this steady state and identifies two parameters that influence the size of capital per person (and therefore GDP per person) in the steady state.

An economy that has a very high saving rate should also have very high levels of capital and GDP per person. As conjectured earlier, high investment should cause high growth. But the model predicts instead that high investment raises the level of GDP per person but does not influence the growth rate in the steady state. This is because the economy always grows to the point at which new investment is just sufficient to replace worn-out capital. If there is any investment left over, after replacing depreciated capital, the economy will grow further. But as it grows, it will need to devote a greater amount of investment to replacing worn-out capital and there will be less left over for further growth. In the steady state, investment is just sufficient to replace depreciated capital, and at this point growth comes to a halt.

13.10 $k = k(1 - \delta) + Ask^\alpha$

> The steady state is found by solving the neoclassical growth equation (when $k_{t+1} = k_t = k$) in terms of the parameters of the model.

> The steady state value of k will be bigger if the savings rate is bigger.

$$\bar{k} = \left(\frac{sA}{\delta}\right)^{\frac{1}{1-\alpha}}$$

> The steady state value will be smaller if depreciation is bigger.

The fact that the flow of saving, in the steady state, is just sufficient to replace depreciated capital implies a second feature of the neoclassical model. An economy with a higher depreciation rate needs to devote more of its savings to replacing worn-out capital, so there is less left over for growth. For a given savings rate, higher depreciation will tend to lower the steady state stock of capital because more savings will be needed to maintain any given stock. An economy with a very high depreciation rate will tend to have a *low* level of per capita GDP.

❹ THE EFFECTS OF PRODUCTIVITY GROWTH

We have seen how the neoclassical growth model behaves for a given initial stock of capital. We have also learned that per capita output cannot grow forever. The key to understanding growth is to explain how the input of labor per person can grow, even when the number of hours per person remains fixed. The neoclassical growth model explains how labor can grow by distinguishing labor supply measured in hours from labor supply measured in efficiency units.

Measuring Labor in Efficiency Units

Not all workers are alike. An hour of work supplied by a brain surgeon, for example, contributes more to the GDP than an hour of work supplied by a laborer. The brain surgeon has a considerable investment in training. A laborer, on the other hand, performs unskilled tasks that are relatively easy for anyone to carry out. One way of capturing the fact that the brain surgeon produces goods with a higher market value is to argue that an hour of the surgeon's labor provides a bigger input to the production function than an hour of work by a laborer. The surgeon supplies the same amount of labor measured in units of time but supplies more labor measured in **efficiency units.**

It is a short step from recognizing that some types of labor are more productive at a point in time to the observation that the average productivity of labor is different at different points in time. The average U.S. worker in the 1990s, for example, is highly skilled relative to his or her counterpart in the nineteenth century. Most workers today are literate, are able to operate complicated machinery, and possess a range of skills that were unknown even a few decades ago. For this reason labor hours may not be a good measure of the true input to the production function. A better measure would be labor measured in efficiency units; that is, labor hours multiplied by labor efficiency.

13.11 $$E = N \times Q$$

> E is total labor supplied, measured in efficiency units.

Equation 13.11 defines labor supply in efficiency units. This measure of labor supply, E, is equal to the number of people, N, each of whom supplies one unit of time, multiplied by their efficiency, Q. Although we have assumed that the population is constant and that each person supplies a fixed number of hours, it will still be possible for the labor supplied by each person to increase, as long as we measure labor in efficiency units. This observation is very important because increases in labor efficiency, according to the neoclassical theory, are ultimately responsible for economic growth.

Measuring Variables Relative to Labor

Earlier, we derived the neoclassical growth equation in per capita terms. A similar equation can be used to describe growth in an economy in which population and productivity are both increasing from one year to the next. The idea is to redefine the state variable of the growth model. Instead of letting k represent capital relative to population, we let it represent capital relative to the labor supply of the population, measured in efficiency units.

Table 13.1 lays out the definitions of the variables used to describe growth in the model. We reinterpret the variables y and k in the first two rows of the table and add some new terms to define the rate at which labor efficiency, population, and productivity[12] are growing.

The derivation of the growth equation has a couple more steps in the case of growth in population and labor efficiency; these steps are laid out in the appendix. The equation that describes growth is very similar to the simpler case that we have already studied.

13.12 $$k_{t+1} = k_t \frac{(1 - \delta)}{(1 + g_E)} + \frac{sA}{(1 + g_E)} k_t^{\frac{1}{3}}$$

> The neoclassical growth equation

Equation 13.12 is a difference equation that behaves in the same way as Equation 13.9. The state variable k, however, is now interpreted as the ratio of capital to labor measured in efficiency units. Beginning with a low level of k, the economy invests in additional capital until it converges to a steady state. If k starts out above the steady state, the economy will not invest enough each period to maintain the high initial stock, and capital per efficiency unit of labor will decline. In either case, the economy will converge to a steady state value of k. Unlike the model with no growth, a steady state value of k does not mean that GDP per

---

12. **Mathematical Note:** Productivity can be derived from labor efficiency and population because the growth factor of labor $(1 + g_E)$ is just the product of their growth factors. It is approximately true that the growth *rate* of labor is equal to the sum of the growth rate of population and productivity. The exact formula that defines the relationship between the three rates is given by

$$(1 + g_E) = (1 + g_Q)(1 + g_N)$$

which can be expanded to give the expression $g_E = g_N + g_Q + g_N g_Q$. Because g_Q and g_N are small numbers, the product $g_Q g_N$ is an order of magnitude less than g_N and g_Q, and it is approximately true that $g_E = g_N + g_Q$.

TABLE 13.1
The Labels Used to Measure Growth Rates

Variable	Formula	Definition
k_t	$\dfrac{K_t}{Q_t N_t}$	Capital per efficiency unit of labor
y_t	$\dfrac{Y_t}{Q_t N_t}$	Output per efficiency unit of labor
$(1 + g_Q)$	$\dfrac{Q_{t+1}}{Q_t}$	g_Q is the growth rate of labor efficiency
$(1 + g_N)$	$\dfrac{N_{t+1}}{N_t}$	g_N is the growth rate of population
$(1 + g_E)$	$\dfrac{E_{t+1}}{E_t} = \dfrac{Q_{t+1}}{Q_t}\dfrac{N_{t+1}}{N_t}$	g_E is the growth rate of labor measured in efficiency units

person will be constant. Rather, it means that GDP per person will grow at a rate fast enough to exactly keep up with the exogenous improvements in productivity.

We have shown that the neoclassical growth equation converged to a steady state, and we used this fact to argue that the model could not explain sustained growth in GDP per person. Now we have redefined the state variable of this equation and argued that, even though this new variable converges to a steady state, the model can explain growth. Equations 13.13 show how we can resolve this apparent paradox.

This variable is defined as k_t. It converges to a constant in the steady state.

$$\left(\frac{K_t}{N_t}\right)\frac{1}{Q_t} = \bar{k} \qquad \left(\frac{Y_t}{N_t}\right)\frac{1}{Q_t} = \bar{y}$$

This is the variable defined as y_t. It also converges to a constant in the steady state.

13.13 $\qquad \left(\frac{K_t}{N_t}\right) = Q_t \bar{k} \qquad \left(\frac{Y_t}{N_t}\right) = Q_t \bar{y}$

If k_t and y_t are constant, then K_t/N_t and Y_t/N_t must be growing at the same rate as Q_t.

Equations 13.13 use the symbols $\bar{k}$ and $\bar{y}$ to represent the steady state values of capital and GDP per efficiency unit of labor. The logic of the model forces each of these variables to settle down to a steady state. But the fact that output per unit of labor converges to a steady state says nothing about output per person when there is positive productivity growth. Output per person and per unit of labor are not the same. In the steady state, capital per person must grow, because labor, measured in efficiency units, is growing. As exogenous technological progress causes improvements in the efficiency of labor, households accumulate capital to keep the relative proportions of capital and labor constant.

CONCLUSION

The neoclassical theories of production and distribution can be used to measure the sources of growth in GDP per person. Growth in capital and labor cannot in themselves account for growth in GDP per person. Instead, much of the cause of growth must be due to improvements in the efficiency of labor. But although not all of growth is accounted for by increases in capital and labor, some of it is. It might still be possible to grow faster by investing more in new capital. To see whether this is possible, we construct a model of economic growth that links the components of growth and explains how they are related to each other.

The neoclassical growth model begins with three facts. First, GDP per capita has grown at an average rate of 1.64% over the past century. Second, the share of wages in GDP has been constant. Third, consumption has been a constant fraction of GDP. The model assumes the latter two facts. The logic of the model itself then allows us to explain the first fact.

To explain economic growth, we use a difference equation, in which the state variable is the ratio of capital to labor, measured in efficiency units. This state variable converges to a steady state. Whether or not the model predicts that output per person will grow depends on whether we allow for exogenous growth in productivity. Using the distinction between these two cases, we can show that the ultimate source of growth of GDP per person is exogenous increases in the efficiency of labor.

Productivity growth is central to the neoclassical model because constant returns to scale means that proportional increases in output require proportional increases in both capital and labor. An economy that applies more and more capital to a fixed stock of labor will eventually suffer from a diminishing marginal product of capital, and its output will increase less than proportionately. Investment is a fixed fraction of output, but in each successive period output will increase by less than in the previous period. Growth must eventually come to a halt as the stock of capital approaches a steady state. The neoclassical model circumvents the fact that labor hours per person are in fixed supply by assuming that labor measured in efficiency units increases as a result of exogenous improvements in productivity.

KEY TERMS

Capital elasticity
Cobb-Douglas function
Constant returns to scale
Efficiency units
Endogenous growth theory
Exogenous growth theory
Growth accounting
Human capital
Labor elasticity

Marginal products
Neoclassical growth equation
Neoclassical growth model
Neoclassical theory of distribution
Penn World Table
Per capita production function
Solow residual
Total factor productivity

PROBLEMS FOR REVIEW

1. The economies of A-land and B-land are identical in all respects except that A-land has a higher depreciation rate. In both economies there is no growth. Will A-land or B-land have a higher value of GDP per capita? Can you explain, in words, why this is so?

2. Suppose that the economies of A-land and B-land from question 1 are both experiencing exogenous growth in labor productivity of 5% per year. Which economy will experience faster growth in GDP per capita? Draw a graph with GDP per capita in A-land and B-land on the vertical axis and time on the horizontal axis. You can assume that in both economies that capital per efficiency unit of labor is at its steady state.

3. In the Kingdom of Slovenia the saving rate is 0.16, the depreciation rate is 0.1, and the share of labor in GDP is 50%. Assuming that Slovenia is experiencing zero productivity growth, what is the steady value of k? Assume $A = 1$.

4. Draw a graph of x_{t+1} against x_t for the difference equation

$$x_{t+1} = 2x_t - 3x_t^{\frac{1}{2}} + 2$$

How many steady states does this equation have? Find the value of each steady state and determine whether it is stable.

5. This question refers to the neoclassical growth equation

$$K_{t+1} = (1 - \delta)K_t + sK_t^\alpha N^{1-\alpha}$$

Suppose that $\alpha = 1$ and $N = 1$. Draw a graph of K_{t+1} against K_t. Does this equation have a stable steady state? Does it have an unstable steady state? Suppose that $\delta = 0.1$ and $s = 0.2$. Can this economy grow? If so, can you explain, in words, why this example is different from the model in the chapter? What would be labor's share of GDP in this economy?

6. You are hired as a summer intern at the Council of Economic Advisers. Your immediate superior asks you to write a brief outlining what you know about policies for promoting growth. Explain to her, in two paragraphs or less, why neoclassical economic theory has no answer to this question.

7. Explain what is meant by *constant returns to scale*. How is this related to the idea of a diminishing marginal product of capital?

8. Consider the production function

$$Y = KL^{\frac{1}{2}}$$

Does this function display constant returns to scale? Does it display diminishing returns to capital? Calculate the share of GDP that would go to capital and the share that would go to labor if the real wage and the real rental rate were equal to the marginal products of labor and capital.

9. Briefly explain why economists use the Cobb-Douglas production function. What feature of the data does it describe accurately? [*Hint:* You will need to combine the Cobb-Douglas function with the neoclassical theory of distribution.]

10. What three facts was the neoclassical growth theory designed to explain?

APPENDIX: THE GROWTH EQUATION WITH PRODUCTIVITY GROWTH

The following equations show the steps used to derive Equation 13.12.

$$\left(\frac{K_{t+1}}{N_{t+1}Q_{t+1}}\right)\left(\frac{Q_{t+1}N_{t+1}}{Q_t N_t}\right) = \left(\frac{K_t}{Q_t N_t}\right)(1-\delta) + \left(\frac{I_t}{Q_t N_t}\right)$$

This is the investment identity that defines how capital accumulates. Variables are measured relative to labor in efficiency units (rather than relative to population).

$$k_{t+1}(1+g_E) = k_t(1-\delta) + sAy_t$$

When efficiency units grow through time, a term is added on the left side of the equation to account for growth.

$$k_{t+1} = k_t \frac{(1-\delta)}{(1+g_E)} + \frac{sA}{(1+g_E)}k_t^{\frac{1}{3}}$$

The neoclassical growth equation with productivity and population growth differs from the model without growth in two ways.
1. The variable k measures capital relative to efficiency units of labor, not capital per capita.
2. The term $(1+g_E)$ appears in the denominator on the righthand side.

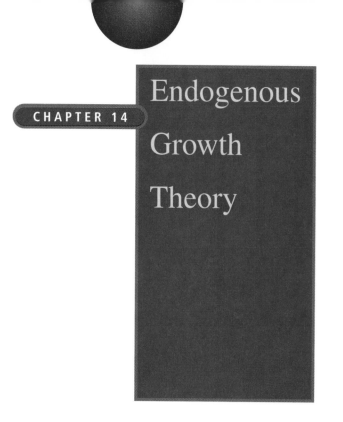

CHAPTER 14

Endogenous Growth Theory

❶ INTRODUCTION

The neoclassical growth model was constructed in the 1950s to fit some stylized facts from the U.S. economy. At that time relatively few countries in the world collected economic data in a systematic way. Recently this situation has begun to change, and we now have evidence from most countries that extends back to 1960. To check the robustness of neoclassical growth theory, researchers have begun to compare this data with the model's predictions. They have investigated the behavior of growth rates and GDP per person across countries and have looked at the relationship among saving rates, growth rates, and relative standards of living. They have found that a number of predictions of the simplest version of the neoclassical model are inconsistent with the evidence.

The neoclassical and endogenous growth models both make the simplifying assumption that each country in the world produces the same homogenous commodity. For this reason they do not allow for international trade in commodities, but the models do allow for trade in capital as countries borrow and lend to each other.

Endogenous and exogenous growth theories explain growth by increases in the efficiency of labor, Q. Whereas the neoclassical model assumes that Q is exogenous, endogenous growth theory explains why Q increases from one year to the next. The main idea is that Q measures the knowledge and skills of the workforce that are acquired in the process of producing goods. As the economy builds more complicated machines and workers learn to operate these machines, they acquire knowledge. This knowledge accumulates through time and contributes to the process of growth.

❷ THE NEOCLASSICAL MODEL AND THE INTERNATIONAL ECONOMY

The neoclassical growth model features a single commodity, but in the real world there are many kinds of goods and services. The diversity in the abilities of different countries to produce these goods and services is one of the major motives for international trade.[1] For example, the Japanese export cars to the United States and import beef. Trade in commodities is excluded from the neoclassical growth model because the model deals with a world in which there is only one good.

A second kind of trade is *intertemporal*—trade between different points in time. **Intertemporal trade** occurs when one country's consumption plus investment is greater than its gross domestic product. It pays for the excess by borrowing from abroad. There are three possible reasons for intertemporal trade. First, people in one country might be more patient than those in another. In the neoclassical growth model this would imply that one country has a higher saving rate. The citizens of the more patient country would lend to those of the less patient countries by trading in the international capital market. A second reason is that one country may have a higher rate of population growth than another. The high population growth country would need to invest at a faster rate than other countries in order to maintain a fixed capital-labor ratio. We would expect to see investment in that country by citizens of foreign countries as world saving flows in to meet the demand for new capital goods. A third reason for intertemporal trade is that one country might be richer than the others. The citizens of the richer country would lend to the relatively poor countries by investing in capital in these countries.

There is a fourth possible reason for intertemporal trade that we will exclude by assumption: the possibility that different countries use different production functions. If one country had access to a superior technology, savers from other countries would try to invest there in order to take advantage of the higher potential profit opportunities. But although differences in technology can account for short-run international lending opportunities, they cannot account for long-run patterns of borrowing and lending, because technologies are relatively easy to copy. For this reason we assume that all countries use the same production function.

In this chapter we model the world as a collection of countries, each of which produces the same homogenous commodity using the same production function. Countries differ for only three reasons: They have different saving rates, different rates of population growth, or different initial stocks of capital.

Modeling World Trade

We can model trade in the international capital markets in two ways. The first is by assuming that world capital markets are open, meaning that an American can borrow and

---

1. In international economics this idea is called *comparative advantage.* Comparative advantage means that each country exports those commodities that it is relatively efficient at producing.

lend freely in any country in the world. The opposite assumption is that world capital markets are closed, meaning that an American can borrow and lend only within the geographical borders of the United States. The real situation is somewhere in between the two extremes; the international capital market is not completely open, but it is not completely closed either. Because the two extremes are easy to model, we look at the implications of the neoclassical model for the behavior of the data in these two extremes.

The Neoclassical Growth Model with Open Capital Markets

The assumption that the world capital market is open is referred to as **perfect capital mobility.** When there is perfect capital mobility, GDP per person should be the same in every country in the world. The Penn World Table shows that the model with perfect capital mobility makes a number of predictions that are contradicted by the data. We can infer that perfect capital mobility is not a good description of the facts. Clearly, the neoclassical model must be amended.

Our first task in amending the neoclassical model is to allow for the fact that countries can borrow and lend internationally. In an open economy, domestic saving need not equal domestic investment because savings in one country could be directed to the accumulation of domestic capital *or* the accumulation of foreign capital. Instead we should observe that world saving equals world investment.

This idea is expressed in Equation 14.1. S and I represent domestic saving and investment, and S^f and I^f are foreign saving and investment. When individuals in each country are free to invest at home or abroad, there should be no tendency for saving in one country to equal investment in that same country. But the evidence suggests that this is exactly what we do see.

14.1 $$S + S^f = I + I^f$$

> World saving should equal world investment.

Figure 14.1 presents evidence from nine countries, year by year. This data shows that in each year domestic saving in each of these countries is very close to domestic investment. There is nothing special about the countries we have selected—all of the countries in the world exhibit this same pattern. Because the neoclassical model cannot explain why domestic saving in an open capital market should be so closely linked to domestic investment, this piece of evidence gives us a reason to question the assumptions of the theory.

A second implication of the neoclassical model is that investment in a perfect capital market should flow freely between countries to equalize the interest rate. If one country has a higher interest rate than another, capital should flow to the high-rate country as investors try to take advantage of the high rate by building factories and machines there. But, as capital flows into a country, the marginal product of capital will fall. Firms equate the rental rate to the marginal product of capital; as the marginal product of capital falls, the rental rate that investors can charge for capital also falls. Free flow of capital between countries should equalize rates of return around the world.

FIGURE 14.1
Investment and Savings as a Percentage of GDP for Nine Countries, 1960–1988
Investment rates and savings rates move very closely together.

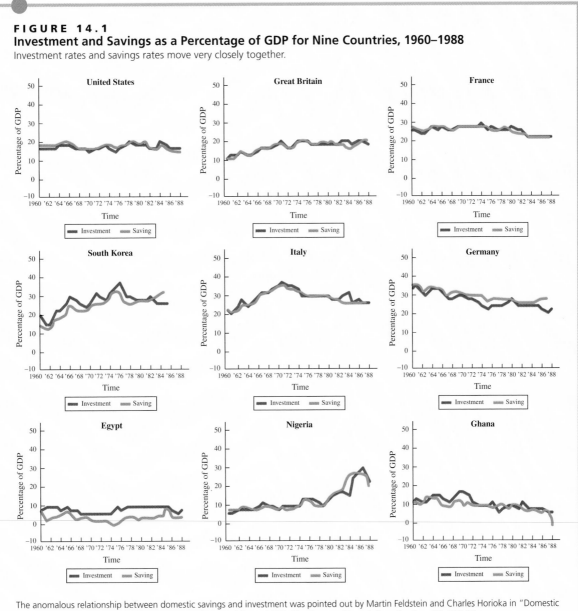

The anomalous relationship between domestic savings and investment was pointed out by Martin Feldstein and Charles Horioka in "Domestic saving and international capital flows." *Economic Journal* (June, 1980). The data used here is from the Penn World Table.

14.2 $$MPK = \alpha \left(\frac{K}{NQ} \right)^{\alpha - 1} = MPK^f = \alpha \left(\frac{K^f}{QN^f} \right)^{\alpha - 1}$$

> If capital markets are per-
> fect, marginal products
> should be equal across
> countries. This implies that
> capital per person should
> also be equalized.

> This is the formula for the marginal
> product of capital when the production
> function is Cobb-Douglas.

For the neoclassical production function the rate of return depends only on the ratio of capital to labor.[2] It follows that if the rate of return is equal in different countries, the capital-labor ratio must also be equal. In Equation 14.2 K and N represent capital and population in the home country, and K^f and N^f are the corresponding variables in the foreign country. The efficiency of labor, Q, and the capital elasticity of the production function, α, are assumed to be the same in both countries. We have also assumed that employment per person is equal to 1.[3]

How could we test whether the marginal product of capital is equalized across countries? One indirect test follows from the fact that equalization of capital-labor ratios implies equalization of GDP per person across countries because per capita GDP depends only on capital per person.

14.3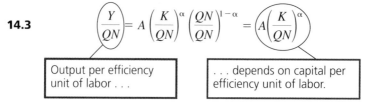

> Output per efficiency
> unit of labor . . .

> . . . depends on capital per
> efficiency unit of labor.

Figure 14.2 presents evidence from five countries, the United States, Great Britain, Mexico, Turkey, and India. The vertical axis records the GDP per person in each country relative to per capita GDP in the United States. If the neoclassical model with perfect capital markets were correct, we would expect to see GDP per person equalized across all of these countries as capital flows to find its highest return. In reality we see that poor countries, like India, tend to stay poor, and rich countries, like the United States, tend to stay rich.

The Neoclassical Model with Closed Capital Markets

Although the evidence suggests that capital does not flow freely between countries, it may still be that a different version of the neoclassical model can explain the facts. As a way of exploring this possibility, we look at the case of **zero capital mobility,** the assumption that capital markets are closed. In a world of zero capital mobility there is no possibility of bor-

---

2.   **Mathematical Note:** This property follows from the assumption of constant returns to scale. We get the formula for the marginal product of capital from the production function by finding the partial derivative with respect to capital. For the Cobb-Douglas function, given by the formula $AK^\alpha L^{1-\alpha}$, the marginal product of capital is represented by the expression $\alpha A(K/L)^{\alpha-1}$, the formula used in the text.
3.   This argument will work as long as employment is proportional to population and the constant of proportionality is the same in the two countries. This constant can always be set equal to 1 by choosing the units of measurement appropriately.

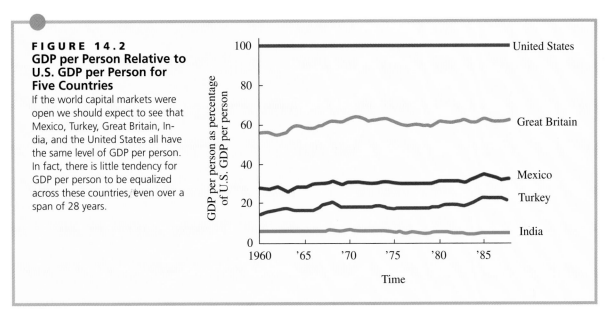

FIGURE 14.2
GDP per Person Relative to U.S. GDP per Person for Five Countries
If the world capital markets were open we should expect to see that Mexico, Turkey, Great Britain, India, and the United States all have the same level of GDP per person. In fact, there is little tendency for GDP per person to be equalized across these countries, even over a span of 28 years.

rowing or lending abroad, and therefore domestic saving must equal domestic investment in each country.[4] As with the assumption of open capital markets, we confront the assumption of closed capital markets with the international evidence.

To begin with, we look at the predicted relationship between capital and GDP per person in two countries that are different in only one respect—one country saves more than the other. To make this comparison we need to recall how the neoclassical model explains the level of capital in the steady state. To obtain an expression for the steady state capital stock, we can use Equation 14.4, the neoclassical equation.

14.4

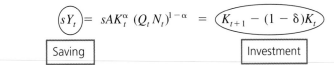

$$\left(sY_t\right) = sAK_t^{\alpha}\,(Q_t N_t)^{1-\alpha} = \left(K_{t+1} - (1-\delta)K_t\right)$$

Saving   Investment

If we let g_E be the growth rate of labor in efficiency units, we can use an algebraic expression to determine the value of capital per efficiency unit of labor in the steady state.[5] We want to establish which factors are responsible for determining the amount of capital in a country, relative to the amount of labor.

The algebraic expression for the capital-labor ratio in the steady state uncovers four factors that determine this value. These are the saving rate, the depreciation rate, the

4.   How can world economies be closed when some countries export as much as 60% of their GDP? The answer is that the major motives for trade involve comparative advantage in the production of different commodities. We are not capturing this motive in our model because we are making the very strong simplifying assumption that there is a single commodity. The fact that domestic saving equals domestic investment implies that exports equal imports; it does not imply that exports or imports constitute a small percentage of GDP.
5.   This is the algebra that we used in Chapter 13 to derive the steady state of neoclassical growth equation.

growth rate of labor in efficiency units, and the capital elasticity of output. The expression that shows how these factors influence the capital labor ratio is given in Equation 14.5.

14.5
$$\frac{K}{QN} = \left(\frac{sA}{g_E + \delta}\right)^{\frac{1}{1-\alpha}}$$

This term measures capital per efficiency unit of labor in the steady state.

This term is a constant that depends on the saving rate, s, and the growth rate of labor, g_E.

Because we have assumed that every country uses the same production function, the depreciation rate, δ, and the capital elasticity, α, are ruled out as possible factors that are different across countries. The two factors that are left are the saving rate and the growth rate of labor, measured in efficiency units.

Equation 14.5 predicts that countries that save more should accumulate more capital per unit of labor in the steady state. But how can we turn this into an observable prediction about living standards? Equation 14.6 gives the relationship between GDP per unit of labor and capital per unit of labor. This equation shows that GDP per person depends positively on the saving rate. In other words, if the saving rate goes up, steady state GDP per person should go up also.

14.6
$$\frac{Y}{QN} = A\left(\frac{sA}{g_E + \delta}\right)^{\frac{\alpha}{1-\alpha}}$$

Output per unit of labor depends (in part) on the saving rate.

In the case of open capital markets, output per person should be equalized in every country in the world. When capital markets are closed, output per person should not be equalized, because it depends on the relative amounts of capital used in different countries and capital per person may differ if countries have different saving rates. If country A has a higher saving rate than country B

$$\frac{Y^A}{N^A} > \frac{Y^B}{N^B}$$

GDP per person > **GDP per person**
in country A　　**in country B**

As a test of this prediction, panel A of Box 14.1 plots average GDP per person from 1960 to 1988 against the average investment-GDP ratio for 17 countries. If the neoclassical model is correct, we should expect to see a positive correlation between these numbers; in fact there is little or no correlation between them.

Perhaps panel A is missing the fact that countries do not differ only in their saving rates. They also differ in their population growth rates. To check for the possibility that population growth rates are hiding the true relationship, panel B corrects the data for population growth. Once again, this figure shows that there is no strong tendency for countries to display the relationship suggested by the steady state of the neoclassical model.

The neoclassical model predicts that GDP per person should be correlated with saving rates, but in the data it is not. The model also falls short in its predictions about growth rates

BOX 14.1
FOCUS ON THE FACTS:
Investment and GDP per Person

The neoclassical growth model predicts that countries with a high saving and investment rate should have a high steady state level of GDP per person. Panel A shows that this prediction is not borne out in the data. There is no tendency for countries with high investment ratios to have a higher standard of living.

Panel B adjusts investment ratios to allow for population growth in a way that is predicted by the steady state formula from the model.[1] This figure shows that the lack of a correlation between investment ratios and GDP per capita cannot be explained by differences in population growth rates.

1.   Investment adjusted for population growth is defined as $s/(g_N + \delta)$, where s is the investment-GDP ratio, g_N is the population growth rate, and δ is set to 0.06.

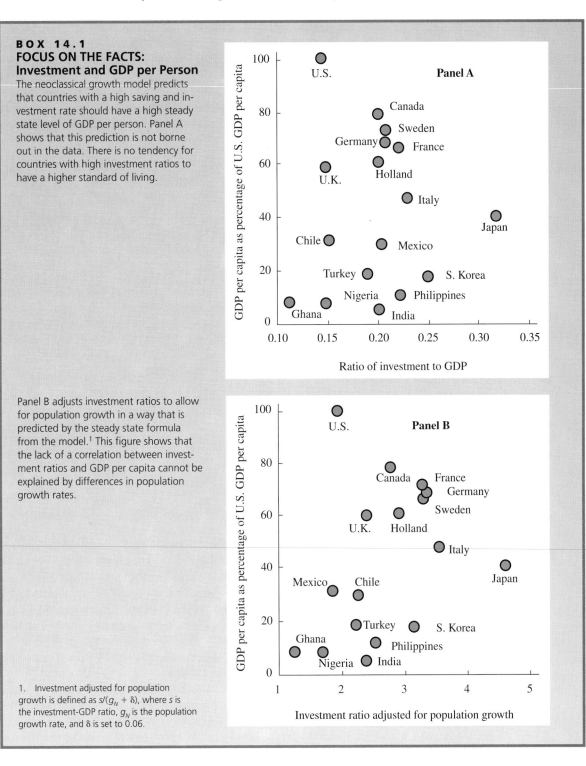

of GDP per person. Although the neoclassical model allows the level of GDP per person to be higher in countries with higher saving rates, it implies that the growth rates of GDP per person should be the same. This implication follows from the fact that all growth is ultimately due to exogenous technical progress.

Suppose that two countries, A and B, have different saving rates and different rates of population growth. Equation 14.7 illustrates the fact that these countries will converge to different levels of GDP per unit of labor in the steady state. We have called these different steady states $\bar{y}_A$ and $\bar{y}_B$.

14.7
$$\frac{Y_A}{N_A Q} = \bar{y}_A$$

> Output per unit of labor in country A will converge to a constant.

$$\frac{Y_B}{N_B Q} = \bar{y}_B$$

> Output per unit of labor in country B will converge to a different constant.

Although the steady state levels are different, they are both constant. How will the growth rate of GDP per person differ in the two countries? Because both countries use the same production function, they must both experience the same growth rate of labor efficiency as measured by changes in Q. These changes in Q are ultimately responsible for growth. Equation 14.8 illustrates that in the steady state, output per person will grow at the same rate in each country, because countries that have the same production function should experience the same increases in the efficiency of labor.

14.8
$$\frac{\Delta(Y_A / N_A)}{(Y_A / N_A)} = \frac{\Delta Q}{Q} \qquad \frac{\Delta(Y_B / N_B)}{(Y_B / N_B)} = \frac{\Delta Q}{Q}$$

> Countries A and B have different levels of GDP per person. But in each case the rate of growth of GDP per person is equal to the rate of growth of labor efficiency.

How does this prediction square with the facts? Figure 14.3 presents the frequency distribution of per capita GDP growth rates (relative to the growth in GDP per person in the United States) for our sample of 17 countries. Two countries in the sample (Japan and South Korea) experienced average growth rates from 1960 through 1988 that were 4 to 5% greater than the U.S. rate. Ghana grew 2% slower. The data shows that annual growth rates of GDP per person in the world economy have differed by as much as 7% over a span of thirty years. The prediction of the simple neoclassical model does not do a good job of explaining these facts because it assumes that all countries use the same production function and will therefore grow at the same rate in the steady state.

One implication of the neoclassical model is that countries with high saving rates should have high levels of GDP per person. A second implication is that all countries should grow at the same rate. The facts, however, suggest otherwise. In other words, the neoclassical model does not do a good job of explaining the data, even under the extreme assumption that capital markets are closed.

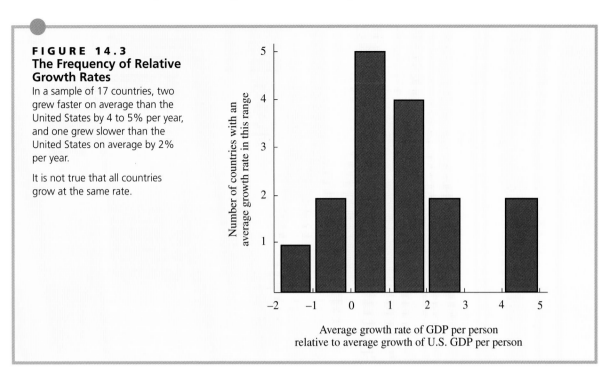

FIGURE 14.3
The Frequency of Relative Growth Rates

In a sample of 17 countries, two grew faster on average than the United States by 4 to 5% per year, and one grew slower than the United States on average by 2% per year.

It is not true that all countries grow at the same rate.

Number of countries with an average growth rate in this range

Average growth rate of GDP per person relative to average growth of U.S. GDP per person

Convergence

The neoclassical model predicts that countries should grow at the same rate. Some authors have noted that this prediction holds only if all countries in the world have attained their steady states. Economies may differ in GDP per person if they are in the process of converging to this steady state. If this is the case, we should expect to see that, after controlling for factors, such as saving and population growth, that determine what steady state a country is converging to, countries that begin with a low initial stock of capital should grow faster than countries that begin with a high stock of capital.

One example of the possibility that the initial stock of capital may matter is provided by Japan, Germany, and Italy, three countries that grew rapidly in the postwar period. All three of these countries experienced considerable destruction of capital equipment during World War II. It is possible that these countries grew faster than the United States in the postwar period because they were catching up by rebuilding capital. This idea is called the **reconstruction hypothesis.** But although the reconstruction hypothesis sounds plausible, two recent studies by Fumio Hayashi of the University of Pennsylvania and Lawrence Christiano of Northwestern University have shown that, at least for Japan, it doesn't explain the facts. Christiano shows that the standard model predicts GDP per person should converge much more quickly to the steady state than was the case in the postwar Japanese experience.[6]

6.   Fumio Hayashi. "Is Japan's savings rate high?" *Federal Reserve Bank of Minneapolis: Quarterly Review* (Spring, 1989): 3–9. Lawrence J. Christiano. "Understanding Japan's savings rate: The reconstruction hypothesis." *Federal Reserve Bank of Minneapolis: Quarterly Review* (Spring, 1989): 10–25. Both of these articles are easy to read and are recommended supplements to this chapter.

A second way of testing whether initial conditions matter is to look for evidence that levels of GDP per person are moving closer together in larger groups of countries. The neoclassical model predicts that countries that begin with low levels of GDP per person should grow faster than countries that begin with high levels of GDP per person. This idea is called the **convergence hypothesis**. A number of authors have tested the convergence hypothesis by looking at the statistical relationship between growth rates of GDP per person and initial levels of GDP per person. Most authors who have studied this relationship have concluded that the convergence hypothesis does not hold across all of the countries in the world. However, there is some evidence of **conditional convergence.** This means that if we include variables such as years of schooling, political stability, and type of government as additional factors, we can explain some of the differences in growth rates. A major finding from studies that have investigated this question is that even when growth rates converge, as predicted by the theory, this convergence occurs at a much slower rate than the simple neoclassical model predicts.[7]

❸ THE MODEL OF LEARNING BY DOING

Several new theories have been put forward to explain the anomalies in the neoclassical model.

Endogenous and Exogenous Theories of Growth

The neoclassical theory attributes growth to increases in labor efficiency. Because increases in labor efficiency are not explained by other economic variables, the neoclassical theory of growth is an exogenous theory. More recently economists have begun to study an alternative approach that assumes workers acquire skills as they learn how to operate a technology. The skills that they acquire in this way are called human capital and, according to endogenous growth theory, it is the accumulation of human capital that is responsible for growth in GDP per person.

The acquisition of human capital allows a worker to operate complicated machinery or to interact with other skilled workers in a team. A doctor, for example, has more human capital than a garbage collector, and the output that a doctor produces is correspondingly more valuable. Human capital can be accumulated in the same way that physical capital is accumulated, by devoting resources to the act of investment. In the case of physical capital, investment means building factories and machines. In the case of human capital, it means spending time acquiring knowledge.

Although human capital is similar to physical capital, there is an important sense in which it is different. Human capital is acquired, not only through the active pursuit of learning, but also through the act of production itself. This way of acquiring knowledge is called **learning by doing.** When new products are invented or new techniques are intro-

---

7.   See, for example, N. Gregory Mankiw; David Romer; and David N. Weil. "A contribution to the empirics of growth." *Quarterly Journal of Economics* 100 (February, 1992): 225–251; and Robert J. Barro and Xavier Sala-i-Martin. "Convergence." *Journal of Political Economy* 100 (April, 1995): 223–251.

duced, the cost of production declines as companies learn the best way to produce these items. This knowledge is acquired by workers through their experience in the workplace.

The Technology of Endogenous Growth

Endogenous growth theory makes a relatively minor change to the neoclassical production function. It assumes that the aggregate production function is described by a Cobb-Douglas technology in which the capital elasticity of GDP is equal to 1. The technology of endogenous growth is given in Equation 14.9:

14.9
$$Y = K^1 L^{1-\alpha}$$

> According to the theory of endogenous growth, the coefficient on capital in the production function is equal to 1.

The fact that the capital elasticity of output is equal to 1 (rather than ⅓) means that the economy is no longer subject to a diminishing marginal product of capital. Proportional increases in capital are associated with proportional increases in GDP. As a consequence of this modification, per capita GDP can grow forever without the additional units of capital becoming relatively less productive. Growth can occur even when there is no exogenous technical progress to continually increase the efficiency of labor.

Why was the theory not proposed earlier? The answer lies in the foundation of exogenous growth theory. Recall that the neoclassical model uses the equation:

$$Y = A K^{\alpha} (QL)^{1-\alpha}$$

where the parameter α is equal to ⅓. This value of ⅓ comes from the neoclassical theory of distribution, which implies that α must equal capital's share of income. If endogenous growth theory is to propose a different value for this important parameter, it must explain how this alternative value can be made consistent with the fact that capital's share of income is only ⅓. This is the role of the theory of learning by doing.

Social and Private Technology

The theory of learning by doing reconciles the assumption of constant returns to capital with the theory of distribution. It does so by drawing a distinction between the production function that faces society as a whole—the **social technology**—and the production function faced by each individual firm—the **private technology**. Labor becomes more productive, not because of exogenous improvements in technology, but because of the accumulation of knowledge. As a society builds new factories and machines, individuals learn new techniques and their knowledge becomes embodied in human capital. The acquisition of human capital is a social process whose effects go beyond the individual's own productivity. One firm produces an idea, another firm copies it. As one individual learns a quick and easy way of solving a problem, another individual can duplicate it. The theory of learning by doing captures this idea by arguing that technical progress, Q, is a function of the level of industrialization of the society.

Let's suppose that an economy consists of M firms. Each firm produces output using a private technology that is identical to the Cobb-Douglas production function of the neoclassical growth model. Letting Y, K, and L be aggregate GDP, capital, and labor, the private production function is given by Equation 14.10.

14.10
$$\frac{Y}{M} = A \left(\frac{K}{M}\right)^{\alpha} \left(\frac{QL}{M}\right)^{1-\alpha}$$

M is the number of firms

Because we can cancel M from both sides of this equation, it follows that aggregate output, aggregate capital, and aggregate labor must be described by the equation[8]

14.11
$$Y = AK^{\alpha}(QL)^{1-\alpha}$$

In the theory of learning by doing, the private production function is the same function that is used in the neoclassical growth model

which is the same as the production function used by each firm in the neoclassical theory.

The new element in the theory of learning by doing is an explicit model of what determines Q. The efficiency of labor is assumed to be determined by the aggregate level of industrialization. Because industrialization increases as society becomes more capital-intensive, the value of Q is assumed to be proportional to aggregate capital per worker, K/N. By appropriately choosing the units by which we measure variables, we can set the constant of proportionality equal to 1. The resulting **knowledge function** is defined in Equation 14.12.

14.12
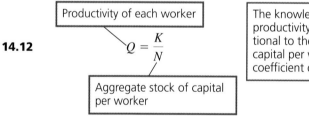

The knowledge function says that the productivity of each worker is proportional to the aggregate stock of physical capital per worker. We have chosen the coefficient of proportionality to equal 1.

In other words, the efficiency of each individual worker depends on the aggregate level of capital in the economy as a whole. This relationship determines how knowledge is propagated through society as a result of increases in the stock of capital.

The accumulation of capital has two effects. The first is the private effect that is present in both endogenous and exogenous growth theory. This gives rise to the term K^{α} in the social production function. The second effect operates through the education of the workforce. As workers learn to use the new technology in one firm, they acquire skills that can be transferred to another firm. This gives rise to the term $K^{1-\alpha}$ on the right-hand side of the social production function. To the individual producer this second effect is an externality, because the producer does not have to pay for the education of the work force. It is acquired from the workers' exposure to ideas in society at large, and the degree of exposure grows with the social acquisition of capital.

8.   Because $M^{a} \times M^{b} = M^{a+b}$.

Substituting the knowledge function into the private production function, we can write the social production function as Equation 14.13.

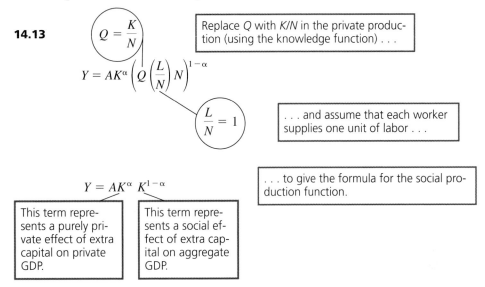

14.13

$$Q = \frac{K}{N}$$

Replace Q with K/N in the private production (using the knowledge function) . . .

$$Y = AK^{\alpha} \left(Q\left(\frac{L}{N}\right) N \right)^{1-\alpha}$$

$$\frac{L}{N} = 1$$

. . . and assume that each worker supplies one unit of labor . . .

$$Y = AK^{\alpha} K^{1-\alpha}$$

. . . to give the formula for the social production function.

This term represents a purely private effect of extra capital on private GDP.

This term represents a social effect of extra capital on aggregate GDP.

The two effects by which aggregate capital affect GDP are collected into a single term.[9] The production function that results is called the **social production function** and is given by Equation 14.14.

14.14

| Aggregate GDP |—| Y | = | A | K |—| Aggregate capital |

The difference between the social and private effects is illustrated in panels A and B of Figure 14.4. Panel A shows that as the economy adds capital to the same stock of labor, GDP increases in proportion to the increase in capital. Panel B, on the other hand, shows what happens to an individual firm if it increases its capital, holding constant the stock of capital of every other firm in the economy. As the firm adds capital to the same stock of labor, each unit of capital becomes relatively less productive than the one before it. This is a consequence of a diminishing marginal product of capital, the same assumption that we met in the neoclassical model.

What economic reasoning is responsible for the difference between the geometry of the two pictures? The answer is that when the individual firm expands its use of capital, it captures only the private impact of this additional capital. But the second effect, on the education of its workforce, cannot be appropriated by the individual firm. As the firm trains its workers in the use of new equipment, most of this benefit is lost when the workers leave to take new jobs. The effect of their education on the job is disseminated widely to friends and colleagues who work at other firms.

An immediate and important implication of the theory of learning by doing is that a firm will be more productive if it is part of a society with a high level of capital. Contrast this with the neoclassical model. The neoclassical model assumes that if a firm were

9.   This rearrangement uses the fact that $K^{\alpha} \times K^{1-\alpha} = K$.

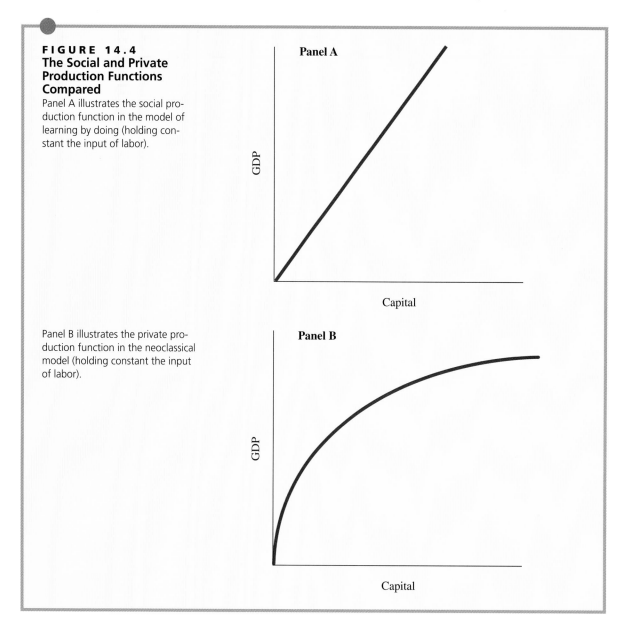

FIGURE 14.4
The Social and Private Production Functions Compared
Panel A illustrates the social production function in the model of learning by doing (holding constant the input of labor).

Panel B illustrates the private production function in the neoclassical model (holding constant the input of labor).

transported from the United States to Ghana, it would still employ the same technology. Learning by doing argues that the firm would be less productive because the skills of the Ghanaian workforce are lower than the skills of the U.S. workforce as a direct result of the lower degree of industrialization of the Ghanaian economy.

To sum up, endogenous growth theory makes a distinction between the production function used by an individual firm and the function that applies to the society as a whole.

If one firm uses more capital, it gains proportionately less output than if the whole society uses more capital. The difference between the two situations may be traced to the increased knowledge that is acquired by workers who use new technology. This effect is spread widely over the whole society and cannot be appropriated by the individual firm. If all firms expand together, however, each benefits from the increased knowledge that is gained, not only as a result of its own expansion, but also as the result of the expansion of all of the other firms.

❹ LEARNING BY DOING AND ENDOGENOUS GROWTH

Endogenous Growth

As with the neoclassical theory, endogenous growth theory must take a stand on how to model world capital markets. Because the evidence suggests that there is relatively little international borrowing and lending, we examine the extreme assumption that the world capital markets are closed. Assuming that saving is a fixed fraction of GDP and that saving equals investment, we can write an expression that explains how capital is accumulated, Equation 14.15.

14.15

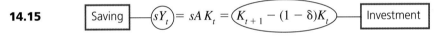

$$\boxed{\text{Saving}} \quad (sY_t) = sA\,K_t = (K_{t+1} - (1-\delta)K_t) \quad \boxed{\text{Investment}}$$

Equation 14.15 looks similar to the expression that describes growth in the neoclassical model, but there is a big and important difference. If we plot a graph of capital next year against capital this year, this graph is a straight line instead of a curve. If we rearrange Equation 14.15, we can find an expression for the growth equation, Equation 14.16.

14.16 $K_{t+1} = (1 - \delta + sA)K_t$ | In a learning-by-doing economy, the growth equation is a straight line.

The endogenous growth equation is very different from the neoclassical growth equation because its graph is a straight line. As the economy applies more and more capital to the same fixed stock of labor, the additional output produced grows in proportion. The economy does not experience diminishing returns to capital. Each period households save a fixed fraction of GDP, and capital expands along a straight line, like the one pictured in Figure 14.5, instead of along a curve as in the neoclassical theory.

Predictions of Comparative Growth Rates

We began this chapter by pointing to several stylized facts that characterize the growth experiences of a number of countries. Let's see how endogenous theory explains these facts.

We begin by examining the implication of the endogenous growth model for the behavior of two economies that have the same saving rates, country A and country B. Recall that countries with similar saving rates do not have similar levels of GDP per person. Figure 14.6 illustrates how the theory of learning by doing explains the fact that relative standards of living do not converge over time.

FIGURE 14.5
Endogenous Growth

The difference equation that describes growth has only one steady state at a value of $K = 0$, and that steady state is unstable. Suppose the economy begins at K_0. Each period more and more capital is accumulated and the economy moves along the trajectory depicted in this graph, without ever reaching a new steady state.

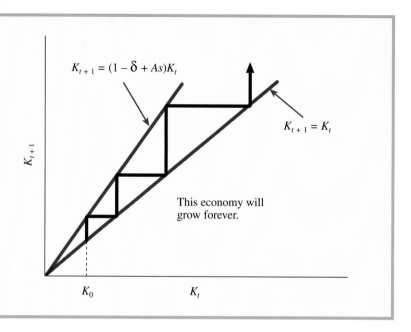

$$K_{t+1} = (1 - \delta + As)K_t$$

$$K_{t+1} = K_t$$

This economy will grow forever.

K_0 K_t

FIGURE 14.6
Two Economies with the Same Growth Rate but Different Initial Conditions

This graph illustrates the growth path of two economies that have the same growth rate but that begin with different initial stocks of capital.

Economy B begins with more capital, and, as a result, residents of this economy always have a higher standard of living than residents of economy A.

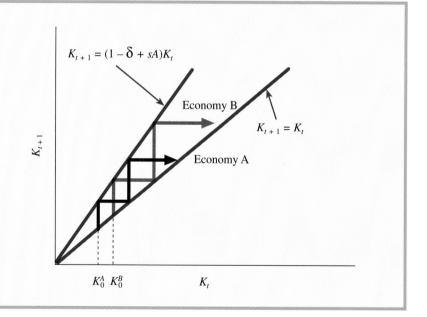

$$K_{t+1} = (1 - \delta + sA)K_t$$

Economy B

$$K_{t+1} = K_t$$

Economy A

K_0^A K_0^B K_t

In Figure 14.6, both countries have the same saving rate and both follow the same endogenous growth equation. Suppose that country A begins with an initial level of capital, K_0^A and B begins with a higher level, K_0^B. Notice that country B begins from a higher initial position, so it will always remain ahead of country A but both countries will grow at

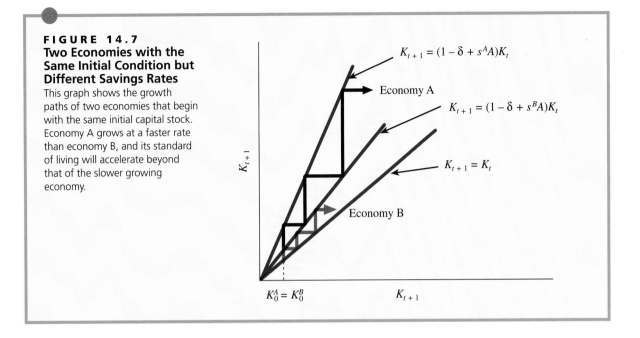

FIGURE 14.7
Two Economies with the Same Initial Condition but Different Savings Rates
This graph shows the growth paths of two economies that begin with the same initial capital stock. Economy A grows at a faster rate than economy B, and its standard of living will accelerate beyond that of the slower growing economy.

the same rate. This is the endogenous growth explanation for the fact that countries like India, the United Kingdom, Mexico, and Turkey, countries with similar saving rates, grow at about the same rate.

A second piece of evidence concerns two countries with different saving rates. Once again we refer to these countries as A and B, but we suppose that A has a higher saving rate. Figure 14.7 illustrates the predictions of the endogenous growth theory. Both countries start from the same initial condition, but A follows a different difference equation because it saves and invests more in every period. The difference equation followed by country A is given by

$$K_{t+1} = K_t(1 - \delta + s^A A)$$

and the equation for country B is:

$$K_{t+1} = K_t(1 - \delta + s^B A)$$

Because we have assumed that the saving rate is higher in A than B, the slope of the endogenous growth function for country A is also higher. But this implies that country A will grow faster than country B, because it will accumulate more capital in every period. This is illustrated in Figure 14.7 as the black zigzag line, describing A, deviates more in each successive period from the gray zigzag line, representing economy B.

As a way of comparing the predictions with the facts, Figure 14.8 shows a scatter plot of the average ratio of investment to GDP against the average growth rate from 1960 through 1988. Each point represents a country from the same sample of 17 nations that we examined earlier. Clearly countries with high investment to GDP ratios tend to grow faster.

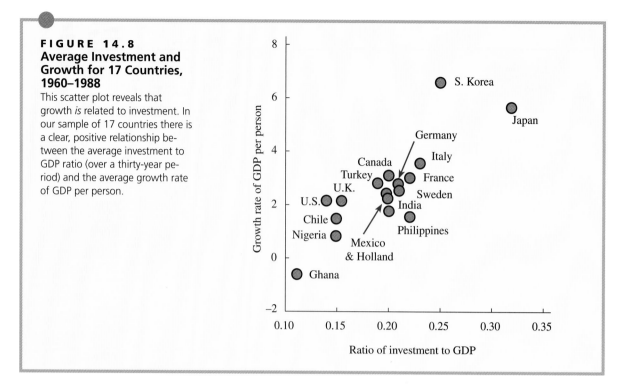

FIGURE 14.8
Average Investment and Growth for 17 Countries, 1960–1988
This scatter plot reveals that growth *is* related to investment. In our sample of 17 countries there is a clear, positive relationship between the average investment to GDP ratio (over a thirty-year period) and the average growth rate of GDP per person.

Look, for example, at Mexico, Holland, India, and Canada. Although these countries have very different levels of GDP per person (see Box 14.1), they have similar growth rates. South Korea and Japan, on the other hand, have experienced very rapid growth that has been associated with very high saving and investment rates.

Endogenous Growth and Economic Policy

One issue that concerns contemporary policy makers is the fact that growth of GDP per capita was a little slower in the 1970s than in the immediate postwar period. If the neoclassical theory is correct, not much can be done about this. The theory of learning by doing, on the other hand, suggests that growth is related to investment—both public and private.

Does this mean that the United States, with the highest standard of living in the world, can grow at the same rate as a country like China, which is emerging from fifty years of a centrally planned economy? The answer to this question is almost certainly no. Chinese growth reflects a large catch-up element. Under the Chinese centrally planned system, the pursuit of individual profit was actively discouraged. For example, farmers were unable to sell their produce on the open market. With the reforms of Deng Xiaoping, all of this changed. The individual accumulation of wealth is now not only permitted, it is encouraged. A large part of the very rapid growth that has occurred in the past decade is a result of a reorganization of institutions that allows Chinese production techniques to catch up with those of the West.

The history of world growth from the eighteenth century to the present is a history of leaders and followers. From the mid-1700s through to the early 1800s the Netherlands was the world leader in terms of GDP per person. From the 1800s through the early 1900s the British took over. The current situation, in which the United States enjoys the highest GDP per person, has persisted from around 1920 to the present. It is likely that the possibilities for increasing a country's standard of living are different depending on whether the country is the leader or a follower. For example, the United States, the world leader, can increase GDP per person only by inventing new techniques that are more efficient than existing ones. Ghana or Nigeria, on the other hand, can potentially realize big increases in the welfare of their citizens by copying the techniques that are already used in the industrialized world. The experience of Japan and South Korea suggests that the route to growth involves a high level of saving and investment as the society industrializes. But the fact that Japan, South Korea, and China are able to follow this route does not necessarily imply that the United States could achieve a similar increase in growth. In fact, the Japanese growth rate has recently slowed considerably as the Japanese GDP per person level gets closer to that of the United States.

Where does all of this leave the current debate on public policy? The evidence suggests that investment promotes growth. However, there are reasons to believe that the increases in growth that can be achieved through increased investment are not as great for the United States as for countries that are behind in terms of relative standard of living. But even if the potential for promoting growth is not as great as the East Asian experience suggests, the possibility that there are big social externalities to the accumulation of knowledge points strongly toward public subsidization of research and development. This is why the U.S. government is so heavily involved in subsidizing education. Investment in human capital has potentially large public benefits. This argument drove much of the rhetoric of Bill Clinton's 1992 presidential campaign. The outcome of the Clinton experiment is still undetermined.

Modified Theories of Learning by Doing

Although there is wide agreement that the neoclassical model does not do a good job of explaining the cross-country evidence, not everyone is willing to accept the extreme form of the learning by doing hypothesis. Some do not accept the assumption that a country could permanently increase its growth rate above that of other countries simply by increasing its investment rate. They believe a more likely hypothesis is that, as a country gets close to the frontier of world knowledge, part of its investment will spill over and improve growth in other countries in the world. There is considerable international movement of human capital between advanced nations, which suggests that the externalities we modeled with the knowledge function can cross international boundaries.

A weaker form of the learning by doing hypothesis argues that the knowledge function for each country may display decreasing returns. In other words, a 1% increase in factories and machines leads to a less than 1% increase in labor efficiency through the spread of knowledge. This weaker form of the learning by doing hypothesis leads to a model that behaves a lot like the neoclassical growth model. GDP per capita is predicted to converge across countries, just as in the Solow model, but the speed at which it converges is much slower. The modified learning by doing hypothesis can explain many of the anomalies of the neoclassical model. It predicts that countries that invest more can grow faster temporarily, but eventually they will catch up with the world leaders, and at that point their growth rates will slow down.[10]

CONCLUSION

One way in which the neoclassical growth model might be extended to allow for international trade in capital is to assume that capital markets are open (perfect capital mobility), and that Americans can borrow and lend freely in every country in the world. If this were a good characterization of the world, we should expect to see GDP per person equalized across countries, as capital flows in search of high rates of return. In the real world we see no tendency for this equalization of living standards to occur.

A second way to extend the model is to assume that capital markets are closed (zero capital mobility). This assumption is at least consistent with the fact that investment and saving tend to be equal within each country. However, the neoclassical growth model predicts that countries with high saving rates will tend to have high levels of GDP per person. The evidence is that there is no such connection. A second prediction of the neoclassical model is that the growth rate of GDP per person should be equal throughout the world. In practice we see divergence in per capita growth rates of as much 7% for long periods of time. Because of the failure of the neoclassical model to explain these facts, we turn to an alternative model of growth, the model of learning by doing.

Learning by doing builds on the neoclassical growth model but allows proportional increases in capital to cause proportional increases in GDP. To explain how the coefficient on capital in the production function can be different from capital's share of income, the theory distinguishes between the private and social production functions. The private production function places a weight of ⅓ on capital; the social production function places a weight of 1. Private firms do not take account of the effect of their actions on the social acquisition of knowledge.

The learning-by-doing theory explains growth endogenously instead of relying on the assumption of an exogenous increase in technical progress. It is able to explain why GDP per person is not equalized across countries. It also explains why countries with high saving rates tend to grow faster than countries with low rates. A modified, weaker form of the learning-by-doing model behaves like the exogenous growth model but predicts much slower convergence.

KEY TERMS

Conditional convergence
Convergence hypothesis
Intertemporal trade
Knowledge function
Learning by doing
Perfect capital mobility

Private technology
Reconstruction hypothesis
Social production function
Social technology
Zero capital mobility

10.   Mankiw, Romer, and Weil. Op cit.

PROBLEMS FOR REVIEW

1. What are the four parameters that influence the steady state level of GDP per person in the neoclassical growth model? For each of these four parameters, explain whether an increase in the factor would cause an increase or a decrease in steady state GDP per person. Explain your answer by appealing to the economic intuition.

2. What three parameters influence the rate of growth in the theory of learning by doing? For each of these parameters, explain the effect of an increase in the parameter on the rate of growth of the economy.

3. The endogenous growth model predicts that

$$K_{t+1} = K_t(1 - \delta + sA)$$

Suppose that $A = 1$, $\delta = 0.1$, and $s = 0.2$. What would you predict would be the growth rate of capital? (*Hint:* The growth rate is $\dfrac{K_{t+1}}{K_t} - 1$).

4. The following table gives saving rates for five economies:

United States	0.16
Philippines	0.17
Mexico	0.18
Japan	0.25
Ghana	0.09

a. Assume that in all of these countries, $\delta = 0.1$ and $A = 1$. Assuming that the neoclassical growth model is true, compute the level of GDP in the steady state for each of these countries as a fraction of U.S. GDP per person.

b. Assume that the endogenous growth theory is correct. Compute the predicted growth rate of GDP per person in each of these countries relative to the growth rate of U.S. GDP per person.

5. You have been appointed as economic advisor to a U.S. senator who is preparing to make a television appearance explaining why he favors a $10 billion stimulus package that would build new highways in his state. Write a brief of 500 words or less outlining the economic arguments in favor of a national policy to increase investment.

6. Suppose that two countries are alike in all respects except that one has a higher saving rate. Suppose that the endogenous growth theory is correct. What would you predict about the relative marginal products of capital in the two countries? If you were to assume that there is perfect capital mobility, would you expect to see a flow of investment from the country with the high saving rate to the country with the low saving rate or vice versa? Would you expect to see any flow from one country to the other at all? (*Hint:* compute the relative marginal products of capital in the two countries.)

7. Explain why economists often assume that world capital markets are closed. What puzzling feature of the data, pointed out by Feldstein and Horioka (see Figure 14.1), leads to this conclusion?

8. Explain what economists mean by an *externality*. How are externalities used to reconcile the theory of endogenous growth with the neoclassical theory of distribution?

9. Suppose that, instead of a Cobb-Douglas function, the production function takes the form

$$Y = (aK^\rho + (1 - a)N^\rho)^{1/\rho}$$

where a is a parameter between 0 and 1 and ρ is a parameter between 1 and $-\infty$.

    a. Find the per capita form of this production function (find $Y/N = y$ as a function of $K/N = k$).

    b. Find the marginal products of capital and labor.

    c. Find an expression for labor's share of income, and show that this expression is not constant. Is there a value of ρ for which it is constant?

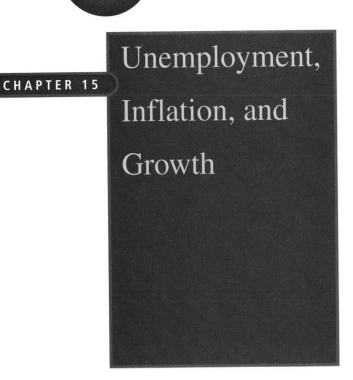

CHAPTER 15

Unemployment, Inflation, and Growth

1 INTRODUCTION

In Chapters 4, 5, and 6 we studied a model of the complete economy based on the ideas of the classical economists. At that point we said little about economic growth, and the theory we discussed was static. Now that we have introduced difference equations, tools that describe how the economy changes from one period to the next, we are ready to study inflation and growth. Our starting point is the classical model of aggregate demand, which we combine with the Keynesian theory of aggregate supply.

We study the classical theory of aggregate demand rather than the Keynesian theory because the classical theory is simpler. This has advantages and disadvantages. The major disadvantage is that the classical theory makes the false assumption that the propensity to hold money does not depend on the interest rate, which means the theory is unable to capture the channels through which fiscal policy influences aggregate demand. The major advantage of using the classical aggregate demand curve, instead of the more complex (and realistic) Keynesian approach, is that we can highlight the most important advances in economic dynamics that have occurred over the past twenty years, without getting bogged down in details. More realistic models have the same features and describe the interactions of the interest rate and fiscal policy with inflation, employment, and growth.

We are now going to develop a model of the whole economy and use it to explain the relationship between unemployment, inflation, and growth. Our model is built from the classical aggregate demand curve (from Chapter 5), the Keynesian aggregate supply curve (from Chapter 7), and the neoclassical wage equation, which explains how the nominal wage is adjusted from one period to the next. The neoclassical wage equation is an essential part of a *dynamic theory,* unlike the static theories we have studied so far.

First we must alter the classical aggregate demand curve and the Keynesian aggregate supply curve to explain how variables change over time. We do this largely by allowing for productivity growth.[1] By writing the classical aggregate demand curve and the Keynesian aggregate supply curve in terms of proportional changes, instead of levels, we can plot a downward-sloping line (the dynamic aggregate demand curve) and an upward-sloping line (the short-run dynamic aggregate supply curve) on a graph of inflation against growth. Using these curves (with a little help from the neoclassical wage equation), we can show how aggregate demand and aggregate supply interact, to determine all of the endogenous variables of our theory: unemployment, growth, inflation, and the nominal wage.

❷ THE CLASSICAL APPROACH TO INFLATION AND GROWTH

We build the dynamic neoclassical theory of aggregate demand and supply in two stages. First, we ask how the dynamic model would work if markets were extremely efficient, that is, if the nominal wage were always chosen to eliminate any possible gains from trade between firms and workers. Another way of saying the same thing is that unemployment is always at the natural rate. We call this version of our theory the **classical approach,** and we study it first to give ourselves an idea of what must be added to a static theory to allow for growth.

Once we understand how the model operates when unemployment is always chosen efficiently, we study the neoclassical wage equation, a theory that explains how the nominal wage changes through time when unemployment is temporarily different from its natural rate. The theory of wage adjustment allows us to describe an economy as Keynesian when the nominal wage moves very slowly in response to differences between unemployment and its natural rate, or as classical when it moves very fast.

Natural Paths and Natural Rates

To discuss the concept of the natural rate of unemployment in a growing economy we need some new ideas. The most important of these is the idea that output has a **natural path,** Y^*. We will show shortly that Y is bigger than Y^* whenever unemployment is less than its natural rate.

We learned in Chapter 7 that there is a natural unemployment rate, a natural level of the real wage, a natural level of employment, and a natural level of output. Now we need to amend the theory of unemployment to account for technical progress. In a dynamic growing economy, when search is costly, the natural unemployment rate and the natural level of employment remain constant each period, just as in the static economy. But the natural level of output and the natural real wage grow from one year to the next as tech-

---

1.   We adopt the exogenous growth theory from Chapter 13. The interaction of aggregate demand and supply with endogenous theories of growth is a very new area of research. We will not have much to say about it in this book.

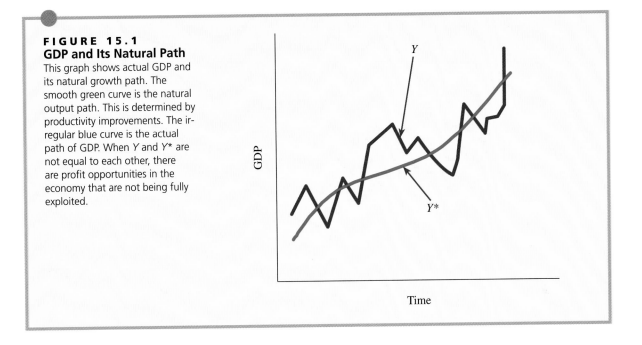

FIGURE 15.1
GDP and Its Natural Path
This graph shows actual GDP and its natural growth path. The smooth green curve is the natural output path. This is determined by productivity improvements. The irregular blue curve is the actual path of GDP. When Y and Y^* are not equal to each other, there are profit opportunities in the economy that are not being fully exploited.

nology improves. We call the list of natural levels of output, one for each year, the **natural output path,** and we call the list of levels of the natural real wage the **natural real wage path.**

Figure 15.1 illustrates the idea that GDP may have a natural path. On panel A this is the smooth green curve labeled Y^*. The irregular blue curve is the path of actual GDP. We refer to Y^* and Y as paths because they are different from one year to the next. The natural path of GDP is determined by factors like the invention of new technology and discoveries of natural resources that make technology more productive from one year to the next.[2]

The Classical Dynamic Aggregate Demand Curve

We write the classical aggregate demand curve in the form of proportional changes in Equation 15.1:

15.1
$$\frac{\Delta P}{P} = \frac{\Delta M}{M} - \frac{\Delta Y}{Y}$$

Rate of price inflation · Money growth rate · Natural GDP growth rate

2. Because inventions arrive randomly, the natural growth path may also fluctuate up and down erratically from one year to the next. In this chapter we ignore these fluctuations in the natural rate in order to keep our presentation as simple as possible.

The variables $\Delta P/P$, $\Delta M/M$, and $\Delta Y/Y$ are the proportional changes in the price level, the proportional change in the money supply, and the proportional change in GDP. We also refer to these variables as the rate of price inflation, the money growth rate, and the GDP growth rate. When it is clear from context what we mean, we refer to the rate of price inflation (as opposed to wage inflation) as the inflation rate and the rate of GDP growth as growth.

Equation 15.1 is a dynamic version of the quantity theory of money. The static version of the quantity theory, which was explained fully in Chapter 5, makes three assumptions: 1) the quantity of money demanded is proportional to income; 2) the quantity of money demanded is equal to the quantity supplied; and 3) the propensity to hold money is constant. When we write the theory in growth rates, the outcome is the **dynamic theory of aggregate demand**.

The Classical Dynamic Aggregate Supply Curve

What are the factors that cause growth and inflation to vary over the business cycle? To answer this question, we amend the search model of unemployment to allow for changes in productivity from one year to the next. We assume that productivity growth arises from the exogenous discovery of new technologies, which increase the quantity of output produced from any given input of labor. The theory that arises from our assumptions is called the **dynamic theory of aggregate supply** because it predicts that GDP will grow each year even if employment does not. We study two versions of this theory. In the classical version we assume that the real wage always grows at the natural rate of productivity growth. This assumption implies that unemployment is always at its natural rate. In the neoclassical version of the theory, we assume instead that real wage growth may differ from its natural rate.

Figure 15.2 shows how the classical dynamic theory of aggregate supply can be derived from a labor market diagram and a production function diagram. The figure illustrates the production function, on panel A, and the labor market, on panel B, in two consecutive years. Panel A shows that in year 2, a given input of labor can produce more output than in year 1. Suppose that employment is equal to its natural rate, L^*.[3] This would be true if the costs of finding a worker are not affected by changes in technology, and it is probably a good first approximation to the way the labor market operates. We see from panel A that, even if L^* is the same in year 1 and year 2, the natural level of output grows from Y_1^* to Y_2^*. In the static model, the fact that employment is equal to L^* implies that there is a single natural level of output, Y^*. In the dynamic model, natural output follows a growing path, even when employment is fixed, because the productivity of labor increases each year as new technologies are discovered. Employment remains at its natural level, L^*, in every period, but output grows at the rate g.

The classical dynamic aggregate supply curve is represented by Equation 15.2. The terms $\Delta Y/Y$ and $\Delta Y^*/Y^*$ represent the proportional change in GDP and the proportional

---

3.   To keep our analysis as simple as possible, we assume that there is no population growth. This assumption is reflected in the fact that the vertical blue line representing the labor supply is the same in the two consecutive years. We also retain the simplifying assumption that labor supply does not depend on the real wage. Allowing for population growth would not be difficult, but it would complicate our analysis without adding additional insights.

FIGURE 15.2
Growth and the Real Wage

These graphs show how the natural level of output and the natural real wage grow as a result of exogenous productivity gains.

Panel A shows the production function in two consecutive years. The production function in year 2 is everywhere higher than the production function in year 1. This reflects the fact that productivity has increased as new technologies are discovered. In the neoclassical model, the rate of productivity growth is exogenous.

Panel B shows how technology growth affects the natural real wage. The figure assumes that population is constant (the labor force does not change).

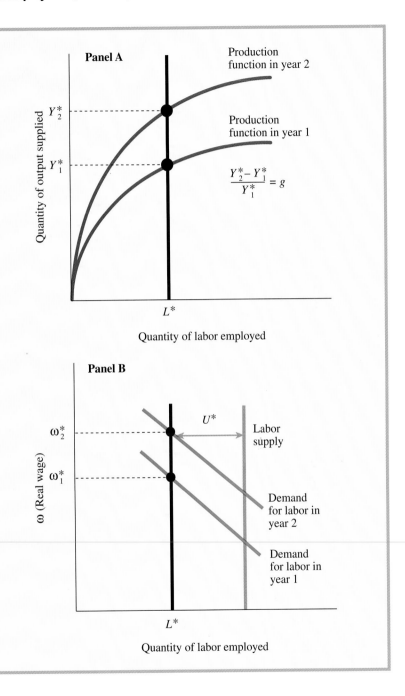

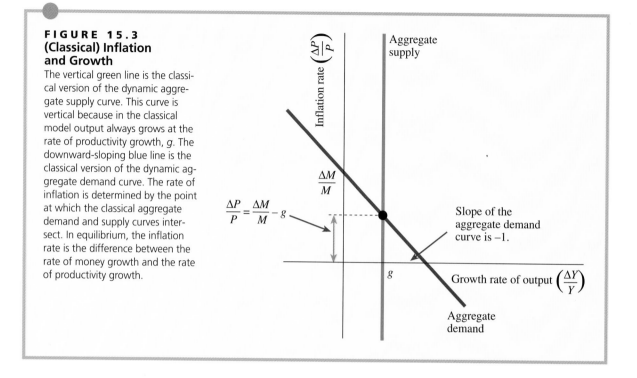

FIGURE 15.3
(Classical) Inflation and Growth

The vertical green line is the classical version of the dynamic aggregate supply curve. This curve is vertical because in the classical model output always grows at the rate of productivity growth, g. The downward-sloping blue line is the classical version of the dynamic aggregate demand curve. The rate of inflation is determined by the point at which the classical aggregate demand and supply curves intersect. In equilibrium, the inflation rate is the difference between the rate of money growth and the rate of productivity growth.

change in the natural rate of output. The natural rate g is determined by exogenous factors that govern the process of innovation and discovery.

15.2

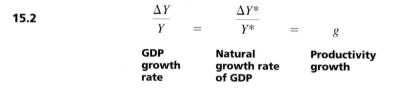

$$\frac{\Delta Y}{Y} = \frac{\Delta Y^*}{Y^*} = g$$

| GDP growth rate | Natural growth rate of GDP | Productivity growth |

Figure 15.3 combines the dynamic theories of aggregate demand and supply on a graph that plots inflation on the vertical axis and growth on the horizontal axis. The dynamic aggregate demand curve is a downward-sloping line with a slope of -1. This graph intersects the vertical axis at the rate of money growth $\Delta M/M$. The dynamic aggregate supply curve is the vertical green line at the rate of productivity growth g. The classical dynamic aggregate supply curve is vertical because we have assumed that employment is always at the natural rate and GDP grows each period at an exogenous rate determined by the rate at which society discovers new technologies.

The Wage Equation in the Classical Model

How is the real wage chosen each period in the dynamic classical theory? Panel B of Figure 15.2 graphs the labor market. We represent the constant natural level of employment by a vertical green line. As technological improvements make each worker more productive, the firm's labor demand curve shifts up, firms compete with each other to hire from the existing pool of workers, and they bid up the natural real wage from ω_1^* in year 1 to ω_2^* in year 2; these are two points on the natural real wage path. Because the labor demand curve shifts at rate g and employment is constant, the real wage also grows at rate g. Equation 15.3 governs wage growth in the classical model.

15.3
$$\frac{\Delta w}{w} - \frac{\Delta P}{P} = \frac{\Delta \omega^*}{\omega^*} = g$$

Difference between   **Growth rate**   **Productivity**
wage inflation   **of natural**   **growth**
and price inflation   **real wage**

According to the data on productivity and the real wage in the United States, presented in Box 15.1, from 1929 to 1983, the assumption that productivity and the real wage grow at the same rate is a good one, because the two variables have moved very closely in the past seventy years.

❹ THE NEOCLASSICAL APPROACH TO INFLATION AND GROWTH

Now that we have developed a dynamic apparatus for analyzing aggregate demand and supply, we are ready to study the **neoclassical theory of aggregate supply.** This theory is more realistic than the classical theory and allows unemployment to temporarily differ from its natural rate.

The neoclassical approach to aggregate supply has three elements. First, is a theory of wage determination, which we return to later. Second is a theory that explains how inflation and growth are related to each other in the short run, the period during which the real wage is temporarily different from its natural growth path. Third is a theory of how inflation and growth are related to each other when the real wage is on its natural growth path—the classical aggregate supply curve. In the neoclassical model, GDP may depart from its natural path for short periods, but it tends to return to this path in the long run.

Aggregate Supply and the Real Wage

We begin by explaining the short-run neoclassical dynamic aggregate supply curve. Because the real wage can differ from its natural path, changes in the real wage will be related to changes in employment and therefore to growth. If the real wage grows more slowly than its natural rate, firms will increase employment. If the real wage grows faster, they will lower employment. Expansions or contractions of employment raise or lower GDP growth above or below its natural rate. An economist observing data generated by this economy would expect to see that output growth is inversely related to real wage growth along the aggregate supply curve.

Figure 15.4 illustrates the relationship between changes in the real wage and changes in GDP. Panel A graphs the production function, and panel B the labor market, in two consecutive periods. The graphs show that if the real wage increases too quickly, GDP growth will be lower than its natural rate.

FIGURE 15.4
Real Wage Growth and Aggregate Supply: The Neoclassical Model
This graph shows what happens to growth of GDP when the real wage grows faster than its natural rate.

On panel A, Y_1^* represents output in year 1, when output is on its natural path. In year 2, the natural path of output increases to Y_2^* but actual output is lower at Y_2. Output between years 1 and 2 has grown at less than the natural rate, g.

Panel B shows why output growth has slipped below g. Growth is low between years 1 and 2 because the real wage has grown too fast and unemployment, in year 2, is above the natural rate.

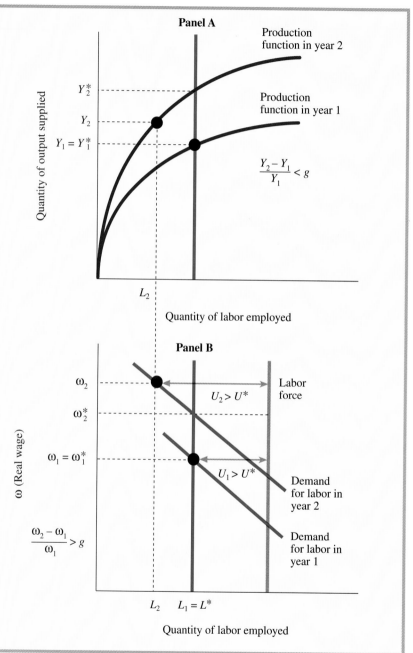

On Panel B the real wage in year 1 is on its natural path at ω_1^*, and employment is equal to its natural level, L^*. In year 2 the labor demand curve shifts up in response to exogenous productivity gains that are sufficient to justify an increase in the real wage to ω_2^*. If the real wage were to increase to ω_2^*, output would grow at its natural rate. But

BOX 15.1
FOCUS ON THE FACTS:
The Third Industrial Revolution

Classical theory assumes that productivity improvements are translated into growth in the real wage. How realistic is this assumption? Productivity is defined as output produced per unit of labor used in production. This graph shows that productivity and the real wage from 1929 through 1993[1] grew, on average, at the same rate over the whole period. Notice, however, that since 1974, both productivity and real wage growth have slowed down.

One possible reason for this is that productivity has slowed as workers adapted to a new technology. If this view is correct, we will soon see a big increase in productivity that will wipe out the apparent losses in wage growth of the past two decades.

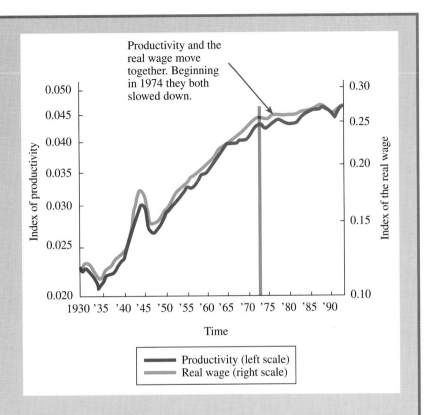

Productivity and the real wage move together. Beginning in 1974 they both slowed down.

Index of productivity

Index of the real wage

Time

Productivity (left scale)
Real wage (right scale)

Economic historians have identified two major industrial revolutions in the last two centuries. The first began in 1760 and the second in 1860. We may be entering a third.

In the two decades beginning in 1760 there were several technological miracles. The introduction of new spinning technology and the invention of energy-efficient steam engines led to tremendous changes in society that generated big increases in living standards. A second jump in technological efficiency began in the seventy-year period beginning in the 1860s. This era saw the introduction of electricity, the modern chemical plant, and the automobile.

In both industrial revolutions, the discovery of new technologies led to initial reductions in productivity, and in the wages of the unskilled, that were later reversed. These reductions were necessary because the introduction of a new technology requires a long period of innovation as firms and workers learn to exploit the new ideas. Jeremy Greenwood of the University of Rochester has argued that we may now be in the throes of a third industrial revolution based on cheap computing power.[2]

Greenwood argues that the productivity slowdown that occurred in 1974 results from the same process that we saw in 1760 and again in 1860. We are entering a third industrial revolution associated with information technology. Initially, the new jobs fueled by computers were highly skill-intensive and there was a big increase in the relative wages of those people who had the skills necessary to develop them. Low-skilled workers, those who form the major part of the labor force, were worse off during the initial adoption phase as there were fewer routine jobs suited to their abilities. But as society learns to use the new information technologies, the new skills will themselves become routine and many more people will become familiar with the operation of the new machines. As this occurs we can expect to see productivity once more increase at the higher rate. Experience with the last two industrial revolutions suggests that it may be forty years before the wage of the unskilled catches up and overtakes the wage that they might have expected if the revolution had not occurred.

1.   The real wage is constructed by dividing compensation to employees by national income and multiplying that by an index of hours of employment supplied to the market. Productivity is defined as output per unit of labor input.
2.   Jeremy Greenwood. *The Third Industrial Revolution*. American Enterprise Institute for Public Policy Research, Washington D.C., 1997.

instead panel B graphs what happens if the real wage increases to ω_2, a level that is greater than ω_2^*. In this case, because the real wage has grown too fast, firms lower employment and output increases by less than the natural rate.

Panel A illustrates the implications of excessive wage growth for GDP growth. In year 1 output is on its natural path at Y_1^*. Between years 1 and 2, productivity increases at rate g. If employment were to remain at its natural level, L^*, output would grow by its natural rate and GDP would increase from Y_1^* to Y_2^*. But because real wage growth between years 1 and 2 exceeds its natural rate, firms reduce employment in year 2 and output grows more slowly. If the real wage grows more quickly than its natural rate, GDP will grow more slowly.

Although Figure 15.4 illustrates the case where real wage growth exceeds the natural rate, it is clear that a similar graph could be used to show that if the real wage grows by less than the natural rate then output growth will be greater than g. Similarly, when real wage growth is equal to the natural rate, output growth will also grow at this rate.

The Dynamic Neoclassical Aggregate Supply Curve

Because the change in the real wage is the difference between wage inflation and price inflation, a theory that explains how changes in the real wage are related to growth can also be used to show how price inflation is related to growth. Let's begin by assuming that wage inflation is given and ask how price inflation is related to GDP growth. The relation between price inflation and growth, implied by the neoclassical theory, is given by Equation 15.4.

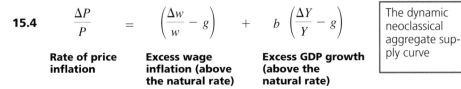

15.4 $$\frac{\Delta P}{P} = \left(\frac{\Delta w}{w} - g\right) + b\left(\frac{\Delta Y}{Y} - g\right)$$

| **Rate of price inflation** | **Excess wage inflation (above the natural rate)** | **Excess GDP growth (above the natural rate)** | The dynamic neoclassical aggregate supply curve |

The left side of Equation 15.4 is the rate of price inflation. The first term on the right side is **excess wage inflation** (increases in the nominal wage over and above those that are justified by productivity gains) and the second is **excess GDP growth** (growth in GDP over and above productivity gains). Let's suppose that the nominal wage grows at the rate of productivity growth, g. In this case Equation 15.4 tells us to expect price inflation whenever GDP grows faster than g and **price deflation** (prices fall) whenever GDP grows more slowly than g.

When price inflation is too high, the real wage increases by less than productivity growth, employment rises, and output growth exceeds the natural rate. When inflation is too low, the real wage grows by more than productivity growth, employment falls, and output grows by less than the natural rate. How much GDP growth exceeds or falls short of natural productivity growth for a given rate of price inflation depends on preferences, endowments, and technology, and it is captured in Equation 15.4 by the parameter b.

Table 15.1 summarizes the channels by which inflation and growth are related to each other. In each row of the table the nominal wage grows by the natural rate of productivity growth, but each row makes a different assumption about price inflation. The first row assumes positive price inflation. We see from column 3 that price inflation causes the real

TABLE 15.1
The Link Between Inflation and Growth When Wage Inflation Equals _g_

Wage inflation	Price inflation	Real wage	Employment	Growth
$\dfrac{\Delta w}{w} = g$	$\dfrac{\Delta P}{P} > 0$	$\dfrac{\Delta \omega}{\omega} < g$	$\dfrac{\Delta L}{L} > 0$	$\dfrac{\Delta Y}{Y} > g$
$\dfrac{\Delta w}{w} = g$	$\dfrac{\Delta P}{P} < 0$	$\dfrac{\Delta \omega}{\omega} > g$	$\dfrac{\Delta L}{L} < 0$	$\dfrac{\Delta Y}{Y} < g$
$\dfrac{\Delta w}{w} = g$	$\dfrac{\Delta P}{P} = 0$	$\dfrac{\Delta \omega}{\omega} = g$	$\dfrac{\Delta L}{L} = 0$	$\dfrac{\Delta Y}{Y} = g$

wage to grow by less than the rate of productivity growth; hence (column 4) employment rises and (column 5) output growth exceeds the natural rate. The second row assumes price inflation is negative. In this case the real wage rises by more than the natural rate, employment falls, and output growth is less than the natural rate. The third row of the table assumes zero price inflation, and the real wage and GDP both grow at the natural rate.

In Table 15.1 we assume that excess wage inflation is equal to zero (wage inflation equals g). What would happen if excess wage inflation did not equal g? If excess wage inflation is positive, say 2%, the real wage will fall, but only if price inflation _exceeds_ 2%. If excess wage inflation is negative, say -2%, the real wage will fall, but only if price inflation exceeds -2%. Price inflation greater than excess wage inflation causes output growth to exceed g. Price inflation lower than excess wage inflation causes output growth to be lower than g.

Figure 15.5 graphs the aggregate supply curve implied by our theory. The vertical purple line is the natural rate of output growth, the long-run aggregate supply curve (LRAS). We use the label long-run because, in the neoclassical theory of wage adjustment, there are forces that cause the rate of wage inflation to change whenever output differs from its natural growth path. Because of these forces, output growth cannot depart from its natural rate for long periods of time.

The upward-sloping line is the dynamic neoclassical short-run aggregate supply curve (SRAS). Its position depends on excess wage inflation, $(\Delta w/w) - g$. The short- and long-run curves cross when price inflation equals excess wage inflation; in this case the real wage and output both grow at the natural rate, g. If price inflation exceeds excess wage inflation, output must grow faster than g, and if price inflation is less than excess wage inflation, output growth must be less than g. The theory says nothing about what determines excess wage inflation; for this we must turn to the neoclassical wage equation.

The Neoclassical Wage Equation

The neoclassical wage equation is best understood by comparing it with its classical counterpart. In the classical theory, the real wage follows its natural path, and there are never any opportunities for firms to make extra profits by offering to trade with workers either at

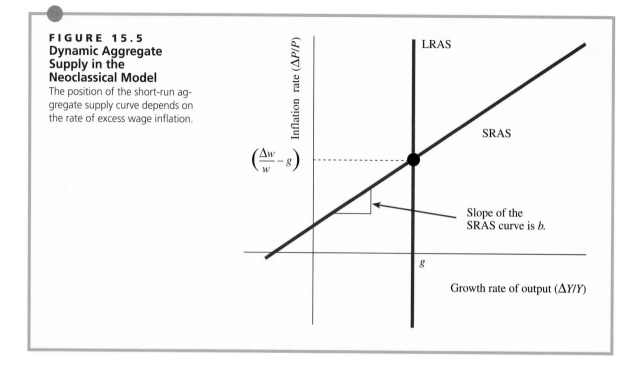

FIGURE 15.5
Dynamic Aggregate Supply in the Neoclassical Model
The position of the short-run aggregate supply curve depends on the rate of excess wage inflation.

a lower real wage or at a higher real wage. In the neoclassical version of the theory, firms sometimes have opportunities to make extra profits either because the real wage is too high, and unemployment is above its natural rate, or the real wage is too low, and unemployment is below its natural rate. The real wage is always moving toward its natural path, but in the neoclassical theory adjustment takes time.

The **neoclassical wage equation,** Equation 15.5, models the idea that, when there are profit opportunities (unemployment differs from its natural rate), the nominal wage moves in a direction that causes these opportunities to be eliminated.

15.5 $$\left(\frac{\Delta w}{w} - g\right) \quad = \quad \frac{\Delta P^E}{P} \quad - \quad c\,(U - U^*)$$

| Excess wage inflation (above natural growth rate) | Expected price inflation | Excess unemployment (above its natural rate) |

On the left side of the neoclassical wage equation the term $(\Delta w/w) - g$ represents excess wage inflation (over and above natural productivity growth). On the right side the amount by which unemployment exceeds its natural rate is subtracted from expected price inflation. The constant c determines how fast the nominal wage moves to restore balance between the real wage and the natural real wage.

In other words, because it takes time for firms and workers gather information about labor market conditions, the real wage may temporarily deviate from its natural path, but there should be strong forces pushing it back. In the neoclassical theory, two factors influence wage inflation: expected price inflation and the difference between unemployment and its natural rate.

Expected price inflation influences wage inflation because wages are typically set for a period of time; wage contracts in the United States often last for two years or more, and firms do not know future demand conditions at the time they hire workers. They must form an expectation of the rate of price inflation because this will affect the real value of the nominal wage. Unemployment influences wage inflation because if U is different from U^*, all of the possible gains from trade between workers and firms have not been exploited, leaving an opportunity for firms to profit.

The neoclassical model is a natural compromise between the classical model, in which the nominal wage adjusts immediately to eliminate excess unemployment, and the Keynesian model, in which the nominal wage does not adjust at all. The two theories, classical and Keynesian, are polar cases of the neoclassical model that occur when the parameter c, the speed of adjustment, is either very large (infinite in the limiting case) or very small (zero in the limiting case). If firms are very quick to react to profit opportunities, parameter c will be very large and the model will behave like the classical model; that is, profit opportunities will quickly disappear. If firms are slow to react to profit opportunities, parameter c will be small, unemployment may deviate from its natural rate for long periods of time, and profit opportunities will be persistent.

Wage Adjustment and the Phillips Curve

What evidence do we have for the neoclassical theory of wage adjustment? We could check the theory by searching for the existence of a relationship between wage inflation and unemployment of the kind predicted by the neoclassical wage equation. One problem with this approach is that Equation 15.5 contains the variable $\Delta P^E/P$ (expected price inflation), and it is difficult to get accurate measures of expectations. Suppose, however, we choose to study the relationship between wage inflation and unemployment in a period when expected price inflation might reasonably be expected to have been constant. The two decades beginning in 1949 were one such period.

From the graphs in Figure 15.6, price inflation from 1949 through 1969, we can see that price inflation hovered at around 2% per year. Some years prices rose faster than 2% and some years they rose slower. A family living through this period would not have gone far wrong if they had forecast that price inflation would equal 2%. After 1965, inflation began to increase at a faster rate, but it seems reasonable to assume that it took workers and firms some time to adjust their expectations to the changing conditions.

Let's assume that expected price inflation was constant and equal to 2% from 1949 through 1969. If this assumption is correct, and if the neoclassical wage equation (Equation 15.5) is correct, we would expect to see a negative relationship between wage inflation and unemployment. Figure 15.7 presents evidence on the relationship between wage inflation and unemployment from 1949 through 1969. Notice that we see exactly the negative relationship predicted by the neoclassical theory, and, furthermore, the relationship that fits the data in the 1950s also fits the data in the 1960s.

FIGURE 15.6
The History of Inflation, 1949–1969
Panels A and B illustrate the history of price inflation in the United States, in the 1950s and the 1960s. During this period inflation exceeded 2% about as often as it was less than 2%.

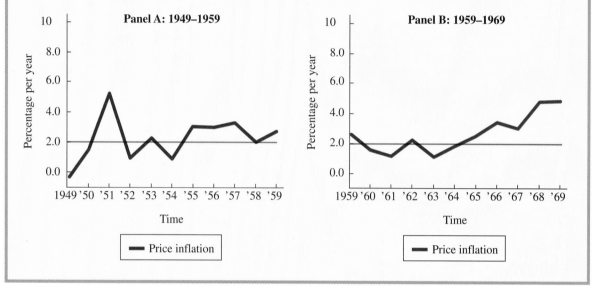

The stability of the relationship between wage inflation and unemployment was first noticed by New Zealand economist A. W. Phillips.[4] Economists in America replicated Phillips' study using U.S. data and got similar results. The relationship between the unemployment rate and wage inflation uncovered by Phillips, known as the **Phillips curve,** provided an important stimulus to the research of theorists working on the neoclassical model.

❺ THE NEOCLASSICAL MODEL

Our theory of growth and inflation makes a number of predictions about the behavior of data. Mostly, these predictions are simple extensions, in a dynamic context, of the static theory of aggregate demand and supply that we studied in the earlier sections of the book. What is new is an explicit account of the way that wages evolve through time. We added the neoclassical wage equation to account for the dynamics of wage inflation.

Figure 15.8 illustrates the three main pieces of the neoclassical model: Panel A is the dynamic theory of aggregate demand, panel B is the dynamic theory of aggregate supply, and panel C is the neoclassical wage equation. Now we examine how these pieces interact to determine inflation and growth over the business cycle.

4.   A. W. Phillips. "The relation between unemployment and the rate of change of money wage rates in the United Kingdom, 1861–1957." *Economica* 25 (November, 1958): 283–299.

FIGURE 15.7
Wage Inflation and Unem-ployment

A. W. Phillips argued that there is a stable relationship between unemployment and inflation. Subsequent authors called this relationship the Phillips curve.

Panel A illustrates the relationship between unemployment and wage inflation (the annual percentage increase in the nominal wage) from 1949 to 1959. Panel B illustrates the same relationship from 1959 through 1969. Notice that the same curve fits both sets of points.

In both cases the slope of the Phillips curve is –2. This implies that if unemployment falls by 1%, wage inflation will increase by 2%.

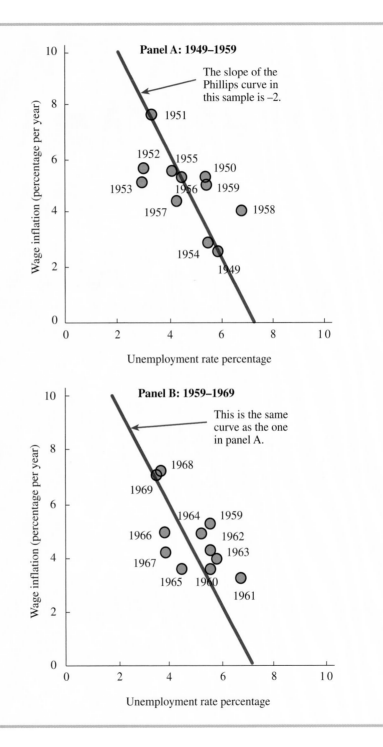

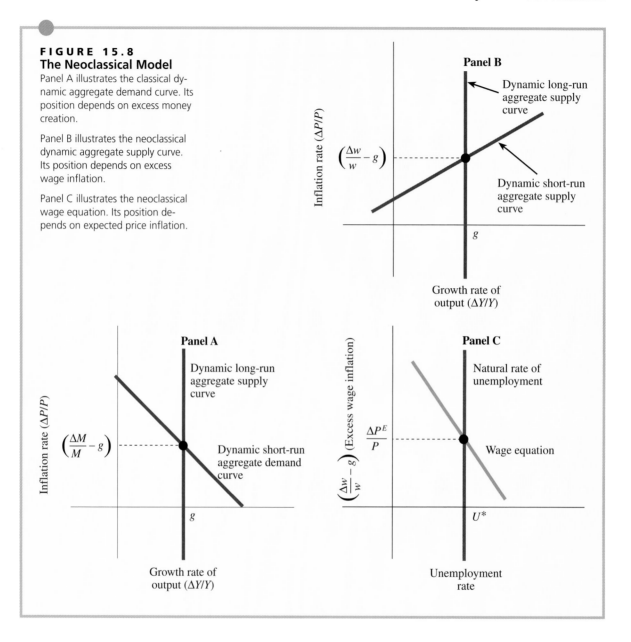

FIGURE 15.8
The Neoclassical Model
Panel A illustrates the classical dynamic aggregate demand curve. Its position depends on excess money creation.

Panel B illustrates the neoclassical dynamic aggregate supply curve. Its position depends on excess wage inflation.

Panel C illustrates the neoclassical wage equation. Its position depends on expected price inflation.

Inflation and Growth When Expectations Are Fixed

The first element of the neoclassical theory is the determination of wage inflation. Let's concentrate, for now, on a period of stable prices like the one that we experienced in the United States in the 1950s. It is reasonable, in a period like this, to assume that expected price inflation is constant and equal to 2%. Under these conditions, excess wage inflation depends only on whether the unemployment rate is currently higher or lower than its natural rate. Because wages are typically set in advance for a period of time, the determination of nominal wage inflation occurs *before* the determination of price inflation and growth, and it interacts with inflation and growth by influencing the position of the short-run aggregate supply curve. The way that current unemployment influences wage inflation is given by the neoclassical wage equation depicted on panel C of Figure 15.8.

Once the rate of wage inflation is known, we can draw the short-run aggregate supply curve on panel B. Inflation and growth are then determined at the point where the short-run aggregate supply curve (on panel B) intersects the aggregate demand curve (on panel A). Typically, both the demand and the supply curves fluctuate from one year to the next. If money growth is higher than average, the aggregate demand curve will shift to the right, and growth and inflation will be higher than average. If the rate of money creation is lower than average, the aggregate demand curve will shift to the left, and growth and inflation will be lower than average. The Federal Reserve Board is aware that changes in its policy position can affect the economy in this way, so in recent years the open market committee has deliberately tried to avoid causing unpredictable changes in demand that might either over-stimulate or under-stimulate the economy.

It is not only aggregate demand that may shift from one year to the next. A second important source of fluctuations occurs as a result of random fluctuations in the natural rate of productivity growth, g. If the natural rate of productivity growth is higher than average, the short-run aggregate supply curve will shift to the right, and inflation and growth will again be higher than average. If the rate of productivity growth is lower than average, the short run aggregate supply curve will shift to the left, and inflation and growth will be lower than average. Real productivity shifts of this kind were responsible for the recessions in 1973 and 1979, when supply shifted as a result of sharp increases in the price of oil.

Inflation and Growth Under Changing Expectations

The dynamic model of aggregate demand and supply, as explained, implies that inflation and growth may fluctuate over the business cycle for two reasons. Shocks to aggregate demand cause growth to fluctuate around its natural rate. Demand shocks generate procyclical movements in inflation. Shocks to aggregate supply cause the natural growth rate itself to fluctuate, and these fluctuations result in countercyclical movements in inflation.

To derive these predictions we assumed that inflationary expectations would be constant and equal to 2%. As long as actual inflation is equal, on average, to 2%, this is a good assumption. But if realized inflation were to exceed 2% for a long period of time, the assumption that expectations are fixed would no longer make sense. If price expectations start to exceed 2%, these expectations feed into actual wage inflation, and the position of the short-run aggregate supply curve will shift. Up to this point, we have taken expectations as given and asked how the other variables of the model behave. In Chapter 16 we relax this assumption and study theories of the endogenous determination of expectations.

More Realistic Theories of Aggregate Demand

In the introduction, we justified our use of the classical theory of aggregate demand, rather than the Keynesian theory, on the grounds of simplicity. You may wonder how the conclusions of the neoclassical model change if we were to go beyond the simple theory. The answer is that the long-run properties of the more complicated model are the same as the

BOX 15.2
Alan Greenspan on the Economy
Several times a year, the Chairman of the Board of Governors, Alan Greenspan, testifies before Congress. His speeches are available on the Web at the Board of Governors site,

http://www.bog.frb.fed.us/boarddocs/testimony/

The following excerpts are from Greenspan's testimony to Congress on October 8, 1997.

Alan Greenspan, Chairman of the Board
of Governors of the Federal Reserve.
©Tom Sobolik/Black Star Publishing Company

Quote	Quick Summary
The long-term outlook for the American economy presents us with . . . uncertainties. There can be little doubt that the American economy in the last several years has performed far better than the history of business expansions would have led us to expect. Labor markets have tightened considerably without inflation emerging as it has in the past. Encouraged by these results, financial markets seem to have priced in an optimistic outlook, characterized by a significant reduction in risk and an increasingly benevolent inflation process.	Unemployment and inflation are both low right now. This has caused investors in the stock market to be optimistic.
[But] ..... continuously digging ever deeper into the available working-age population is not a sustainable trajectory for job creation. The unemployment rate has a downside limit, if for no other reason than unemployment, in part, reflects voluntary periods of job search and other frictional unemployment, and includes people whose skills are not well adapted to work today and would be very costly to employ.	I'm worried that unemployment is *too* low . . .
Thus, the performance of the labor markets this year suggests that the economy has been on an unsustainable track. That the marked rate of absorption of potential workers since 1994 has not induced a more dramatic increase in employee compensation per hour and price inflation has come as a major surprise to most analysts.	. . . and most of us would have expected more wage and price inflation by now.
To be sure, there is still little evidence of wage acceleration. To believe, however, that wage pressures will not intensify as the group of people who are not working, but who would like to, rapidly diminishes, strains credibility.	It hasn't happened, but this can't continue.
The law of supply and demand has not been repealed. If labor demand continues to outpace sustainable increases in supply, the question is surely when, not whether, labor costs will escalate more rapidly.	Wage inflation will take off sooner or later.

Quote	Quick Summary
Of course, a fall-off in the current pace of demand for goods and services could close the gap and avoid the emergence of inflationary pressures. So could a sharp improvement in productivity growth, which would reduce the pace of new hiring required to produce a given rate of growth of real output.	If the dynamic aggregate demand curve shifts left . . . or the dynamic aggregate supply shifts right . . . inflation may not be a problem,
However, to reduce the recent two million plus annual rate of job gains to the one million rate consistent with long-term population growth would require, all else equal, a full percentage point increase in the rate of productivity growth. While not inconceivable, such a rapid change is rare in the annals of business history, especially for a mature industrial society of our breadth and scope.	but don't hold your breath.
An acceleration of productivity growth, should it materialize, would put the economy on a higher trend growth path than [has been] projected. The development of inflationary pressures, on the other hand, would doubtless create an environment of slower growth in real output than that projected by OMB or CBO.[1] A reemergence of inflation is, without question, the greatest threat to sustaining what has been a balanced economic expansion virtually without parallel in recent decades. In this regard, we at the Federal Reserve recognize that how we handle monetary policy will be a significant factor influencing the path of economic growth and, hence, fiscal outcomes.	An increase in the natural rate of productivity growth would be fabulous, but if inflation reemerges we're in trouble, because getting rid of it could be really costly in terms of future growth. The Federal Reserve System has a big role in preventing this from happening.
If economic growth and rising living standards, fostered by investment and price stability, are our goal, fiscal policy in my judgment will need to be biased toward surpluses in the years immediately ahead. This is especially so given the inexorable demographic trends that threaten huge increases in outlays beyond 2010. We should view the recent budget agreement, even if receipts and outlays evolve as expected, as only an important down payment on the larger steps we need to take to solve the harder problem—putting our entitlement programs on a sound financial footing for the twenty-first century.	Congress should keep the budget deficit down and preferably run a budget surplus, because in the next century there will be more old people claiming pensions, and we need to make sure the money is there to pay them.

1.   OMB is the Office of Management and Budget (professional economists employed by the President). CBO is the Congressional Budget Office (professional economists employed by Congress).

simple one. Inflation is determined by the rate of money creation, and output growth is determined by its natural rate. In the short run, many variables, other than the rate of money creation, can shift the dynamic aggregate demand curve. These other variables can influence growth and inflation in a way that is more complicated than the model described in this chapter. In the more complete model, changes in the interest rate interact with money creation and inflation, and these interactions add additional dynamic elements to the adjustment path from the short run to the long run.

> **WEBWATCH 15.1** **Past Federal Reserve Board Governors**
>
> In September of 1995, *The Region* (the magazine of the Federal Reserve Bank of Minneapolis) ran a series of interviews with nine past members of the Board of Governors of the Federal Reserve System. You can read these interviews at http://woodrow.mpls.frb.fed.us/pubs/region/reg959c.html.
>
> The following quote is from the introduction to the article:
>
> > In the Federal Reserve's 82-year history, 74 people have had the privilege of serving on the Board of Governors. This group has played an important role in fostering the nation's economic growth. We invited former Board members to reflect on their experience and share their thoughts on current monetary policy direction as well as career highlights after leaving the Board. We posed the following questions.
>
> > 1) What have been some of the highlights of your career since leaving the Board?
> > 2) What are your views on the Fed's strong emphasis on price stability in recent years?
> > 3) As you reflect on your tenure as a Federal Reserve governor, what was your most memorable experience?
> > 4) With Chairman Greenspan's term expiring next March, what advice would you give to the new chairman, whether it is Greenspan or someone else?
>
> You may find some of these interviews interesting—particularly the answers to question 2. As you read the interviews, see if you can interpret the policy stance of the previous Federal Reserve Board governor's, using the dynamic aggregate demand and supply framework.

CONCLUSION

There were three parts to the dynamic theory of aggregate demand and supply: a dynamic theory of aggregate demand, a dynamic theory of aggregate supply, and a theory of wage adjustment.

We need a dynamic theory of wage adjustment because the static theory was capable of explaining deviations of unemployment from its natural rate, but only if we could assume that the nominal wage was fixed. A theory in which the nominal wage was fixed is unsatisfactory because wages have grown at 2 to 3% per year for the past century. Our theory of wage adjustment accords well with the data from the 1950s and the 1960s, a period when expected price inflation was constant. The theory can also account for more recent data, but we need to think more carefully about what determines expectations.

The static theory of aggregate demand and supply was incomplete in two dimensions: It assumed that the nominal wage and expected inflation were fixed. In the dynamic theory we relaxed the assumption that the nominal wage is fixed. In Chapter 16 we show how the theory can be amended to make expectations endogenous also.

KEY TERMS

Classical approach to inflation and growth   Natural path

Dynamic theory of aggregate demand   Natural real wage path

Dynamic theory of aggregate supply   Neoclassical theory of aggregate supply

Excess GDP growth   Neoclassical wage equation

Excess wage inflation   Phillips curve

Natural output path   Price deflation

PROBLEMS FOR REVIEW

---

1. Explain, in words, why the dynamic AD curve slopes down. Why does an increase in the rate of money creation shift the AD curve? Trace out the economic mechanism that causes this shift.

2. What two factors determine wage inflation in the classical version of the dynamic theory of aggregate supply? Explain, in words, why each of them is important.

3. In its current policy stance, the Federal Reserve Board is committed to preventing the emergence of inflation. But it hasn't always been that way. Read the interviews with past Federal Reserve Board governors at **http://woodrow.mpls.frb.fed.us/pubs/region/reg959c.html**. How many of them agree with the current focus of the Federal Reserve Board on price stability?

4. Assume that expected price inflation is fixed at 2%, the natural rate of unemployment is 5%, and the natural rate of productivity growth is 3%. What rate of unemployment is compatible with zero wage inflation? What rate is consistent with zero price inflation? Explain why these two rates are different. (*Hint:* Assume that $c = 2$.)

5. Suppose that the natural rate of productivity growth is constant and equal to 3%, and that expected inflation is constant and equal to 4%. What rate of money creation is consistent with price inflation of 4% and output growth at its natural rate? What would be the rate of wage inflation in this scenario?

6. Using the data from question 4, explain what would happen if the Federal Reserve Board were to raise the rate of money creation above the rate consistent with price inflation of 4%. Do you think this situation would persist for long? If not, why not?

7. In the 1970s productivity growth has slowed down considerably, and as a consequence real wages have almost stopped growing. How would your answer to question 4 differ if productivity growth were equal to zero?

8. According to Alan Greenspan, what are the two possible events that could prevent the emergence of inflation?

9. How much of an increase in productivity growth is necessary, according to Greenspan, if we are to avoid inflation in the immediate future? Do you think that growth of this magnitude is likely? (Read Box 15.1 as well as Box 15.2 before answering this question.)

10. What is meant by the Phillips curve and how is it related to the neoclassical wage equation? What do you predict would happen to the Phillips curve if inflation were to become very high?

11. Download the entire text of Alan Greenspan's testimony to Congress on October 8, 1997, and write a one-page summary of what he said. Pretend that you are preparing a short item for an evening news report and try to make your summary understandable to the general public. (Do not use jargon.)

12. Repeat the exercise in question 11, but this time write your report for a fellow student in your macroeconomics class. Use as many of the concepts that you learned in Chapter 15 as possible. For example, you can use terms like *neoclassical wage equation* and *dynamic short-run aggregate supply curve.*

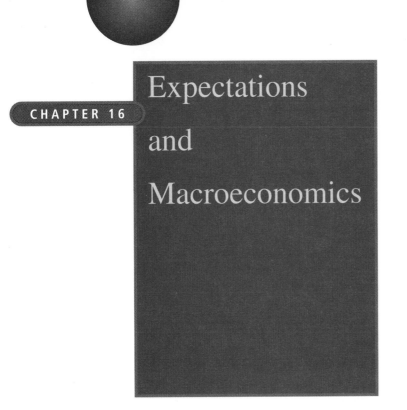

Expectations and Macroeconomics

CHAPTER 16

❶ INTRODUCTION

We have put together a complete model of aggregate demand and supply in steps and, at each step, we have broadened the theory by explaining more of the variables of the model endogenously. For example, in Chapter 15 we introduced the neoclassical wage equation to explain how the nominal wage adjusts when unemployment differs from its natural rate. So far, we have maintained the assumption that expectations of future inflation are exogenous. Now we relax this final assumption and study the endogenous determination of expectations.

This topic has occupied some of the best economists of the postwar period. The history of the theory of expectations is a history of the interaction of economic events with economic theory. Several approaches to modeling expectations were tried and rejected, and eventually one approach, rational expectations, came to dominate the way that expectations are modeled in practice.

❷ POSTWAR ECONOMIC HISTORY OF THE UNITED STATES

Immediately after the end of World War II, the United States experienced a surge in inflation that resulted from the lifting of wartime price controls. Because our theory may not apply when the government directly controls prices, as it did during World War II, we begin our narrative in 1949. We use neoclassical theory to show that a model in which expectations are fixed cannot account for the experience of the 1970s and 1980s.

Inflation

The assumption that expectations of price inflation are constant was not unreasonable during the 1950s and the 1960s, when inflation exceeded 2% about as often as it fell short of 2%. After 1965, inflation began to climb, and by 1969 it was a little higher than 4%. No one who lived through this period could have known what was coming next; a period of temporarily high inflation in the late 1960s might reasonably have been expected to decline in subsequent years.

The history of the 1970s and 1980s was very different from that of the two preceding decades. From 1969 through 1981 inflation climbed in almost every year. By 1981, inflation, as measured by the rate of growth of the GDP deflator, reached a peak of 9%. Some measures of inflation (the CPI for example) indicated inflation even greater than this.

Box 16.1 shows the history of price inflation decade by decade. It is a history of a gradual build-up and equally gradual decline. After reaching its peak in 1981, inflation began to fall and by 1996 it had returned to the levels of the 1950s.

The Phillips Curve

The neoclassical wage adjustment equation that we studied in Chapter 15 was not an established part of economic theory in the 1960s. The role of expectations was poorly understood, and expected price inflation was typically omitted from the right side of the equation. This led to a crisis in economic theory when, as inflation took hold, the previously stable Phillips curve began to break down.

Equation 16.1 is the neoclassical wage adjustment equation. Recall that, according to the neoclassical theory, wage inflation occurs for two reasons. First, households and firms may expect inflation; this is why the term $\Delta P^E/P$ appears on the right side of the equation. Second, if unemployment is currently too high, the real wage must be too high, and households and firms will negotiate for wage contracts that lower the expected real wage to bring unemployment down to its natural rate. This is why the term $(U - U^*)$ appears on the right side of the equation.

16.1
$$\left(\frac{\Delta w}{w} - g\right) = \frac{\Delta P^E}{P} - c\,(U - U^*)$$

Excess wage inflation (above the natural rate)   **Expected price inflation**   **Excess unemployment (above its natural rate)**

As long as expectations of inflation remain fixed at 2% per year, the neoclassical wage equation predicts a relationship exactly like the Phillips curve between nominal wage inflation and unemployment. But in the 1970s and 1980s inflation did not remain at 2%, and individuals living through this period needed to revise their expectations. Because we do not have good measures of expected inflation, one approach to testing the validity of the

BOX 16.1
FOCUS ON THE FACTS: Inflation in the United States Since World War II

Panels A through D illustrate the history of price inflation in the United States, decade by decade, since 1949. In each case, the green line represents a baseline case of 2% inflation.

In the first two decades (panels A and B) it would not have been unreasonable to expect that price inflation would equal 2% per year. At least through 1965, inflation exceeded 2% about as often as it was less than 2%.

In the mid 1960s things began to change, and by the 1970s (panel C) inflation was consistently above 2%.

Anyone expecting that price inflation would equal 2% in the 1970s would have been seriously mistaken. Only recently has inflation been reduced to the levels of the 1950s.

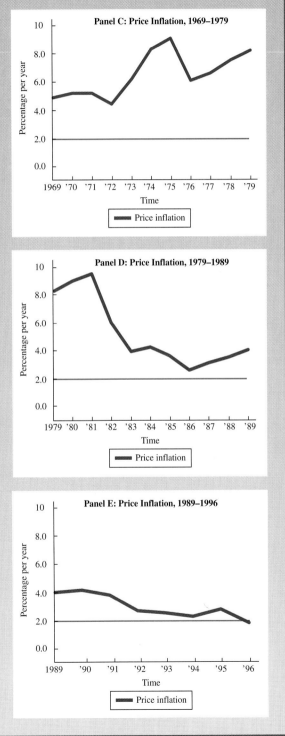

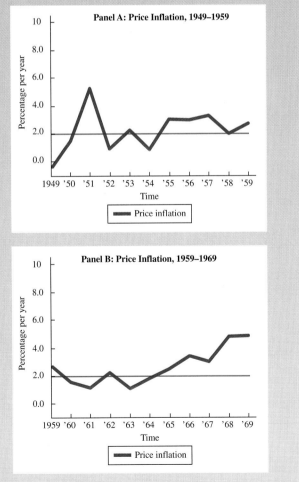

BOX 16.2
FOCUS ON THE FACTS: The Phillips Curve Since World War II
The left columns show graphs of nominal wage inflation plotted against unemployment for each decade since 1949. The right columns show graphs of real wage inflation (the proportional growth rate of the real wage) plotted against unemployment.

In the 1970s, the Phillips curve relationship began to break down. Notice in the left column that during this decade the points are above and to the right of the curve as the U.S. economy experienced high wage inflation and high unemployment simultaneously. This occurred because it was no longer reasonable to expect that price inflation would remain at 2%.

We do not have good measures of expected price inflation. Instead, the right column shows the relationship that would hold between wage inflation and unemployment if firms and households formed accurate predictions of price inflation. These graphs show how *actual* real wage inflation was related to unemployment. The graphs show that the relationship between *real* wage inflation and unemployment has remained constant during the five decades since the end of World War II.

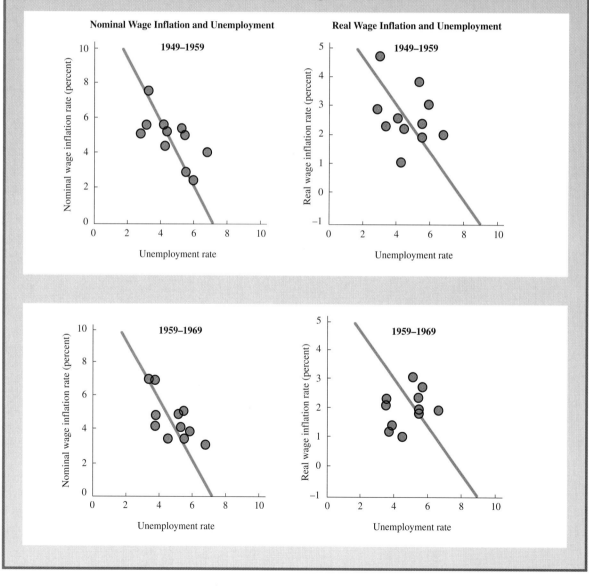

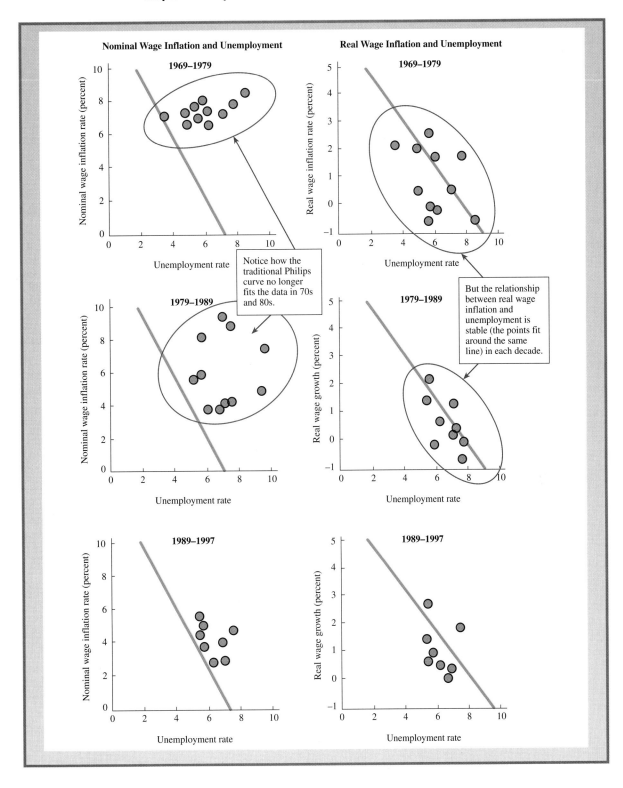

Nominal Wage Inflation and Unemployment

Real Wage Inflation and Unemployment

1969–1979

1969–1979

Notice how the traditional Philips curve no longer fits the data in 70s and 80s.

1979–1989

1979–1989

But the relationship between real wage inflation and unemployment is stable (the points fit around the same line) in each decade.

1989–1997

1989–1997

neoclassical wage equation would be to replace expected inflation by actual inflation. If we replace $\Delta P^E/P$ with $\Delta P/P$, we can write Equation 16.1 as

16.2 $$\left(\frac{\Delta w}{w} - \frac{\Delta P}{P} - g\right) \qquad = \qquad -c\,(U - U^*)$$

Excess real wage inflation   **Excess unemployment**
(above the natural rate)   **(above its natural rate)**

Stated in this way, the equation predicts that unemployment above its natural rate should cause the *real* wage to grow at a lower rate than natural productivity growth, and unemployment below the natural rate should cause it to grow more quickly. Assuming that U^* and g are constant, a graph of real wage inflation against unemployment should be a downward-sloping line.

Box 16.2 shows the history of nominal wage inflation and unemployment in the left column and real wage inflation and unemployment in the right column. Although the Phillips curve as a graph of nominal wage inflation against unemployment is unstable, the graph of **real wage inflation** against unemployment retains its position throughout the history of the postwar period.

Why the Phillips Curve Shifted Its Position

The macroeconomics journals in the 1960s discussed the idea that the Phillips curve offers a trade-off. Policy makers were thought to be able to choose a low rate of inflation and a high level of unemployment, or a high rate of inflation and a low rate of unemployment, but not both. According to this view, the goal of economic policy was to pick a point on the Phillips curve through choosing the rate of money creation. If the Federal Reserve Board chose rapid monetary expansion, so it was asserted, high inflation but low unemployment would result. If it chose a low rate of money creation, low inflation but high unemployment would result.

Over the period from 1949 to 1969 real wages grew at 2.4%, on average, as new inventions made labor more productive. Because real wages were growing, economists argued that nominal wages could be allowed to grow at 2.4% without risking price inflation. But, reading from the graph of the Phillips curve, economists estimated that if they wanted to eliminate price inflation entirely they would have to incur unemployment of at least 5.8%.

This estimate is found by reading from the Phillips curve (see Figure 16.1) the level of unemployment that would occur if the rate of wage inflation were equal to 2.4%, the same as productivity growth in the period from 1949 to 1969. When productivity is growing, nominal wages can increase at the rate of productivity growth without generating price inflation. Some economists argued that, if the government were willing to accept a positive rate of inflation, policy makers would be able to reduce unemployment below the equilibrium level of 5.8%, consistent with zero price inflation. These economists suggested that the Phillips curve should be viewed as an exploitable trade-off between inflation and unemployment.

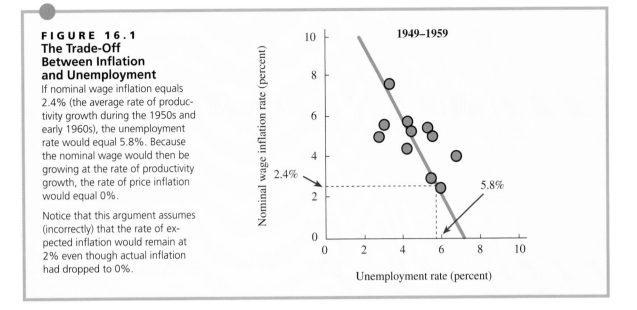

FIGURE 16.1
The Trade-Off Between Inflation and Unemployment
If nominal wage inflation equals 2.4% (the average rate of productivity growth during the 1950s and early 1960s), the unemployment rate would equal 5.8%. Because the nominal wage would then be growing at the rate of productivity growth, the rate of price inflation would equal 0%.

Notice that this argument assumes (incorrectly) that the rate of expected inflation would remain at 2% even though actual inflation had dropped to 0%.

The Natural Rate Hypothesis (NAIRU)

The view of the Phillips curve as a trade-off led to a fierce debate in the 1960s. Two prominent critics of the trade-off view were Edmund Phelps of Columbia University and Milton Friedman of the University of Chicago.[1] Phelps and Friedman believed that permanently low unemployment is unsustainable in the long run because eventually workers and firms would build expectations of price inflation into their wage-setting behavior. They argued that the observed relationship between inflation and unemployment occurred as a result of mistaken expectations on the part of households and firms. Any attempt to exploit the trade-off between inflation and unemployment would eventually be frustrated as households and firms came to expect higher levels of inflation.

Friedman and Phelps argued that the economy has a **natural rate of unemployment** independent of the variables that shift the aggregate demand curve. Unemployment can only be above or below this natural rate as a result of mistaken expectations on the part of private decision makers. If policy makers were to try to maintain unemployment below its natural rate, Phelps and Friedman argued that the inflation rate would accelerate with each successive attempt to reduce unemployment. The result would be a self-fulfilling spiral of wage and price increases. Some economists refer to the natural unemployment rate as the **non-accelerating inflation rate of unemployment (NAIRU).**

Economists did not have to wait long for spectacular confirmation of the Phelps-Friedman hypothesis. Beginning in the mid 1960s the Federal Reserve System began to expand the money supply at a faster rate than it had done in previous decades. During the 1950s and early 1960s GDP grew at almost 4% per year. The Federal Reserve Board was

1.   Milton Friedman's ideas on this topic appeared in his presidential address to the American Economic Association, published in the *American Economic Review* (March, 1968). Edmund Phelps wrote "Phillips curves, expectations of inflation and optimal unemployment over time." *Economica* (August, 1967).

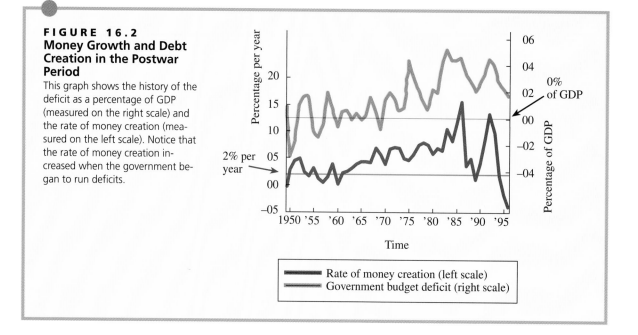

FIGURE 16.2
Money Growth and Debt Creation in the Postwar Period
This graph shows the history of the deficit as a percentage of GDP (measured on the right scale) and the rate of money creation (measured on the left scale). Notice that the rate of money creation increased when the government began to run deficits.

committed to keeping interest rates low, but as the economy expanded and the demand for money increased, this policy led to an ever-increasing rate of money growth.

Figure 16.2 shows the rate of money growth from 1949 through 1993, measured on the left scale.[2] This figure also shows what was happening to the government budget deficit over this period, measured as a percentage of GDP on the right scale.

In the early 1970s the government began to run larger deficits, partly because lower economic growth reduced the revenues available from taxation. In addition, a number of government spending programs, such as Medicare and Social Security, began to increase as the population aged and claimed pensions and medical benefits. A second reason was the build-up of defense expenditures to pay for the Vietnam War. Because the Vietnam War was domestically unpopular, it would have been difficult to finance the required military expenditures by raising taxes. Increased expenditures were financed by new government bonds, and some of these new bond issues were bought by the Federal Reserve as it tried to keep down the nominal interest rate. As the Federal Reserve System bought government debt, it created new money to pay for it, and the rate of money creation began to climb. Increases in the money supply eventually led to higher inflation as the aggregate demand curve shifted to the right.

If the Phillips curve did indeed represent an exploitable policy trade-off, then the increase in inflation in the 1970s should have resulted in a movement along the Phillips curve to a point further to the northwest; that is, the increase in aggregate demand should have resulted in higher inflation but lower unemployment. The facts were very different.

2.   The money supply in Figure 16.2 is the M1. This is a relatively narrow measure of the money stock that includes currency in the hands of the public and various kinds of checkable deposits. Different definitions of the money supplied are explained in Chapter 9.

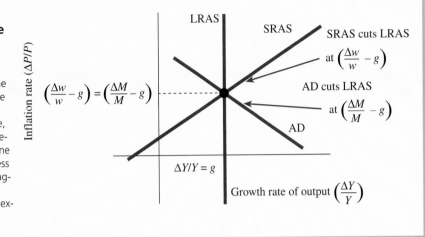

FIGURE 16.3
Fixing the Position of the Aggregate Demand and Supply Curves
We measure the position of the aggregate demand curve and the short-run aggregate supply curve by the point where they cut the long-run aggregate supply curve, the vertical green line. The aggregate demand curve cuts the g line when price inflation equals excess money creation. The short-run aggregate supply curve cuts the g line when price inflation equals excess wage inflation.

Box 16.2 illustrates that during the 1970s and 1980s the stable Phillips curve of the previous decades proved to be an illusion, as higher money growth led to higher inflation but the economy experienced higher unemployment at the same time. The experience of **stagflation** (simultaneously high unemployment and inflation) convinced many economists that the natural rate hypothesis was correct and that the Phillips curve represents only a short-run relationship between unemployment and inflation that relies on misperceptions of future inflation.

❸ THE NEOCLASSICAL MODEL

If we learned one lesson from the events of the postwar period about using the neoclassical model of aggregate demand and supply, it is that expectations cannot be modeled using mechanical rules. Instead, we must use a more sophisticated approach. First we study the implications of the neoclassical model in the short run, then its implications in the long run.

Determining Growth and Inflation

Figure 16.3 illustrates two equations of the neoclassical model on the same diagram. The downward-sloping line is the aggregate demand curve (labeled AD) and the upward-sloping line is the short-run aggregate supply curve (labeled SRAS). Growth and inflation are determined at the point where these two curves intersect. In Figure 16.3 growth is equal to its natural rate, g, as can be seen from the fact that SRAS and AD intersect where $\Delta Y/Y = g$. We call the line $\Delta Y/Y = g$ the long-run aggregate supply curve; if growth deviates from its natural rate, there will be forces that push the economy back to the long-run supply curve over time.

We can use Figure 16.3 to make short-run predictions about the effects of policy on growth and inflation. First, we must be clear about how the position of the AD and SRAS curves depend on policy and on expectations. Figure 16.3 shows that the aggregate demand curve cuts the LRAS curve when inflation equals $\Delta M/M - g$. We call this term **excess money growth.** If GDP grows at its natural rate, inflation will equal the difference between the money growth rate and g. If the Federal Reserve System creates money faster than the natural growth rate, the economy will experience inflation. If the Federal Reserve System creates money more slowly than the natural growth rate, it will experience deflation.

Figure 16.3 shows that the short-run aggregate supply curve cuts the line $\Delta Y/Y = g$ when inflation equals excess wage inflation, $\Delta w/w - g$. If price inflation equals excess wage inflation, the real wage will grow at its natural rate and output will grow at rate g.

Short-Run Growth and Inflation

Now that we understand how the position of the aggregate demand and supply curves are determined, we can use the AD–AS diagram to explain how changes in monetary policy influence inflation and growth in the short run.

Let's consider what would happen if the rate of money growth were to increase. We'll begin with a baseline case in which wage inflation and money growth are equal.

16.3
$$\frac{\Delta w}{w} - g \quad = \quad \frac{\Delta M}{M} - g$$

Excess wage inflation   **Excess money growth**

When wage inflation equals money growth, GDP must grow at its natural rate. Remember that the aggregate demand curve cuts the $\Delta Y/Y = g$ line when price inflation equals excess money growth. The aggregate supply curve cuts the $\Delta Y/Y = g$ line when price inflation equals excess wage inflation. If nominal wage inflation equals money growth, these two curves both cut at the same point and output growth equals g.

Price inflation must equal excess money creation to keep the propensity to hold money constant. When GDP grows at its natural rate, the demand for real balances also grows at the rate g, because households and firms need more money each year to finance the growing demand for transaction services. When nominal money grows faster than g, price inflation keeps real balances growing at the same rate as GDP. This is the demand side of the equation. On the supply side, price inflation must equal the rate of excess wage inflation to keep the real wage growing at the natural rate of growth. When nominal wage inflation exceeds the rate of productivity growth, price inflation keeps the real wage growing at its natural rate. Putting these two pieces together, we can see that when wage inflation (which determines the position of aggregate supply) equals money creation (which determines the position of aggregate demand), aggregate demand and short-run aggregate supply are equated at exactly the natural rate of GDP growth, g.

Figure 16.4 shows what happens when the rate of money growth increases so that $\Delta M/M$ and $\Delta w/w$ are no longer equal. The increase in the rate of money growth shifts the aggregate demand curve from AD_0 to AD_1. Because we have assumed that wage inflation does not change in the short run, the increase in aggregate demand causes price inflation to increase from $(\Delta P/P)_0$ to $(\Delta P/P)_1$. But now the real wage has fallen below its natural path, and firms increase employment above its natural rate, causing growth to be faster in year 1 than in year 0, and GDP growth goes up from $(\Delta Y/Y)_0$ to $(\Delta Y/Y)_1$.

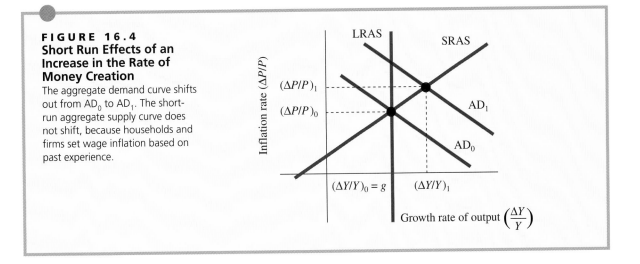

FIGURE 16.4
Short Run Effects of an Increase in the Rate of Money Creation
The aggregate demand curve shifts out from AD_0 to AD_1. The short-run aggregate supply curve does not shift, because households and firms set wage inflation based on past experience.

We started with the assumption that the rate of wage inflation is given. The neoclassical wage equation assumes wages to be determined in advance by expectations of price inflation and by pressure on wages from differences of unemployment from its natural rate. Given that households and firms expect price inflation to remain at historical levels, and given that there is no excess unemployment in the initial period, wage inflation will be equal to the same level that it was at historically. This was the situation during the 1950s and the first part of the 1960s.

Suppose now that the rate of money creation increases, as it did in the second half of the 1960s. We model this in Figure 16.4 as a shift of the aggregate demand curve from AD_0 to AD_1. The neoclassical model predicts that the increase in the rate of money creation should initially lead to an increase in inflation, a reduction in unemployment, and GDP that grows faster than its natural rate. This is exactly what happened between 1965 and 1970 as inflation increased and unemployment fell.

Long-Run Growth and Inflation

The Federal Reserve System can (and did) increase employment and growth in the short run. But what would be the long-run effect of a policy that increases the rate of money growth? Can a change in the rate of money growth permanently affect the rate of unemployment—or would the effect be temporary?

Figure 16.5 illustrates, on an aggregate demand and supply diagram, the effects of an increase in the rate of money creation in the long run predicted by the neoclassical model. We assume in this figure that the aggregate demand curve remains at AD_1 and initially, after the increase in the rate of money creation, the economy temporarily grows faster than the natural rate. The period immediately following the increase in the rate of money growth is represented as point **A** on the graph.

Now two factors cause upward pressure on the rate of wage inflation. First, at point **A**, because output is growing faster than its natural rate, unemployment is below its natural rate

FIGURE 16.5
**Long-Run Effects of
an Increase in the Rate
of Money Creation**
We assume that the aggregate demand curve remains at AD_1. As
long as unemployment is below its
natural rate, wage inflation increases and the aggregate supply
curve shifts up. In the long run,
growth returns to its natural rate
and inflation increases to equal
the new rate of excess money
creation.

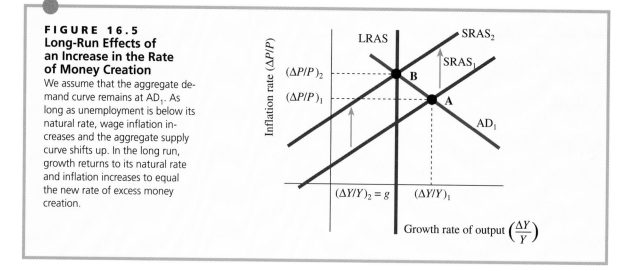

and the rate of wage inflation will begin to increase. The second factor causing additional
wage inflation is that firms and households have been surprised by the level of price inflation and revise upward their expectations of future price inflation. Both of these factors cause
the short-run aggregate supply curve to begin to shift upward. As this happens, the rate of inflation increases and the rate of growth begins to decrease until the economy ends up in a
new long-run equilibrium, depicted in Figure 16.5 as point **B.**

❹ EXPLAINING EXPECTATIONS ENDOGENOUSLY

A key element of the explanation of historical events is the idea that expectations adjusted
endogenously when actual inflation was higher than expected inflation. In order for our
theory to be useful we must be able to model this process and understand the factors that
determine expected inflation. If expectations are left unexplained, any observed pattern of
correlation between inflation, unemployment, and growth could be consistent with the theory and any discrepancy between theory and data would be attributed to the unobserved
variable, expectations.

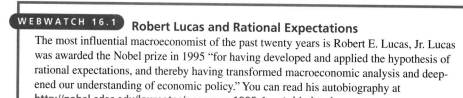

WEBWATCH 16.1   **Robert Lucas and Rational Expectations**
The most influential macroeconomist of the past twenty years is Robert E. Lucas, Jr. Lucas
was awarded the Nobel prize in 1995 "for having developed and applied the hypothesis of
rational expectations, and thereby having transformed macroeconomic analysis and deep-
ened our understanding of economic policy." You can read his autobiography at
http://nobel.sdsc.edu/laureates/economy-1995-1-autobio.html.
You will find an interview with Lucas in the *Region* magazine at
http://woodrow.mpls.frb.fed.us/pubs/region/int936.html.

Early theories of price formation provided mechanical rules to represent the process whereby households and firms formed their beliefs. This approach proved unsatisfactory because it failed to capture the innovative ways in which thinking human beings adapt to their circumstances. Any given rule for forecasting the future may work well in a given environment, but when the environment changes, people change the way in which they forecast the future. The fact that human beings adapt to their environment led to the theory of *rational expectations*.

Rational Expectations

The key to **rational expectations** is the idea that the world is a lot like a casino. In reality, nothing is certain, and sometimes there are unpredictable changes in either aggregate demand or aggregate supply as a result of wars and famines, political disputes, new inventions, and a host of other uncertainties that affect our lives. Some of these events have a primary effect on aggregate demand, and some influence aggregate supply. To keep our narrative simple, let's focus on cases in which all uncertainty is associated with aggregate demand, such as a war that causes the Federal Reserve System to print money to help pay for armament. If the Federal Reserve System expands the money supply faster than average, the aggregate demand curve will shift to the right. In another example, the Federal Reserve open market committee might be dominated by cautious men and women who are afraid that excessive monetary expansion might lead to inflation, if so the money supply increases less quickly than it otherwise might and aggregate demand shifts to the left.

The idea that aggregate demand may be random is a powerful one, because it lets us handle the expectation of inflation in the same way that a casino handles risk. Suppose that you bet a dollar that a coin will come up heads on a single flip. Statisticians say that the **expected value** of this gamble is zero, and they compute the expected value by adding the different possible outcomes and weighting them by probabilities. Half of the time you will gain a dollar ($+1 \times 0.5$) and half of the time you will lose a dollar (-1×0.5); adding up these two possibilities gives an expected value of zero. The expected value of a variable is a statistical term for the average.

The theory of rational expectations models beliefs of individuals in the same way that a statistician calculates averages. We say that it is rational to calculate inflation using probabilities. If half the time the money supply grows faster than $\Delta M/M$, then half the time the aggregate demand curve will shift to the right. If half the time the money supply grows slower than $\Delta M/M$, then half the time the aggregate demand curve will shift to the left. The actual inflation rate is determined by the intersection of an aggregate demand curve with the short-run aggregate supply curve. When the money supply grows faster than average, inflation is higher than average. When it grows slower than average, inflation is lower. The rational expectation of the inflation rate is equal to the high rate, multiplied by the probability that it will be high, plus the low rate, multiplied by the probability that it will be low.

We can illustrate this idea by showing how the neoclassical theory of aggregate demand and supply would explain the determination of inflation and growth in a hypothetical world in which expectations were not rational. We use two cases, one in which inflationary expectations are too low and one in which they are too high. These extreme examples lead naturally to a theory of the factors that determine whether an expectation of price inflation is rational. In our example, all of the uncertainty in the economy is associated with

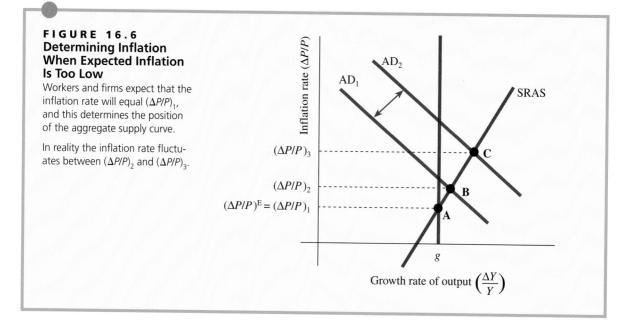

FIGURE 16.6
Determining Inflation
When Expected Inflation
Is Too Low
Workers and firms expect that the
inflation rate will equal $(\Delta P/P)_1$,
and this determines the position
of the aggregate supply curve.

In reality the inflation rate fluctu-
ates between $(\Delta P/P)_2$ and $(\Delta P/P)_3$.

aggregate demand, and the aggregate supply curve is fixed but the aggregate demand curve
fluctuates.

Expected Price Inflation Is Too Low

Figure 16.6 illustrates what would be observed if workers and firms expected the inflation
rate to equal some arbitrary value that we denote $(\Delta P/P)_1$. Expectations of price inflation
affect the position of the aggregate supply curve because they influence actual wage inflation. When expected price inflation is low, the position of the aggregate supply curve is
also low. In the figure, the expectation $(\Delta P/P)^E = (\Delta P/P)_1$ is too low; that is, if workers
and firms believe that inflation is equal to $(\Delta P/P)_1$, they are mistaken and their mistakes
are systematically in one direction.

Consider a situation in which unemployment is equal to the natural rate, firms and
workers expect that inflation will equal $(\Delta P/P)_1$, and the money supply is, on average,
growing at a rate $\Delta M/M$. Because unemployment is equal to the natural rate, excess wage
inflation equals expected price inflation. This is reflected on Figure 16.6 by the fact that
the short-run aggregate supply curve cuts the long-run curve (the line $(\Delta Y/Y) = g$) at the
expected rate of price inflation, $(\Delta P/P)_1$.

Given these beliefs, what will actually happen depends on the rate of money creation.
In Figure 16.6 the money supply fluctuates randomly between two levels. When the
money supply grows quickly, the aggregate demand curve is at AD_2, and when the money
supply grows slowly, it is at AD_1. The actual rate of inflation is determined by the intersection of the aggregate demand curve with the short-run aggregate supply curve, and half
of the time the equilibrium is at **B** and the rest of the time it is at **C**. A worker or a firm that

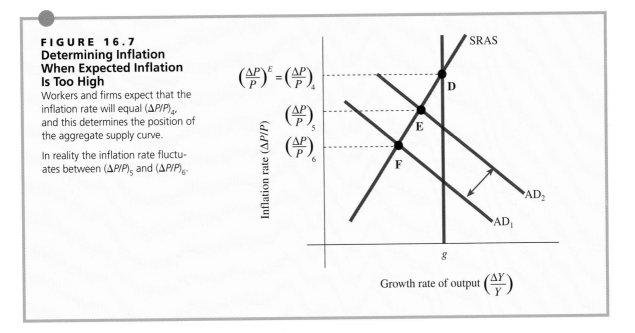

FIGURE 16.7
Determining Inflation When Expected Inflation Is Too High
Workers and firms expect that the inflation rate will equal $(\Delta P/P)_4$, and this determines the position of the aggregate supply curve.

In reality the inflation rate fluctuates between $(\Delta P/P)_5$ and $(\Delta P/P)_6$.

lived in this economy would observe that sometimes inflation is equal to $(\Delta P/P)_3$, and sometimes it is equal to $(\Delta P/P)_2$. But notice that both of these possible outcomes lead to higher inflation than the worker or the firm was expecting.

Expected Price Inflation Is Too High

Figure 16.7 illustrates what would happen if workers and firms had instead expected the higher inflation rate $(\Delta P/P)_4$. In this case the aggregate supply curve would cross the natural rate line at **D**. Once again, we assume that the only shocks are to aggregate demand. If the aggregate demand shock is equal to its highest value, equilibrium will occur at **E** and the actual inflation rate will be $(\Delta P/P)_5$. If it is equal to its lowest value, the equilibrium will occur at **F** and the actual inflation rate will be $(\Delta P/P)_6$. In reality, the aggregate demand curve fluctuates between these two extremes, and the observed inflation rate varies between $(\Delta P/P)_5$ and $(\Delta P/P)_6$. Notice, however, that if firms and workers expect the price level to equal $(\Delta P/P)_4$, the actual inflation rate will turn out to be lower than they expected. Clearly, in this case, the expected inflation rate is too high.

Rational Expectations of Price Inflation

Rational expectations, a method of modeling expectations that captures the ability of human beings to adapt to their environment was first suggested in 1961 by John Muth.[3] Muth's concept of rational expectations was introduced into macroeconomics in 1972 by

3.   J. F. Muth. "Rational expectations and the theory of price movements." *Econometrica* 29 (1961).

FIGURE 16.8
The Rational Expectation of Inflation

Workers and firms expect that the inflation rate will equal $(\Delta P/P)_7$, and this determines the position of the aggregate supply curve. The actual inflation rate fluctuates between $(\Delta P/P)_8$ and $(\Delta P/P)_9$. The rational expectation depends on monetary policy.

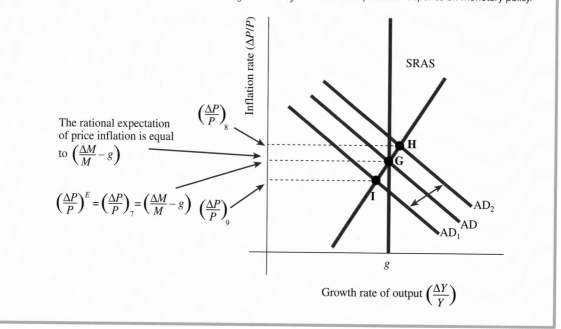

Robert Lucas.[4] It has since become standard as a way of treating expectations. Rational expectations assumes that the beliefs of workers and firms will be right on average.

Figure 16.8 illustrates rational expectations of inflation. The figure depicts the same two aggregate demand curves that we saw in Figures 16.6 and 16.7. In addition, we have depicted the average aggregate demand curve, the one that will hold if the monetary shock is equal to its average value of zero. The inflation rate at which this average aggregate demand curve cuts the aggregate supply curve is the rational expectation of inflation and is equal to $(\Delta P/P)_7$. Notice that this is also the point at which the aggregate supply curve intersects the natural rate line.

In Figures 16.6 and 16.7 the expected inflation rate was either too high or too low; the actual inflation rate would either be consistently above or consistently below the expected inflation rate. In Figure 16.8, however, the expectations of firms and households are rational: the expected inflation rate is such that, whatever random events occur in the future, the observed inflation rate will sometimes turn out to be higher than expected and sometimes lower.

The rational expectation of the inflation rate is equal to its average value. This value, in turn, depends on the factors that alter the set of positions of the aggregate demand

---

4.   Robert E. Lucas Jr. "Expectations and the neutrality of money." *Journal of Economic Theory* (1972).

curve—the factors that determine $\Delta M/M$. Therefore, rational expectations implies that beliefs depend on the policy pursued by the Federal Reserve Board.

The major insight of the rational expectations literature is that what individuals expect has consequences for the set of outcomes that actually occurs. A few observations of an inflation rate higher than expected might be consistent with bad luck, much as a gambler could throw a string of ones on a die. But a consistent string of outcomes higher than expected would cause workers and firms to revise their expectation of inflation upwards. Rational expectations means that in our economic models we should assume expectations are chosen so that they are not systematically wrong.

Rational Expectations and Learning

Most economists today accept some version of the rational expectations hypothesis, but not all are comfortable with the strictest form of the hypothesis. Rational expectations ascribes a degree of knowledge to households and firms that many economists find implausible. In order to form a rational expectation of the future inflation rate, people must be able to predict accurately the future rate of money growth. Predicting future money growth is difficult because the policy of the Federal Reserve Board is constantly changing as policy makers respond to changing circumstances. Many economists believe that rational expectations is a sensible way of modeling the equilibrium of an economy, but that the assumption must be supplemented by a description of how individuals learn about their environment.

❺ FEDERAL RESERVE SYSTEM MONETARY POLICY

The theory outlined in this chapter, supplemented by a more sophisticated version of the dynamic theory of aggregate demand, is extremely influential among policy makers in the Federal Reserve System. Rational expectations is now accepted by most economists as a constraint on policy, and it is widely thought that the credibility of economic policy is an important determinant of its effects. But the Federal Reserve System did not arrive at this position overnight. The economy had some tough lessons to teach first.

Arthur Burns and the Build-Up of Inflation

Inflation did not become a problem in the United States until the 1970s. Prices remained relatively stable for thirty years following World War II, but by the mid 1970s the inflation rate was following a detectable trend. Figure 16.9 illustrates the history of the money growth rate and the inflation rate over this period. The figure indicates a clear upward trend in both rates. Because economic theory states that inflation can be controlled by constraining the rate of money growth, one might ask why the Federal Reserve System allowed inflation to occur.

In 1970 the chairmanship of the Federal Reserve Board was taken over by Arthur Burns. Under Burns, inflation built up from 5% in 1970 to 9% in 1980. Evidence that Arthur Burns was aware of the consequences of the actions of the Federal Reserve Board can be found in a speech he made in 1977:

FIGURE 16.9
The Build-Up of Inflation
Under Arthur Burns

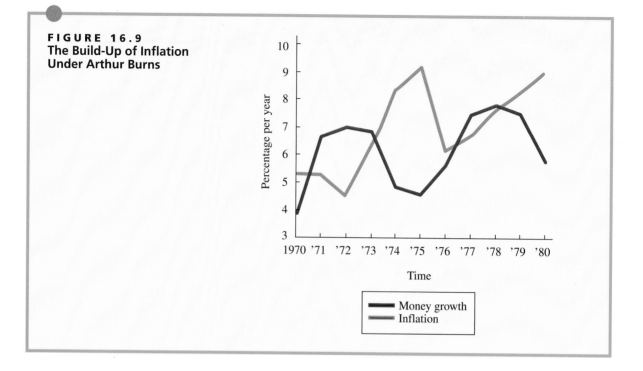

Neither I nor, I believe, any of my associates would quarrel with the proposition that money creation and inflation are closely linked and that serious inflation could not long proceed without monetary nourishment. We well know—as do many others—that if the Federal Reserve stopped creating new money, or if this activity were slowed drastically, inflation would soon either come to an end or be substantially checked.[5]

But Burns chose to accommodate inflationary expectations rather than accept a costly recession. Burns put it this way in testimony before the Committee on Banking and Currency of the House of Representatives on July 30, 1974:

. . . an effort to use harsh policies of monetary restraint to offset the exceptionally powerful inflationary forces in recent years would have caused serious financial disorder and economic dislocation. That would not have been a sensible course for monetary policy.[6]

In other words, Burns deliberately allowed the money supply to grow in order to avoid a recession. The probable cause of the inflationary forces that Burns refers to was a large increase in the world price of oil in 1973. The oil price increase can be interpreted as a negative supply shock that shifted the aggregate supply curve to the left.[7] In

5.   Arthur F. Burns, "Reflections of an economic policy maker, speeches and congressional statements: 1969–78." American Enterprise Institute for Public Policy Research, Washington D.C. p. 417. These passages are cited in a recent discussion paper, "Expectation traps and discretion," by V. V. Chari, Lawrence Christiano, and Martin Eichenbaum.
6.   Burns, op. cit. p. 171.
7.   In 1973 oil became much more expensive and firms used less of it. This caused other factors to become less productive: the effect on our model would be to shift the aggregate supply curve.

the language of macroeconomics, we would say that the Federal Reserve Board reacted to the oil price increase by conducting **a discretionary monetary policy.** A discretionary policy is one that allows the rate of monetary growth to react to contemporaneous shocks. Some economists, notably Milton Friedman of the University of Chicago, have argued that the Federal Reserve System has no business trying to stabilize recessions and that the best way to conduct monetary policy is to fix a target for the rate of monetary growth and stick to it. Discretionary monetary policy, according to Friedman, only adds to uncertainty and creates additional sources of shocks that exacerbate business cycles.

A second argument against discretion is raised by V. V. Chari of the University of Minnesota and Lawrence Christiano and Martin Eichenbaum of Northwestern University. They argue that it is the fact that the Federal Reserve Board was allowed to run a discretionary monetary policy that was responsible for the inflation of the 1970s. According to this view, agents formed expectations of inflation precisely because they believed that the Federal Reserve System would accommodate those expectations rather than permit a recession; these inflationary expectations then became self-fulfilling. Chari, Christiano, and Eichenbaum argue that if the Federal Reserve Board were to be given less discretionary power, the situation that Burns described could have been avoided.

The Volcker Recession and the Removal of Inflation

Burns's term as chairman of the Federal Reserve Board ended in October of 1979 when Paul Volcker took over. Under Volcker's chairmanship, the Federal Reserve Board reduced inflation in the United States economy by lowering the rate of monetary growth. In effect, the Federal Reserve Board engineered a leftward shift of the aggregate demand curve. Initially the policy of lowering the rate of monetary growth was perceived as a temporary shock that shifted the aggregate demand curve to the left. But firms and workers did not initially expect that this policy would continue, and a lower expected inflation rate was not built into contracts. As a consequence, the reduction in aggregate demand resulted in a recession.

Figure 16.10 illustrates the behavior of key economic variables from 1977 through 1983. Panel A illustrates the growth in M1 and panel B indicates the behavior of the interest rate. Money growth slowed from 9% in 1978 to 5% in 1981, while the interest rate on six-month loans increased from 7% in 1978 to a peak of 14% in 1981. Undoubtedly the Federal Reserve Board could have prevented the increase in the short-term interest rate by allowing narrow measures of money to grow at a faster rate. Minutes of the Federal Reserve Board meetings from the period indicate that it chose not to. Instead, the Federal Reserve Board allowed a sharp rise in the interest rate because it wanted to lower the inflation rate.

Panel C of Figure 16.10 indicates an initial consequence of the reduction in the monetary growth rate—a sharp recession as GDP growth went from 4% in 1978 to −2% in 1982. The modern interpretation of these events is that households and firms did not expect the Federal Reserve Board to tighten the rate of money growth when they negotiated their wage contracts. As a consequence, the inflation rate in the early 1980s was lower than the rate that firms and workers had anticipated. The Federal Reserve System's monetary contraction caused a movement down the aggregate supply curve, leading to a loss of

FIGURE 16.10
Removing Inflation from the Economy
These graphs illustrate the behavior of money growth, inflation growth, and the rate of interest from 1977 to 1983.

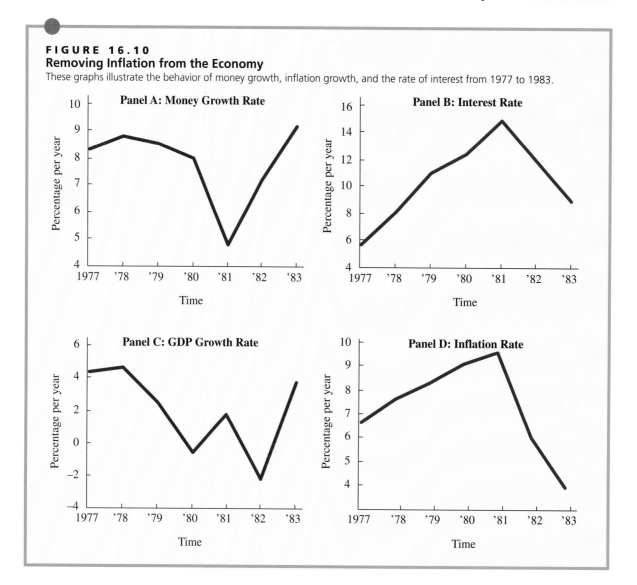

output in the short run. The payoff did not occur until 1982–83, when the inflation rate finally fell from a peak of almost 10% in 1981 to 4% in 1983 (panel D).

Monetary Policy Under Alan Greenspan

Most economists believe that the disinflation of the early 1980s was costly in terms of output foregone, because it took time for households and firms to build a lower expectation of inflation into contracts. Because it is costly to remove inflation from the economy, the Federal Reserve Board is constantly alert to the possibility that inflationary expectations are building up.

Monetary policy under Alan Greenspan, the current chairman of the Federal Reserve Board, is best viewed as a balancing act between the use of monetary policy to offset adverse shocks to the economy and the worry that monetary policy should not be too expansionary. Expansionary monetary policy might lead to a build-up of inflationary expectations in a way that becomes self-fulfilling.

The current view of policy makers, under Greenspan's chairmanship, is that discretionary monetary policy is an important means of offsetting shocks that occur elsewhere in the economy. For example, suppose that a negative supply shock hits the economy and is expected to persist for a year or more, such as an increase in the price of oil of the kind that occurred in the 1970s. If households and firms had already negotiated contracts, a negative supply shock of this kind would tend to raise inflation and lower GDP growth. If the Federal Reserve Board is able to observe the shock in time and react to it with an offsetting monetary disturbance, then the impact of the supply shock on GDP growth could be completely offset. The Federal Reserve Board would shift up the aggregate demand curve at the same time that the aggregate supply curve shifted up. This would result in temporarily higher inflation than would otherwise have occurred, but it would prevent the shock from causing increased unemployment and reducing growth.

The danger of using discretionary policy in this way is that the Federal Reserve Board may not be able to recognize adverse supply shocks in time to take the correct action. As a consequence, an attempt to run discretionary policy may actually exacerbate the business cycle. In addition, if the Federal Reserve System stimulates the economy too often, it may contribute to an increase in inflationary expectations that could be difficult to remove without a costly recession in the future.

CONCLUSION

A complete dynamic model of aggregate demand and supply can be used to explain the joint determination of price and GDP in the long run and the short run. According to modern theory, the short run is a period over which expectations of future inflation are fixed. The long run is the period over which expectations adjust. In the short run, monetary policy has real effects because expectations have already been written into wage contracts. Over longer periods, wage contracts change to reflect new expectations and increases in the supply of money are totally absorbed by price increases.

The Phillips curve is a stable relationship between wage inflation and unemployment when expectations are fixed. The Phillips curve does not work when expectations of inflation are determined endogenously. The modern theory of aggregate demand and supply explains why the Phillips curve appeared to be stable before 1970, and why the apparently stable relationship disappeared in the 1970s and 1980s. The theory argues that the Phillips curve shifted when policy makers tried to exploit the relationship by raising growth above its natural rate. As inflation became anticipated, it was built into expectations and the Phillips curve shifted up. Policy makers are now aware of the importance of preventing the build-up of inflationary expectations. This awareness causes them to be cautious in using monetary policy to offset the effects of adverse supply shocks on employment and growth.

Discretionary monetary policy   Rational expectations
Excess money growth   Real wage inflation
Expected value   Stagflation
Natural rate of unemployment
Non-accelerating inflation rate of unem-
   ployment (NAIRU)

PROBLEMS FOR REVIEW

1. Describe the history of inflation in the United States, decade by decade, since 1949. What was the highest value of inflation during this period? What was the lowest? When did each occur?

2. What is the Phillips curve? What is the neoclassical wage equation? Under what conditions does the neoclassical wage equation predict that you should observe a Phillips curve in actual data?

3. What is the role of the parameter c in the neoclassical wage equation? Prove that as c gets very large, the neoclassical and classical models are the same.

4. Suppose that expected inflation is equal to 4%. Use the Phillips curve to predict the rate of unemployment that is consistent with 2% price inflation. (*Hint:* Use Figure 16.1 to estimate the natural rate of unemployment and assume that agents have rational expectations).

5. What is meant by the *natural rate of employment?* How does the natural rate of employment differ from the natural rate of unemployment? What are the factors that determine each of these concepts? Can you think of circumstances under which the natural rate of unemployment and the natural rate of employment would both increase?

6. Why did money growth increase in the 1970s? Use the Keynesian theory of aggregate demand (from Chapters 8 through 10) to explain why, if the Federal Reserve Board were to try to keep down the nominal interest rate, it would need to expand the money supply.

7. Suppose that you are the dictator of a small country able to conduct any monetary and fiscal policy you wanted. (You can ignore ethical issues for the time being.) How would you design an experiment that would enable you to test the dynamic neoclassical theory of aggregate supply?

8. Suppose that expectations are not rational but instead are equal to last year's actual inflation. That is, $\left(\dfrac{\Delta P}{P}\right)^E_t = \left(\dfrac{\Delta P}{P}\right)_{t-1}$. Show that it is possible to design a monetary policy for which unemployment is permanently below the natural rate.

9. Explain the factors that determine the position of the dynamic aggregate demand curve.

10. Explain the factors that determine the position of the short-run aggregate supply curve.

11. The theory of rational expectations says that actual inflation always equals expected inflation. Is this true or false? Explain your answer.

12. You have been appointed as a policy advisor to Alan Greenspan. Prepare a brief outlining how you think he should run monetary policy. Your brief should include the main lessons of this chapter.

13. Read the article "Formulating a Consistent Approach to Monetary Policy" by Gary Stern, President of the Federal Reserve Bank of Minneapolis. This article is available online at **http://woodrow.mpls.frb.fed.us/pubs/ar/ar1995.html**. Answer the following questions:

    a. How is inflation related to long-run growth?

    b. Which central banks have recently announced low inflation targets? Why?

    c. Why does Stern believe that the Federal Reserve Board should not "act aggressively in most circumstances" to stabilize business cycles?

    d. Briefly summarize Stern's three proposals for running monetary policy on a day-to-day basis.

14. You are asked to explain the modern theory of aggregate supply to your brother's high school class in economics. Prepare a ten-minute presentation in which you outline the main features of this theory.

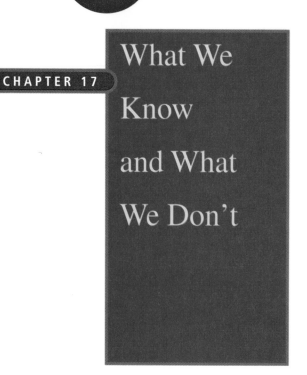

CHAPTER 17

What We Know and What We Don't

❶ INTRODUCTION

Economists have a unique approach to social problems that sets them apart from most other social scientists. This approach, called methodological individualism,[1] begins with the assumption that societies consist of large numbers of individuals, each of whom makes choices over what to produce and what to consume. The defining aspect of the economic approach is that the preferences of individuals can be taken as fixed for the purposes of analyzing economic questions. Economic choices are made to achieve a goal—either the maximization of profits, in the case of firms, or the maximization of utility, in the case of households.

❷ WHAT WE KNOW

The Cause of Economic Growth

We learned in Chapter 1 that U.S. GDP per person has grown at roughly 1.6% per year for the past hundred years. But a number of countries, among them Japan, South Korea, and, more recently, China have achieved much more rapid rates of growth.

---

1.   Not all economists subscribe to this approach, although there is a much greater consensus in economics than in other social sciences.

Probably the most useful thing to remember is that technology advances at different rates in different countries. The history of the world is a history of leaders and followers, and currently, the United States is at the very frontier in the production of knowledge. It is much easier to grow by catching up with the world leader than by pushing forward the frontier. The main reason for the recent rapid growth of the East Asian countries is their ability to emulate the organization and production techniques already in place in the West. China is now undergoing a very rapid change from a rural economy to a modern industrial economy, and along the way it is developing a market economy and a modern trading system. This reorganization is in part responsible for the very rapid growth in the Chinese economy over the last two decades.

Until very recently, we did not really know what causes growth in advanced industrialized economies. Economic theory predicts that GDP per person cannot grow unless the technology improves each year. We must continually discover new and more productive ways of producing commodities to avoid the stagnation that comes from diminishing returns to capital. For over two hundred years the advanced industrialized countries have been discovering new technologies at a rate permitting increases in their standard of living of 1.6% per year, but only recently have we begun to collect data on growth across different countries that allows us to understand which countries have grown faster and why.

The data set collected by Alan Heston and Robert Summers has caused a burst of intellectual activity among economists who argue that growth is the result of externalities stemming from the acquisition of knowledge. If these economists are right, the immediate future looks very promising: the invention of the computer and the construction of the Internet are the most significant advances in the technology of knowledge production since the printing press. The invention of moveable type was, arguably, the single most important cause of the industrial revolution. There are many signs in the current world economy that we will shortly enter a similar period of rapid economic growth.

Market capitalism can deliver growth, but there are alternative ways of organizing social and economic policy within a capitalist society. The Western European economies, for example, have grown at about the same rate as the United States, but they have chosen, so far at least, a greater degree of government intervention in markets. In the mid-twentieth century the economies of the former Soviet Union and its satellite nations in Eastern Europe achieved relatively rapid industrialization under a centrally planned system. But the comparative performance of East and West Germany suggests that the communist model was much less successful at delivering sustained increases in the standard of living of its citizens than the market capitalist model. When the Berlin Wall fell in November of 1989, it quickly became apparent that the standards of living in East and West Germany, a single country with a single culture and comparable infrastructure only 45 years earlier, had diverged dramatically. China has grown rapidly by adopting a market system; whether this will inevitably lead to a democratic political system remains to be seen.

Studying Business Cycles

The main advances in business cycle theory over the past two decades have been theoretical. We have begun to understand how to use the tools of supply and demand analysis to study dynamic problems, and for the first time in a very long while, a consensus is developing amongst macroeconomists. Textbooks on macroeconomics written five or ten years ago divided macroeconomists into different schools of thought: monetarists and Keynesians, classicals and neoclassicals, real business cycle economists and new Keynesians. At research meetings throughout the world, these divisions have become a thing of the past. The progress is slow but discernible, and these days there is far more consensus than conflict.

How has this consensus developed? First and foremost, the dominant method of analyzing problems in macroeconomics today is to apply the microeconomic tools of supply and demand. The problems that we study are often more complex than the problems of a single industry or a single market, but the methods we use are the same. Economies are conceptualized as collections of rational thinking human beings who interact in markets. The simplest way of applying this idea is to assume that households and firms can trade as much as they wish of any commodity at a given price: perfect competition. But more complicated models have also been studied. Firms might be modeled as monopolists that can influence the price at which they sell by restricting quantity. Markets might involve search or random matching of buyers and sellers. By constructing model economies, based around the paradigm of the rational actor, economists can look at what causes business cycles. By constructing simulations of economic models, and checking the predictions of the models for other observable facts, we ask whether the explanation that is given by the model is the right one.

The Causes of Business Cycles

Although economists are broadly agreed as to the right method for analyzing business cycles, there is still tremendous disagreement about their causes. One school of economists, led by Edward Prescott at the University of Minnesota, argues that 70% of post–World War II business cycles have been caused by random shocks to technology. More recently, these findings have been challenged by a group of economists motivated by Keynes' view that animal spirits might be partly the cause of fluctuations in both the pre- and postwar periods.[2] What differentiates this recent debate from arguments between macroeconomists of the 1960s is that today's arguments are couched in the same language, the language of demand and supply, and these alternative theories can therefore potentially be resolved by confrontation with scientific evidence.

A modern theory of the business cycle is a system of difference equations, which models the propagation mechanism and a hypothesis about the nature of the impulse. Real business cycle economists and their opponents disagree about both of these components. These disagreements are relevant to policy makers because, if business cycles are caused by shocks to productivity, and if the propagation mechanism that causes persistence operates through the equalization of demand and supply in competitive markets, there is probably no reason for governments to intervene in the economy in order to stabilize the cycle.

If, on the other hand, business cycles arise from the animal spirits of investors, perhaps the Federal Reserve Board should act in ways that prevent wild fluctuations in

2.   Quantitative research on animal spirits as a cause of business cycles is relatively recent, and there is still no easily accessible source. For the adventurous, a collection of research papers in the *Journal of Economic Theory* 63 (1994), deals with quantitative applications of economic models in which animal spirits are the main cause of business fluctuations.

beliefs from being transmitted to employment and GDP. These questions are hard to analyze because no one can tell whether wild swings in beliefs are justifiable until after the fact. A good example of this is the current activity in the stock market. The market has realized high real returns in recent years mainly as a consequence of beliefs that there will be very high future profits. Currently, the ratio of the price of a stock to the average dividend paid by a stock is at historically high levels. Because investors in the stock market are buying claims to future dividends, the market is betting that these dividends will themselves become very big very soon. If they are wrong, the average value of stocks could fall dramatically, and that, in turn, might have repercussions for employment and growth.

Economists agree that business cycles are caused by shocks to aggregate demand and supply, and that these shocks persist for long periods of time in part because households try to smooth their consumption through saving. But there is considerable disagreement over how much of business fluctuations is caused by demand shocks, how much by supply shocks, and whether the market mechanism does or does not cause shocks to persist for longer than they should.

The Causes of Inflation

In Chapter 1, we pointed out that the trend rate of inflation has been quite a bit higher since 1945 than before 1945. The cause seems clear. In the period before 1945 the world inflation rate was limited by discoveries of gold because currencies were tied to each other, and to gold, at fixed rates under the gold standard. In 1948, with a move to the gold exchange standard, currencies became tied to the U.S. dollar, and the link to gold gradually eroded. This move from a commodity-based monetary system to a purely fiat system allowed governments throughout the world to choose their rates of monetary expansion without limit. As different countries chose to expand their money supplies at different rates, the gold exchange standard itself collapsed, and since 1973 we have lived in world of floating exchange rates in which the only check on inflation is the conservative nature of central banks.

The consensus amongst economists as to the cause of inflation is relatively new. In the 1970s an influential "cost-push" school argued that the main cause for inflation was the growth of strong trade unions. It was relatively controversial for Milton Friedman in the 1950s to argue that inflation is caused by excessive creation of money, largely because the quantity theory of money had been discredited by the observation that the propensity to hold money is not a constant. Proponents of the utility theory of the demand for money argued not that the propensity to hold money is constant, but that it is a stable function of the rate of interest, and the incorporation of this idea into modern macroeconomics has led to a consensus that money growth is essential to the maintenance of a sustained increase in the general level of prices. Friedman coined the then-controversial phrase "inflation is always and everywhere a monetary phenomenon." Today this statement is accepted as scientific fact.

The most recent episode of inflation in the United States was relatively mild on a world scale, but is was important enough to cause significant disruption in economic activity and was partly responsible for the downfall of the Carter presidency. Inflation began to build up in the late 1960s and reached a peak of 10% in the 1980s. It was caused by a monetary policy in which the Federal Reserve Board was committed to keeping interest rates low during a period in which fiscal deficits were increasing. This low interest rate policy forced the Federal Reserve System to monetize government debt at an increasing rate, leading to an excessive monetary expansion and an eventual collapse of the policy itself as inflationary expectations were fed into the capital markets.

How Inflation Is Related to Growth

Perhaps the most difficult and least understood area of macroeconomics is the relationship of money to growth. It is widely believed that maintaining a low inflationary environment to promote growth is important, largely because we know that countries with very high inflation rates like Argentina, Brazil, and Bolivia suffer from systemic employment problems stemming from the disruption of financial markets with the erosion of the currency. There seems to be some evidence from the United States in the 1960s, and from the United Kingdom over the last century, that low inflation rates are associated with low unemployment and with high growth. Modern explanations of this phenomenon suggest that inflation causes growth in the short run through mistaken expectations on the part of households and firms. For this reason, the Federal Reserve System no longer tries to stimulate GDP on a short-run basis through monetary expansion. The exact connection between the short run and the long run is the subject of modern research in macroeconomics, and the natural rate hypothesis, which we studied in Chapters 15 and 16, is itself once more under attack.

❸ THE RESEARCH FRONTIER

What are the "hot topics" these days in universities and research institutes? If you were to study macroeconomics in graduate school, what kinds of things would you learn and how might you contribute to the advancement of knowledge?

WEBWATCH 17.1   **How to find Economic Sites on the Net**

Throughout this book we have given interesting Web sites that you can use to supplement the material in the book. But Web sites are constantly being built, updated, and changed. One site that will probably have a degree of permanence is Bill Goffe's Resources for Economists on the Internet, at

http://econwpa.wustl.edu/EconFAQ/EconFAQ.html.

Resources for Economists on the Internet is the most comprehensive list of economic resources available. It lists university departments and institutions, teaching tools, and research material. If it's available and economic, the address is probably somewhere on Bill Goffe's site.

Research on Growth Theory

A recent topic of study is the endogenous theory of growth. To see why, take a look at the article "Making a Miracle" by Robert E. Lucas, Jr.,[3] in which he analyzes the potential increase in social welfare that could be brought about in a country like India or Ghana if it were to emulate the experience of Hong Kong or Japan. For all of recorded history, up until the seventeenth century in Europe, growth in GDP resulted in growth in population. As more was produced, more people were born, but most of these people lived a miserable existence relative to the average citizen of an advanced industrialized nation in the 1990s. It was only with the onset of the Renaissance in sixteenth-century Europe that this began to change. The world economy has not looked back.

How is knowledge disseminated? What is the difference between the process of discovery and the process of innovation whereby new discoveries are applied? How does investment in research and education influence the production of knowledge? Should research be left to the private sector, or should it be actively encouraged through government grants or government research institutions? These are the questions that are being asked in modern growth theory. As new data emerges that allows us to compare the results of social experiments, such as the development of a market economy in China, reliable answers are increasingly likely. The theory of economic growth has been the single most important research topic in macroeconomics in the last two decades, and is likely to occupy the minds of many of our best researchers for several decades to come.

Research on Business Cycles

For 25 years, following World War II, most macroeconomists were occupied with attempts to reconcile Keynes' book, *The General Theory of Employment, Interest, and Money,* with the microeconomic paradigm of supply and demand. Initially, the ideas in *The General Theory* seemed to work, and many economists believed that the problem of understanding business cycles had been solved. But the shifting of the Phillips curve in the 1970s and 1980s led to a re-evaluation. To paraphrase Robert Lucas, many economists began to feel that as practical advisors to policy makers, we were "in over our heads."

The arrival of the idea of rational expectations in the 1970s changed all that. Macroeconomists began to question the foundations of the Keynesian model and to search for explanations of business cycles that were more firmly rooted in the microeconomic paradigm of supply and demand. The culmination of this was the real business school, which in its strongest form denies the need for active government intervention. By this time the pendulum had swung the other way and academic economists completed a move from interventionists with cures for all social ills, to introverts who, in political circles, were not really sure that they belonged at the party.

The rational expectations revolution has been a healthy development for macroeconomic science. It has forced us to make sure that our economic theories are internally consistent and to adopt the view that the microeconomic model of behavior should also be used to explain the macroeconomy. Not surprisingly, the early models of this idea were crude and could not capture the rich complexity of the real world. But more recently,

---

3.   Robert E. Lucas Jr. "Making a miracle." *Econometrica* 61(2): 251–272.

research that combines explicit dynamic models with supply and demand analysis has been much more widely embraced, as economists have realized that the method itself permits many explanations. The static Keynesian analysis that guided policy advisors in the 1960s is dead. But the combination of Keynesian insights into the role of market failures and the discipline of the demand and supply model of the RBC school, is likely to prove very fruitful in the next few years.

Inflation, Growth, and the Monetary Transmission Mechanism

One of the more interesting areas under study today is the monetary transmission mechanism. We know that an increase in the rate of monetary expansion leads to lower unemployment in the short run and to higher inflation in the long run. Our theories suggest that there is a natural rate of unemployment independent of policy, but evidence is accumulating from the European experience and from long series of observations in the United States that the natural rate of unemployment can change substantially from one decade to the next. It is a short step to ask whether the natural rate is itself a function of monetary policies that influence the long-run rate of inflation.

Many economists are today researching why an increase in the monetary growth rate lowers unemployment in the short run. In our theoretical models this can only happen if the nominal wage (or some other nominal price) is slow to respond to monetary changes. But understanding why rational economic agents choose to engage in behavior that seems to lead to bad outcomes for society in the short run is not easy to explain. Several competing theories are currently being analyzed, and perhaps in the next few years an academic consensus on this issue may provide an alternative model to policy makers than can improve the dynamic demand and supply model.

❹ THE FUTURE

The study of macroeconomics is more exciting today than ever. Because economists are unable to conduct experiments, we are forced to search for regularities in data in which many different variables are changing at the same time. It is only relatively recently, with the invention of the personal computer, that the analysis of huge amounts of data has become practical. When A. W. Phillips wrote his seminal article on wage inflation and unemployment in the 1950s, he analyzed his data with a hand calculator. Today, an analysis that would have taken weeks of painstaking calculations just thirty years ago can be carried out in seconds by an undergraduate using a laptop. The invention of the personal computer is doing for economics what the invention of the telescope did for astronomy.

Along with the ability to analyze data has come an extensive collection of economic statistics. Before World War II, very few countries collected national income data in a comprehensive way. Today, we have amassed thirty years of data on every country in the world, and the quality of the data is improving yearly. As we accumulate better data on economic time series, we will get a much better feel for the way that economies work. We cannot design experiments, but politicians often conduct them for us. As countries experiment with different economic and social policies, and as we observe and measure the results, we will naturally accumulate a wealth of observations that will enable us to discriminate between different hypotheses. We are indeed "living in interesting times."

Utility Theory and Indifference Curves

How do people choose to allocate scarce resources between competing ends? In economics we model choice by assuming that households maximize a utility function—a mathematical formula that tells us how happy a family will be if it receives bundles of different commodities. Suppose that there are two commodities, X and Y. The formula:

A.1
$$U = X \times Y$$

is an example of a utility function. A household with this utility function would get 1 utility unit (called a util) if it consumed 1 unit of good X and 1 of good Y. There are other combinations of X and Y that give the same utility; for example, 2 units of good X and 0.5 units of good Y would also give the household 1 util as would 0.5 units of X and 2 units of Y. We can plot a graph of Y against X for all combinations of X and Y that give the same utility. This graph is called an indifference curve. Figure A.1 plots the indifference curve that gives 1 util.

Not every combination of X and Y gives the same utility. For example, if the household consumes 2 units of X and 2 units of Y it will get 4 utils. Because we assume that people prefer more to less, the household would prefer 4 utils to 1 util. Just as we drew an indifference curve for all combinations of X and Y that yield 1 util, so we can draw an indifference curve corresponding to a utility level of 4 utils. Figure A.2 illustrates an indifference map, a set of indifference curves each of which corresponds to a different utility level.

The indifference curve U_1 represents all combinations of goods X and Y that yield 1 util, U_2 shows combinations that yield 4 utils, and U_3 shows combinations that yield 9

359

FIGURE A.1
An Indifference Curve for the
Utility Function $U = X \times Y$

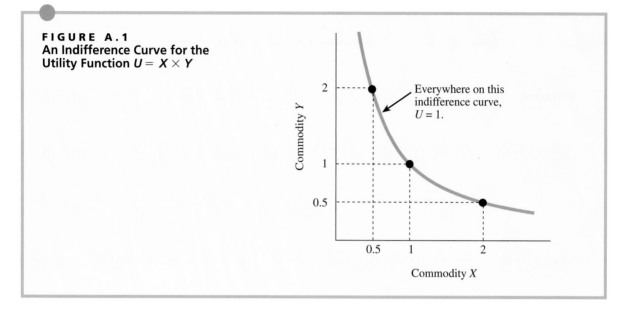

utils. They are called indifference curves because the household is indifferent between choices of X and Y that lie on the same curve; all such bundles give the same utility. A curve that lies strictly above and to the right of another represents strictly preferred bundles. For example, in Figure A.2 the household would prefer any bundle on curve U_2 to any bundle on curve U_1. It would prefer combinations on U_3 to both U_1 and U_2.

FIGURE A.2
Three Indifference Curves

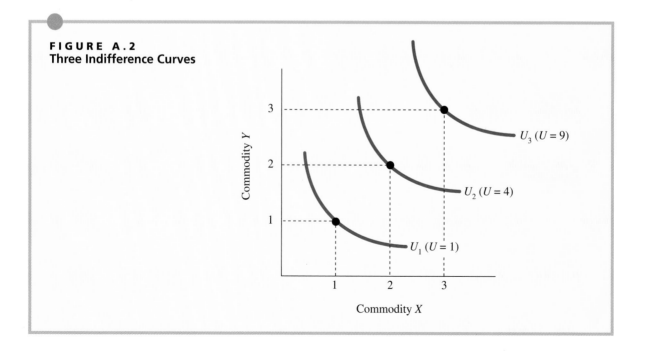

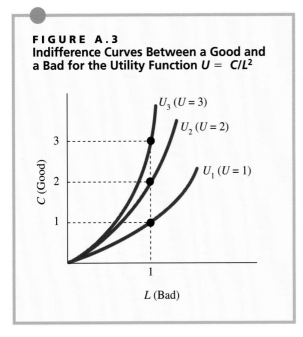

FIGURE A.3
Indifference Curves Between a Good and a Bad for the Utility Function $U = C/L^2$

Some commodities give us disutility rather than utility; selling our time to the market to earn income is an example. When a commodity gives disutility, we call it a bad rather than a good. We can still draw indifference curves between goods and bads but these curves slope up instead of down. Figure A.3 gives an example of indifference curves for the utility function

A.2
$$U = \frac{C}{L^2}$$

where C is a good (C stands for consumption) and L is a bad (L stands for labor supply). On Figure A.3 indifference curves that are higher (more consumption) and to the left (less labor) give more utility.

Logarithms

Logarithms are often used to measure variables that grow through time. A logarithm is defined relative to its base. Two commonly used bases are base 10 and base e. The logarithm of a number in base ten is the power that 10 must be raised to give the number—for example, the logarithm of 100 is 2 because we multiply 10 by itself 2 times to get 100. Similarly, the logarithm of 1000 is 3, and the logarithm of 10,000 is 4.

10	=	10^1	$\log(10) = 1$
$100 = 10 \times 10$	=	10^2	$\log(100) = 2$
$1000 = 10 \times 10 \times 10$	=	10^3	$\log(1000) = 3$
$10,000 = 10 \times 10 \times 10 \times 10$	=	10^4	$\log(10,000) = 4$

Any number can be used as the base of logarithms; a particularly good choice is e, which is equal to 2.7182 up to four decimal places. The logarithm base e of a number is called its natural logarithm and it is denoted with the symbol 1n.

2.7182	=	e	$1n(2.7182) = 1$
$7.3890 = e \times e$	=	e^2	$1n(7.3890) = 2$
$54.5981 = e \times e \times e$	=	e^3	$1n(54.5981) = 3$
$2980.9580 = e \times e \times e \times e$	=	e^4	$1n(2980.9580) = 4$

Natural logarithms are used a lot in economics because the difference of the natural logarithm of a variable is approximately equal to its growth rate. Suppose that a variable X is growing through time, then

$$\frac{X_t - X_{t-1}}{X_{t-1}} = \frac{\Delta X}{X} \cong \ln(X_t) - \ln(X_{t-1})$$

If, for example, X is the value of a bank account that earns interest at 6% per year, then a graph of $\ln(X)$ against time will be a straight line with a slope equal to 1.06 (1 plus the growth rate).

The following rules of logarithms are useful to remember:

Rule 1: $\ln \dfrac{X}{Y} = \ln(X) - \ln(Y)$

Rule 2: $\ln(X \times Y) = \ln(X) + \ln(Y)$

Rule 3: $\ln(X^a) = a \times \ln(X)$

Data for the United States Economy

Year	Real GDP	GDP Deflator	Cons.	Inv.	Gov. Exp.	Imports	Exports	Net Exports
1890	218.21	6.26	126.14	64.92	26.91	11.79	12.03	0.24
1891	227.81	6.15	135.20	63.37	28.72	12.83	13.35	0.51
1892	250.13	5.92	141.59	75.73	30.84	13.57	15.54	1.97
1893	237.89	6.05	142.29	65.34	30.12	13.49	13.62	0.13
1894	231.30	5.67	138.08	60.45	29.61	11.71	14.88	3.16
1895	258.65	5.59	155.36	70.08	32.23	12.64	13.62	0.98
1896	253.17	5.44	154.94	64.27	31.79	13.87	16.05	2.18
1897	277.71	5.47	167.09	73.14	34.46	14.43	17.45	3.02
1898	283.43	5.65	169.90	70.44	36.20	12.18	19.08	6.90
1899	309.93	5.82	189.98	72.38	41.38	12.58	18.76	6.19
1900	317.83	6.10	191.74	79.12	40.32	13.66	20.31	6.66
1901	354.68	6.05	215.27	87.06	44.14	13.71	21.93	8.22
1902	357.93	6.26	217.09	91.81	43.55	14.10	19.57	5.47

Year	Real GDP	GDP Deflator	Cons.	Inv.	Gov. Exp.	Imports	Exports	Net Exports
1903	375.80	6.33	230.09	95.73	45.74	15.50	19.74	4.24
1904	371.15	6.41	233.11	86.91	46.22	15.64	20.55	4.91
1905	398.91	6.54	246.45	99.32	48.57	16.45	21.01	4.57
1906	445.03	6.71	273.70	113.81	53.00	18.25	22.77	4.52
1907	451.67	6.99	278.83	116.27	53.45	20.40	23.52	3.12
1908	414.77	6.94	261.27	96.72	50.97	17.91	23.72	5.81
1909	465.75	7.17	289.86	116.26	56.25	17.51	20.88	3.38
1910	478.35	7.37	295.19	124.39	57.24	20.02	21.54	1.52
1911	493.84	7.29	309.45	121.52	58.87	20.26	24.26	4.00
1912	518.39	7.59	317.53	135.22	60.93	20.66	25.36	4.71
1913	523.17	7.56	327.99	127.46	61.90	22.81	28.62	5.81
1914	503.80	7.71	323.92	115.94	59.91	23.15	27.17	4.02
1915	498.05	8.06	318.30	110.92	59.24	20.86	30.44	9.59
1916	535.50	9.02	347.03	105.33	61.69	30.91	52.36	21.45
1917	544.28	11.12	339.51	111.48	72.21	28.67	49.75	21.08
1918	629.15	12.17	337.97	103.45	167.25	23.32	43.80	20.48
1919	589.15	14.31	352.93	24.09	188.33	25.50	49.31	23.81
1920	551.42	16.60	370.21	75.56	93.71	31.23	43.17	11.94
1921	513.84	13.53	393.87	24.52	89.20	21.63	27.88	6.25
1922	590.56	12.56	408.41	95.03	85.91	24.69	25.89	1.20
1923	638.29	13.06	445.50	105.46	89.05	28.75	27.03	−1.71
1924	659.59	12.87	478.51	88.71	89.65	27.89	30.62	2.73
1925	710.01	13.14	464.53	148.13	94.31	30.15	33.19	3.04
1926	750.56	12.95	502.53	149.64	98.98	32.64	32.06	−0.58
1927	754.26	12.60	513.83	139.27	99.04	31.65	33.77	2.12
1928	762.00	12.75	521.00	133.43	100.54	30.42	37.47	7.04
1929	821.80	12.50	554.50	152.80	112.60	34.10	36.01	1.91
1930	748.90	12.10	520.00	107.20	122.00	30.10	29.80	−0.30
1931	691.30	11.00	501.00	67.20	125.50	27.00	24.70	−2.30
1932	599.70	9.70	456.60	25.00	120.50	22.00	19.60	−2.40
1933	587.10	9.50	447.40	26.60	116.10	22.90	19.90	−3.00
1934	632.60	10.30	461.10	41.10	131.40	23.40	22.30	−1.10
1935	681.30	10.60	487.60	65.20	135.70	31.10	23.90	−7.20

Year	Real GDP	GDP Deflator	Cons.	Inv.	Gov. Exp.	Imports	Exports	Net Exports
1936	777.90	10.60	534.40	89.90	158.60	30.40	25.30	−5.10
1937	811.40	11.20	554.60	106.40	152.20	33.80	31.90	−1.90
1938	778.90	10.90	542.20	69.90	162.50	26.50	30.70	4.20
1939	840.70	10.80	568.70	93.40	174.00	28.10	32.70	4.60
1940	906.00	11.00	595.20	121.80	180.70	29.20	37.50	8.30
1941	1070.60	11.70	629.30	149.40	289.10	36.30	39.10	2.80
1942	1284.90	12.30	628.70	81.40	586.00	37.40	26.30	−11.10
1943	1540.50	12.50	647.30	53.50	867.70	50.40	22.30	−28.10
1944	1670.00	12.60	671.20	59.80	968.00	53.50	24.60	−28.90
1945	1602.60	13.30	714.60	82.60	829.40	56.70	32.80	−23.90
1946	1272.10	16.70	779.10	195.50	271.00	40.20	66.70	26.50
1947	1252.80	18.70	793.30	198.80	218.80	37.10	79.10	42.00
1948	1300.00	20.00	813.00	229.80	240.60	44.10	60.70	16.60
1949	1305.50	19.90	831.40	187.40	269.30	42.50	59.90	17.40
1950	1418.50	20.20	874.30	256.40	284.50	49.70	53.00	3.30
1951	1558.40	21.30	894.70	255.60	397.00	53.20	64.30	11.10
1952	1624.90	21.50	923.40	261.60	467.60	59.90	62.30	2.40
1953	1685.50	22.00	962.50	240.30	489.80	66.60	59.50	−7.10
1954	1673.80	22.20	987.30	234.10	454.70	64.40	62.20	−2.20
1955	1768.30	22.90	1047.00	284.80	441.70	72.90	67.70	−5.20
1956	1803.60	23.60	1078.70	282.20	444.00	79.20	78.00	−1.20
1957	1838.20	24.40	1104.40	266.90	465.30	83.40	85.00	1.60
1958	1829.10	24.90	1122.20	245.70	476.00	88.50	73.70	−14.80
1959	1928.80	25.60	1178.90	296.40	475.30	95.60	73.80	−21.80
1960	2025.38	26.00	1210.80	290.80	476.90	96.10	88.40	−7.70
1961	2071.48	26.30	1238.40	289.40	501.50	95.30	89.90	−5.40
1962	2175.46	26.90	1293.30	321.20	524.20	105.50	95.00	−10.50
1963	2269.85	27.20	1341.90	343.30	536.30	107.70	101.80	−5.90
1964	2393.50	27.70	1417.20	371.80	549.10	112.90	115.40	2.50
1965	2532.04	28.40	1497.00	413.00	566.90	124.50	118.10	−6.40
1966	2679.59	29.40	1573.80	438.00	622.40	143.70	125.70	−18.00
1967	2751.16	30.30	1622.40	418.60	667.90	153.70	130.00	−23.70

Year	Real GDP	GDP Deflator	Cons.	Inv.	Gov. Exp.	Imports	Exports	Net Exports
1968	2863.52	31.80	1707.50	440.10	686.80	177.70	140.20	−37.50
1969	2940.72	33.40	1771.20	461.30	682.00	189.20	147.80	−41.40
1970	2942.05	35.20	1813.50	429.70	665.80	196.40	161.30	−35.10
1971	3033.42	37.10	1873.70	475.70	652.40	207.80	161.90	−45.90
1972	3188.92	38.80	1978.40	532.20	653.00	230.20	173.70	−56.50
1973	3347.70	41.30	2066.70	591.70	644.20	244.40	210.30	−34.10
1974	3333.85	44.90	2053.82	543.00	655.40	238.40	234.40	−4.00
1975	3314.23	49.20	2097.50	437.60	663.50	209.80	232.90	23.10
1976	3478.01	52.30	2207.30	520.60	659.20	249.70	243.40	−6.30
1977	3625.94	55.90	2296.60	600.40	664.10	274.70	246.90	−27.80
1978	3800.00	60.30	2391.80	664.60	677.00	300.10	270.20	−29.90
1979	3904.58	65.50	2448.40	669.70	689.30	304.10	293.50	−10.60
1980	3883.12	71.70	2447.10	594.40	704.20	289.90	320.50	30.60
1981	3949.18	78.90	2476.90	631.10	713.20	304.10	326.10	22.00
1982	3868.85	83.80	2503.70	540.50	723.60	304.10	296.70	−7.40
1983	4030.39	87.20	2619.40	599.50	743.80	342.10	285.90	−56.20
1984	4288.35	91.00	2746.10	757.50	766.90	427.70	305.70	−122.00
1985	4428.71	94.40	2865.80	745.90	813.40	454.60	309.20	−145.40
1986	4563.67	96.90	2969.10	735.10	855.40	484.70	329.60	−155.10
1987	4539.90	100.00	3094.50	747.20	992.80	507.10	364.00	−143.10
1988	4731.80	103.61	3232.99	746.93	996.04	525.70	421.60	−104.10
1989	4863.00	107.94	3330.30	768.19	1014.52	545.40	471.80	−73.60
1990	5099.46	112.64	3408.61	709.99	1044.17	565.10	510.50	−54.60
1991	5053.21	117.09	3394.97	628.76	1046.99	531.48	513.97	−17.51
1992	5189.10	120.34	3506.65	656.82	1050.22	555.94	531.34	−24.60
1993	5307.55	123.47	3607.56	705.54	1045.15	583.56	532.78	−50.78
1994	5489.11	126.35	3720.43	802.83	1040.49	643.83	569.12	−74.71
1995	5592.76	129.96	3781.74	819.69	1045.14	694.04	621.25	−72.79
1996	5768.67	132.37	3934.12	843.46	1062.70	729.50	657.92	−71.62
1997	5973.54	135.32	4056.00	914.57	1074.42	780.00	708.54	−71.46

A

Absence of arbitrage opportunities A situation in which there are no opportunities to profit by buying commodities or financial securities in one market and selling them in another. *Chapter 11*

Animal spirits The idea that mass psychology can be an independent cause of economic fluctuations. *Chapter 6*

Appreciation (of a foreign country's currency) A decrease in the number of foreign currency units that can be purchased for a dollar in a flexible exchange rate system. (*See also* **Devaluation**; **Depreciation**; **Revaluation**.) *Chapter 11*

B

Balance of payments The change in the foreign exchange reserves of the government. *Chapter 11*

Balance of trade The difference between the values of exports and imports of goods and services. *Chapter 2*

Balance sheet accounting A system for measuring the assets and liabilities of an economic unit, such as a household or a firm. *Chapter 2*

Banknote A paper claim to assets on deposit at a financial institution that is transferable from one individual to another. *Chapter 9*

Barter economy An economy in which all trade must be accomplished through bilateral exchange of commodities. *Chapter 5*

Base year The year whose prices are used to value goods and services in the construction of real GDP. *Chapter 1*

Boom (expansion) A period of time during which the growth rate of real GDP is above trend. *Chapter 1*

Budget constraint An inequality that describes the combinations of commodities that can be purchased and the labor that can be supplied, given a household's wealth and given the wage and the price of commodities determined in the market. *Chapter 4*

Budget deficit An excess of expenditures over revenues. *Chapter 2*

Business cycles The tendency of many economic time series to display coherent, persistent swings from one period to the next. *Chapter 1*

C

Capital elasticity The percent increase in output for a 1% increase in capital employed in production. (*See also* **Labor elasticity**.) *Chapter 13*

Capital market The set of financial institutions that channel savings from households to firms. *Chapter 2*

Capital stock The stock of machines, factories, houses, and unsold goods. *Chapter 8*

Central bank An institution that controls a nation's money supply. In the United States the central bank is the Federal Reserve System. *Chapter 9*

Circular flow of income The idea that GDP and income for the whole economy are different ways of measuring the same thing. *Chapter 2*

Classical aggregate demand curve A curve that illustrates all combinations of GDP and the price level for which the quantity of money demanded equals the quantity supplied. *Chapter 5*

Classical theory of aggregate demand A theory that asserts that the aggregate quantity of goods and services demanded at a given price depends only on the quantity of money in circulation. *Chapter 5*

Classical theory of aggregate supply A theory that asserts that the quantity of output produced is determined only by preferences, technology, and endowments. *Chapter 4*

Closed economy An economy studied in isolation from the rest of the world. *Chapter 2*

Cobb-Douglas production function A formula that describes how much output can be produced for given amounts of labor and capital. $Y = AK^{\alpha}(LQ)^{1-\alpha}$ where Y is output, K is capital, L is labor, A and α are constants, and Q measures labor productivity. *Chapter 13*

Coherence A measure of the degree to which two variables move together over time. (*See also* **Persistence**.) *Chapter 1*

Competitive equilibrium allocation A list of the quantities of commodities and labor demanded and supplied by every household and firm in a competitive equilibrium. *Chapter 4*

Competitive equilibrium A property of a model economy in which the quantities of all commodities demanded (including labor) equal the quantities supplied. *Chapter 4*

Compound growth A process of growth by which a variable increases each period by a fixed percentage of its level. *Chapter 3*

Conditional convergence hypothesis The proposition that per capita incomes of countries that have the same characteristics should grow closer together over time. *Chapter 14*

Constant returns to scale A property of a production function whereby if all inputs are multiplied by a positive number, output produced is multiplied by the same number. *Chapter 13*

Consumer Price Index (CPI) A measure of the cost of a standard bundle of consumer goods in a given year. *Chapter 1*

Consumption goods Commodities used to meet immediate needs. *Chapter 2*

Consumption smoothing The process of borrowing and lending in the capital market in order to distribute consumption more evenly through time. *Chapter 6*

Contraction (recession) A period of time during which the growth rate of GDP is below trend. *Chapter 1*

Convergence hypothesis The proposition that per capita incomes of countries should grow closer together over time irrespective of national characteristics. *Chapter 14*

Corporate bond A promise by a firm to make a series of fixed payments over time. *Chapter 8*

Correlation coefficient A measure of the strength of association between two variables. *Chapter 3*

Countercyclical variable One that tends to decrease when real GDP increases and increase when real GDP decreases. *Chapter 1*

Coupon The fixed periodic payment by a firm to the owner of one of its bonds. *Chapter 8*

Cycle (*See* **High frequency component**.) *Chapter 3*

D

Deficit An excess of expenditures over revenues. (*See also* **Surplus**.) *Chapter 9*

Demand for money An equation that shows how much money the household would like to hold each week as a function of income and (in some theories) the interest rate. *Chapter 5*

Demand management Active government intervention—through fiscal or monetary policy—designed to maintain a steady rate of economic growth. *Chapter 8*

Depreciation (of a foreign country's exchange rate) An increase in the number of foreign currency units that can be purchased for a dollar in a flexible exchange-rate system. (*See also* **Appreciation; Devaluation; Revaluation**.) *Chapter 11*

Depreciation (of capital) The portion of gross investment devoted to replacing worn out capital. *Chapter 2*

Detrending The process of separating a time series into two components—a trend and a cycle. *Chapter 1*

Devaluation (of a foreign country's exchange rate) An increase in the number of foreign currency units that can be purchased for a dollar in a fixed exchange-rate system. (*See also* **Appreciation; Depreciation; Revaluation**.) *Chapter 11*

Difference equation An equation that relates the current value of a variable to its own past values. *Chapter 1*

Differencing The process of calculating the changes in a time series variable from one period to the next. *Chapter 3*

Diminishing returns The idea that as more and more labor is added to a fixed quantity of capital, the additional output that can be produced increases at a diminishing rate. *Chapter 4*

Discount rate The interest rate charged by the Federal Reserve System on loans to financial institutions. *Chapter 9*

Discretionary monetary policy A policy (not based on a predetermined rule) whereby the central bank adjusts monetary variables on a day-to-day basis in an attempt to influence the economy. *Chapter 16*

Disposable income National income minus taxes plus transfers. *Chapter 10*

Domestic economy The economy of a single country of interest. *Chapter 2*

Domestic expenditure Expenditure on goods and services produced in the domestic economy. *Chapter 2*

Double coincidence of wants A situation in a barter economy in which the goods that one person wants to sell are the same as those that another wants to buy. *Chapter 5*

Dynamic (economic) analysis The study of how the economy evolves from one period to the next. (*See also* **Static (economic) analysis**.) *Chapter 12*

Dynamic theory of aggregate supply A theory that explains how the growth of GDP is related to wage and price inflation. *Chapter 15*

E

Economic model An artificial economy represented by a graph or a set of equations. *Chapter 1*

Efficiency units A way of measuring labor input that takes account of skill. An hour of time supplied by a surgeon contains more labor measured in efficiency units than an hour supplied by a laborer. *Chapter 13*

Efficiency wage theory The theory that firms pay workers more than their marginal product to induce them to work hard. *Chapter 7*

Employment rate The fraction of the adult population that is employed. *Chapter 3*

Endogenous growth theory The theory that explains growth of per capita income using the assumption that productivity improves each period for reasons that are explained endogenously within the model. (*See also* **Exogenous growth theory**.) *Chapter 13*

Endogenous variable A variable that is explained within an economic model. (*See also* **Exogenous variable**.) *Chapter 4*

Endowments The quantity of resources available to an economy (including the time of its people). *Chapter 4*

ex ante **real interest rate** The nominal interest rate minus the *expected* inflation rate. *Chapter 10*

Excess GDP growth The amount by which GDP growth exceeds growth in total factor productivity. *Chapter 15*

Excess money growth The amount by which the money growth rate exceeds the natural rate of output growth. *Chapter 16*

Excess wage inflation The amount by which wage inflation exceeds the natural rate of output growth. *Chapter 15*

Exchange controls Limits on the amount of a foreign currency that an individual or firm can buy or sell at a point in time. *Chapter 11*

Exchange services The flow of benefits a household gains by holding money because it is generally acceptable in exchange. *Chapter 5*

Exogenous growth theory A theory that explains growth of per capita income using the assumption that productivity improves each period for reasons that are exogenous to the model. (*See also* **Endogenous growth theory**.) *Chapter 13*

Exogenous variable A variable that is not explained within an economic model. (*See also* **Endogenous variable**.) *Chapter 4*

Expected value The value that would be obtained by averaging a random variable over many repeated observations. *Chapter 16*

Expenditure method A method of measuring GDP by adding up all expenditures on final goods and services. *Chapter 2*

ex post **real interest rate** The nominal interest rate minus the *actual* inflation rate. *Chapter 10*

Externality An action by one person or firm that directly affects the utility function or the production function of another person or firm. *Chapter 7*

F

Factor services Services of the factors of production that households supply to firms in exchange for income. *Chapter 2*

Feasible choice A combination of labor demanded and output supplied that is possible, given the available technology. *Chapter 4*

Federal Open Market Committee The body responsible for determining and implementing U.S. monetary policy. *Chapter 9*

Federal Reserve System The central bank of the United States. *Chapter 9*

Fiat money Money that is backed by laws requiring it to be accepted in all legal transactions. *Chapter 9*

Final good One sold directly to the final user. *Chapter 2*

Financial asset A claim to resources that will be delivered in the future. *Chapter 2*

Financial liability An obligation to deliver resources in the future. *Chapter 2*

Firm An economic organization that produces commodities. *Chapter 4*

Fixed exchange-rate system A world monetary system in which the rate that each national currency trades for any other currency is fixed and regulated by the nation's central bank. (*See also* **Floating (flexible) exchange-rate system.**) *Chapter 11*

Flexible trend The low-frequency component that results from decomposing a time series into a trend and a cycle using a flexible detrending method. Flexible detrending is computed using a formula that lets the trend vary slowly over time. *Chapter 3*

Floating (flexible) exchange-rate system A world monetary system in which the value of one national currency in terms of another is freely determined by demand and supply. (*See also* **Fixed exchange-rate system.**) *Chapter 9*

Flow (variable) A variable measured per unit of time. (*See also* **Stock.**) *Chapter 2*

Frictional unemployment Unemployment that results from labor turnover. *Chapter 7*

Fully-funded pension A pension plan in which contributions are invested in stocks or bonds and in which retirees earn claims to the income streams from their invested assets. *Chapter 6*

G

GDP accounting identity An identity linking the components of GDP: $Y = C + I + G + NX$. *Chapter 2*

GDP deflator A price index computed as the ratio of nominal GDP to real GDP. *Chapter 1*

Gold standard A world monetary system in which each nation's currency is convertible to gold at a fixed rate. *Chapter 9*

Gross domestic product (GDP) The value, at market prices, of all final goods and services produced within a nation's borders during a given time period. *Chapter 1*

Growth The increase in real GDP over time. *Chapter 1*

Growth accounting A method of calculating the shares of growth in per capita GDP that are attributable to growth in capital, labor, and productivity. *Chapter 13*

H

High-frequency component (cycle) The part of a time series that remains after removing a linear or a flexible trend or after differencing the series. *Chapter 3*

Household A group of individuals who live together and make collective economic decisions. *Chapter 2*

Human capital The stock of accumulated knowledge. *Chapter 13*

Hyperinflation A period of very rapidly increasing prices. *Chapter 1*

I

Income method A method of measuring GDP by adding up all the income earned by the factors of production. *Chapter 2*

Indifference curve A curve showing combinations of commodities demanded and labor supplied that make a household equally happy. *Chapter 4*

Inflation rate The rate of change of the price level from one year to the next. *Chapter 1*

Intermediate good A good produced by one firm and used as an input by another. *Chapter 2*

International Monetary Fund An organization that acts as an international central bank. *Chapter 11*

Intertemporal budget constraint An equation that describes combinations of present and future household consumption that are feasible at each stage of life by borrowing and lending in the capital market. *Chapter 6*

Intertemporal indifference curve A curve showing combinations of present and future consumption that make a household equally happy. *Chapter 6*

Intertemporal production possibilities set Those combinations of current investment and future production of commodities that are feasible given the state of technology. *Chapter 6*

Intertemporal trade Exchange of commodities at different points in time mediated by borrowing and lending. *Chapter 14*

Intertemporal utility theory A theory that asserts that households allocate their consumption through time in order to maximize their utility. *Chapter 6*

Investment demand curve A curve that shows the quantity of investment goods demanded by firms at different real interest rates. *Chapter 6*

Investment goods Commodities that add to the stock of capital. *Chapter 2*

IS curve A curve that shows all combinations of the nominal interest rate and income at which saving equals investment. *Chapter 10*

IS-LM equilibrium A situation in which the nominal interest rate and income are simultaneously determined at the intersection of the IS and LM curves. *Chapter 10*

Isoprofit line A line showing all combinations of commodities supplied and labor demanded that yield the same profit. *Chapter 4*

K

Keynesian aggregate demand curve A curve showing all combinations of the price level and real GDP that are consistent with IS-LM equilibrium. *Chapter 10*

Knowledge function A function that describes how the productivity of an individual worker depends on the stock of capital in society. *Chapter 14*

L

Labor demand curve A curve showing the quantity of labor that firms are willing to hire at different real wage rates. *Chapter 4*

Labor elasticity The percentage increase in output for a 1% increase in labor employed in production. (*See also* **Capital elasticity**.) *Chapter 13*

Labor force All individuals who are either working or looking for work. *Chapter 3*

Labor force participation rate The fraction of the civilian population over the age of 16 that is in the labor force. *Chapter 3*

Labor income The income earned by supplying labor services. *Chapter 2*

Labor supply curve A curve showing the quantity of labor that households are willing to supply at different real wage rates. *Chapter 4*

Learning by doing Acquisition of knowledge through the act of production. *Chapter 14*

Lender of last resort The central bank's role in lending money to banks that are short of reserves. *Chapter 9*

Linear cycle The component of a time series that remains after removing a linear trend. *Chapter 3*

Linear detrending The process of decomposing a time series into trend and cycle by drawing the best straight line through the data. *Chapter 1*

Liquid assets Assets that pay a lower rate of return than similar assets of equal risk because they are themselves generally acceptable in exchange or because they can quickly be converted into other assets that are generally acceptable in exchange. *Chapter 8*

Liquidity preference A theory of why households and firms hold money when they could be earning interest by holding bonds. *Chapter 8*

LM curve A curve that shows all combinations of the nominal interest rate and income at which the quantity of money demanded equals the quantity supplied. *Chapter 8*

Low-frequency component (trend) A slowly moving component of a time series. *Chapter 3*

M

Macroeconomics The study of the working of the economy as a whole. *Chapter 1*

Macroeconomic variable An economic concept, pertaining to the aggregate economy, that can be measured and that can take on different values. *Chapter 1*

Marginal product (of a factor) The additional output produced by a one-unit increment in a factor of production, holding constant the inputs of all other factors. *Chapter 13*

Market A collection of traders who exchange commodities with each other. *Chapter 4*

Market rate of interest The rate of interest at which households and firms can borrow and lend in a competitive capital market. *Chapter 6*

Menu costs The costs of rewriting price lists in response to an ongoing inflation. *Chapter 7*

Microeconomics The study of the behavior of individual producers and consumers in markets. *Chapter 1*

Monetary base The liabilities of the Federal Reserve System. *Chapter 9*

Monetary policy The direct manipulation of the quantity of money or the nominal interest rate by the Federal Reserve System in order to alter one or more economic variables. *Chapter 8*

Money A commodity or financial asset that is generally acceptable in exchange for goods or services. *Chapter 5*

Money supply The quantity of money in circulation in an economy. *Chapter 5*

Money supply multiplier The ratio of the money supply to the monetary base. *Chapter 9*

N

National Income and Product Accounts (NIPA) A set of data on GDP and its components, published by the U.S. Department of Commerce. *Chapter 2*

Natural (output) path A list of values of output each period when the (output) growth rate equals the total factor productivity growth rate. *Chapter 15*

Natural (real wage) path A list of values of the real wage each period when the (real wage) growth rate equals the total factor productivity growth rate. *Chapter 15*

Natural rate of output The quantity of commodities supplied when unemployment is at its natural rate. *Chapter 10*

Natural rate of unemployment The unemployment rate that occurs in a search equilibrium. At the natural rate of unemployment, no firm or worker can profitably offer to trade at a higher or lower real wage. *Chapter 7*

Neoclassical growth model An exogenous theory of growth developed from the neoclassical theory of distribution. *Chapter 13*

Neoclassical synthesis The idea that the Keynesian theory of aggregate demand and supply holds in the short run and the classical theory of aggregate demand and supply holds in the long run. *Chapter 5*

Neoclassical theory of aggregate supply A dynamic theory of aggregate supply in which output growth may differ temporarily from its natural path. *Chapter 15*

Neoclassical theory of distribution The proposition that each factor of production is paid the value of its marginal product. *Chapter 13*

Neoclassical wage equation An equation used to explain the Phillips curve that relates wage inflation to expected price inflation and unemployment. *Chapter 15*

Net domestic product (NDP) The maximum output that is available for consumption without running down the stock of capital. *Chapter 2*

Net investment The portion of gross investment that contributes to increases in the capital stock. *Chapter 2*

Net worth The value of assets (real and financial) of an economic unit minus the value of its financial liabilities. *Chapter 2*

Neutrality of money The idea that if the money supply is increased (decreased) all nominal variables will increase (decrease) in the same proportion, and all real variables will remain unchanged. *Chapter 5*

Nominal exchange rate The number of units of a foreign currency that can be purchased for each unit of domestic currency. *Chapter 11*

Nominal GDP GDP measured using current prices. (*See also* **Real GDP.**) *Chapter 1*

Nominal interest rate The interest rate on loans expressed in dollars. (*See also* **Real interest rate**.) *Chapter 6*

Nominal rigidity A situation in which a nominal price or wage rate does not adjust quickly in response to disequilibrium. *Chapter 7*

Nominal wage The wage measured in dollars per period of time. *Chapter 4*

Nonaccelerating inflation rate of unemployment (NAIRU) Another name for the natural rate of unemployment. *Chapter 16*

O

Okun's Law The empirical regularity that real GDP falls 3% below trend for each 1% increase in the unemployment rate. *Chapter 7*

Open economy An economy that trades with the rest of the world. *Chapter 2*

Open market operations Federal Reserve purchases or sales of bonds in the capital markets in an effort to influence the money supply. *Chapter 9*

Opportunity cost (of holding money) The opportunities, in terms of goods and services foregone, that are given up by the decision to hold money. *Chapter 5*

P

Peak The point in a business cycle at which the difference of real GDP from trend begins to decline. *Chapter 3*

Per capita production function A function that expresses the output per unit of labor that can be produced from a given input of capital per unit of labor. *Chapter 13*

Perfect capital mobility A property of a model of being able to borrow and lend at the same real interest rate in any country in the world. (*See also* **Zero capital mobility**.) *Chapter 14*

Perfect competition A market in which all traders are able to buy or sell as much of any commodity as they desire at a given price and in which no individual trader is able to influence that price. *Chapter 4*

Perpetuity A bond that promises to make coupon payments forever. *Chapter 8*

Persistence The tendency of a time series to be highly correlated with its own past values. (*See also* **Coherence**.) *Chapter 3*

Phillips curve A negative relationship between unemployment and wage inflation that was first found to hold by A. W. Phillips in U.K. data. *Chapter 15*

Portfolio allocation An allocation of wealth among different kinds of assets. *Chapter 8*

Preferences The factors that cause households to choose one combination of goods over another. *Chapter 4*

Present value The value today of a specific amount of resources to be delivered at a future date. *Chapter 6*

Price deflation A situation of a falling price level (negative price inflation). *Chapter 15*

Primary deficit A measure of how much government expenditures plus transfer payments exceed revenues. The primary deficit *does not* include interest payments on outstanding debt. (*See also* **Reported deficit**.) *Chapter 12*

Private production function (private technology) The production function that faces an individual firm, holding constant the factors of production used by all other firms in the economy. (*See also* **Social production function**.) *Chapter 14*

Private profits Profits that accrue to a firm, before accounting for search costs. *Chapter 7*

Procyclical variable One that tends to increase when real GDP increases and decrease when real GDP decreases. *Chapter 1*

Production function The outer boundary of a production possibilities set. *Chapter 4*

Production possibilities set Those combinations of labor supplied and commodities produced that are feasible, given the state of technology. *Chapter 4*

Product method A method of measuring GDP by summing the value added by every firm in the economy. *Chapter 2*

Profit The income earned by supplying capital services. *Chapter 2*

Propensity to hold money The ratio of money to nominal GDP. *Chapter 5*

Purchasing power parity The idea that the real exchange rate should equal 1.0 in the long run. *Chapter 11*

Q

Quantity equation of money An equation that links the price level to the quantity of money, the level of GDP, and the propensity to hold money. *Chapter 5*

Quantity theory of money (classical theory of the price level) A theory that asserts that the price level is determined by the combination of the classical theories of aggregate demand and supply. *Chapter 5*

R

Rational expectations The idea that agents will learn to forecast future prices and incomes without making systematic errors. *Chapter 10*

Real business cycle model An economic model in which all fluctuations in real GDP are explained in terms of random fluctuations in technology and in which the quantity of labor supplied equals the quantity demanded at every point in time. *Chapter 4*

Real exchange rate The value of a basket of foreign goods relative to a basket of domestic goods. *Chapter 11*

Real GDP GDP measured using base-year prices. (*See also* **Nominal GDP**.) *Chapter 1*

Real interest rate The interest rate on loans expressed in commodities. (*See also* **Nominal interest rate**.) *Chapter 6*

Real money balances The value of money measured in units of commodities. *Chapter 8*

Real wage The wage measured in units of final output per time period. *Chapter 4*

Real wage inflation The percentage rate of increase of the real wage. *Chapter 16*

Recession The period from the peak of a business cycle to the subsequent trough. *Chapter 3*

Reconstruction hypothesis The hypothesis that Japan and Germany grew rapidly after World War II because they needed to replace capital that was damaged during the war. *Chapter 14*

Relative purchasing power parity The idea that the relative values of the GDP deflator between different countries should not change systematically over time. *Chapter 11*

Reported deficit A measure of how much government expenditures plus transfer payments exceed revenues. The reported deficit *does* include interest payments on outstanding debt. (*See also* **Primary deficit**.) *Chapter 12*

Representative agent economy A model in which a single family makes all economic decisions. *Chapter 4*

Required reserve ratio The minimum ratio of reserves to deposits that commercial banks are required to hold by law. *Chapter 9*

Reserves The portion of customers' deposits that private banks retain in their vaults or keep on deposit with the Federal Reserve System. *Chapter 9*

Retained earnings Profits used to purchase new capital rather than being returned to shareholders as dividends. *Chapter 2*

Revaluation (of a foreign country's exchange rate) A decrease in the number of foreign currency units that can be purchased for a dollar in a fixed exchange-rate system. (*See also* **Appreciation**; **Depreciation**; **Devaluation**.) *Chapter 11*

Ricardian equivalence A theoretical proposition that it is irrelevant whether the government finances its expenditures by borrowing or by raising taxes. *Chapter 12*

Risk aversion A preference for a steady income over one that fluctuates. *Chapter 8*

S

Saving The decision not to consume. *Chapter 8*

Saving supply curve A curve showing the quantity of saving supplied by households at different real interest rates. *Chapter 6*

Scatter plot A graph in which each point represents an observation on two different variables at a given point in time. *Chapter 3*

Search theory An economic model of the process by which workers and firms are matched up over time. *Chapter 7*

Social production function (social technology) The production function that faces society as a whole if all firms simultaneously alter their inputs of factors of production. (*See also* **Private production function**.) *Chapter 14*

Solow residual (total factor productivity) The quantity of output produced per unit of factors of production when each factor is weighted by its share of national income. *Chapter 13*

Solution (to a model) A list of values of the endogenous variables of a model as functions of the exogenous variables. *Chapter 4*

Stability A property of the steady state of a difference equation. If a steady state is stable then solutions that begin near the steady state will converge towards it over time. *Chapter 12*

Stagflation A situation of simultaneously high inflation and high unemployment. *Chapter 16*

State variable A variable that is used to summarize how the economy changes through time. In dynamic economic models, other endogenous variables are expressed as functions of the state variables. *Chapter 12*

Static (economic) analysis The study of the economy at a point in time. (*See also* **Dynamic economic analysis**.) *Chapter 12*

Steady-state solution A solution to a difference equation that is the same in every period. *Chapter 12*

Stock (variable) A variable measured at a point in time. (*See also* **Flow**.) *Chapter 2*

Substitution effect The change in the quantity of labor supplied that results from increasing the real wage, holding fixed the household's wealth. *Chapter 4*

Surplus An excess of revenues over expenditures. (*See also* **Deficit**.) *Chapter 9*

T

Technology A method for transforming the factors of production into finished goods. *Chapter 4*

Time series A sequence of numbers that measures an economic variable at consecutive dates. *Chapter 1*

Total factor productivity (*See* **Solow residual**.) *Chapter 13*

Trend (*See* **Low-frequency component**.) *Chapter 3*

Trough The point in a business cycle at which the difference of real GDP from trend begins to increase. *Chapter 3*

U

Uncovered interest rate parity The idea that the expected real interest rate, measured in units of domestic goods, should be the same on bonds issued in all world currencies. *Chapter 11*

Unemployment rate The fraction of the labor force that is unemployed. *Chapter 3*

Utility function A mathematical formula used to represent preferences. *Chapter 4*

Utility theory of money An economic theory that asserts that households hold money to obtain the utility flowing from the services of real money balances. *Chapter 8*

V

Velocity of circulation The ratio of nominal GDP to the nominal money stock; the number of times per period that the average dollar is spent on GDP. *Chapter 8*

Volatility Rapid up-and-down movements of a variable measured by its standard deviation. *Chapter 6*

W

Wealth The sum of the values of money and bonds held by a household. *Chapter 8*

Wealth effect The effect on the quantity of a commodity demanded or supplied as a consequence of an increase in household wealth. *Chapter 4*

World supply of capital curve A curve showing the quantity of funds supplied to a domestic economy by the rest of the world at different values of the real interest rate. *Chapter 6*

Z

Zero capital mobility A property of a model in which it is assumed that households and firms cannot borrow or lend abroad. (*See also* **Perfect capital mobility**.) *Chapter 14*